CONSTERNATION AT THE SIGHT OF FULTON'S MONSTER

D1880419

GREAT FORTUNES

AND

HOW THEY WERE MADE

GREAT FORTUNES
AND
HOW THEY WERE MADE;
OR THE
Struggles and Triumphs of our
Self-Made Men

BY

JAMES D. McCABE, Jr.,

NUMEROUS ILLUSTRATIONS
FROM ORIGINAL DESIGNS BY G.F. & E.B. BENSELL

GYAN

Published by

Gyan Publishing House
5, Ansari Road
Daryaganj, New Delhi-110002
Phone: 011-47034999, 9811692060
E-mail: books@gyanbooks.com

Distribution Network
gyanbooks.com
India, USA, Canada, UK, Australia, France

© **Publisher**
All rights reserved. No part of this work may be reproduced, stored, adapted, or transmitted in any form or by any means, electronic, mechanical, photocopying, micro-filming, recording or otherwise, or translated in any language, without the prior written permission of the copyright owner and the publisher.

ISBN : 978-81-212-6006-0 (PB)
First Published, 1871

2nd Impression 2021

Printed at: Gyan Press, Delhi.

The book is sold subject to the condition that it shall not, by way of trade or otherwise, be lent, resold, hired out, or otherwise circulated without the prior publisher's written consent.

Great Fortunes and How They Were Made
Author: James D. McCabe Jr.,

GREAT FORTUNES,

AND

HOW THEY WERE MADE;

OR THE

Struggles and Triumphs of our Self-Made Men.

BY

JAMES D. McCABE, Jr.,

AUTHOR OF "PLANTING THE WILDERNESS," ETC., ETC.

Numerous Illustrations,

FROM ORIGINAL DESIGNS BY G. F. & E. B. BENSELL.

"MAN, it is not thy works, which are mortal, infinitely little, and the greatest no greater than the least, but only the *spirit thou workest in*, that can have worth or continuance."—CARLYLE.

1871

"The physical industries of this world have two relations in them: one to the actor, and one to the public. Honest business is more really a contribution to the public than it is to the manager of the business himself. Although it seems to the man, and generally to the community, that the active business man is a self-seeker, and although his motive may be self-aggrandizement, yet, in point of fact, no man ever manages a legitimate business in this life, that he is not doing a thousand-fold more for other men than he is trying to do even for himself. For, in the economy of God's providence, every right and well organized business is a beneficence and not a selfishness. And not less is it so because the merchant, the mechanic the publisher, the artist, think merely of their profit. They are in fact working more for others than they are for themselves.

HENRY WARD BEECHER.

PREFACE.

The chief glory of America is, that it is the country in which genius and industry find their speediest and surest reward. Fame and fortune are here open to all who are willing to work for them. Neither class distinctions nor social prejudices, neither differences of birth, religion, nor ideas, can prevent the man of true merit from winning the just reward of his labors in this favored land. We are emphatically a nation of self-made men. and it is to the labors of this worthy class that our marvelous national prosperity is due.

This being the case, it is but natural that there should be manifested by our people a very decided desire to know the history of those who have risen to the front rank of their respective callings. Men are naturally cheered and encouraged by the success of others, and those who are worthy of a similar reward will not fail to learn valuable lessons from the examples of the men who have preceded them.

With the hope of gratifying this laudable desire for information, and encouraging those who are still struggling in the lists of fame and fortune, I offer this book to the reader. I have sought to tell simply and truthfully the story of the trials and triumphs of our self-made men, to show how they overcame where others failed, and to offer the record of their lives as models worthy of the imitation of the young men of our country. No one can hope to succeed in life merely by the force of his own genius, any more than he can hope to live without exerting some degree of influence for good or evil upon the community in which his lot is cast. Success in life is not the effect of accident or of chance: it is the result of the intelligent application of certain fixed principles to the affairs of every day. Each man must make this application according to the circumstances by which he is surrounded, and he can derive no greater assistance or encouragement in this undertaking than by informing himself how other men of acknowledged merit have succeeded in the same departments of the world's industry. That this is true is shown by the fact that many of the most eminent men attribute their great achievements to the encouragement with which the perusal of the biographies of others inspired them at critical periods of their careers. It is believed that the narrations embraced in these pages afford ample instruction and entertainment to the young, as well as food for earnest reflection on the part of those who are safely advanced upon their pathway to success, and that they will prove interesting to all classes of intelligent readers.

Some explanation is due to the reader respecting the title that has been chosen for the work. The term "Great Fortunes" is not used here to designate pecuniary success exclusively. A few of the men whose lives are herein recorded never amassed great wealth. Yet they achieved the highest success in their vocations, and their lives are so full of interest and instruction that this work must have been incomplete and unsatisfactory had they been passed over in silence. The aim of the writer has been to present the histories of those who have won the highest fame and achieved the greatest good in their respective callings, whether that success has brought them riches or not, and above all, of those whose labors have not only opened the way to fortune for themselves, but also for others, and have thus conferred lasting benefits upon their country.

In short, I have sought to make this work the story of the *Genius of America*, believing as I do that he whose achievements have contributed to the increase of the national wealth, the development of the national resources, and the elevation of the national character, though he himself be poor in purse, has indeed won a great fortune, of which no reverse can ever deprive him.

J. D. McC., Jr.

New York, *24th October*, 1870.

LIST OF ILLUSTRATIONS.

CONTENTS.

I. MERCHANTS.

CHAPTER I.

STEPHEN GIRARD.

CHAPTER II.

JOHN JACOB ASTOR.

CHAPTER III.

ALEXANDER T. STEWART.

CHAPTER IV.

AMOS LAWRENCE.

CHAPTER V.

ANDREW V. STOUT.

CHAPTER VI.

JONAS CHICKERING.

CHAPTER VII.

NICHOLAS LONGWORTH.

CHAPTER VIII.

GEORGE PEABODY.

II. CAPITALISTS.

CHAPTER IX.

CORNELIUS VANDERBILT.

CHAPTER X.

DANIEL DREW.

CHAPTER XI.

JAMES B. EADS.

CHAPTER XII.

CYRUS W. FIELD.

III. INVENTORS.

CHAPTER XIII.

ROBERT FULTON.

CHAPTER XIV.

CHARLES GOODYEAR.

CHAPTER XV.

ELI WHITNEY.

CHAPTER XVI.

CHAUNCEY JEROME.

CHAPTER XVII.

ELIAS HOWE, JR.

CHAPTER XVIII.

RICHARD M. HOE.

CHAPTER XIX.

SAMUEL COLT.

CHAPTER XX.

SAMUEL F. B. MORSE.

IV. PUBLISHERS.

CHAPTER XXI.

JAMES HARPER.

CHAPTER XXII.

JAMES T. FIELDS.

V. EDITORS.

CHAPTER XXIII.

JAMES GORDON BENNETT.

CHAPTER XXIV.

ROBERT BONNER.

VI. LAWYERS.

CHAPTER XXV.

JOHN MARSHALL.

CHAPTER XXVI.

JAMES T. BRADY.

VII. ARTISTS.

CHAPTER XXVII.

BENJAMIN WEST.

CHAPTER XXVIII.

JOHN ROGERS.

CHAPTER XXIX.

HIRAM POWERS.

CHAPTER XXX.

EMMANUEL LEUTZE.

VIII. DIVINES.

CHAPTER XXXI.

HENRY WARD BEECHER.

CHAPTER XXXII.

PETER CARTWRIGHT.

IX. AUTHORS.

CHAPTER XXXIII.

HENRY W. LONGFELLOW.

CHAPTER XXXIV.

NATHANIEL HAWTHORNE.

X. ACTORS.

CHAPTER XXXV.

EDWIN BOOTH.

CHAPTER XXXVI.

JOSEPH JEFFERSON.

XI. PHYSICIANS.

CHAPTER XXXVII.

BENJAMIN RUSH.

CHAPTER XXXVIII.

VALENTINE MOTT.

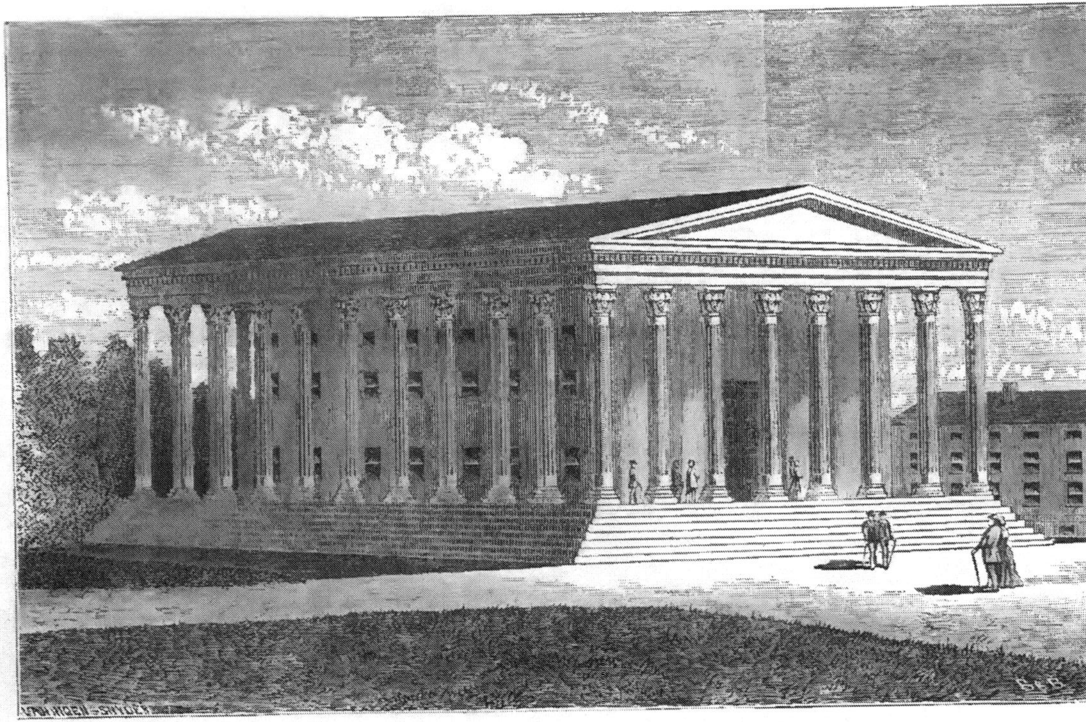

GIRARD COLLEGE

I.

MERCHANTS.

CHAPTER I.

STEPHEN GIRARD.

ONE May morning, in the year 1776, the mouth of the Delaware Bay was shrouded in a dense fog, which cleared away toward noon, and revealed several vessels just off the capes. From one of these, a sloop, floated the flag of France and a signal of distress. An American ship ran alongside the stranger, in answer to her signal, and found that the French captain had lost his reckoning in a fog, and was in total ignorance of his whereabouts. His vessel, he said, was bound from New Orleans to a Canadian port, and he was anxious to proceed on his voyage. The American skipper informed him of his locality, and also apprised him of the fact that war had broken out between the colonies and Great Britain, and that the American coast was so well lined with British cruisers that he would never reach port but as a prize.

"What shall I do?" cried the Frenchman, in great alarm.

"Enter the bay, and make a push for Philadelphia," was the reply. "It is your only chance."

The Frenchman protested that he did not know the way,

and had no pilot. The American captain, pitying his distress, found him a pilot, and even loaned him five dollars, which the pilot demanded in advance. The sloop got under weigh again, and passed into the Delaware, beyond the defenses which had been erected for its protection, just in time to avoid capture by a British war vessel which now made its appearance at the mouth of the bay. Philadelphia was reached in due time, and, as the war bade fair to put an end to his voyages, the captain sold the sloop and her cargo, of which he was part owner, and, entering a small store in Water Street, began the business of a grocer and wine-bottler. His capital was small, his business trifling in extent, and he himself labored under the disadvantage of being almost unable to speak the English language. In person he was short and stout, with a dull, repulsive countenance, which his bushy eyebrows and solitary eye (being blind in the other) made almost hideous. He was cold and reserved in manner, and was disliked by his neighbors, the most of whom were afraid of him.

This man was Stephen Girard, who was afterward destined to play so important a part in the history of the city to which the mere chances of war sent him a stranger.

He was born at Bordeaux, in France, on the 21st of May, 1750, and was the eldest of the five children of Captain Pierre Girard, a mariner of that city. His life at home was a hard one. At the age of eight years, he discovered that he was blind in one eye, and the mortification and grief which this discovery caused him appear to have soured his entire life. He afterward declared that his father treated him with considerable neglect, and that, while his younger brothers were sent to college, he was made to content himself with the barest rudiments of an education, with merely a knowledge of reading and writing. When he was quite young, his mother died, and, as his father soon married again, the severity of a step-mother was added to his other troubles. When about thirteen years of age, he left home, with his father's consent, and began, as a cabin-boy, the life of a mariner. For nine years he sailed between Bordeaux and the French West Indies, rising steadily from his position of cabin-boy to that of mate. He improved his leisure time at sea, until he was not only master of the art of navigation, but generally well informed for a man in his station. His father possessed sufficient influence to procure him the command of a vessel, in spite of the law of France which required that no man should be made master of a ship unless he had sailed two cruises in the royal navy and was twenty-five years old. Gradually Girard was enabled to amass a small sum of money, which he invested in cargoes easily disposed of in the ports to which he sailed. Three years after he was licensed to command, he made his first appearance in the port of Philadelphia. He was then twenty-six years old.

From the time of his arrival in Philadelphia he devoted himself to business with an energy and industry which never failed. He despised no labor, and was willing to undertake any honest means of increasing his subsistence. He bought and sold any thing, from groceries to old "junk." His chief profit, however, was in his wine and cider, which he bottled and sold readily. His business prospered, and he was regarded as a thriving man from the start.

In July, 1777, he married Mary Lum, a servant girl of great beauty, and something of a virago as well. The union was an unhappy one, as the husband and wife were utterly unsuited to each other. Seven years after her marriage, Mrs. Girard showed symptoms of insanity, which became so decided that her husband was compelled to place her in the State Asylum for the Insane. He appears to have done every thing in his power to restore her to reason. Being pronounced cured, she returned to her home, but in 1790 he was compelled to place her permanently in the Pennsylvania Hospital, where, nine months after, she gave birth to a female child, which happily died. Mrs. Girard never recovered her reason, but died in 1815, and was buried in the hospital grounds.

Girard fled from Philadelphia, with his wife, in September, 1777, at the approach of the British, and purchased a house at Mount Holly, near Burlington, New Jersey, where he carried on his bottling business. His claret commanded a ready sale among the British in Philadelphia, and his profits were large. In June, 1778, the city was evacuated by Lord Howe, and he was allowed to return to his former home.

Though he traded with the British, Girard considered himself a true patriot, as indeed he was. On the 27th of October, 1778, he took the oath of allegiance required by the State of Pennsylvania, and renewed it the year following. The war almost annihilated the commerce of the country, which was slow in recovering its former prosperity; but, in spite of this discouraging circumstance, Girard worked on steadily, scorning no employment, however humble, that would yield a profit. Already he had formed the plans which led to his immense wealth, and he was now patiently carrying out the most trying and disheartening preliminaries. Whatever he undertook prospered, and though his gains were small, they were carefully husbanded, and at the proper time invested in such a manner as to produce a still greater yield. Stephen Girard knew the value of little things, and he knew how to take advantage of the most trifling circumstance. His career teaches what may be done with these little things, and shows how even a few dollars, properly managed, may be made to produce as many thousands.

In 1780, Mr. Girard again entered upon the New Orleans and St. Domingo trade, in which he was engaged at the breaking out of the Revolution. He was very successful in his ventures, and was enabled in a year or two to greatly enlarge his operations. In 1782, he took a lease of ten years on a range of frame buildings in Water Street, one of which he occupied himself, with the privilege of a renewal for a similar period. Rents were very low at that time, as business was prostrated and people were despondent; but Girard, looking far beyond the present, saw a prosperous future. He was satisfied that it would require but a short time to restore to Philadelphia its old commercial importance, and he was satisfied that his leases would be the best investment he had ever made. The result proved the correctness of his views. His profits on these leases were enormous.

About this time he entered into partnership with his brother, Captain John Girard, in the West India trade. But the brothers could not conduct their affairs harmoniously, and in 1790 the firm was dissolved by mutual consent. Stephen Girard's share of the profits at the dissolution amounted to thirty thousand dollars. His wealth was greatly increased by a terrible tragedy which happened soon afterward.

At the outbreak of the great insurrection in St. Domingo, Girard had two vessels lying in one of the ports of that island. At the first signal of danger, a number of planters sent their valuables on board of these ships for safe-keeping, and went back to their estates for the purpose of securing more. They never returned, doubtless falling victims to the fury of the brutal negroes, and when the vessels were ready to sail there was no one to claim the property they contained. It was taken to Philadelphia, and was most liberally advertised by Mr. Girard, but as no owner ever appeared to demand it, it was sold, and the proceeds—about fifty thousand dollars—turned into the merchant's own coffers. This was a great assistance to him, and the next year he began the building of those splendid ships which enabled him to engage so actively in the Chinese and East India trades.

His course was now onward and upward to wealth. At first his ships merely sailed between Philadelphia and the port to which they were originally destined; but at length he was enabled to do more than this. Loading one of his ships with grain, he would send it to Bordeaux, where the proceeds of her cargo would be invested in wine and fruit. These she would take to St. Petersburg and exchange for hemp and iron, which were sold at Amsterdam for coin. From Amsterdam she would proceed to China and India, and, purchasing a cargo of silks and teas, sail for Philadelphia, where the final purchase was sold by the owner for cash or negotiable paper. His success was uniform, and was attributed by his brother merchants to *luck*.

Stephen Girard had no faith in luck. He never trusted any thing to chance. He was a thorough navigator, and was perfect master of the knowledge required in directing long voyages. He understood every department of his business so well that he was always prepared to survey the field of commerce from a high stand-point. He was familiar with the ports with which he dealt, and was always able to obtain such information concerning them as he desired, in advance of his competitors. He trusted nothing of importance to others. His instructions to the commanders of his ships were always full and precise. These documents afford the best evidence of the statements I have made concerning his system, as the following will show:

Copy of Stephen Girard's Letter to Mr. ——, Commander and Supercargo of the ship ——, bound to Batavia.

PHILADELPHIA, ——.

SIR—I confirm my letters to you of the — ult., and the — inst. Having recently heard of the decease of Mr. ——, merchant at Batavia, also of the probable dissolution of his house, under the firm of Messrs. ——, I have judged it prudent to request my Liverpool correspondents to consign the ship ——, cargo, and specie on board, to Mr. ——, merchant at Batavia, subject to your control, and have requested said Liverpool friends to make a separate invoice and bill of lading for the specie, which they will ship on my account, on board of the ship ——, and similar documents for the merchandise, which they will ship in the same manner; therefore, I request that you will sign in conformity.

I am personally acquainted with Mr. ——, but not with Mr. ——, but I am on very friendly terms with some particular friends of the latter gentleman, and consequently I give him the preference. I am sorry to observe, however, that he is alone in a country where a partner appears to me indispensable to a commercial house, as well for the safety of his own capital as for the security of the interests of those who may confide to them property, and reside in distant parts of the globe.

The foregoing reflections, together with the detention of my ship V——, at Batavia, from June last, epoch of her arrival at that port, until the 15th of September, ——, when she had on board only nineteen hundred peculs of coffee, are the motives which have compelled me to request of my Liverpool friends to consign the specie and goods, which they will ship on my account, on board of the ship ——, under your command, to said Mr. ——, subject to your control.

Therefore, relying upon your activity, perseverance, correctness, zeal, and attention for my interest, I proceed in pointing out to you the plan of conduct which I wish you to pursue on your arrival at Batavia, and during your stay at that or any port of that island, until your departure for Cowes, on the Isle of Wight, to await my subsequent orders.

First. On your arrival at Batavia, you are to go on shore and ascertain Mr. ——'s residence, and, if you have reason to believe that he is still considered at that place as a man of good credit, and merits full confidence, you are to deliver to him my Liverpool consignees' letters to his address, and also the goods which you have on board, in such proportion as he may request, except the specie, which is to continue on board, as mentioned in the next article.

Second. The specie funds of the ship ——, which will consist of old Carolus dollars, you are to retain on board untouched, and in the said boxes or packages as they were in when shipped from Liverpool, well secured, and locked up in your powder magazine, in the after run of the said ship under the cabin floor.

The bulkhead and floor of said magazine, scuttle, iron bar, staples, etc., must be made sufficiently strong, if not already so, while you are at Liverpool, where you are to procure a strong padlock and key, for the purpose of securing said specie in the most complete and safest manner; and when you have the certainty that it is wanted to pay for the coffee purchased on account of the ship ——, then you are to receive the said coffee, and pay or deliver to your consignee Spanish dollars to the amount of said purchase, and no more, having due regard to the premium or advance allowed at Batavia on old Spanish dollars; and in that way you are to continue paying or delivering dollars as fast as you receive coffee, which is not to exceed the quantity which can be conveniently stowed on board said ship ——, observing to take a receipt for each payment, and to see that the net proceeds of the goods, which will have been shipped at Liverpool, must be invested in coffee, as far as the sales will permit, and shipped on board of said ship.

Should it happen that on your arrival at Batavia you should find that death, absence, etc., should deprive you of the services of Mr. ——, or that, owing to some causes before mentioned, it would be prudent to confide my interests elsewhere, in either case you are to apply to Messrs. ——, merchants of that place, to communicate your instructions relative to the disposal of the Liverpool cargo, on board of the ship ——, the loading of that ship with good merchantable coffee, giving the preference to the first quality whenever it can be purchased on reasonable terms for cash, or received in payment for the sales of the said Liverpool cargo, or for a part thereof, observing that I wished said coffee to be purchased at Samarang, or any other out-port, if practicable; and in all cases it must be attentively examined when delivered, and put up in double gunny bags.

If the purchase of said cargo is made at an out-port, the ship —— must proceed there to take it in.

On the subject of purchasing coffee at government sales, I have no doubt that it is an easy way to obtain a cargo, but I am of opinion that it is a very dear one, particularly as the fair purchaser, who has no other object in view but to invest his money, does not stay on the footing of competitors, who make their payments with Netherland bills of exchange, or wish to raise the prices of their coffee which they may have on hand for sale.

Under these impressions, I desire that all the purchases of coffee on my account be made from individuals, as far as practicable, and if the whole quantity necessary to load the ship can not be obtained at private sale, recourse must then be had to government sales.

In many instances I have experienced that whenever I had a vessel at Batavia, the prices of coffee at the government sales have risen from five to ten per cent., and sometimes higher.

On the subject of coffee I would remark that, owing to the increase of the culture of that bean, together with the immense imports of tea into the several ports of Europe, the price of that leaf has been lowered to such a degree as to induce the people of those countries, principally of the north, to use the latter article in preference to the first.

That circumstance has, for these past three years, created a gradual deduction from the consumption of coffee, which has augmented the stock on hand throughout every commercial city of the northern part of the globe, so as to present a future unfavorable prospect to the importers of that article. Indeed, I am convinced that, within a few months from this date, coffee will be ten per cent. cheaper in the United States than what it has been at Batavia for these two years past; nevertheless, being desirous to employ my ships as advantageously as circumstances will permit, and calculating also that the price at Java and other places of its growth will fall considerably, I have no objection to adventure.

Therefore, you must use every means in your power to facilitate the success of the voyage.

Should the invoice-cost of the entire cargo of coffee shipped at Java, on board of the ship ——, together with the disbursements of that ship (which must be conducted with the greatest economy), not amount to the specie funds and net proceeds of her Liverpool cargo, in that event you are to deliver the surplus to your consignee, who will give you a receipt for the same, with a duplicate, expressing that it is on my account, for the purpose of being invested on the most advantageous terms, in good dry coffee, to be kept at my order and disposal.

Then you will retain the original in your possession, and forward to me the duplicate by first good vessel to the United States, or via Europe, to care of my correspondents at Liverpool, London, Antwerp, or Amsterdam, the names of whom you are familiar with.

If you should judge it imprudent, however, to leave that money at Batavia, you are to bring it back in Spanish dollars, which you will retain on board for that purpose.

Although I wish you to make a short voyage, and with as quick dispatch at Java as practicable, yet I desire you not to leave that island unless your consignee has finally closed the sales of the Liverpool cargo, so that you may be the bearer of all the documents, and account-current, relative to the final transactions of the consignment of the ship —— and cargo. Duplicate and triplicate of said documents to be forwarded to me by your consignees, by the two first safe conveyances for the ports of the United States.

Being in the habit of dispatching my ships for Batavia from this port, Liverpool, or Amsterdam, as circumstances render it convenient, it is interesting to me to be from time to time informed of the several articles of produce and manufactures from each of those places which are the most in demand and quickest of sale at Java. Also of the quantity of each, size of package, and the probable price which they may sell for, cash, adding the Batavia duty, charges for selling, etc. Please to communicate this to your Batavia consignee.

The rates of commission I will allow for transacting the business relative to the ship and cargo at Java are two and a half per cent. for selling, and two and a half per cent. for purchasing and shipping coffee and other articles.

The consignees engaging to place on board of each prow one or two men of confidence, to see that the goods are safely delivered on board of the ship, to prevent pilfering, which is often practiced by those who conduct the lighter.

I am informed that the expenses for two men are trifling, comparatively, to the plunder which has been committed on board of the prows which deliver coffee on board of the ships.

No commissions whatever are to be allowed in the disbursements of my ships, whenever ship and cargo belong to me, and are consigned to some house.

While you remain at Batavia, I recommend you to stay on board of your ship, and not to go on shore except when the business of your ship and cargo may render it necessary.

Inclosed is an introductory letter to ——, which I request you to deliver, after you have made the necessary arrangements with Mr. —— for the consignment of the ship and cargo, or after the circumstance aforementioned has compelled you to look elsewhere for a consignee. Then you are to call upon said Messrs. ——, deliver them the aforesaid letter and the consignment of the ship —— and cargo, after having agreed with them in writing, which they will sign and deliver to you, that they engage to transact the business of the ship and cargo on the terms and conditions herein stated; and when that business is well understood and finally closed, you are to press them in a polite manner, so that they may give you a quick dispatch, without giving too great a price for the coffee, particularly at this present moment, when its price is declining throughout those countries where it is consumed.

Indeed, on the subject of purchasing coffee for the ship ——, the greatest caution and prudence should be exercised. Therefore, I request that you will follow the plan of conduct laid down for you throughout. Also, to keep to yourself the intention of the voyage, and the amount of specie you have on board; and in view to satisfy the curious, tell them that it is probable that the ship will take in molasses, rice, and sugar, if the price of that produce is very low, adding that the whole will depend on the success in selling the small Liverpool cargo. The consignees of said cargo should follow the same line of conduct, and if properly attended to by yourself and them, I am convinced that the cargo of coffee can be purchased ten per cent. cheaper than it would be if it is publicly known there is a quantity of Spanish dollars on board, besides a valuable cargo of British goods intended to be invested in coffee for Stephen Girard, of Philadelphia.

During my long commercial experience, I have noticed that no advantage results from telling one's business to others, except to create jealousy or competitors when we are fortunate, and to gratify our enemies when otherwise.

If my remarks are correct, I have no doubt they will show you the necessity of being silent, and to attend with activity, perseverance, and modesty, to the interests of your employer.

As my letters of instruction embrace several interesting objects, I request you to peruse them in rotation, when at sea in fine climates, during your voyage to Batavia, and to take correct extracts, so as to render yourself master of the most essential parts. I conclude by directing your attention to your health and that of your crew.

I am yours, respectfully, STEPHEN GIRARD.

Mr. Girard was not only rigidly precise in his instructions, but he permitted no departure from them. He regarded it as dangerous to allow discretion to any one in the execution of *his* plans. Where a deviation from his instructions might cause success in one case, it would cause loss in ninety-nine others. It was understood among all his employés that a rigid obedience to orders, in even the most trifling particulars, was expected, and would be exacted. If loss came under such circumstances, the merchant assumed the entire responsibility for it.

Upon one occasion one of his best captains was instructed to purchase his cargo of teas at a certain port. Upon reaching home he was summoned by the merchant to his presence.

"Captain ——," said Mr. Girard, sternly, "your instructions required you to purchase your cargo at ——."

"That is true, Mr. Girard," replied the Captain, "but upon reaching that port I found I could do so much better at ——, that I felt justified in proceeding to the latter place."

"You should have obeyed your orders, sir," was the stern retort.

"I was influenced by a desire to serve your interests, sir. The result ought to justify me in my act, since it puts many thousands more into your pocket than if I had bought where I was instructed."

"Captain ——," said Girard, "I take care of my own interests. You should have obeyed your orders if you had broken me. Nothing can excuse your disobedience. You will hand in your accounts, sir, and consider yourself discharged from my service."

He was as good as his word, and, though the captain's disobedience had vastly increased the profit of the voyage, he dismissed him, nor would he ever receive him into his service again.

To his knowledge of his business Mr. Girard joined an unusual capacity for such ventures. He was, it must be said, hard and illiberal in his bargains, and remorseless in exacting the last cent due him. He was prompt and faithful in the execution of every contract, never departed in the slightest from his plighted word, and never engaged in any venture which he was not perfectly able to undertake. He was prudent and cautious in the fullest sense of those terms, but his ventures were always made with a boldness which was the sure forerunner of success.

His fidelity to his word is well shown by a circumstance which had occurred long after he was one of the "money kings" of the land. He was once engaged with his cashier in a discussion as to the length of time a man would consume in counting a million of dollars, telling out each dollar separately. The dispute became animated, and the cashier declared that he could make a million of dots with ink in a few hours.

"I'll tell you what I'll do," said Girard, who was thoroughly vexed by the opposition of the other, "I'll wager five hundred dollars that I can ride in my gig from here to my farm, spend two hours there, and return before you can make your million of dots with ink."

The cashier, after a moment's reflection, accepted the wager, and Mr. Girard departed to his farm. He returned in a few hours, confident that he had won. The cashier met him with a smile.

"Where is my money?" asked Girard, triumphantly.

"The money is mine," replied the cashier. "Come and see."

He led the merchant to an unused room of the bank, and there, to his dismay, Girard saw the walls and ceiling covered with spots of ink, which the cashier had dashed on them with a brush.

"Do you mean to say there are a million of dots here?" he cried, angrily.

"Count them, and see," replied his subordinate, laughing. "You know the wager was a million of dots with ink."

"But I expected you would make them with the pen."

"I did not undertake any thing of the kind."

The joke was too good, and the merchant not only paid the amount of the wager, but the cost of cleaning the walls.

In 1810 the question of renewing the charter of the old Bank of the United States was actively discussed. Girard was a warm friend of that institution, which he believed had been the cause of a very great part of the prosperity of the country, and was firmly convinced that Congress would renew the charter. In this belief he ordered the Barings, of London, to invest all his funds in their hands in shares of the Bank of the United States, which was done, during the following year, to the amount of half a million of dollars. When the charter expired, he was the principal creditor of that institution, which Congress refused to renew. Discovering that he could purchase the old Bank and the cashier's house for one hundred and twenty thousand dollars, he at once secured them, and on the 12th of May, 1812, opened the Girard Bank, with a capital of one million two hundred thousand dollars, which he increased the next year by one hundred thousand dollars more. He retained all the old officers of the Bank of the United States, especially the cashier, Mr. Simpson, to whose skill and experience he was greatly indebted for his subsequent success.

Finding that the salaries which had been paid by the Government were higher than those paid elsewhere, he cut them down to the rate given by the other banks. The watchman had always received from the old Bank the gift of an overcoat at Christmas, but Girard put a stop to this. He gave no gratuities to any of his employés, but confined them to the compensation for which they had bargained; yet he contrived to get out of them service more devoted than was received by other men who paid higher wages and made presents. Appeals to him for aid were unanswered. No poor man ever came full-handed from his presence. He turned a deaf ear to the entreaties of failing merchants to help them on their feet again. He was neither generous nor charitable. When his faithful cashier died, after long years spent in his service, he manifested the most hardened indifference to the bereavement of the family of that gentleman, and left them to struggle along as best they could.

Yet from the first he was liberal and sometimes magnificent in the management of his bank. He would discount none but good paper, but it was his policy to grant accommodations to small traders, and thus encourage beginners, usually giving the preference to small notes, by this system doing very much to avert the evils that would of necessity have sprung from the suspension of the old Bank of the United States. The Government credit was almost destroyed, and money was needed to carry on the war. He made repeated advances to the treasury, unsolicited by the authorities, and on more than one occasion kept the Government supplied with the sinews of war. In 1814, when our prospects, both military and financial, were at their lowest ebb, when the British forces had burned Washington and the New England States were threatening to withdraw from the Union, the Government asked for a loan of five millions of dollars, with the most liberal inducements to subscribers. Only twenty thousand dollars could be obtained, and the project seemed doomed to failure, when it was announced that Stephen Girard had subscribed for the whole amount. This announcement at once restored the public confidence, and Mr. Girard was beset with requests from persons anxious to take a part of the loan, even at an advanced rate. They were allowed to do so upon the original terms. When the Government could not, for want of funds, pay the interest on its debt to him, he wrote to the Secretary of the Treasury:

"I am of opinion that those who have any claim for interest on public stock, etc., should patiently wait for a more favorable moment, or at least receive in payment treasury notes. Should you be under the necessity of resorting to either of these plans, as one of the public creditors, I shall not murmur."

"A circumstance soon occurred, however, which was a source of no little discomfiture to the financial arrangements of his individual institution. This fact was the suspension of specie payments by the State banks, resulting from the non-intercourse act, the suspension of the old bank, and the combined causes tending to produce a derangement of the currency of the country. It was then a matter of great doubt with him how he should preserve the integrity of his own institution, while the other banks were suspending their payments; but the credit of his own bank was effectually secured by the suggestion of his cashier, Mr. Simpson, who advised the recalling of his own notes by redeeming them with specie, and by paying out the notes of the State banks. In this mode not a single note of his own was suffered to be depreciated, and he was thus enabled, in 1817, to contribute effectually to the restoration of specie payments."

He was instrumental in securing the establishment of the new Bank of the United States, and was its largest stockholder and one of its directors. He even offered to unite his own institution with it upon certain liberal conditions, which were refused. Yet he was always a firm friend to it.

"One of the characteristics of Mr. Girard was his public spirit. At one time he freely subscribed one hundred and ten thousand dollars for the navigation of the Schuylkill; at another time he loaned the company two hundred and sixty-five thousand eight hundred and fifty dollars. When the credit of the State of Pennsylvania was prostrated by what was believed to have been an injudicious system of internal improvement, and it was found expedient for the Governor to resort to its metropolis in order to replenish its coffers, he made a voluntary loan to Governor Shultz of one hundred thousand dollars. So far was his disposition to promote the fiscal prosperity of the country manifested, that, as late as 1831, when the country was placed in extreme embarrassment from the scarcity of money, he perceived the cause in the fact that the balance of trade was against us to a considerable extent, and he accordingly drew upon the house of Baring Brothers & Co. for bills of exchange to the amount of twelve thousand pounds sterling, which he disposed of to the Bank of the United States at an advance of ten per cent., which draft was followed up by another for ten thousand, which was disposed of in like manner to other institutions. This act tended to reduce the value of bills, and the rate of exchange suddenly fell. The same spirit which he manifested toward the national currency he exhibited to the corporation of Philadelphia, by erecting new blocks of buildings, and beautifying and adorning its streets; less, apparently, from a desire of profit than from a wish to improve the place which was his adopted home, and where he had reaped his fortunes. His subscription of two hundred thousand dollars to the Danville and Pottsville Railroad, in 1831, was an action in keeping with the whole tenor of his life; and his subscription of ten thousand dollars toward the erection of an exchange looked to the same result."

The war of 1812, which brought financial ruin to so many others, simply increased Girard's wealth. He never lost a ship, and as war prices prevailed, his profits were in accordance with them. One of his ships was taken by a British cruiser at the mouth of the Delaware, in the spring of 1813. Fearing that his prize would be recaptured by an American ship of war if he attempted to send her into port, the English admiral dispatched a flag of truce to Mr. Girard, and proposed to him to ransom the vessel for one hundred and eighty thousand dollars in coin. Girard consented, paid the money, and the ship was allowed to come up to the city. Her cargo consisted of silks, nankeens, and teas, and afforded her owner a profit of half a million of dollars.

Yet in the midst of all his wealth, which in 1828 was estimated at ten millions of dollars, he was a solitary old man.

He lived in a dingy little house in Water Street. His wife had died in an insane asylum, and he was childless. He was repulsive in person. He was feared by his subordinates—by all who had dealings with him—and liked by none. He was mean and close in his personal habits, living on less, perphaps, than any of his clerks, and deriving little or no benefit from his vast wealth, so far as his individual comfort was concerned. He gave nothing in charity. Lazarus would have lain at his doors a life-time without being noticed by him. He was solitary, soured, cold, with a heart of stone, and fully conscious of his personal unpopularity. Yet he valued wealth—valued it for the power it gave him over men. Under that cold, hardened exterior reigned an ambition as profound as that which moved Napoleon. He was ambitious of regulating the financial operations of the land, and proud of his power in this respect, and it should be remembered in his favor that he did not abuse that power after it had passed into his hands.

He had no vices, no dissipations; his whole soul was in his business. He was conscious that his only hope of distinction above his fellow-men was in his wealth, and he was resolved that nothing should make him swerve from his endeavor to accumulate a fortune which should make him all powerful in life and remembered in death. He sought no friends, and was reticent as to his career, saying to those who questioned him about it, "Wait till I am dead; my deeds will show what I was."

Religion had no place in his heart. He was an avowed unbeliever, making a boast of his disbelief. He always worked on Sunday, in order that he might show his disapproval of the observance of it as a day of rest. Rest, he said, made a man rusty, and attendance upon the worship of God he denounced as worse than folly. His favorite books were the works of Voltaire, and he named his best ships after the most celebrated French infidels.

Yet this man, so unloved, so undeserving of love, is said to have once had a warm heart. His early troubles and his domestic griefs are said to have soured and estranged him from mankind.

"No one who has had access to his private papers can fail to be impressed with the belief that these early disappointments furnish the key to his entire character. Originally of warm and generous impulses, the belief in childhood that he had not been given his share of the love and kindness which were extended to others, changed the natural current of his feelings, and, acting on a warm and passionate temperament, alienated him from his home, his parents, and his friends. And when in after time there were superadded years of bitter anguish, resulting from his unfortunate and ill-adapted marriage, rendered even more poignant by the necessity of concealment, and the consequent injustice of public sentiment, marring all his cherished expectations, it may be readily understood why constant occupation became a necessity and labor a pleasure."

This is the testimony of Mr. Henry W. Arey, the distinguished secretary of Girard College, in whose keeping are the papers of the subject of this memoir, and it must be confessed that his view of Girard's character is sustained by the following incidents, the narration of which I have passed over until now, in order that the history of his commercial career might not be interrupted:

In the summer of 1793 the yellow fever broke out with fearful violence in Philadelphia. The citizens fled in dismay, leaving the plague-smitten city to its fate. Houses were left tenantless, and the streets were deserted. It was a season of horror and dread. Those who could not get away avoided each other, and the sufferers were left to languish and die. Money could not buy nurses in sufficient numbers, and often the victims lay unburied for days in the places where they had died. So terrible was the panic that it seemed that nothing could stay it.

On the 10th of September the *Federal Gazette*, the only paper which had not suspended its publication, contained an anonymous card, stating that of the visitors of the poor all but three had succumbed to the disease or fled from the city, and begging assistance from such benevolent citizens as would consent to render their aid. On the 12th and 14th, meetings were held at the City Hall, at the last of which a volunteer committee was appointed to superintend the measures to be taken for checking the pestilence. Twenty-seven men volunteered to serve, but only twelve had the courage to fulfill their promise. They set to work promptly. The hospital at Bush Hill was reported by the physician to be in a deplorable state—without order, dirty and foul, and in need of nurses. The last, he stated, could not be had for any price. Two of the committee now stepped forward and nobly offered themselves as managers of the hospital. They were Stephen Girard and Peter Helm.

Girard was now a man of wealth and influence, and with a brilliant commercial career opening before him. Above all, he was a foreigner, and unpopular in the city. Yet he did not hesitate to take the post from which others shrank. He and Helm were regarded as doomed men, but they did not falter from their self-imposed task. They went to work at once. Girard chose the post of honor, which was the post of danger—the management of the interior of the hospital. His decisive character was at once felt. Order began to appear, medicines and nurses were procured, and the very next day the committee were informed that the hospital had been cleaned and reorganized, and was prepared to receive patients.

Girard opened his purse liberally, and spared no expense where money would avail. But this was not all. Besides personally superintending the interior of the hospital, he went about through the city seeking the sick and conveying them to the hospital.

"In the great scarcity of help, he used frequently to receive the sick and dying at the gate, assist in carrying them to their beds, nurse them, receive their last messages, watch for their last breath, and then, wrapping them in the sheet on which they had died, carry them out to the burial ground and place them in the trench. He had a vivid recollection of the difficulty of finding any kind of fabric in which to wrap the dead, when the vast number of interments had exhausted the supply of sheets. 'I would put them,' he would say, 'in any old rag I could find.'

"If he ever left the hospital, it was to visit the infected districts, and assist in removing the sick from the houses in which they were dying without help. One scene of this kind, witnessed by a merchant who was hurrying past with camphored handkerchief pressed to his mouth, affords us a vivid glimpse of this heroic man engaged in his sublime vocation. A carriage, rapidly driven by a black man, broke the silence of the deserted and grass-grown street. It stopped before a frame house, and the driver, first having bound a handkerchief over his mouth, opened the door of the carriage, and quickly remounted to the box. A short, thick-set man stepped from the coach and entered the house. In a minute or two the observer, who stood at a safe distance watching the proceedings,

GIRARD'S HEROISM.

heard a shuffling noise in the entry, and soon saw the stout little man supporting with extreme difficulty a tall, gaunt, yellow-visaged victim of the pestilence. Girard held round the waist the sick man, whose yellow face rested against his own; his long, damp, tangled hair mingled with Girard's; his feet dragging helpless upon the pavement. Thus he drew him to the carriage door, the driver averting his face from the spectacle, far from offering to assist. Partly dragging, partly lifting, Girard succeeded, after long and severe exertion, in getting him into the vehicle. He then entered it himself, closed the door, and the carriage drove away toward the hospital."*

For sixty days Mr. Girard continued to discharge his duties, never absenting himself from his post, being nobly sustained by Peter Helm.

Again, in 1797 and 1798, when the city was scourged a second and a third time with the fever, he volunteered his services, and more than earned the gratitude of his fellow-citizens. In the absence of physicians, he took upon himself the office of prescribing for the sick, and as his treatment involved careful nursing and the use of simple remedies only, he was very successful. In 1799 he wrote to his friend Devize, then in France, but who had been the physician at the Bush Hill Hospital in 1793:

"During all this frightful time I have constantly remained in the city, and, without neglecting any public duties, I have played a part which will make you smile. Would you believe it, my friend, that I have visited as many as fifteen sick people in a day, and what will surprise you still more, I have lost only one patient, an Irishman, who would drink a little. I do

* James Parton.

not flatter myself that I have cured one single person, but you will think with me that in my quality of Philadelphia physician I have been very moderate, and that not one of my confreres have killed fewer than myself."

Such acts as these should go far in his favor in estimating his character, for they are the very height of true heroism.

Mr. Girard was never idle. Work, as has before been said, was a necessity with him. Nothing would draw him from his labors. His only recreation was to drive to his little farm, which lay a few miles out of the city, and engage with his own hands in the work of tilling it. He was very proud of the vegetables and fruits he raised himself, and took great interest in improving their growth. During the visit of the present head of the house of Baring Bros. (then a young man) to this country, that gentleman supposed he would give Mr. Girard pleasure by informing him of the safe arrival of one of his ships, the Voltaire, from India. Engaging a carriage, he drove to the banker's farm, and inquired for Mr. Girard.

"He is in the hay-loft," was the answer.

"Inform him that I wish to see him," said Mr. Baring; but almost before the words had left his lips Girard was before him.

"I came to inform you," he said, addressing the banker, "that your ship, the Voltaire, has arrived safely."

"I knew that she would reach port safely," said Girard; "my ships always arrive safe. She is a good ship. Mr. Baring, you must excuse me; I am much engaged in my hay." And so saying, he ascended to the loft again.

To the last he was active. In 1830, having reached the age of eighty, he began to lose the sight of his eye; yet he would have no assistance. In attempting to cross a crowded street, he was knocked down by a passing wagon and injured severely. His ear was cut off, his face bruised, and his sight entirely destroyed. His health now declined rapidly, and on the 26th of December, 1831, he died, in the back room of his plain little house in Water Street.

His immense wealth was carefully divided by his will. He gave to his surviving brother and eleven of his nieces sums ranging from five to twenty thousand dollars, and to his remaining niece, who was the mother of a very large family, he gave sixty thousand dollars. He gave to each of the captains then in his employ who had made two voyages in his service, and who should bring his ship safely into port, fifteen hundred dollars. To each of his apprentices he gave five hundred dollars. To his old servants he gave annuities, ranging from three to five hundred dollars each.

He gave thirty thousand dollars to the Pennsylvania Hospital, in which his wife had been cared for; twenty thousand to the Deaf and Dumb Asylum; ten thousand to the Orphan Asylum; ten thousand to the Lancaster schools; ten thousand for the purpose of providing the poor in Philadelphia with free fuel; ten thousand to the Society for the Relief of Distressed Sea-Captains and their Families; twenty thousand to the Masonic Grand Lodge of Pennsylvania, for the relief of poor members; six thousand for the establishment of a free school in Passyunk, near Philadelphia; five hundred thousand dollars to the Corporation of Philadelphia for certain improvements in the city; three hundred thousand to the State of Pennsylvania for her canals; and a portion of his valuable estates in Louisiana to the Corporation of New Orleans, for the improvement of that city.

The remainder of his property, worth then about six millions of dollars, he left to trustees for the erection and endowment of the noble College for Orphans, in Philadelphia, which bears his name.

Thus it will be seen that this man, who seemed steeled to resist appeals for private charity in life, in death devoted all the results of his unusual genius in his calling to the noblest of purposes, and to enterprises of the most benignant character, which will gratefully hand his name down to the remotest ages of posterity.

CHAPTER II.

JOHN JACOB ASTOR.

THOSE who imagine that the mercantile profession is incapable of developing the element of greatness in the mind of man, find a perfect refutation in the career of the subject of this memoir, who won his immense fortune by the same traits which would have raised him to eminence as a statesman. It may be thought by some that he has no claim to a place in the list of famous Americans, since he was not only German by birth, but German in character to his latest day; but it must be borne in mind that America was the theater of his exploits, and that he owed the greater part of his success to the wise and beneficent institutions of the "New Land," as he termed it. In his own country he would have had no opportunity for the display of his great abilities, and it was only by placing himself in the midst of institutions favorable to progress that he was enabled to make use of his talents. It is for this reason, therefore, that we may justly claim him as one of the most celebrated of American merchants.

John Jacob Astor was born in the village of Waldorf, near Heidelberg, in the Grand Duchy of Baden, on the 17th of July, 1763. This year was famous for the conclusion of the Treaties of Paris and Hubertsburg, which placed all the fur-yielding regions of America, from the Gulf of Mexico to the

Frozen Sea, in the hands of England. He was the youngest of four sons, and was born of Protestant parents. He was early taught to read Luther's Bible and the Prayer-book, and throughout his whole life remained a zealous Protestant. He was trained to the habit of rising early, and giving the first of his waking hours to reading the Bible and Prayer-book. This habit he continued all through life, and he often declared that it was to him the source of unfailing pleasure and comfort. His religious impressions were mainly due to his mother, who was a pious, thrifty, and hard-working woman, given to saving, and devoted to her family.

His father, on the contrary, was a jolly "ne'er do well," a butcher by trade, and not overburdened with industry. The business of a butcher in so small a village as Waldorf, where meat was a luxury to the inhabitants, was merely a nominal calling. It knew but one season of real profit. It was at that time the custom in Germany for every farmer to set apart a calf, pig, or bullock, and fatten it against harvest time. As that season approached, the village butcher passed from house to house to slaughter the animal, cure its flesh, or make sausage meat of it, spending, sometimes, several days at each house. This season brought Jacob Astor an abundance of work, and enabled him to provide liberally for the simple wants of his family; but during the rest of the year it was with difficulty that he could make bread for them. Yet Jacob took his hard lot cheerfully. He was merry over his misfortunes, and sought to forget them in the society of companions who gathered at the village beer-house. His wife's remonstrances against such a course of life were sometimes so energetic that the house became any thing but a pleasant place for the children.

Here John Jacob grew up to boyhood. His brothers left home to earn their livelihood elsewhere, as soon as they were old enough to do so, and he alone remained under the paternal roof. His father destined him for his own calling, but the boy shrank from it with disgust. To crown his misfortunes, his mother died, and his father married again, and this time a woman who looked with no favor upon the son. The newly-married pair quarreled continually, and the boy was glad to escape occasionally to the house of a schoolmate, where he passed the night in a garret or outhouse. By daylight he was back at his father's slaughter-house, to assist in carrying out the meat. He was poorly clad and badly fed, and his father's bad reputation wounded him so keenly that he shrank from playing with other boys, and led a life of comparative isolation.

Fortunately for him, he had a teacher, Valentine Jeune by name, the son of French Protestants, who was better fitted for his position than the majority of the more liberally-patronized Catholic instructors. He was well taught by Valentine Jeune in the rudiments of a plain education, and the tutor and the Protestant minister of the village together succeeded so well in his religious instruction that at the age of fourteen he was confirmed. Confirmation is the decisive point in the career of the German youth. Until then he is only a child. Afterward he is regarded as on the threshold of manhood, and is given to understand that the time has come for him to make choice of a career in life.

To the German peasant two courses only lie open, to learn a trade or go out to service. John Jacob was resolved not to do the latter, and he was in no condition to adopt the former. He was already familiar with his father's trade, but he shrank from it with disgust, and he could not hope to obtain money enough to pay for his tuition as an apprentice in any other calling. No workman in the village would receive him as an apprentice for less than fifty dollars, and fifty dollars were then further beyond his reach than as many millions in after years. The harvest was approaching, and Jacob Astor, seeing an unusual amount of work in store for him at that season, decided the matter for his son by informing him that he must prepare to settle down as his assistant. He obeyed, but discontentedly, and with a determination to abandon his home at the earliest practicable moment.

His chief desire was to leave Germany and emigrate to America. The American Revolution had brought the "New Land" into great prominence; and one of the brothers, Henry Astor, had already settled in New York as a butcher, and his letters had the effect of increasing John Jacob's desire to follow him. It was impossible to do so then, for the war which was raging in this country made it any thing but inviting to an emigrant, and the boy was entirely ignorant of the English language. Nevertheless, he knew that the war could not last always, and he resolved to go as soon as peace would allow him. Meanwhile he wished to join his elder brother, who had removed to London, and was now engaged with his uncle in the manufacture of musical instruments. In London he thought he could acquire a knowledge of English, and save from his wages the amount necessary to pay his passage from England to America. He could reach some of the seaports of the Continent by walking. But he needed money to pay his passage from there to Great Britain. His determination thus formed, he made no secret of it, and succeeded at length in extorting a reluctant consent from his father, who was not inclined to expect very much from the future career of his son. His teacher, however, had more faith in him, and said to the butcher, on the morning of the lad's departure: "I am not afraid of John Jacob; he'll get through the world. He has a clear head, and every thing right behind the ears."

He was seventeen years old when he left home; was stout and well built, and had a constitution of iron. He was possessed of a good plain education, and a remarkable degree of common sense. He had no vicious habits or propensities, and was resolved that he would never set foot again in his native town until he could do so as a rich man.

Ardently as he was bent on seeking his fortune in distant lands, it cost him a struggle to go away, for he was a true German in his attachment to his home and family. This attachment he never lost. After providing liberally for his relatives in his will, he made a munificent donation to his native village for the benefit of its poor children.

With his scanty wardrobe in a bundle, which he slung over his shoulder by a stick, and a mere pittance in his purse, he set out from Waldorf, on foot, for the Rhine. "Soon after I left the village," said he, in after-life, "I sat down beneath a tree to rest, and there I made three resolutions: to be honest, to be industrious, and not to gamble." He had but two dollars in his pocket; but this was enough for his purpose. The Rhine was not far distant from his native village, and this part of his journey he easily accomplished on foot. Upon reaching the river, he is said to have secured a place as oarsman on a timber raft. The timber which is cut in the Black Forest for shipment is made up into rafts on the Rhine, but instead of being suffered to float down the stream, as in this country, is rowed by oarsmen, each raft having from sixty to eighty men attached to it. As the labor is severe and attended with some risk, the wages are high, and the lot of the oarsmen not altogether a hard one, as they manage to have a great deal of sport among themselves. The amount paid as wages on these voyages is about ten dollars, besides the coarse fare furnished the men, and the time occupied is about two weeks.

Upon reaching the Dutch seaport at the mouth of the Rhine, young Astor received his wages—the largest sum he had ever possessed—and took passage in a vessel for London, where he was welcomed cordially by his brother, and provided with employment in his manufactory.

He now set to work to prepare himself for his emigration to America. His industry was unflagging. He worked literally from dawn till dark, and practiced the most rigid economy in his expenditures. His leisure time, which was brief, was spent in trying to master the English language, and in acquiring information respecting America. He had anticipated great difficulty in his efforts to learn English, but succeeded beyond his hopes. In six weeks he could make himself understood in that language, and some time before starting for America could speak it with ease, though he never could at any period of his life rid himself of his strong German accent. He was never able to write English correctly, but after being some years in this country acquired a style which was striking and to the point, in spite of its inaccuracy. England, however, was not a favorable place for acquiring information respecting America. The Colonies had exasperated the mother country by their heroic struggle for freedom, which was just drawing to its close, and the New World was pictured to the imagination of the young German in any thing but a favorable light. His most accurate information was gained from those who had returned from America, and these persons, as often as chance threw them in his way, he questioned with eagerness and precision; their answers were carefully stored up in his memory.

In September, 1783, the news of the peace which established the independence of the United States was published in Europe. Young Astor had now been in London two years, and had saved money enough to take him to America. He was the possessor of a suit of good clothes, besides his ordinary wearing apparel, and fifteen guineas in English money, which he had saved from his slender earnings by the absolute denial to himself of every thing not essential to his existence. The way to America was now open, and he resolved to set out at once. For five guineas he bought a steerage passage in a ship bound for Baltimore, and reserving about five pounds sterling of the remainder of his capital in money, invested the rest in seven German flutes, which he bought of his brother, and embarked for the "New Land."

The winter was memorable on land and sea for its severity, and our hero's first voyage was a stormy one. It is said that on one occasion, when the tempest was unusually violent, and the ship in imminent danger, he made his appearance in his Sunday clothes. In reply to those who asked his reason for so strange an act, he said that if he should reach land he would save his best clothes, and that if he was drowned it was immaterial what became of them.

Although the ship sailed in November, it did not reach the Chesapeake until near the end of January, and there, when only one day distant from Baltimore, was caught in the ice, where it was compelled to remain until late in March. This delay was very vexatious to the young emigrant, but it proved in the end the greatest blessing that could have befallen him. During the voyage Astor had made the acquaintance of one of his fellow passengers, a German, somewhat older than himself, and, while the ship lay fast in the ice, the two were constantly together. As a consequence of the intimacy which thus sprung up between them, they exchanged confidences, told each other their history, and their purpose in coming to America. Astor learned that his friend had emigrated to the New World a few years before, friendless and penniless, but that, beginning in a little way, he had managed to become a fur trader. He bought his furs from the Indians, and from the boatmen plying on the Hudson River. These he sold at a small profit to larger dealers, until he had accumulated a considerable sum for one in his position. Believing that he could find a better market in Europe than in America, he had embarked all his capital in skins, which he had taken to England and sold at a heavy advance. The proceeds he had invested in toys and trinkets valued by the savages, and was now on his way back with them, intending to go into the wilderness himself and purchase an additional stock of furs from the Indians. He recommended Astor to enter upon the same business; gave him valuable information as to the value of peltries in America and in England; told him the best way of buying, packing, preserving, and shipping the skins, and gave him the names of the leading furriers in New York, Montreal, and London. Astor was deeply impressed with the views of his friend, but he could not see his own way clear to such a success, as he had no capital. His friend assured him that capital was unnecessary if he was willing to begin in an humble way. He could buy valuable furs on the wharves of New York for toys and trinkets, and even for cakes, from the Indians who visited the city, and these he could sell at an advance to the New York dealers. He advised the young man, however, not to be satisfied with the American market, but to work for a position which would enable him to send his furs to England, where they would bring four or five times as much as in this country. Astor carefully treasured up all that his friend said to him, and quietly resolved that he would lose no time in entering upon this business, which seemed to promise so much.

The two friends traveled together from Baltimore to New York, where they were warmly received by Astor's brother,

Henry, who had succeeded in laying the foundation of a prosperous business as a butcher, in which he afterward made a large fortune. Both brothers were men of business habits, and on the very first evening after the arrival of the new-comer they began to discuss plans for his future. Astor's friend stated all the advantages of the fur trade, and convinced Henry Astor that it was a fine field for the energies of his brother; and it was agreed that it would be best for the young man to seek employment in the service of some furrier in the city, in order that he might thoroughly learn the business, and familiarize himself with the country and its customs. To his great delight, young Astor learned that, so far from being compelled to pay his employer for learning him the business, as in Europe, he would be certain here to receive his board and nominal wages from the first. The next day the three started out, and succeeded in obtaining a situation for the young man in the store of Mr. Robert Bowne, a Quaker, and a merchant of long experience in the business, as well as a most estimable man. He is said to have engaged Astor at two dollars per week and his board.

Astor was at once set to work by his employer to beat furs, this method of treating them being required to prevent the moths from lodging in and destroying them. From the first he applied himself to the task of learning the business. He bent all the powers of his remarkable mind to acquiring an intimate knowledge of furs, and of fur-bearing animals, and their haunts and habits. His opportunities for doing so were very good, as many of the skins were sold over Bowne's counters by the hunters who had taken them. These men he questioned with a minuteness that astonished them, and the result was that in a few years he was as thoroughly familiar with the animals, their habits, their country, and the mode of taking them, as many of the trappers themselves. He is said to have been in his prime the best judge of furs in America. He appreciated the fact that no man can succeed in any business or profession without fully understanding it, and he was too much determined upon success to be satisfied with a superficial knowledge. He was resolved that there should be no detail in the business, however minute, with which he was unfamiliar, and he toiled patiently to acquire information which most salesmen in his place would have esteemed trivial. Nothing was trivial with him, however, and it is remarkable that he never embarked in any scheme until he had mastered its most trifling details. Few men have ever shown a deeper and more far-reaching knowledge of their profession and the issues involved in it than he. He fully understood that his knowledge would give him a power which a man of less information could not obtain, and he never failed to use that knowledge as a power. His instructions to his subordinates were always drawn up with the strictest regard to details, and show not only how thoroughly he had mastered the subject before him, but also how much importance he attached to the conscientious fulfillment of a well-digested plan of operations. He recognized no such thing as luck. Every thing with him was the result of a deliberate plan based upon knowledge. In this respect his career affords one of the best models to be found in our history.

Astor's employer was not insensible to his merits, and soon promoted him to a better place. In a little while the latter intrusted him with the buying of the furs from the men who brought them to the store, and he gave such satisfaction to his employer that he was rewarded with a still more confidential post. Montreal was at that time the chief fur depot of the country, and it was the custom of Mr. Bowne to make an an-

ASTOR'S FIRST TRIP FOR FURS.

nual journey to that city for the purpose of replenishing his stock. The journey was long and fatiguing, and as soon as the old gentleman found that he could intrust the mission to his clerk, he sent him in his place. Ascending the Hudson to Albany, Astor, with a pack on his back, struck out across the country, which was then almost unsettled, to Lake George, up which he passed into Lake Champlain. Sailing to the head of the lake, he made his way to Montreal. Then returning in the same way, he employed Indians to transport his furs from Lake George to Albany, and dropped down the Hudson in the way he had come. Mr. Bowne was delighted with the success of his clerk, who proved more than a match for the shrewd Indians in his bargains. It was doubtless here that Mr. Astor obtained that facility in "driving a hard bargain" for which he was afterwards noted.

As soon as Mr. Astor felt himself master of his business, he left the employ of Mr. Bowne, and began life on his own account. The field upon which he purposed entering was extensive, but it was one of which he had made a careful survey. Previous to the peace of 1763, the French and English divided the control of the fur-bearing regions of America. The British possessions, extending from Canada to the unexplored regions of the North, had been granted by a charter of Charles II. to Prince Rupert, and were, by virtue of that instrument, under the exclusive control of the Hudson Bay Company. Large quantities of furs were obtained in this region, and collected at the principal settlement, York Factory, from which they were shipped to England.

South of this region was Canada, then possessed by the French, who carried on an extensive trade with the Indians, who brought their furs down to Montreal in their birch canoes. The French finally settled in the country of the savages, and married among the natives, thenceforward entirely devoting themselves to the life of the trapper and hunter. These marriages produced a race of half-breeds who were especially successful in securing furs. The cession of Canada to England was a severe blow to the French traders, as it opened the country to the enterprise of the English, a few of whom were quick to avail themselves of its advantages. The French and Indians at first regarded them with hostility, but gradually became reconciled to their presence.

Under the French rule the savages had not been furnished with liquors, but the English soon sold whisky and rum in great quantities to them, receiving the best furs in return. As a consequence, intemperance spread rapidly among the savages, and threatened to put an end to their industry as gatherers of furs. To check the evil results of this irregular trading, a company was established in 1785, called the North-west Company. It was managed by twelve partners, some of whom resided at Montreal, and others at the trading posts in the interior. Their chief station was at Fort William, on Lake Superior. Here, at stated times, the agents would come up from Montreal and hold a consultation for the purchase of furs. These meetings always drew crowds of French and Indian trappers, boatmen, and others, who brought in large quantities of skins.

A few years later a third company was organized, with its principal station at Michilimackinac, near Lake Huron. It was called the Mackinaw Company, and its field of operations was the country bordering Lake Superior, and that lying between the Mississippi and the Rocky Mountains. The company was English, but did not hesitate to operate in American territory, so little regard did Great Britain pay to the rights of the infant republic.

"Although peace had been concluded, the frontier forts had

not been given up. Oswego, Niagara, Detroit, Michilimackinac, and other posts were still in the hands of the English. The Indian tribes continued hostile, being under English influence. No company had as yet been formed in the United States. Several French houses at St. Louis traded with the Indians, but it was not until 1807 that an association of twelve partners, with a capital of forty thousand dollars, was formed at St. Louis, under the name of the Missouri Company.

"The trade, it will thus be seen, was almost wholly in the hands of the English companies—the Hudson's Bay Company in the north, the North-west Company in the Canadas, the Mackinaw Company in the territories of the United States—and the few American traders in the field had to rely on their individual resources, with no aid from a Government too feeble in its infancy to do more than establish a few Indian agencies, and without constitutional power to confer charter privileges."

The voyage of Captain Cook had brought to the notice of the fur dealers of the world the sea otter of the northern Pacific, and the announcement made upon the return of the expedition drew large numbers of adventurers to the west coast of America, in search of the valuable skins of these animals. In 1792, there were twenty-one vessels, principally American, on the coast.

It was into this field, already occupied by powerful and hostile corporations, that the young German entered. He was perfectly aware of the opposition his efforts would encounter from them, but he was not dismayed. He began business in 1786, in a small store in Water Street, which he furnished with a few toys and notions suited to the tastes of the Indians who had skins to sell. His entire capital consisted of only a few hundred dollars, a portion of which was loaned him by his brother. He had no assistants. He did all his own work. He bought his skins, cured, beat, and sold them himself.

Several times during the year he made journeys on foot through western New York, buying skins from the settlers, farmers, trappers, savages, wherever he could find them. He tramped over nearly the entire State in this way, and is said to have had a better knowledge of its geography and topography than any man living.

"He used to boast, late in life, when the Erie Canal had called into being a line of thriving towns through the center of the State, that he had himself, in his numberless tramps, designated the sites of those towns, and predicted that one day they would be the centers of business and population. Particularly he noted the spots where Rochester and Buffalo now stand, one having a harbor on Lake Erie and the other upon Lake Ontario. He predicted that those places would one day be large and prosperous cities; and that prediction he made when there was scarcely a settlement at Buffalo, and only wigwams on the site of Rochester."

During these tramps his business in the city was managed by a partner, with whom he was finally compelled to associate himself.

As soon as he had collected a certain number of bales of skins he shipped them to London, and took a steerage passage in the vessel which conveyed them. He sold his skins in that city at a fine profit, and succeeded in forming business connections which enabled him afterward to ship his goods direct to London, and draw regularly upon the houses to which they were consigned. He also made an arrangement with the house of Astor & Broadwood, in which his brother was a partner, by which he became the agent in New York for the sale of their musical instruments, a branch of his business which became quite profitable to him. He is said to have been the first man in New York who kept a regular stock of musical instruments on hand.

Slowly, and by unremitting industry, Mr. Astor succeeded in building up a certain business. His personal journeys made him acquainted with the trappers, and enabled him to win their good will. The savages sold their skins to him readily, and he found a steady market and a growing demand for his commodities in the Old World.

It was about this time that he married Miss Sarah Todd, of New York. She was a connection of the Brevoort family, and was of better social position than her husband. She entered heartily into his business, doing much of the buying and beating of the furs herself. She was a true helpmate to him, and long after he was a millionaire, he used to boast of her skill in judging furs and conducting business operations.

In 1794, Jay's treaty placed the frontier forts in the hands of the Americans, and thus increased the opportunities of our own traders to extend their business. It was of the greatest service to Mr. Astor. It enabled him to enlarge the field of his operations, and, at the same time, to send his agents on the long journeys which he formerly made, while he himself remained in New York to direct his business, which by this time had grown to considerable proportions.

He was now on the road to wealth. He had scores of trappers and hunters working for him in the great wilderness, and his agents were kept busy buying and shipping the skins to New York. As soon as he was able to do so he purchased a ship, in which he sent his furs to London, occasionally making a voyage thither himself. He manifested the greatest interest in the markets of the Old World, especially in those of Asia, and informed himself so accurately concerning them that he was always enabled to furnish his captains with instructions covering the most minute detail of their transactions in those markets; and it is said that he was never unsuccessful in his ventures there, except when his instructions were disobeyed.

In this again, as in the fur trade, we see him patiently acquiring knowledge of the eastern trade before venturing to engage in it. His first step was always to fully comprehend his task, to examine it from every possible point of view, so that he should be prepared to encounter any sudden reverse, or ready to take advantage of good fortune. Here lay the secret of his success—that he never embarked in an enterprise until he had learned how to use it to advantage.

Under his skillful management his business grew rapidly; but he avoided speculation, and confined himself to legitimate commerce. He was plain and simple in his habits, carrying this trait to an extreme long after economy had ceased to be necessary to him. He worked hard, indulged in no pleasures except horseback exercise and the theater, of both which he was very fond. It was only after he had amassed a large fortune that he ever left his business before the close of the day. Then he would leave his counting-room at two in the afternoon, and, partaking of an early dinner, would pass the rest of the day in riding about the island. So plain was his style of living that, before he became generally known as a wealthy man, a bank clerk once superciliously informed him that his indorsement of a note would not be sufficient, as it was not likely he would be able to pay it in case the bank should be forced to call upon him.

"Indeed," said Mr. Astor, "how much do you suppose I am worth?"

The clerk named a moderate amount, at which the merchant smiled quietly.

"Would the indorsement of Mr. ——, or Mr. ——, be sufficient?" asked Mr. Astor, naming several well-known merchants who lived in great style.

"Entirely sufficient," was the reply. "Each one of them is known to be wealthy."

"How much do you think each is worth?"

The clerk named large sums in connection with each of the gentlemen.

"Well, my friend," said the merchant, "I am worth more than any of them. I will not tell you how much I am worth, but it is more than any sum you have named."

The clerk looked at him in surprise, and then said, bluntly, "Then you are a greater fool than I took you for, to work as hard as you do."

Mr. Astor was very fond of telling this story, which he regarded as one of the best jokes of the day.

All this time Mr. Astor had lived over his store, but in 1800, after he had been in business fifteen years, he moved his dwelling to 223 Broadway, on the site of the Astor House of to-day. He lived here, with one removal, for upwards of twenty-five years. The house was plain and simple, but he was satisfied with it. He was now worth a quarter of a million dollars, and his business was growing rapidly. The fur trade was exceedingly profitable. A beaver skin could be bought from the trappers in western New York for one dollar and sold in London for six dollars and a quarter. By investing this amount in English manufactures, the six dollars and a quarter received for the skin could be made to produce ten dollars paid for the English goods in New York.

The Chinese trade was also very profitable. China was an

excellent market for furs. They brought high prices, and the proceeds could always be invested in teas and silks, which sold well in New York. His profit on a voyage would sometimes reach seventy thousand dollars, and the average gain on a lucky venture of this kind was thirty thousand dollars. The high prices produced by the war of 1812–15 were also in Mr. Astor's favor. His ships were all remarkably lucky in escaping capture by the enemy, and he was almost the only merchant who had a cargo of tea in the market. Tea having reached double its usual price, he was enabled to reap immense profits from his ventures.

Mr. Francis, in his *Old Merchants of New York*, makes the following revelation of the manner in which Mr. Astor found it possible to carry on such an immense business. He says:

"A house that could raise money enough, thirty years ago, to send $260,000 in specie, could soon have an uncommon capital; and this was the working of the old system. The Griswolds owned the ship Panama. They started her from New York in the month of May, with a cargo of perhaps $30,000 worth of ginseng, spelter, lead, iron, etc., and $170,000 in Spanish dollars. The ship goes on the voyage, reaches Whampoa in safety (a few miles below Canton). Her supercargo, in two months, has her loaded with tea, some chinaware, a great deal of cassia, or false cinnamon, and a few other articles. Suppose the cargo mainly tea, costing about thirty-seven cents (at that time) per pound on the average.

"The duty was enormous in those days. It was twice the cost of the tea, at least; so that a cargo of $200,000, when it had paid duty of seventy-five cents per pound (which would be $400,000), amounted to $600,000. The profit was at least fifty per cent. on the original cost, or $100,000, and would make the cargo worth $700,000.

"The cargo of teas would be sold almost on arrival (say eleven or twelve months after the ship left New York in May), to wholesale grocers, for their notes at four and six months—say for $700,000. In those years there was *credit given by the United States* of nine, twelve, and eighteen months! So that the East India or Canton merchant, after his ship had made one voyage, had the use of Government capital to the extent of $400,000, on the ordinary cargo of a China ship.

"No sooner had the ship Panama arrived (or any of the regular East Indiamen), than her cargo would be exchanged for grocers' notes for $700,000. These notes could be turned into specie very easily, and the owner had only to pay his bonds for duty at nine, twelve, and eighteen months, giving him time actually to send two more ships, with $200,000 each, to Canton, and have them back again in New York before the bonds on the first cargo were due.

"John Jacob Astor, at one period of his life, had several vessels operating in this way. They would go to the Pacific, and carry furs from thence to Canton. These would be sold at large profits. Then the cargoes of tea to New York would pay enormous duties, which Astor did not have to pay to the United States for a year and a half. His tea cargoes would be sold for good four and six months paper, or perhaps cash; so that, for eighteen or twenty years, John Jacob Astor had what was actually a free-of-interest loan from Government of over *five millions* of dollars."

It is estimated that Mr. Astor made about two millions of dollars by his trade in furs and teas. The bulk of his immense fortune was made by investments in real estate. His estate was estimated at twenty millions of dollars at the time of his death, and has now increased to over forty millions. He had a firm faith in the magnificent future of New York as the greatest city of the continent, and as fast as his gains from his business came in, they were regularly invested in real estate. A part was expended in leasing for a long period property which the owners would not sell, and the rest in buying property in fee simple. These leases, some of which have but recently expired, were extremely profitable. In his purchases of land Mr. Astor was very fortunate. He pursued a regular system in making them. Whenever a favorable purchase could be made in the heart of the city, he availed himself of the opportunity, but as a rule he bought his lands in what was then the suburb of the city, and which few besides himself expected to see built up during their lifetime. His sagacity and foresight have been more than justified by the course of events. His estate now lies principally in the heart of New York, and has yielded an increase greater even than he had ventured to hope for. Seventy hundred and twenty houses are said to figure on the rent roll of the Astor estate at present, and besides these are a number of lots not yet built upon, but which are every day increasing in value. When Mr. Astor bought Richmond Hill, the estate of Aaron Burr, he gave one thousand dollars an acre for the hundred and sixty acres. Twelve years later, the land was valued at fifteen hundred dollars per lot.

In 1810, he sold a lot near Wall Street for eight thousand dollars. The price was so low that a purchaser for cash was found at once, and this gentleman, after the sale, expressed his surprise that Mr. Astor should ask only eight thousand for a lot which in a few years would sell for twelve thousand.

"That is true," said Mr. Astor, "but see what I intend doing with these eight thousand dollars. I shall buy eighty lots above Canal Street, and by the time your one lot is worth twelve thousand dollars, my eighty lots will be worth eighty thousand dollars."

His expectations were realized.

During the war of the Revolution, Roger Morris and his wife, Mary, of Putnam County, were obliged to flee from the country to England for adhering to the cause of King George, and, being attainted by the authorities as public enemies, their immense estate, consisting of fifty-one thousand one hundred and two acres, was seized by the State of New York, and sold in small parcels to farmers, who believed the title thus acquired valid. In 1809, there were upwards of seven hundred families residing on this land. Mr. Astor, having learned that Roger and Mary Morris possessed only a life interest in their property, and having ascertained to his satisfaction that the State could not confiscate the rights of the heirs, purchased their claim, which was good not only for the land, but for all the improvements that had been put upon it. He paid twenty thousand pounds sterling for it. A few years previous to the death of Mrs. Morris, who survived her husband some years, Mr. Astor presented his claim. The occupants of the land were thunderstruck, but the right was on his side. The State of New York had simply robbed the heirs of their rights. There was no weak point in the claim. Having given defective titles to the farmers, the State was of course responsible for the claim; and upon finding out their mistake, the authorities asked Mr. Astor to name the sum for which he would be willing to compromise. The lands were valued at six hundred and sixty-seven thousand dollars, but Mr. Astor expressed his willingness to sell for three hundred thousand dollars. His offer was refused. In 1819, a second proposition was made to Mr. Astor by the Legislature of the State. He replied: "In 1813 or 1814 a similar proposition was made to me by the commissioners then appointed by the Honorable the Legislature of this State, when I offered to compromise for the sum of three hundred thousand dollars, which, considering the value of the property in question, was thought very reasonable, and, at the present period, when the life of Mrs. Morris is, according to calculation, worth little or nothing, she being near eighty-six years of age, and the property more valuable than it was in 1813. I am still willing to receive the amount which I then stated, with interest on the same, payable in money or stock, bearing an interest of — per cent., payable quarterly. The stock may be made payable at such periods as the Honorable the Legislature may deem proper. This offer will, I trust, be considered as liberal, and as a proof of my willingness to compromise on terms which are reasonable, considering the value of the property, the price which it cost me, and the inconvenience of having so long *lain out* of my money, which, if employed in commercial operations, would most likely have produced better profits."

This offer was not accepted by the Legislature, and the cause was delayed until 1827, when it was brought before the courts. It was argued by such men as Daniel Webster and Martin Van Buren, on the part of the State, and by Thomas Addis Emmett, Ogden, and others for Astor. The State had no case, and the matter was decided in Astor's favor. Then the State consented to compromise. The famous Astor stock, which paid that gentleman about five hundred thousand dollars, was issued, and the titles of the possessors of the lands confirmed.

The most important of all of Mr. Astor's undertakings was his effort at founding the settlement of Astoria, on the coast of Oregon. This enterprise has been made so familiar to the majority of readers by the pen of Washington Irving, that I can only refer to it here. "His design," says a writer of thirteen years ago, "was to organize and control the fur trade from the lakes to the Pacific, by establishing trading posts along the Missouri and Columbia to its mouth. He designed establishing a central depot and post at the mouth of the Columbia. He proposed sending regular supply-ships to the Pacific posts around the Horn. By these, stores were to be sent also to the Russian establishments. It was part of his plan, if possible, to obtain possession of one of the Sandwich Islands as a station, for from the Pacific coast he knew that the Chinese market for his peltries could be most conveniently reached, and thus the necessity for a long and circuitous voyage be avoided. Instead of bringing the furs intended for China to New York, they could be sent from the Pacific. By the supply-ships, too, the stock of goods suitable for the Indian trade would be kept up there, and the cargoes purchased with the proceeds of the furs sold in China brought back to New York. The line of posts across the continent would become a line of towns; emigration would follow, and civilization would belt the continent.

"In this grand scheme, Mr. Astor was only anticipating the course of events which, fifty years later, we are beginning to witness. When he laid his plans before the Government, Mr. Jefferson, who was then President, 'considered as a great acquisition,' as he afterward expressed himself in a letter to Mr. Astor, 'the commencement of a settlement on the western coast of America, and looked forward with gratification to the time when its descendants should have spread themselves through the whole length of that coast, covering it with free and independent Americans, unconnected with us except by ties of blood and interest, and enjoying, like us, the rights of self-government.' Even Jefferson's mind, wide as it was, could not take in the idea of a national unity embracing both ends of the continent; but not so thought Astor. The merchant saw farther than the statesman. It was precisely this political unity which gave him hope and chance of success in his world-wide schemes. When the Constitution was adopted, the chief source of apprehension for its permanence with men like Patrick Henry, and other wise statesmen, was the extent of our territory. The Alleghanies, it was thought, had put asunder communities whom no paper constitution could unite. But at that early day, when Ohio was the far West, and no steamboat had yet gone up the Mississippi, Astor looked beyond the Ohio, beyond the Mississippi, and the Rocky Mountains, and saw the whole American territory, from ocean to ocean, the domain of one united nation, the seat of trade and industry. He saw lines of trading posts uniting the Western settlements with the Pacific; following this line of trading posts, he saw the columns of a peaceful emigration crossing the plains, crossing the mountains, descending the Columbia, and towns and villages taking the places of the solitary posts, and cultivated fields instead of the hunting-grounds of the Indian and the trapper.

"No enterprise, unless it be the Atlantic telegraph, engages more deeply the public attention than a railroad communication with the Pacific coast.* The rapid settlement of Oregon and California, the constant communication by steam to the Pacific coast, render it easy now to feel the nearness of that region, and the oneness of the nationality which covers the continent. But to Astor's eye the thing was as palpable then as now. And yet but two or three attempts had then been made to explore the overland routes."

It would be deeply interesting to examine the details of this vast scheme of colonization and trade, for it is certain that Mr. Astor was as anxious to do an act which, by building up the continent, should hand his name down to posterity as a national benefactor, as to increase his business; but the limits of this article forbid more than a mere glance at the subject.

* The reader will bear in mind that the above extract was written in 1857.

A company was formed, at the head of which stood Mr. Astor, and an elaborate and carefully-arranged plan of operations prepared. Two expeditions were dispatched to the mouth of the Columbia, one by land and the other by sea. Many hardships were encountered, but the foundation of a settlement was successfully made on the Columbia. In spite of the war with England (1812–15), which now occurred, the enterprise would have been successful had Mr. Astor's positive instructions been obeyed. They were utterly disregarded, however, and his partners and agents not only betrayed him in every instance, but sold his property to a rival British company for a mere trifle. His pecuniary loss was over a million of dollars, and his disappointment bitter beyond expression. When the enterprise was on the point of failure, and while he was still chafing at the conduct of his treacherous subordinates, he wrote to Mr. Hunt, the most faithful of all his agents: "Were I on the spot, and had the management of affairs, I would defy them all; but as it is, every thing depends on you and your friends about you. Our enterprise is grand, and deserves success, and I hope in God it will meet it. *If my object was merely gain of money*, I should say, think whether it is best to save what we can, and abandon the place; but the very idea is like a dagger to my heart." When the news of the final betrayal reached him, he wrote to the same gentleman: "Had our place and property been fairly captured, I should have preferred it; I should not feel as if I were disgraced."

Mr. Astor remained in active business for fifty years. During that entire period he scarcely committed an error of judgment which led to a loss in business. He was thorough master of every thing pertaining to his affairs, and his strength and accuracy of judgment was remarkable. The particulars of his transactions were indelibly impressed upon his mind. His intellect was vigorous and quick, and he grasped a subject with a readiness which seemed like intuition. He was always careful of the present, but he loved to undertake enterprises which extended far into the future. He was a man of the utmost punctuality in all his habits. He rose early, and, until he was fifty-five years old, was always in his office before seven o'clock. His capacity for work was very great, so that, in spite of his heavy labors, he was always able to leave his office by two o'clock, while many of his associates, who really did less than he, were compelled to remain in their counting-rooms until four or five. He was noted for his unvarying calmness, which he doubtless owed to his German temperament. In the midst of disaster and loss he was cooler and more cheerful than ever. To those who chafed at their troubles, he would say, smilingly, "Keep quiet; keep cool." This was his safeguard.

He was a devoted citizen of the United States, and, though he took no active interest in politics, was a steady supporter of the Whig party. Henry Clay was his personal friend, and his last donation to any political cause was a subscription of fifteen hundred dollars to aid the election of his old friend to the Presidency.

About the year 1830, Mr. Astor, now the possessor of millions, began to withdraw from active business, confining his efforts chiefly to such investments as the management of his immense estate made necessary. He now put into execution an enterprise which he had long cherished. When a poor stranger in the city, he had once stopped in Broadway to notice a row of buildings which had just been erected, and which were considered the finest in the street, and had then made a vow that he would one day build a larger and finer house than any in Broadway. He now set to work to carry out the plan he had cherished ever since. He owned the entire block on Broadway, between Vesey and Barclay streets, with the exception of one house, which was the property of a Mr. Coster, a merchant who had amassed a large fortune and retired from business. Mr. Astor made him many offers for his house, but the old gentleman was unwilling to remove. Mr. Astor offered him the full value of his house, which was thirty thousand dollars, and increased the bid to forty thousand, but Mr. Coster was obstinate. At length Mr. Astor, in despair, was compelled to reveal his plan to his neighbor.

"I want to build a hotel," said he. "I have got all the other lots. Now name your own price."

Mr. Coster replied that he would sell for sixty thousand dollars if his wife would consent, and that Mr. Astor could see her the next morning. Mr. Astor was punctual to the appointment, and his offer was accepted by the good lady, who said to him, condescendingly, "I do n't want to sell the house, but we are such old friends that I am willing for your sake."

Mr. Astor used to remark with great glee that any one could afford to exhibit such condescension after receiving double the value of a piece of property.

Having got possession of the entire block, he commenced the demolition of the old buildings, and on their site reared the Astor House, then the largest and most elegant hotel in the country. This building, when completed, he gave to his eldest son, William B. Astor.

In 1832, Mr. Astor sailed for Europe to visit one of his daughters, who had married a nobleman, and remained abroad until 1835. In that year he was compelled to return home by the action of General Jackson with regard to the Bank of the United States. "He reached Havre," says Mr. Parton, "when the ship, on the point of sailing, had every stateroom engaged, but he was so anxious to get home, that the captain, who had commanded ships for him in former years, gave up to him his own stateroom. Head winds and boisterous seas kept the vessel beating about and tossing in the channel for many days. The great man was very sick, and still more alarmed. At length, being persuaded that he should not survive the voyage, he asked the captain to run in and set him ashore on the coast of England. The captain dissuaded him. The old man urged his request at every opportunity, and said, at last, 'I give you tousand dollars to put me aboard a pilot boat.' He was so vehement and importunate, that one day the captain, worried out of all patience, promised him that if he did not get out of the channel before next morning, he would run in and put him ashore. It happened that the wind changed in the afternoon and wafted the ship into the broad ocean. But the troubles of the sea-sick millionaire had only just begun. A heavy gale of some days' duration blew the vessel along the western coast of Ireland. Mr. Astor, now thoroughly panic-stricken, offered the captain ten thousand dollars if he would put him ashore anywhere on the wild and rocky coast of the Emerald Isle. In vain the captain remonstrated. In vain he reminded the old gentleman of the danger of forfeiting his insurance.

"'Insurance!' exclaimed Astor, "can't I insure your ship myself?'

"In vain the captain mentioned the rights of the other passengers. In vain he described the solitary and rock-bound coast, and detailed the dangers and difficulties which attended its approach. Nothing would appease him. He said he would take all the responsibility, brave all the perils, endure all the consequences, only let him once more feel the firm ground under his feet. The gale having abated, the captain yielded to his entreaties, and engaged, if the other passengers would consent to the delay, to stand in, and put him ashore. Mr. Astor went into the cabin, and proceeded to write what was expected to be a draft for ten thousand dollars in favor of the owners of the ship on his agent in New York. He handed to the captain the result of his efforts. It was a paper covered with writing that was totally illegible.

"'What is this?' asked the captain.

"'A draft upon my son for ten thousand dollars,' was the reply.

"'But no one can read it.'

"'O yes, my son will know what it is. My hand trembles so that I can not write any better.'

"'But,' said the captain, 'you can at least write your name. I am acting for the owners of the ship, and I can not risk their property for a piece of paper that no one can read. Let one of the gentlemen draw up a draft in proper form; you sign it, and I will put you ashore.'

"The old gentleman would not consent to this mode of proceeding, and the affair was dropped."

During the last twenty years of his life Mr. Astor lived in the retirement of his family, leaving even the greater part of the management of his estate to the hands of others. He was exceedingly fond of literary men. Irving was his friend, and Halleck his business manager. He died at the age of eighty-four years and eight months, literally from old age. He was buried in St. Thomas's Church, on Broadway.

His immense estate was left to his children, the bulk of it being bequeathed to his eldest son. All of his relatives were made comfortable. The village of Waldorf, his native place, received a legacy of fifty thousand dollars for the benefit of its poor, and an amount in land and funds equal to four hundred thousand dollars was left to certain trustees to establish the Astor Library in the city of New York. Besides these, several charitable and benevolent associations received handsome donations from him.

His career has been related in these pages as an example to those who are seeking to rise in legitimate commerce. It is the best instance on record of the facility with which success may be won by patient and intelligent industry. In his capacity for grasping and carrying out an enterprise, in his prudent and economical management of his business, in his tact, courage, sagacity, Mr. Astor's example is one which will lead many to success, and none to injury.

He was a thoroughly upright man, his transactions were rigidly honest; but as a man, candor compels the acknowledgment that he was not a safe or admirable model. He was utterly devoid of generosity. Liberal to an extreme with his own family, he was close and hard with others. He paid small wages to his employés, and never gave more than the man bargained for, no matter what extra service might be rendered. He carried his economy to a degree of meanness painful to contemplate. At his death, out of his vast estate, he left to his friend and faithful manager an annuity of only two hundred dollars, which his son increased to fifteen hundred.

One of his captains once succeeded in saving for him property in China to the amount of seven hundred thousand dollars, which had become jeopardized by the sudden death of the agent in charge of it. This service was purely voluntary, and was one which required the greatest skill, determination, and courage on the part of the captain, and Astor acknowledged it, frequently saying: "If you had not done just as you did, I should never have seen one dollar of my money; no, not one dollar of it." This was the only acknowledgment he made, however. He was worth ten millions of dollars, and the captain had only his pay—twelve hundred dollars a year—and a family. At his father's death Mr. William B. Astor sent a considerable sum to the old seaman in return for this service.

"We have all heard much of the closeness, or rather the meanness, of this remarkable man. Truth compels us to admit that he was not generous, except to his own kindred. His liberality began and ended in his own family. Very seldom during his lifetime did he willingly do a generous act, outside of the little circle of his relations and descendants. To get all he could, and to keep nearly all that he got—those were the laws of his being. . . . . He enjoyed keenly the consciousness, the feeling, of being rich. The roll-book of his possessions was his Bible. He scanned it fondly, and saw, with quiet but deep delight, the catalogue of his property lengthening from month to month. The love of accumulation grew with his years, until it ruled him like a tyrant. If at fifty he possessed his millions, at sixty-five his millions possessed him. Only to his own children and to their children was he liberal; and his liberality to them was all arranged with a view to keeping his estate in the family, and to cause it at every moment to tend toward a final consolidation in one enormous mass."

This is the estimate of his character formed by Mr. James Parton. His friend Dr. Coggswell presents him in quite a different light. He says:

"Mr. Astor lived to the good old age of four score and four years and eight months. For some years previous to his death, which happened March 29, 1848, his manly form was bowed down by age, and his bodily strength greatly enfeebled, but his mind retained much of its original vigor and brightness. Considering his extraordinary activity until a late period of his life, he submitted to the helplessness of age with uncommon resignation. When his impaired eye-sight no longer permitted him to read, his principal relief from the wearisomeness of unoccupied time was in the society of his friends and near relatives. All who knew him well were strongly attached to him, and none but those who were ignorant of his true character believed him unamiable and repulsive.

"His smile was peculiarly benignant and expressive of genuine kindness of heart, and his whole manner cordial and courteous to every one entitled to his respect. There was something so impressive in his appearance, no one could stand before him without feeling that he was in the presence of a superior intelligence. His deep, sunken eye, beneath his overarched brow, denoted the prophetic—it might almost be said the inspired—mind within. Although he lived many years beyond the age when the grasshopper is a burden, and was the victim of much suffering, he did not murmur, nor did he become unreasonable and peevish. He was not wont to talk much on the subject of religion, or freely communicate his views in relation to the life beyond the grave; but it can not be doubted that such tranquillity as he exhibited in his near approach to it must have been derived from 'that peace which the world can neither give nor take away.'"

Perhaps a medium between Mr. Parton's bitterness and Dr. Coggswell's enthusiasm will be as correct an estimate of his personal character as can be formed. It is a singular fact that Mr. Astor managed, in spite of the closeness which marked his operations, in spite of the small wages he paid, to inspire his employés with a zeal in his service that made them willing to undertake any thing, to endure any amount of labor, for him.

"He once lost seventy thousand dollars by committing a piece of petty injustice toward his best captain. This gallant sailor, being notified by an insurance office of the necessity of having a chronometer on board his ship, spoke to Mr. Astor on the subject, who advised the captain to buy one.

"'But,' said the captain, 'I have no five hundred dollars to spare for such a purpose; the chronometer should belong to the ship.'

"'Well,' said the merchant, 'you need not pay for it now; pay for it at your convenience.'

"The captain still objecting, Astor, after a prolonged higgling, authorized him to buy a chronometer and charge it to the ship's account, which was done.

"Sailing day was at hand. The ship was hauled into the stream. The captain, as is the custom, handed in his account. Astor, subjecting it to his usual close scrutiny, observed the novel item of five hundred dollars for the chronometer. He objected, averring that it was understood between them that the captain was to pay for the instrument. The worthy sailor recalled the conversation, and firmly held to his recollection of it. Astor insisting on his own view of the matter, the captain was so profoundly disgusted that, important as the command of the ship was to him, he resigned his post. Another captain was soon found, and the ship sailed for China.

"Another house, which was then engaged in the China trade, knowing the worth of this 'king of captains,' as Astor himself used to style him, bought him a ship and dispatched him to Canton two months after the departure of Astor's vessel. Our captain, put upon his mettle, employed all his skill to accelerate the speed of his ship, and had such success that he reached New York, with a full cargo of tea, just seven days after the arrival of Mr. Astor's ship. Astor, not expecting another ship for months, and therefore sure of monopolizing the market, had not yet broken bulk, nor even taken off the hatchways. Our captain arrived on a Saturday. Advertisements and handbills were immediately issued, and on the Wednesday morning following, as the custom then was, the auction sale of the tea began on the wharf—two barrels of punch contributing to the *eclat* and hilarity of the occasion. The cargo was sold to good advantage, and the market was glutted. Astor lost in consequence the entire profits of the voyage, not less than the sum previously named. Meeting the captain some time after in Broadway, he said:

"'I had better have paid for that chronometer of yours.'"

Yet he could do a kind act when he was in the humor. When he was poor and struggling for fortune, he had a friend in the city named Pell, a coachmaker. As he advanced in the world he lost sight of his friend. One day a young man called on him to ask if he would sell one of his leases which he (the visitor) then held. He replied promptly and decidedly that he would not sell.

"But what is your name?" he asked.

"It is Pell," was the reply.

"Pell—Pell—" said the old man, hesitating a moment, "I knew a man by that name once; he was a dear friend of mine, but I have not seen him for years."

"That man," said the visitor, "was my father."

"Indeed," exclaimed the old man, warmly; "your father? Why, he used to give me rides in his coaches. How I should like to see him."

Then pausing a moment, and smiling as he recalled the past to his mind, he said:

"You shall have the lease, young man. Go home, have the papers drawn, come here at eleven o'clock on Thursday, and I'll sign them. But don't put in any consideration."

The engagement was kept punctually by both parties.

"Have you got the papers?" asked the merchant. "Did

you put in the consideration? Well, let it be one hundred dollars. Have you got the money about you? Well, no matter, Bruce will keep the lease till you come and pay. I've given you two thousand dollars, young man. Don't you buy any more, for I sha'n't do it again. You tell your father that I remember him, and that I have given you two thousand dollars."

Mr. Astor dearly liked a joke, and occasionally indulged in a sly bit of humor himself. On one occasion a committee called upon him to solicit a donation for some charitable object. The old man took the subscription list, and, after examining it, signed it and gave the committee a check for fifty dollars. They had expected much more, and one of them ventured to say:

"We did hope for more, Mr. Astor. Your son gave us a hundred dollars."

"Ah!" replied the old man, drily, "William has a rich father. Mine was very poor."

CHAPTER III.

ALEXANDER T. STEWART.

IN the year 1818, a European vessel anchored in the harbor of New York, after a long and weary voyage from the Old World. She brought many passengers to the young metropolis, the majority of whom came with the intention of seeking fortunes in this land of promise.

Among them was a young Irishman who had left his home in his native land to seek in America the means of bettering his condition. This was ALEXANDER T. STEWART. He was the son of Scotch-Irish parents, and was born in Belfast in 1802. Being only three years old when his father died, his grandfather took charge of him, and proved a kind and judicious guardian. As he was designed for the ministry by his relative, and as his own tastes inclined him to that profession, he was given a good common school education, and placed at college, where he made favorable progress in his class. He was particularly successful in the classics, and is said to retain his relish for them at the present day.

During his second term his grandfather died, and he was by this event obliged to leave college. Abandoning the idea of entering the ministry, he embarked for America, determined to make a fortune in the New World. He came sufficiently supplied with ready money to insure him against immediate want, and with letters of introduction which at once secured him an excellent social position.

After trying in vain for some time to secure employment in a business house, he obtained a position as assistant in a commercial school. This he soon resigned for a similar place in a more celebrated school. His salary here was $300, which was considered ample compensation in those days.

Not wishing to continue in this career, however, he opened a small retail dry goods store in New York, and began business on a humble scale. Here he remained until the age of twenty-one, manifesting no extraordinary business capacity, and in no way distinguished from the many small dealers around him. Upon reaching his majority he returned to Ireland, to look after the inheritance left him by his grandfather. The amount which thus came to him was nearly one thousand pounds, and the greater part of this he invested in "insertions" and "scollop trimmings," which he shipped to America by the vessel in which he returned. He rented a little store, on his return, at 283 Broadway, and there displayed his stock, which met with a ready sale at a fair profit.

Without mercantile experience, and possessing little advantage, save his own Scotch-Irish energy and courage, Mr. Stewart started boldly on what proved the road to fortune. No young merchant ever worked harder than he. From fourteen to eighteen hours each day were given to his business. He was his own book-keeper, salesman, and porter. He could not afford to employ help. Credit was hard to obtain in those days, and young merchants were not favorites with those who had such favors to bestow. Mr. Stewart was one of the least favored, inasmuch as he was almost a total stranger to the business community in which he lived. He kept a small stock of goods on hand, which he purchased for cash chiefly at the auction sales. He was a regular attendant at these sales, and his purchases were invariably "sample lots"—that is, collections of small quantities of various articles thrown together in confusion, and sold in heaps for what they would bring. He had these purchases conveyed to his store, and after the business of the day was over, he and his wife would take these "sample lots," and by carefully assorting them, bring order out of the confusion. Every article was patiently gone over. Gloves were redressed and smoothed out, laces pressed free from the creases which careless bidders had twisted into them, and hose made to look as fresh as if they had never been handled. Each article being good in itself, was thus restored to its original excellence. The goods were then arranged in their proper places on the shelves of the store, and by being offered at a lower price than that charged by retail dealers elsewhere in the city, met with a ready sale. Even at this low price the profit was great, since they had been purchased for a mere trifle. For six years Mr. Stewart continued to conduct his business in this way, acquiring every day a larger and more profitable trade. Here he laid down those principles of business and personal integrity from which he has never departed, and which have led him to the honorable position he now holds.

"His first rule was *honesty* between seller and buyer. His career is a perfect exemplification of Poor Richard's maxim: 'Honesty is the best policy,' and of the poet's declaration: 'Nothing can need a lie.' His interest consorted with his inclination, his policy with his principles, and the business with the man, when he determined that the truth should be told over his counter, and that no misrepresentation of his goods should be made. He never asked, he never would suffer, a clerk to misrepresent the quality of his merchandise. Clerks who had been educated at other stores to cheat customers, and then to laugh off the transaction as 'cuteness,' or defend it as 'diamond cut diamond,' found no such slipshod morality at Stewart's little store, and learned frankness and fairness in representation at the peril of dismissal. Their employer asked no gain from deceit in trade. On his part, too, in buying, he rarely gave a seller a second opportunity to misrepresent goods to him.

"A second innovation of the young dry goods dealer was selling at *one price*—a custom which has also lasted without interruption, and which has spread to all the great houses. He fixed his price, after careful consideration, at what he thought the goods could and would bring, and would not deviate from it for any haggling, or to suit individual cases. Of course, he followed the fluctuations of the market, and marked his goods up or down in accordance with it; but no difference in the price was made to different people. Perhaps those who had some art in 'beating down' prices were offended, but people in general were pleased.

"The third principle he adopted was that of *cash on delivery*. It is said that his own early experience of buying on credit, and selling on credit, drove him to this rule.

"A fourth principle with him was to conduct business *as* business—not as sentiment. His aim was honorable profit, and he had no purpose of confusing it by extraneous considerations."

While still engaged in his first struggles in his little store, Mr. Stewart found himself called on to make arrangements to pay a note which would soon become due. It was for a considerable sum, and he had neither the money nor the means of borrowing it. It was a time when the mercantile community of New York regarded a failure to pay a note as a crime, and when such a failure was sure to bring ruin to any new man. Mr. Stewart knew this, and felt that he must act with greater resolution and daring than he had ever before exhibited, if he would save himself from dishonor. To meet the crisis he adopted a bold and skillful maneuver. He marked down every article in his store far below the wholesale price. This done, he had a number of handbills printed, announcing that he would sell off his entire stock of goods below cost, within a given time. He scattered these handbills broadcast through the city, and it was not long before purchasers began to flock to his store to secure the great bargains which his advertisements offered them. His terms were "cash," and he had little difficulty in selling. Purchasers found that they thus secured the best goods in the market at a lower figure than they had ever been offered before in New York, and each one was prompt to advise relatives and friends to avail themselves of the favorable opportunity. Customers were plentiful; the little Broadway store was thronged all day, and long before the expiration of the period he had fixed for the duration of his sales, Mr. Stewart found his shelves empty and his treasury full. He paid his note with a part of the money he had thus received, and with the rest laid in a fresh stock of goods. He was fortunate in his purchases at this time, for, as the market was extremely dull and ready money scarce, he, by paying cash, bought his goods at very low prices.

The energy, industry, patience, and business tact displayed by Mr. Stewart during these first years of his commercial life brought him their sure reward, and in 1828, just six years after commencing business, he found his little store too small and humble for the large and fashionable trade which had come to him. Three new stores had just been erected on Broadway, between Chambers and Warren Streets, and he leased the smallest of these and moved into it. It was a modest building, only three stories high and but thirty feet deep, but it was a great improvement on his original place. He was enabled to fill it with a larger and more attractive stock of goods, and his business was greatly benefited by the change. He remained in this store for four years, and in 1832 removed to a two-story building located on Broadway, between Murray and Warren Streets. Soon after occupying it, he was compelled, by the growth of his business, to add twenty feet to the depth of the store and a third story to the building. A year or two later a fourth story was added, and in 1837 a fifth story, so rapidly did he prosper.

His trade was now with the wealthy and fashionable class of the city He had surmounted all his early difficulties, and laid the foundation of that splendid fortune which he has since won. The majority of his customers were ladies, and he now resolved upon an expedient for increasing their number. He had noticed that the ladies, in "shopping," were given to the habit of gossiping, and even flirting with the clerks, and he adopted the expedient of employing as his salesmen the handsomest men he could procure, a practice which has since become common. The plan was successful from the first. Women came to his store in greater numbers than before, and "Stewart's nice young men" were the talk of the town.

The great crisis of 1837 found Mr. Stewart a prosperous and rising man, and that terrible financial storm which wrecked so many of the best of the city firms did not so much as leave its mark on him. Indeed, while other men were failing all around him, he was coining money. It had always been his habit to watch the market closely, in order to profit by any sudden change in it, and his keen sagacity enabled him to see the approach of the storm long before it broke, and to prepare for it.

He at once marked down all his goods as low as possible, and began to "sell for cost," originating the system which is now so popular. The prices were very low, and the goods of the best quality. Every body complained of the hard times, and all were glad to save money by availing themselves of "Stewart's bargains." In this way he carried on a retail cash trade of five thousand dollars per day in the midst of the most terrible crisis the country has ever seen. Other merchants were reduced to every possible expedient, and were compelled to send their goods to auction to be sold for what they would bring, so great was their need of ready money. Stewart attended all these auctions regularly, and purchased the goods thus offered. These he sold rapidly by means of his "cost system," realizing an average profit of forty per cent. It is said that he purchased fifty thousand dollars worth of silks in this way, and sold the whole lot in a few days, making a profit of twenty thousand dollars on the transaction. Thus he not only passed through the "crisis," but made a fortune in the midst of it.

From that time to the present day his march to fortune has been uninterrupted. Nearly a quarter of a century ago he purchased the property which is now the site of his wholesale store, and commenced to erect the splendid marble warehouse which he still occupies. His friends were surprised at his temerity. They told him it was too far up town, and on the wrong side of Broadway, but he quietly informed them that a few years would vindicate his wisdom, and see his store the center of the most flourishing business neighborhood of New York. His predictions have been more than realized.

He moved into his new store in 1846, and continued to expand and enlarge his business every year. Some years ago he purchased the old Ninth-Street Dutch Church and the lots adjacent to it, comprising the entire block lying between Ninth and Tenth Streets, Broadway and Fourth Avenue. When he found the retail trade going up town, and deserting its old haunts below Canal Street, he erected a fine iron building at the corner of Broadway and Tenth Street, to which he removed the retail department of his business, continuing his wholesale trade at his old store on Chambers Street. This new "upper store" has increased with the business. The building now covers the entire block upon which it is erected, and is the largest, most complete, and magnificent establishment of its kind in the world.

Though he took no active part in politics, he was too much interested in public affairs, by reason of his immense wealth, not to watch them closely. He was satisfied, some time before our late troubles began, that war must come, and quietly made contracts with nearly all the manufacturers for all their productions for a considerable period of time. Accordingly, when the war did come, it was found that nearly all the articles of clothing, blankets, etc., needed for the army had been monopolized by him. His profits on these transactions amounted to many millions of dollars, though it should be remarked that his dealings with the Government were characterized by an unusual degree of liberality. The gains thus realized by him more than counterbalanced the losses he sustained by the sudden cessation of his Southern trade.

Fifty years have now passed away since the young schoolteacher landed in New York, and he stands to-day at the head of the mercantile interests of the New World. In the half-century which has elapsed since then, he has won a fortune which is variously estimated at from twenty-five to forty millions of dollars. He has gained all this wealth fairly, not by trickery and deceit, or even by a questionable honesty, but by a series of mercantile transactions the minutest of which bears the impress of his sterling integrity, and by a patience, energy, tact, and genius of which few men are possessed. Surely, then, it must be a proud thought to him that he has done all this *himself*, by his own unaided efforts, and that amid all his wonderful success there does not rest one single stain upon his good name as a man or a merchant.

It is said that Mr. Stewart regards himself as a "lucky man," rather than as one who has risen by the force of his own genius. A writer in the New York *Herald* relates the following incident, as illustrative of the superstition which this feeling of "luck" has given rise to with him: "When he kept his store on Broadway, between Murray and Warren Streets, there sat on the sidewalk before it, on an orange box, an old woman, whose ostensible occupation was the selling of apples. This business was, however, merely a pretense; the main object being beggary. As years rolled on, Mr. Stewart became impressed with the idea that the old dame was his guardian angel of good luck, and this impression took so firm a hold upon his mind that when he removed to Chambers Street, he, in person, took up the old woman's box, and removed her to the front of his new establishment. In further illustration of Mr. Stewart's faith in the Irish traditional belief in 'lucky' and 'unlucky' persons, it may be mentioned that, after the completion of the St. Nicholas Hotel in this city, an undertaking in which he was largely interested, and when the building was just about to be opened for the reception of guests, the millionaire, standing in the drawing-room, ejaculated, 'It is now finished; I hope its first visitors may be lucky people.'

"A gentleman present, who had heard of Mr. Stewart's care for the aged apple vender, remarked, 'I presume, sir, you do not in reality care about lucky or unlucky persons;' to which he immediately replied, 'Indeed, I do. There are persons who are unlucky. I sometimes open a case of goods, and sell the first from it to some person who is unlucky, and lose on it to the end. I frequently see persons to whom I would not sell if I could avoid it.'"

The first incident, if true, doubtless illustrates the quiet kindness with which Mr. Stewart watches over the poor that he takes under his care—and they are many. He has won his success too fairly to be a believer in mere *luck*. There is no such thing as chance in this world. Men are the architects of their own fortunes.

One of the principal reasons of his success is the rigid system with which he conducts his business. He has a place for every thing, and a time for every duty, and requires the same regularity from his subordinates. His salesmen and managers are thoroughly versed in their duties, and the more important of them are selected with great care. Every thing works smoothly under the master's eye, and there is a penalty for each and every delinquency, which is rigidly exacted.

Mr. Stewart is one of the hardest workers in his establishment. His partners relieve him of the details, but the general management of his immense business he trusts to no other hands. His eye is on every thing. He is familiar with every detail, though he does not take upon himself its direction. He goes to his business between nine and ten in the morning, stopping first at his upper store. He makes a brief but thorough inspection here, and learns the general progress of the day, and then repairs to his lower or wholesale store, where he remains during business hours, and returns home between five and six in the afternoon, stopping again at the upper store. He works hard, and is never absent from his post unless detained by sickness.

His time is valuable, and he is not willing to waste it.

Many persons endeavor to see him merely to gratify their impertinent curiosity, and others wish to intrude upon him for purposes which would simply consume his time. To protect himself, he has been compelled to resort to the following expedient: A gentleman is kept on guard near the main door of the store, whose duty is to inquire the business of visitors. If the visitor wishes to see Mr. Stewart, the "sentinel" informs him that he must first state his business to him. If the visitor urges that it is private, he is told that Mr. Stewart has no private business. If his errand meets the approval of the gentleman on guard, he is allowed to go up stairs, where he is met by the confidential agent of the great merchant, to whom he must repeat the object of his visit. If this gentleman is satisfied, or can not get rid of the visitor, he enters the private office of his employer and lays the case before him. If the business of the visitor is urgent he is admitted, otherwise, he is refused an interview. If admitted, the conference is brief and to the point. There is no time lost. Matters are dispatched with a method and promptitude which astonish strangers. If the visitor attempts to draw the merchant into a friendly conversation, or indulges in useless complimentary phrases, after the matter on which he came is settled, Mr. Stewart's manner instantly becomes cold and repelling, and troublesome persons are sometimes given a hint which hastens their departure. This is his working time, and it is precious to him. He can not afford to waste it upon idlers. In social life he is said to be exceedingly affable.

The greater portion of Mr. Stewart's immense fortune is invested in real estate. Besides his two stores on Broadway, he owns the Metropolitan Hotel and the New York Theater, also on Broadway; nearly all of Bleecker Street from Broadway to Depauw Row, several churches, a number of buildings, and many valuable lots. He resides at the north-east corner of the Fifth Avenue and Thirty-fourth Street. Immediately opposite he is building one of the finest residences in the world, and the most superb in America. He owns more real estate than any man in America except William B. Astor, and is the most successful merchant in the world.

Mr. Stewart is said to be extremely liberal in his donations to objects which meet with his sympathy. The majority of these donations are quietly made, as he has a repugnance to public charities. He gave liberally to the cause of the Union during the war. During that struggle he sent a cargo of provisions to Ireland, where much distress existed, and then invited as many emigrants as the vessel would carry to take passage to America in her, free of charge. One hundred and thirty-nine persons availed themselves of his offer, and upon reaching America were all provided with good situations by him. At present he is engaged in erecting on the Fourth Avenue a large building, in which homes will be provided for poor working females, at a small expense to them. It is said that this noble project will require an outlay of several millions of dollars. His friends—and he has many—speak of him as exceedingly kind and liberal, and seem much attached to him.

As I have said before, Mr. Stewart has not cared for political distinction, but has rather shunned it. He was a member of the Union Defense Committee during the war, and in 1866 was one of the signers of the Saratoga address, calling on the people of the country to sustain the policy of President Johnson. His warm friendship for General Grant caused him to be one of the earliest advocates of the election of the latter to the Presidency. He was a candidate for Presidential Elector on the Republican ticket for the State of New York, but was defeated, with his associates, by the Democracy.

His intimate relations with General Grant, together with his vast financial experience, induced many persons to believe that he would be offered a place in the Cabinet of the new President. These expectations were realized by his nomination to the post of Secretary of the Treasury, on the 5th of March, 1869, and his immediate and unanimous confirmation by the Senate. He was about to enter upon his new duties, when it was discovered that there existed an old and almost forgotten law forbidding any merchant from becoming the head of the Treasury Department. As soon as this discovery was made, Mr. Stewart expressed his desire to withdraw from the position, and thus relieve the President of all embarrassment upon the subject, but the latter, wishing, if possible, to retain him in the Cabinet, urged him to delay his action, with the hope that the difficulty might be obviated. Willing to oblige his friend, and anxious to serve the country, Mr. Stewart consented to do this, but finding that certain persons were seeking to make his nomination a source of trouble to the Administration, offered either to resign the place or to relinquish his entire interest in his business during the period of his Secretaryship, and to donate his immense profits for that time to the poor of the city of New York. This sacrifice, he hoped, would render him eligible; but the President was unwilling to accept the princely offer—the noblest ever made by any man—and Mr. Stewart finally withdrew from the contest.

There can be no doubt that he would have been the best Secretary that could have been placed at the head of the Treasury. His great financial experience and his unquestioned ability were better qualifications than those possessed by any politician in the land. Perhaps the best proof of the satisfaction which his appointment produced in the minds of the thinking men of the country is the manner in which the news affected the money market. Gold fell as soon as the announcement was made.

Few strangers ever come to New York and depart without visiting Stewart's famous store at the corner of Tenth Street and Broadway. The lower, or wholesale store, is far more important to its owner; but it conducts its operations exclusively with dealers, and in such a quiet and systematic way that it seems to attract but little attention among the masses. It is the upper or retail store that is the wonder of the great city in which it is located.

It is constructed of iron, in the style of arcade upon arcade, and is lighted by numerous windows. It fronts two hundred feet on Broadway, and three hundred feet on Ninth and Tenth Streets. It covers an area of about two acres, is five stories and an attic in height, and has two cellars underneath. It is warmed by steam, and contains several steam-engines for hoisting goods, running the machines employed in the manufacturing department, and forcing water into the immense tank at the top of the building. Six elevators and several handsome stairways connect the various floors. Three of the elevators are used for conveying customers up and down, and the others for hoisting and lowering goods. The building is lighted by several thousand gas jets, which are all set aflame simultaneously by electricity.

The various floors, with the exception of the first, are broken only by a rotunda, which extends to the roof, and is inclosed at each floor by a massive iron balustrade. Leaning over one of these balustrades, and looking up or down, the sight is brilliant and attractive. Thousands of persons are scattered about the floors making purchases. Hundreds of clerks, salesmen, and cash boys are busy serving them, and the buz and hum of human voices under the vast roof sounds like the droning of a hive of bees.

The service of this immense establishment is arranged as follows: There is one general superintendent, with nineteen assistants, each of whom is at the head of a department. Nine cashiers receive and pay out money; twenty-five book-keepers keep the record of the day; thirty ushers direct purchasers to the department they seek; two hundred cash boys receive the money and bring back the change of purchasers; four hundred and seventy clerks, a few of whom are females, make the sales of the day; fifty porters do the heavy work, and nine hundred seamstresses are employed in the manufacturing department. Besides these, there are usually about five hundred other persons employed about the establishment in various capacities, bringing the total strength of the *personelle* of the house to twenty-two hundred.

The accounts of each department are kept separate, and the sales of each for the day constitute a separate return. These sales will average something like the following figures:

Silks	$15,000
Dress goods	6,000
Muslins	3,000
Laces	2,000
Shawls	2,500
Suits	1,000
Calicoes	1,500
Velvets	2,000
Gloves	1,000
Furs	1,000
Hosiery	600
Boys' clothing	700
Notions	600
Embroideries	1,000
Carpets	5,500

The total daily receipts average $60,000, and have been known to amount to $87,000.

Salaries of subordinate clerks range from $5 to $25 per week. The cash boys receive $5 per week. If not fined for misconduct they receive a reward of $1 per month, and a further reward of $5 at the end of each half year. They are promoted as fast as their conduct and vacancies in the force of salesmen will allow. The number of employés being so large, the proprietor is compelled to keep them under the constant espionage of two experienced detectives, and each evening when they leave the store they are required to do so through a private door on Ninth Street, where the detectives are stationed to see that none of them carry away articles which do not belong to them.

The number of visitors to the establishment in the busy season is very large. On special occasions, such as opening days, it is said to have reached fifty thousand, but the general average is placed at fifteen thousand, and they represent every grade in life. Rich and poor mingle here freely.

The floors are arranged simply, and with regard to business rather than for show, but every thing is elegant and tasteful. The sub-cellar is used as a store-room for goods in cases. Here the fabrics are opened and sent to their departments. The cellar is the carpet sales-room. The first floor is the general sales-room, and is the most attractive place in the building. It is three hundred feet long by two hundred wide, and is provided with one hundred counters, each fifty feet in length. Behind these counters the goods are arranged, with no effort at display, on the shelves, which rise but a few feet above the counters. There is an abundance of light in all parts of the house, especially over the silk counters, which are just under the rotunda. The second floor is taken up with ladies' suits, shawls, curtain goods, etc., and the next floor is devoted to the same purpose. The fourth floor is used as a manufactory for making up the suits, etc., placed on sale or ordered by customers; on the fifth is the fur-room and upholstery manufactory; and the sixth is occupied as a laundry. The most perfect order is maintained in every part of the establishment, the mere direction of which requires administrative ability of a very high character.

As fast as the sales are made, the articles, unless taken away by the purchaser, are sent to the parcel desk, which is located in the cellar. This is the busiest department in the house, and one of the most important. Each order is accompanied by a ticket stating the quality and amount of the goods, the price, and the address of the purchaser. It is remeasured and examined here, so that any error on the part of the salesman may be detected and repaired. Errors of this kind, however, are rare, and the burden of the labor in this department consists of making the goods up into secure packages and sending them to their destinations. The tickets delivered at the parcel desk are then sent to the checking desk, which is also in the basement, where they are compared with those delivered by the salesmen to the cashiers, and if no error is discovered, the goods are sent to the wagons for delivery.

The wagon department constitutes a very important branch of the business. The vehicles and horses are accommodated in a fine stable on Amity Street, near Broadway. The building was formerly a Baptist church, and was presided over by the Rev. Dr. Williams. When the congregation went higher up town, they sold the old church, which found a purchaser in Mr. Stewart. He converted it into a stable, and has since more than doubled its size. The floor was taken up, a sewer built to carry off the waste water, and the place paved with brick and cement. It is now one of the best stables in the city. It contains over forty horses, and five grooms are on hand to attend to them. There are eight wagons employed at the up-town store to deliver parcels to purchasers, while thirteen single wagons are used by the lower store to cart single cases around town. In addition to these, there are ten double trucks to haul heavy goods. Twenty-seven drivers are employed, and thirteen hundred bushels of oats and fifty tons of hay are fed out during a year. The place is in charge of a watchman at night, and during the day is managed by a superintendent. At half-past eight the trucks report at the down-town store, and remain there all day. At the same moment one of the light wagons is dispatched to the retail store, and at once takes out the early sales. In an hour another wagon follows it, and this course is pursued all day until six o'clock, when the last wagon takes the last sales. By this system purchasers receive their parcels with dispatch, and the immense business of the day is entirely finished. Every week the superintendent of the stables makes a report of the condition of the horses and wagons, and this "stable report" is carefully inspected at head-quarters. In case of sickness or stubborn lameness, the horses are sent to the country to recruit.

Mr. Stewart has a farm at Tuckahoe, where the invalid horses are kept, and where much of their provender is raised. This farm is noted for the valuable marble quarry which furnished the stone from which his new mansion on Fifth Avenue is built.

The retail store contains fabrics of every description and price. The wife of a millionaire can gratify her fancy here to its utmost limit, while the poor sewing-girl can obtain her simple necessities at the same price which is demanded for them from the rich. In the shawl department, there are "wraps" worth as much as $4,500, but not more than one or two find a purchaser in the course of a year. Shawls at $3,000 find a sale of about twenty a year, and the number of purchasers increases as the price diminishes. The wealthy ladies of New York deal here extensively. One of the clerks of the establishment recently made a statement that a fashionable lady ran up a bill of $20,000 here in two months.

Mr. Stewart, though leaving the details of the retail business in the hands of Mr. Tuller, the general superintendent, yet keeps himself thoroughly informed respecting it, and exercises over it a general supervision, to which its increasing success is due. He knows exactly what is in the house, how much is on hand, and how it is selling. He fixes the prices himself, and keeps them always at a popular figure. He is said to have an aversion to keeping goods over from one season to another, and would rather sacrifice them than do so. He has no dead stock on hand. His knowledge of the popular taste and its variations is intuitive, and his great experience enables him to anticipate its changes.

"There can not be so much selling without proportionate buying, and Stewart is as systematic in the latter as the former. Of late he has not acted personally in making purchases, but has trusted to the system which he organized some years ago, and which he has found to admirably answer as his substitute. He has branch establishments exercising purchasing functions only in Boston and Philadelphia, in the United States; in Manchester, England; and in Paris and Lyons, France. But while these are his agencies, his buyers haunt the marts of the whole world. There is no center of commerce or manufacture of the wide range of articles in which he deals, on either of the continents, where he is not always present by deputy to seize upon favorable fluctuations of the market, or pounce upon some exceptionally excellent productions. He owns entire the manufactory of the celebrated Alexandre kid-glove. He has a body of men in Persia, organized under the inevitable superintendent, chasing down the Astrachan goat heavy with young, from which the unborn kids are taken and stripped of their skins, thus sacrificing two animals for every skin obtained. He rifles Lyons of its choicest silks, the famous productions of Bonnet and Ponson. Holland and Ireland yield him the first fruits of their looms. Belgium contributes the rarest of her laces, and the North sends down the finest of its Russian sables. All the looms of France, England, Belgium, and the United States are closely watched, and the finest fabrics in dress goods, muslins, carpets, and calicoes are caught up the moment the workmen put on the finishing touches. He buys for cash the world over, and is a customer every-where so recognized as desirable that he has his choice of industrial productions, and on more advantageous terms than his rivals can purchase what he leaves. He has been so long in the business, and has become so thoroughly versed in the productions of different looms in different countries, that it is now his practice to select certain mills noted for excellence of work, and take their entire supply, and thus it happens that there are many looms in the busiest haunts of the Old and New Worlds that toil unceasingly on his account.

"By buying thus largely in foreign lands, he is, of course, the largest importer in the nation, and his duties average $30,000 gold per day. Every year his business steadily increases, and there is apparently no practical limit at which it will stop. As prudent in vast affairs as other men are in small, he insures liberally, and has policies renewed every third day throughout the year. But, while leaning upon the insurance companies, he is utterly independent of the banks; he has never asked one of them to 'carry' him through a crisis, and should such a contingency arise, there is no bank in the world competent to the task."

Mr. Stewart is now sixty-eight years old, but looks much younger, being still as vigorous and active, both mentally and physically, as most men of forty-five. He is of the medium size, has light-brown hair and beard, which are closely trimmed. His features are sharp, well cut, his eye bright, and his general expression calm and thoughtful. His manner is reserved, and to all but his intimate friends cold. He dresses with great simplicity, but with taste, and in the style of the day. His habits are simple, and he avoids publicity in all things. Standing as he does at the head of the mercantile interests of the country, he affords a fine example of the calm and dignified manner in which a man of true merit may enjoy his legitimate success, and of the good use he may make of its fruits.

CHAPTER IV.

AMOS LAWRENCE.

AMOS LAWRENCE was born at Groton, Massachusetts, on the 22d of April, 1786. His ancestor came of a good English family, and was one of the company which sailed from England for the New World under Governor Winthrop, in 1630, and which, according to Grahame, contained "several wealthy and high-born persons, both men and women, who expressed their determination to follow truth and liberty into a desert, rather than to enjoy all the pleasures of the world under the dominion of superstition and slavery." This Lawrence settled in Watertown, and was one of the original proprietors of the town of Groton, which was founded in 1655. Samuel Lawrence, the father of the subject of this memoir, was the fifth in descent from the founder of the family, and was himself a gallant officer of the American army in the War of the Revolution, the close of which found him the possessor of a small farm, which yielded a modest support for his family.

Young Amos was brought up on the farm, with none of the advantages of wealth, and with but a limited education, which he gained at the village schools, and which was seriously interfered with by his delicate health. He received his final training at the Groton Academy, to which, in after life, he became a liberal patron. "As we children came forward," he wrote, late in life, "we were carefully looked after, but were taught to use the talents intrusted to us; and every nerve was strained to provide for us the academy which is now doing so much there." Toward the close of the year 1799, when but a little over thirteen years of age, he took his final departure from school, and entered a store in the village of Dunstable, as clerk.

He remained there but a few months, and then returned to Groton, where he obtained a place as apprentice in the store of a Mr. Brazer. This was the largest establishment in the place, and conducted a very important trade with the country for miles around. Boston was so far, and so difficult to reach in those days, that Groton came in for nearly all the business of its vicinity which the railroads have now taken to the city. Mr. Brazer's establishment, which was known as a "variety store," came in for the best part of this trade. Every thing was sold there; "puncheons of rum and brandy, bales of cloth, kegs of tobacco, with hardware and hosiery, shared attention in common with silks and threads, and all other articles for female use." Even medicines were sold there; and Dr. Wm. R. Lawrence, the son of our hero, assures us that his father was obliged to sell medicines, not only to customers, but to all the physicians within a circuit of twenty miles, who depended on this establishment for their supplies. "The confidence in his good judgment," he adds, "was such that he was often consulted in preference to the physician, by those who were suffering from minor ails; and many were the extemporaneous doses which he administered for the weal or woe of the patient."

The Brazer store was a prominent feature in Groton. It was a place of general resort, and close by was the tavern where the mail coaches stopped. Travelers were constantly passing through the town, bringing the news of those stirring days when Napoleon was rushing over Europe with his armies, overturning old states and building up new ones, and changing the destinies of the world. The domestic politics of the day were exciting, and it is likely that they aided, together with the events in the Old World, in imparting to the character of Mr. Lawrence the earnestness and gravity for which he was noted when a mere lad.

Mr. Brazer had in his employ a number of clerks, but it was not long before the energy and business talent of young Lawrence made him the most trusted of all. Mr. Brazer did not give much personal attention to the store, and when he found that his young clerk was so admirable and reliable a manager, he left the business entirely in his hands. This was a post of unusual responsibility for one so young, but Amos Lawrence accepted it promptly, and labored to discharge its duties faithfully. He at once established the character for probity and fairness which distinguished him through life; his simple assertion was sufficient in any matter, being received with implicit trust by all who knew him. His duties kept him constantly employed, and though he lived within a mile of his father's house, weeks sometimes passed without giving him the opportunity of visiting it.

Drunkenness was at that day the curse of New England. Every body drank, and such fiery fluids as brandy, whisky, rum, and gin were the favorites. Men, women, and children were addicted to the vice, and Groton was no exception to the rule. Mr. Brazer's store was famous for the good liquors served out to its customers, and his clerks were aware that their employer did not object to their helping themselves when they felt thirsty. Amos Lawrence fell into the habit to which all were given, and for some time went along with the rest; but at length he came to the conclusion that such indulgence was wantonly ruining his health, and he resolved to abstain entirely. "We five boys," said he, years afterward, "were in the habit, every forenoon, of making a drink compounded of rum, raisins, sugar, nutmegs, etc., with biscuit—all palatable to eat and drink. After being in the store four weeks, I found myself admonished by my appetite of the approach of the hour for indulgence. Thinking the habit might make trouble if allowed to grow stronger, without further apology to my seniors, I declined partaking with them. My first resolution was to abstain for a week, and, when the week was out, for a month, and then for a year. Finally, I resolved to abstain for the rest of my apprenticeship, which was for five years longer. During that whole period I never drank a spoonful, though I mixed gallons daily for my old master and his customers."

At the same time, Mr. Lawrence determined that he would not use tobacco in any form. He was very fond of the odor of "the weed," and at one period of his life always kept a fine Havana in his drawer that he might enjoy the scent of it; but he was totally free from our disgusting national vice in any of its forms. In this respect, as indeed in all others, he offers a fine example to the rising youth of the present generation.

On the 22d of April, 1807, Mr. Lawrence completed his twenty-first year, and his seven years' apprenticeship with Mr. Brazer came to an end. He was now of an age to enter into business for himself, and it was his intention to open a small store in Groton, in connection with a brother apprentice, but before doing so he decided to visit Boston for the purpose of establishing a credit. He reached the city with but twenty dollars in his pocket, richer, he subsequently declared, in his own estimation, than he ever felt before or afterward. While in the city, he received the offer of a clerkship from a mercantile house of good standing. It was entirely unsolicited, and took him by surprise, but he decided to accept it, and abandoned his idea of going into business for himself in Groton; and this act led to a career entirely different from that to which he had looked forward.

Boston, in 1807, had a population of about thirty thousand, and the commercial position of the city was relatively much greater than at present. The foreign trade of the United States was enormous, and was carried on in American ships, and not, as at present, in foreign vessels. The total tonnage of American shipping engaged in this trade was seven hundred thousand tons, and of this Boston possessed a fair share. Her domestic trade was also important.

"The merchants of Boston had then high places in the estimation of the world. The Perkinses, the Sargeants, the Mays, the Cabots, the Higginsons, and others, were known throughout the world for their integrity, their mercantile skill, and the extent and beneficial character of their operations. These were the golden days of Boston's commerce. . . . . The standard of integrity was high, and though it would be absurd to suppose that there was not the usual amount of evil in the place, it may be assumed that in no part of the world was the young trader more likely to find severer judges of character and conduct, or to be better treated if he should afford unquestionable proofs of capacity and honesty."

It was into this community that Mr. Lawrence now entered, and in which his life was spent. He gave such satisfaction to his employers that, when he had been with them a short time, they astonished him with the offer of a partnership. He was but partially acquainted with their affairs, but their manner of conducting their business did not please him, and he declined their offer. His sagacity was verified by the result. In a few months the firm failed, and the creditors appointed him to settle their affairs, which he did to their satisfaction.

Being now out of employment, he resolved to commence business on his own account in Boston. He had made such a favorable impression upon the merchants of the city that he had no difficulty in obtaining credit. He rented a store in Cornhill, stocked it with dry goods, and began his career as a merchant. Four months after this, his father, who was keenly interested in his son's success, without consulting the latter, mortgaged his farm for one thousand dollars, and, repairing to Boston, placed the money in Amos Lawrence's hands. Mr. Lawrence was profoundly affected by this proof of his father's devotion, but he regretted it none the less, as he knew that his failure would bring ruin to his parent as well as to himself. "I told him," said he, forty years later, "that he did wrong to place himself in a situation to be made unhappy if I lost the money. He told me he *guessed I wouldn't lose it*, and I gave him my note." Mr. Lawrence made a prompt use of the money, and paid the mortgage at the proper time; but he had a narrow escape from loss, as the bank on which he had bills for the amount of the mortgage failed almost immediately after he had obtained specie for them.

"This incident," he said, "shows how dangerous it is to the independence and comfort of families for parents to take pecuniary responsibilities for their sons in trade, beyond their power of meeting them without embarrassment. Had any Hillsborough bank-notes not been paid as they were, nearly the whole amount would have been lost, and myself and my family might have been ruined. The incident was so striking that I have uniformly discouraged young men who have applied to me for credit, offering their fathers as bondsmen; and by doing so I believe I have saved some respectable families from ruin. My advice, however, has sometimes been rejected with anger. A young man who can not get along without such aid will not be likely to get along with it."

He began his business upon principles of prudence and economy, which he rigidly maintained throughout his whole life. He never allowed himself to anticipate his gains, and having fixed his personal expenses at a certain sum, he never went beyond it. His system, which is thus stated by himself, is offered here as a safe and admirable rule for all persons:

"When I commenced, the embargo had just been laid, and with such restrictions on trade that many were induced to leave it. But I felt great confidence that, by industry, economy, and integrity, I could get a living; and the experiment showed that I was right. Most of the young men who commenced at that period failed by spending too much money, and using credit too freely.

"I adopted the plan of keeping an accurate account of merchandise bought and sold each day, with the profit, as far as practicable. This plan was pursued for a number of years, and I never found my merchandise fall short in taking an account of stock, which I did as often at least as once in each year. I was thus enabled to form an opinion of my actual state as a business man. I adopted also the rule always to have property, after my second year's business, to represent forty per cent. at least more than I owed—that is, never to be in debt more than two and a half times my capital. This caution saved me from ever getting embarrassed. If it were more generally adopted, we should see fewer failures in business. Excessive credit is the rock on which so many business men are broken."

Mr. Lawrence was very successful from the first. His profits during his first year were fifteen hundred dollars, and over four thousand during the second. In seven years he made over fifty thousand dollars. He paid the closest attention to his business, and nothing could draw him from it in working hours. After these were over he would take his pleasure. His aim was to keep every thing in the most complete state possible. During the first seven years of his business he never allowed a bill against him to stand unsettled over the Sabbath. If he made a purchase of goods on Saturday, and they were delivered to him that day, he always examined and settled the bill by note, or by crediting it, and leaving it clear, so that there should be no unfinished business to go over to the next week, and make trouble for his clerks in case he should not be at his post. "Thus," said he, "I always kept my business *before* me, instead of allowing it to drive me."

The first years of Mr. Lawrence's mercantile experience covered the darkest period of the history of the Republic. They were marked by the embargo, the crippling of our commerce by the hostility of England and France, and the second war with Great Britain, in all of which there was much to dishearten a beginner, even if he escaped positive loss. Nothing was certain. The events of a single hour might undo the labor of years, and baffle the best laid plans. Yet he persevered, and went steadily on to fortune. He was remarkable for his keen foresight, as well as for his prudence, and was always on the alert to profit by the fluctuations of the market. Yet he abominated speculation. He averred that speculation made men desperate and unfit for legitimate business, and that it led them, when under excitement, to the commission of acts against which their cooler judgment would have warned them. The fair profits of legitimate business were, in his opinion, sure to reward any honest and capable man. His aim was to elevate commerce, and not to degrade it. He introduced into

Boston the system of double-entry in book-keeping, in advance of any other city merchant. He was prompt and faithful in the performance of every contract, and required a similar course toward himself from all indebted to him, as long as they were able to do so. When they became unfortunate, he was kind and generous, ready to compromise upon the most liberal terms, or to give them their own time for payment; and it is recorded of him that he never dealt harshly with a debtor who had failed in business.

As long as such a course was necessary, Mr. Lawrence devoted himself entirely to his business, but after he had placed it on a safe footing, he was careful to reserve to himself time for other duties and for relaxation. No man, he said, had the right to allow his business to engross his entire life. "Property acquired at such sacrifices as I have been obliged to make the past year," he wrote at the commencement of 1826, "costs more than it is worth; and the anxiety in protecting it is the extreme of folly." He never lost sight of the fact that man is a responsible, intelligent being, placed in the world for other purposes than the mere acquisition of wealth.

In October, 1808, his brother, Abbott Lawrence, afterward famous as a merchant and statesman, came to him as an apprentice, and on the 1st of January, 1814, he was admitted to partnership, the style of the firm being A. & A. Lawrence. This partnership was terminated only by the death of the elder brother in 1852. Their business was the importation and sale of foreign manufactures, and the firm soon took its place at the head of the Boston merchants engaged in this trade. The tariffs of 1816 and 1824 gave a new and powerful impetus to the manufacture of woolens and cottons in this country, and the Lawrences entered largely into the sale of these goods on commission. In 1830, they became interested in the cotton mills at

Lowell; and on the establishment of the Suffolk, Tremont, and Lawrence Companies, as well as subsequently in other corporations, they became large proprietors. From this time their business as selling agents was on the most extensive scale, and their income from all sources large in proportion. They amassed large fortunes, and won names which are the most precious heritages of their children.

Perhaps the best exposition of the principles upon which these brothers conducted their commercial operations is found in the following letter from the elder to the younger, written on the 11th of March, 1815, upon the occasion of a visit to England by the latter on business for the firm:

MY DEAR BROTHER—I have thought best, before you go abroad, to suggest a few hints for your benefit in your intercourse with the people among whom you are going. As a first and leading principle, let every transaction be of that pure and honest character that you would not be ashamed to have appear before the whole world as clearly as to yourself. In addition to the advantages arising from an honest course of conduct with your fellow-men, there is the satisfaction of reflecting within yourself that you have endeavored to do your duty; and however greatly the best may fall short of doing all they ought, they will be sure not to do more than their principles enjoin.

It is, therefore, of the highest consequence that you should not only cultivate correct principles, but that you should place your standard of action so high as to require great vigilance in living up to it.

In regard to your business transactions, let every thing be so registered in your books, that any person, without difficulty, can understand the whole of your concerns. You may be cut off in the midst of your pursuits, and it is of no small consequence that your temporal affairs should always be so arranged that you may be in readiness.

If it is important that you should be well prepared in this point of view, how much more important is it that you should be prepared in that which relates to eternity!

You are young, and the course of life seems open, and pleasant prospects greet your ardent hopes; but you must remember that the race is not always to the swift, and that, however flattering may be our prospects, and however zealously you may seek pleasure, you can never find it except by cherishing pure principles and practicing right conduct. My heart is full on this subject, my dear brother, and it is the only one on which I feel the least anxiety.

While here, your conduct has been such as to meet my entire approbation; but the scenes of another land may be more than your principles will stand against. I say *may be*, because young men of as fair promise as yourself have been lost by giving a small latitude (innocent in the first instance) to their propensities. But I pray the Father of all mercies to have you in his keeping, and preserve you amid temptations.

I can only add my wish to have you write me frequently and particularly, and that you will embrace every opportunity of gaining information.

Your affectionate brother,

AMOS LAWRENCE.

TO ABBOTT LAWRENCE.

In his politics, Mr. Lawrence was a Federalist, and then a Whig. He served for one term in the State Legislature as a Representative from Boston, with credit to himself, but afterward avoided any active participation in public events. When his nephew-by-marriage, General Pierce, was a candidate for the Presidency, he was very much gratified personally by the selection of the Democracy, but declined to vote for him. In a letter to a friend, written at this time, he said: "I had a charming ride yesterday with my nephew, Frank Pierce, and told him I thought he must occupy the White House the next term, but that I would go for Scott. Pierce is a fine, spirited fellow, and will do his duty wherever placed. Scott will be my choice for President of the United States."

Regarding himself as a steward of the riches committed to him, Amos Lawrence was liberal in his charities. During the last twenty-four years of his life he kept an accurate account of the sums he thus distributed, but with no idea that the statement, which he intended for his own eye only, would ever be made public. During this period he gave away six hundred and thirty-nine thousand dollars. The greater part of this was given away in ten years, and during a period when his average income was sixty thousand dollars a year. He was a liberal patron of education, giving large sums to its extension; and it was his delight to assist poor clergymen, without regard to denominations. He gave away clothing, food, books, etc., in large quantities, as well as ready money. "Two rooms in his house," says his son and biographer, "and sometimes three, were used principally for the reception of useful articles for distribution. There, when stormy weather or ill-health prevented him from taking his usual drive, he was in the habit of passing hours in selecting and packing up articles which he considered suitable to the wants of those whom he wished to aid." He did not forget the children, and many of his packages contained toys, and books, and other things calculated to promote their enjoyment.

He was beset with beggars of all kinds, many of whom he was compelled to refuse. In his diary, he wrote on the 11th of April, 1849, "Applications come in from all quarters, for all objects. The reputation of giving freely is a very bad reputation, so far as my personal comfort is concerned."

It pained him to have his charities made public, and he frequently requested the recipients to say nothing about them. He once made a present of some books to the Johnson school for girls, and the gift being acknowledged through the columns of a newspaper, he wrote to the principal of the school: "I merely want to say that I hope you will not put me in the newspaper at present, and when my work is done here, if you have any thing to say about me that will not hurt my children and grandchildren, *say on.*" To another party he wrote: "I must request that my name be not thrust forward, as though I was to be a by-word for my vanity. I want to do good, but am sorry to be published, as in the recent case."

As a merchant, Mr. Lawrence was upright, prudent, far-seeing, sagacious, and courageous; as a citizen, he was patriotic, public-spirited, and devoted; and as a man, he was a sincere, earnest, Christian husband, father, and friend. Viewed in any light, his character affords one of the most perfect models to be found in our history. He was the Christian *gentleman* in all things, even in the minutest detail of his business. His standard was very high, but he came up to it. Courteous and dignified in manner, with a face handsome and winning in youth, and gentle and benignant in age, he made scores of friends wherever he went, for it was a true index to his character. It is a significant and interesting fact that, during the hottest passages of the old nullification times, although his views were known to be uncompromisingly opposed to the attitude of the South, he never lost the warmest friendship of some of the most advanced of the South Carolina leaders. When one thinks of the friendships that were wrecked amid the passions of those days, this fact speaks volumes for the personal attributes of Mr. Lawrence.

He was a true American—proud of his country's past, hopeful for her future, and desiring nothing better than to live and die in the land of his birth. He sent his children abroad that they might see the Old World, and profit by the lessons learned there, but he strove earnestly to keep them true to their country. To his son, who was traveling in France in 1829, he wrote:

"Bring home no foreign fancies which are inapplicable to our state of society. It is very common for our young men to come home and appear quite ridiculous in attempting to introduce their foreign fashions. It should be always kept in mind that the state of society is widely different here from that in Europe; and our comfort and character require it should long remain so. Those who strive to introduce many of the European habits and fashions, by displacing our own, do a serious injury to the republic, and deserve censure. An idle person, with good powers of mind, becomes torpid and inactive after a few years of indulgence, and is incapable of making any high effort. Highly important it is, then, to avoid this enemy of mental and moral improvement. I have no wish that you pursue trade; I would rather see you on a farm, or studying any profession.

"It should always be your aim so to conduct yourself that those whom you value most in the world would approve your conduct, if your actions were laid bare to their inspection; and thus you will be pretty sure that He who sees the motive of all our actions will accept the good designed, though it fall short in its accomplishment. You are young, and are placed in a situation of great peril, and are, perhaps, sometimes tempted to do things which you would not do if you knew yourself under the eye of your guardian. The blandishments of a beautiful city may lead you to forget that you are always surrounded, supported, and seen by that best Guardian."

He was an eminently just man, and he carried this trait into the little details of his domestic life. His household adored him; and his friends were bound to him by ties unusually strong. He was firm and positive in his own opinions; but he was tolerant of those who differed from him. He was a man of quick, nervous temperament, but he possessed a powerful self-control. He was a sincere and earnest Christian, and while attaching himself to the sect of his choice, his sympathies and aid went out to the whole Christian Church.

Denominational differences had no place in his heart. He stood on the broad platform of the "faith of Christ crucified."

During the last years of his life, Mr. Lawrence was a constant invalid. To a man of his temperament this was a great trial, but he bore it unflinchingly, exhibiting, in the long years of feeble health which preceded his death, a cheerfulness and patience which plainly showed the aid of the Arm on which he leaned for support. For sixteen years he did not take a meal with his family. His food and drink, of the simplest kind, were regularly weighed, a pair of scales being kept in his chamber for that purpose. He wrote to his friend President Hopkins, of Williams College: "If your young folks want to know the meaning of epicureanism, tell them to take some bits of coarse bread (one ounce or a little more), soak them in three gills of coarse meal gruel, and make their dinner of them, and nothing else; beginning very hungry, and leaving off more hungry."

Mr. Lawrence continued in this condition until December, 1852, when he was seized with a severe attack of the stomachic trouble to which he was a martyr. He died peacefully, on the last day of that month and year, at the age of sixty-six years, eight months, and eight days. He was buried in Mount Auburn Cemetery, and was followed to the grave by a host of friends who mourned him as a brother, and by strangers to whom his kindness in life had brought relief from many a care and suffering.

CHAPTER V.

ANDREW V. STOUT.

THERE are few men in the city of New York who have won more fairly their proud positions in the mercantile world than he whose name stands at the top of this page. For more than forty years he has carried on a large and increasing business with an energy, skill, and probity which could not fail of success.

ANDREW V. STOUT was born in the city of New York, at No. 6 Canal Street, or, as it was then called, Pump Street, about the year 1814. When he was scarcely more than a child he was left fatherless, and thrown upon his own resources for a living. He was a manly little fellow, and, young as he was, was fully alive to the importance of the position he was compelled to assume. He was resolved not only to support himself, but also to acquire a good education, and by studying hard while most boys are at play, mastered the ordinary English branches by the time he was twelve years old.

He had a mother and sister to support, and applied himself manfully to the task of accomplishing this. He was well grown for his age, and was generally supposed to be several years older than he really was. When he was fourteen years old he applied for and received a position as assistant teacher of the English branches in one of the public schools of the city. The trustees of the school supposed he was at least eighteen or nineteen years old. Had his true age been known to them, it is probable he would not have received the appointment. He was not questioned upon the subject, and he was wise enough to keep his own counsel. He performed the duties of his position to the entire satisfaction of the school officials, and made such a good impression on his friends that at the age of sixteen he was made assistant principal in one of the most important and popular private schools of the day, taught by Shepherd Johnson, a name well known to the old residents of New York.

He was very young to fill this position, and, as may be supposed, it was peculiarly trying to one whose learning was mainly self-acquired. He was determined to succeed, however, and he applied himself energetically to master the course he was teaching. He studied harder and more constantly than any of his pupils, and was always fresh on the lessons for the day.

When he was sixteen years old he was so well grown and so mature that he passed for twenty. Having succeeded so well in the management of his English classes, he was offered the position of instructor of Latin, with an increase of his salary. The offer at first dismayed him. He was thoroughly ignorant of the Latin language, and utterly unprepared for the duties demanded of him. He was very anxious to have the place, however, for he needed the increase of salary offered him, and, after hesitating a little while, accepted it. He purchased a Latin grammar, and engaged a private tutor. He studied hard, and soon mastered the rudiments of the language. In this way he managed to keep ahead of his classes. If a question was asked him which he could not answer, he postponed his reply, looked into the matter at night, and explained it the next morning. By such hard study and patient efforts did this boy, himself a mere novice, turn out what was admitted by all to be the best drilled Latin class Shepherd Johnson's school had ever boasted of.

When he was eighteen years old he was made principal of Public School No. 2 of New York. He was living at Bushwick, where he resided with his mother and sister in a cosy little cottage, the garden of which was his pride, since he tended it with his own hands. It was his custom to rise every morning at four o'clock, and work in his garden until seven. Then he rode into the city, and attended to his school duties until four o'clock, when he returned home.

He was now in possession of a comfortable living; but he was not satisfied to do this and nothing more. He was anxious to win fortune, to enter upon a more active and stirring pursuit, and he kept himself always on the watch for an opening. About the time he became the head of the public school we have referred to, he commenced to engage in various ventures of a commercial nature, devoting to them his evenings, and the hours of the day not demanded by his school.

One of his relatives was a builder, with a fair trade, and had made some money by erecting houses in New York. Young Stout, who had saved a little money, proposed to him that they should take out a contract for building a number of dwellings on the then fashionable thoroughfare of East Broadway. The elder man was pleased with the plan, and at once consented to it. The houses were built at a handsome profit; others followed them, and by attending closely to this business, as well as his other duties, Andrew Stout, by the time he was twenty years old, had saved seventeen thousand dollars—a very large sum in those steady-going days.

He was greatly aided by the custom of doing business on time, which then prevailed, but he never allowed one of his notes to be protested, and never asked for an extension. When he began business, he did so with the firm resolve that he would conduct his most insignificant transaction as a Christian man of honor. If he could not make money honestly, he would remain poor. Every body saw the energy and judgment with which he conducted his affairs, and the strict integrity which marked them all, and he was not long in building up a reputation as a business man of which any one might have been proud. The promptness and apparent ease with which he met every contract, and took up every note, caused it to be generally believed that he was a very rich man. Further than this, it was known that he was a zealous and earnest Christian, one who carried his religion into his business, and who lived up to his professions. He was an active member of the Methodist Church, and the business man of the congregation to which he belonged. In his hands its finances prospered as they had never done before. Such was the reputation of this young man, who had not yet attained his majority.

He held his position in the public school for several years after his appointment to it, but the requirements of his business at length compelled him to relinquish it.

In the midst of his prosperity Mr. Stout made one mistake. A friend with whom he had been interested in building wished to procure some money from the bank, and Mr. Stout was induced, with considerable reluctance, to indorse his note for five thousand dollars. One false step in business, as in other affairs of life, leads to another, and, in order to save this money, Mr. Stout was forced to renew his indorsements until his liabilities amounted to twenty-three thousand dollars. To his dismay he was now informed by the builder for whose sake he had incurred this risk, that he (the builder) had failed, without making provision for the payment of the notes, and that Mr. Stout would have to account to the bank for them.

"Several methods of relief were open to Mr. Stout. He was worth seventeen thousand dollars, which he had earned by nights of toil, by economy, and by daily and earnest attention to business. To pay the notes would not only sweep away every penny that he had, but would leave him six thousand dollars in debt. He had never realized one cent from the money, and his name was used simply to accommodate the builder. Besides, he was not of age, though nobody suspected that fact, and he could repudiate his debts as a minor. He took no counsel, made no statement of his affairs to any one, shut himself up in his own room, and considered thoughtfully what he should do, and then followed out the decision that he had reached. Having become bankrupt in money, he concluded he would not be so in character. He had earned seventeen thousand dollars, and could earn seventeen thousand dollars more. He did confide in one friend. He went to a relative, and asked him to lend him six thousand dollars, the sum necessary to take up all the notes. The relative was astonished at the request, and insisted upon knowing the facts in the case. Mr. Stout made a full and frank statement. It was met with the remark, 'Well, Andrew, I thought you would be a rich man, but if this is the way you do your business, you will never be worth any thing.' But Mr. Stout did not want preaching, he wanted money; and as the relative seemed to hesitate about loaning the money, as no security was offered, Mr. Stout curtly told him he could do as he pleased about it; he could get the money somewhere, and pay the notes. The money was promised, and he went on his way.

"The bank watched the young financier with a great deal of

interest. The whole matter had been discussed often in the bank, and the wonder was how young Stout would meet the blow. It was supposed that he would ask for an extension; and it was agreed to give it to him, and to make the time of payment convenient to his ability. Had he proposed to compromise the matter by paying one-half, the bank would have accepted it. That would have left him a capital of nearly eight thousand dollars for a fresh start. Had he offered his seventeen thousand dollars on condition that he was released from all liability, the notes would have been canceled with alacrity. He did neither. He proposed no compromise, asked no extension, and attempted to negotiate no settlement. When the first note became due, he paid it. He did the same with the second and third. After the third payment, he was called into the office of the president. Reference was made to the notes, and to the fact that he had obtained no benefit from the money. The president told him the bank was ready to renew the notes, and to give him any accommodation that he might ask. Mr. Stout simply replied that the blow was a heavy one, but that having assumed the obligation, he should discharge it; that he asked no favors, and as the notes matured he should take them up. He paid every dollar due, and every one was certain that his wealth must be very large. His manliness, pluck, and integrity, which carried him through that crisis, became the sure foundation-stone on which his great fortune was laid. He took the front rank among successful financiers, and his honorable course in that crisis established his fame as an honest man, in whom it would be safe to confide. Years of earnest and active business life have not changed that character, nor allowed a blot or stain to cloud that reputation."*

Some years later, Mr. Stout became a merchant. He estab-

* Matthew Hale Smith.

lished a wholesale boot and shoe store, and engaged actively in that business. He brought to his new calling the energy, prudence, and integrity which had distinguished him all through his life, and was successful from the first. He worked hard. His business hours were from seven in the morning until six in the evening. During his busy season, four months in the year, he worked until ten, and often until twelve, paying his employés extra wages for labor performed after the regular business hours. Sometimes he worked until four in the morning, but that did not deter him from being in the store at the usual hour for opening. He was always the last to go home, never leaving the store until the business of the day was over and the house was closed. He extended his operations into dry goods, meeting with equal success in this department. As his business expanded, he was compelled to form various partnerships, but in all these arrangements he reserved to himself, like Stewart, the exclusive management of the finances.

About eighteen years ago, the shoe and leather merchants of the city decided to organize a bank, in which their interests should be the principal consideration. Mr. Stout engaged in the effort with great enthusiasm, and the Shoe and Leather Bank of New York was at length organized under the most auspicious circumstances. Mr. Stout was the largest stockholder in the new bank, and was elected one of its directors. His influence was potent in directing its first operations, and the next year he was elected vice-president, in which position he really had the control of the enterprise left to him. A year later he was elected president of the bank, a position which he still holds, being in point of service the oldest bank president in New York. Upon questions of banking and finance, his views are listened to with great respect by his associates, who have proof of their soundness in the splendid success of the institution over which he presides; and it may be truly said that there are few men in the city who enjoy so large a share of the public confidence as is bestowed upon him.

As a citizen, he is public-spirited and liberal. Some years ago, he held the office of city chamberlain, and during his administration of it a difficulty arose in regard to paying the police force their wages. Knowing that the men and their families would suffer if the money were not promptly paid them, Mr. Stout generously advanced the necessary sum from his private means, looking to the city to reimburse him. In grateful acknowledgment of this practical sympathy for them, the force presented him with a handsome testimonial. His fortune is immense, and is used liberally in behalf of the cause of the Christian religion. His charities are said to be large, but one rarely hears of them, so quietly are they done. He is married and has a family.

No man's career holds out more encouragement to young men seeking to rise than that of Andrew V. Stout. It shows that courage, patient industry, and business capacity will bring fortune to any honest worker. His uniform success speaks volumes in favor of a young man's striving to lead a Christian life in the midst of his business cares and struggles. God's blessing follows such an one at every step, and he will succeed in the end, whatever trials may beset his path at first. It is a great mistake to suppose that a man's success depends on his "sharpness." Shrewdness is a valuable quality, but it must be coupled with a plain, practical honesty, or it will amount to nothing in the end. A man must be faithful to his God if he would have his work stand.

CHAPTER VI.

JONAS CHICKERING.

ON Tremont Street, in the City of Boston, near the Roxbury line, there stands an immense building of brick, said to be larger than any edifice in the United States, save the Capitol at Washington. It is built in the form of a hollow square, with a large court-yard in the center, and the building and court-yard together cover an area of five acres. It is five stories in height on the outer side, and six on the inner, the court-yard being one story lower than the street. The building is two hundred and sixty-two feet in length from east to west, and two hundred and forty-five from north to south, the shorter distance being the length on Tremont Street. The width of the building all around the court-yard is fifty feet. It contains nine hundred windows, with eleven thousand panes of glass, and when lighted up at night seems almost a solid mass of fire. From five to six hundred men are employed here in various capacities, and an immense steam engine of one hundred and twenty horse-power furnishes the motive power for the machinery. Altogether, it is one of the most prominent and interesting of all the sights of Boston, and the visitor is surprised to learn that it is due entirely to the energy and genius of one who, but thirty-four years previous to its erection, came to Boston a penniless stranger. The building is the famous piano-forte manufactory of Chickering & Sons, and its founder was Jonas Chickering, the subject of this sketch.

JONAS CHICKERING was born at New Ipswich, New Hampshire, on the 5th of April, 1798. His father was a blacksmith by trade, and employed his leisure time in cultivating a small farm of which he was the owner. He was esteemed by his neighbors as an upright, reliable man, and prudent and careful in his temporal affairs. The family being poor, young Jonas was required to do his share toward cultivating the farm, and received only such education as was afforded by the district schools in the vicinity. He was noted at an early age for his passionate love of music. When a mere child, he learned to play on the fife, and was such a proficient performer that he was called upon with the town drummer to furnish music for the militia musters, which were then the pride of the town. These were happy days for the lad, but his pleasure was marred by the ridicule which the contrast between his slender figure and the stalwart frame of the "six-foot drummer" caused the fun-loving towns-people to indulge in. Soon after this he learned to play on the clarionet, and when only seventeen or eighteen years old, was so advanced in his art that he could read at sight music of the most difficult character.

At the age of seventeen he was apprenticed to a cabinet-maker to learn his trade, and remained with him for three years, exerting himself to become thorough master of every detail of the business. Toward the close of his apprenticeship, an event occurred which changed the whole current of his life, and placed him in what proved to him the road to fame and fortune.

One of the wealthiest citizens of New Ipswich was the fortunate owner of a piano, the only instrument of the kind in the place; but his treasure was almost useless to him, for the reason that it was out of tune and seriously damaged in some respects. It had lain in this condition for a long time, no one in or near the place being able to make the necessary repairs. In this extremity the owner bethought him of Jonas Chickering, who had acquired an enviable reputation for skill in his trade, and it was thought that a good cabinet-maker ought of necessity to be a clever piano-maker. Young Chickering, thus appealed to, consented to undertake the task, as much for the purpose of becoming familiar with the instrument as of earning the sum the owner of it proposed to pay for the repairs. He had not the slightest knowledge of its internal organization, but he believed that by patient investigation he could master it, and he knew that the correctness of his ear would enable him to tune it. He made a careful study of the instrument and of every separate part, spent days over the task, discovered the injury and the cause of it, and not only took the instrument to pieces and restored it to its former condition, but did his work so well that the piano was pronounced fully as good in every respect as when it was new. This was not all. He discovered defects in the instrument which even its maker was not able to remedy, and his fertile brain at once suggested to him a plan for removing them.

Here was a chance for him, and he resolved to profit by it. He would abandon cabinet-making and learn the manufacture of pianos. Then, when master of his trade, he would make use of his discoveries, and earn both fame and fortune. When his determination to change his business was made known, his friends attributed it to his desire to be in the midst of musical instruments, and where he could gratify his love of music; but this was only a part of the motive which influenced him. He meant to rise in the world, and he was sure that he held in his hands the means of doing so.

In 1818, when twenty years old, he removed to Boston, and obtained employment with a cabinet-maker. He did this in order to give him time to look about him, to become familiar with the city and city life, and to acquire such other information as would enable him to decide upon the best means of putting his plans into execution. He saved his wages with the greatest care, and at the end of his first year in Boston had accumulated a modest little sum, which he meant should support him while he was learning his new trade.

On the 15th of February, 1819, without the loss of a day, he began work with a piano-maker.

He had now entered upon what he meant should be the business of his life, and he was resolved that he would be master of it. From the first he took rank in his employer's factory as the most careful workman in it. He spared no pains to make his knowledge full in every detail. Time was of no consequence compared with knowledge, and he was never anxious to hurry through with his work. It soon came to be recognized by his employer and fellow-workmen that he was the best fitted for those portions of the work upon the instrument which required the greatest patience as well as the greatest care, and the most difficult and delicate work was always intrusted to him, his wages being, of course, in proportion. Other men had no thought but to earn a living. This man meant to win fame and fortune, and to enlarge the scope of that art to which he was so passionately devoted. He labored with his mind as well as his hands, familiarizing himself with every detail of the manufacture, and devising in silence the means for improving the instrument and the implements used in its construction. He could afford to wait, to be slower than his fellows. Every moment spent over his task made his workmanship the better, and opened to his mind new sources of improvement. He spent three years as a journeyman, and then went into business for himself. He associated himself with a Mr. Stewart, under the firm of Stewart & Chickering.

Fifty years ago the piano-forte was a wretched piece of mechanism compared with the superb instrument of to-day. It was originally a progressive growth from the ancient lyre, through the harp, psaltery, dulcimer, clavictherium, clavichord, virginal, spinet, harpsichord, to the piano of Christofali in the early years of the last century. At the period of Mr. Chickering's entrance into business, it was still very imperfect, and the various manufacturers of the instrument were earnestly endeavoring to discover some means of remedying the defects of which they were all conscious. There are four divisions in the manufacture of a piano, each of which requires great skill and care. These are: First, The making of the framing and the sound-board; Second, The stringing; Third, The keys and action; Fourth, The case and ornamental work. The framing requires strength and simplicity. It is this portion of the instrument which sustains the tension of the strings, which in full to large-sized pianos is not less than from six to twelve tons, and it is a matter of prime necessity that the portions which serve as a strut or stretcher between the ends of the strings, and which are to resist this enormous pull, must be made correspondingly strong and rigid, since by any gradual yielding under the pull of the strings, their lengths and tensions, and hence their tone, must undergo proportionate change. In the old pianos, the frames were of wood, and it was impossible to use any but small, short strings, for the reason given above. Fullness and power were not to be thought of, and builders were obliged to confine themselves to securing truthfulness of tone. A multitude of causes, among which were the changes in the weather, combined to render it impossible to keep the old-fashioned instrument in tune. It was this defect which first attracted the attention of Jonas Chickering, and his first endeavor was to produce an instrument which would withstand the climatic changes which were so troublesome to the old ones. He was fully aware of the fact that the piano trade in this country was then so unimportant that it offered but little inducement to a man who could manufacture only the old instrument; but he believed that by producing an instrument of better proportions, and one fuller, richer, and more lasting in tone, he could create a demand for it which would insure the sale of all he could manufacture. His hope of success lay not in the old, but in an improved and nobler instrument. That he was correct in his belief, the magnificent instrument of to-day which bears his name, and the lucrative business he has left to his sons, amply demonstrate. Others besides himself were working for the same end, and he knew that he would have to bear the test of determined and intelligent competition. He applied himself to his purpose with enthusiasm. He carefully studied the theory of atmospheric vibration and musical combination, as well as an application of the principles of mechanical philosophy to the construction of the instrument. He went deep into the science involved in his work, into the philosophy of melody. Passionately devoted to music, he was ambitious of placing that which has been so truly called "the king of instruments" within the reach of all lovers of harmony, and to give them the best instrument that human invention could produce—an instrument which should not only withstand atmospheric changes, but which should yield the richest, fullest volume of melody, with the least exertion to the performer. His progress was slow, but it was sure. Beginning with an improvement in the action, he accomplished, in a great measure (in 1838), his plan for preserving the permanence and purity of the tone of the instrument by casting the entire iron framing with the parallel bars in one piece. Iron had for some time before this been in general use for framing, but the frame was cast in a few separate parts, which were put together by means of bolts and screws, a plan which is still used to a considerable extent in Europe. By his plan of casting the frame and its supporting bars in one solid piece, Mr. Chickering not only prevented the frame from yielding to the pull of the strings, thus securing permanence and purity of tone, but was enabled to use larger frames and more strings, which greatly increased the capacity of the instrument.

Several other improvements were made by him, the most important of which was the invention, in 1845, of the circular scale for square pianos, which is now in general use in this country and in Europe. "This consists in giving to the row of tuning pins and wrest-planks—previously straight in these instruments—a curved disposition, answering nearly to an arc of a circle, the advantage being that the strings become less crowded, larger hammers, and a more direct blow can be secured, and the tone is both strengthened and improved." With a rare generosity, Mr. Chickering declined to patent this improvement, which would have enabled him to drive competition out of the market. He regarded it as so necessary to a good piano that he declared that all makers ought to have the use of it, as it would thus be within the power of all persons able to purchase a piano to avail themselves of it, whether they bought a "Chickering" or not. Such generosity is too rare to fail to receive the praise it merits.

Mr. Chickering did not continue long in business with Mr. Stewart. The latter withdrew in a few years, and Mr. Chickering carried on the business alone. In 1830 he formed a partnership with Captain John Mackay, a retired ship-merchant. In the new firm Captain Mackay took charge of the finances and the office business, while Mr. Chickering devoted himself entirely to the mechanical department. The operations of the new house were very successful. The improvements made by Mr. Chickering from the first created a demand for their instruments which was sometimes so great that it was difficult to supply it. This demand continued to increase, until the house was perfectly easy as to money matters, and able to enlarge its facilities very greatly. It was Mr. Chickering's design that each separate instrument should be an improvement upon those which had preceded it, and he was careful that this plan should not miscarry. In a few years the firm was enabled to import the foreign materials needed, by the cargo, thus saving the profit which they had hitherto been compelled to pay the importer. Besides this saving, they were enabled to keep on hand a large stock of the woods used in the instrument, and thus it was allowed to become more thoroughly seasoned than that which they had been compelled to purchase, from time to time, in small quantities. In 1841, Captain Mackay sailed from Boston for South America, for the purpose of obtaining a supply of the woods needed by the firm; but he never returned, and as no tidings of him or his ship were ever received, it is supposed that the vessel went down at sea with all on board.

Mr. Chickering now decided to continue the business without a partner. His friends supposed that in assuming the management of the concern, in addition to the direction of the mechanical department, and the constant mental labor to which he subjected himself in his efforts to improve the piano, he was undertaking more than he was capable of performing. They feared his health would break down under it. Besides, it was generally believed that, in spite of Mr. Chickering's undoubted skill in his own department, he was not much of a business man. He was confident of his own ability, however, and did not hesitate to assume the new responsibility.

The business of which he now became the owner was very heavy and extensive. Soon after the beginning of his connection with Captain Mackay, the firm erected a large factory for the purpose of carrying on their business. One hundred hands were employed in it when opened, but in a few years it was necessary to employ more than twice that number, so rapidly did the business increase. The supply of materials needed was ample and of the very best quality, for Mr. Chickering never allowed an inferior article to be used. The warerooms were large and handsomely fitted up, and were filled with instruments ranging in price from a thousand dollars downward. It was generally believed that while Mr. Chickering's genius had created the demand for the pianos, it was Captain Mackay's business knowledge and experience that had placed affairs on their present footing, and when Mr. Chickering proposed to buy Captain Mackay's interest from his heirs, which was valued at several hundred thousand dollars, there was a very general belief, which found expression, that he was incurring certain ruin. The condition of the sale was that the purchase-money should be divided into installments, for each of which Mr. Chickering should give his note, secured by a mortgage on the premises. At Mr. Chickering's request each note was made payable "on or before" a given day. The lawyer who conducted the transaction smiled skeptically as he inserted this clause, and asked the purchaser if he *ever* expected to pay the notes at all.

"If I did not expect to pay them promptly, I should not

give them," was the simple reply. He was as good as his word. The notes were met promptly, and although Captain Mackay's family requested that they might stand as an investment for them, Mr. Chickering took up the last one at its maturity.

With the business in his own hands, Mr. Chickering continued its operations, displaying an ease in his mercantile transactions which astonished and delighted his friends. The business prospered to a greater degree than before, and all the while Mr. Chickering continued his labors for the improvement of his instruments with still greater success than in former years. His pianos were universally regarded as the best in the market, and his competitors were unable to excel him. Although conducting a business which required the constant exercise of the highest mercantile talent, he did not relax his energy in the mechanical department. To the end of his life, long after he had become a wealthy and prominent man, he had his own little working-cabinet, with an exquisite set of tools, with which he himself put the finishing touch to each of his splendid instruments, a touch he would not intrust to any other hands.

His competitors did all in their power to equal him, but he distanced them all. One of them adopted a most startling expedient. He obtained permission from the Legislature of Massachusetts to change his name to *Chickering*, and at once sent out his instruments marked with his new name, his object of course being to deceive the public, and Jonas Chickering had the mortification of seeing the inferior instruments of another maker mistaken for his own. He promptly laid before the Legislature a petition for redress, setting forth the facts of the case and the motives of his rival. The result was that the Legislature reconsidered its action, and compelled the bogus Chickering to resume his original name.

Mr. Chickering was noted for his simplicity and straightforwardness in business transactions. Conscious of his own integrity, he listened to no proposition of a doubtful character, nor would he ever allow his credit as a merchant to be questioned with impunity. Upon one occasion, he applied through his clerk to the bank, with which he had dealt for many years, for an accommodation which he needed. The president of the bank sent for him, and told him that security would be required.

"I shall give you none," he replied. "I have done my business at this bank for a long time, and if you do not know me, I shall apply where I am better known."

The president was firm in his position, and Mr. Chickering applied to another bank, which readily granted him the desired discount, and to which he at once transferred his business, which was worth to the bank about ten thousand dollars a year. Shortly after, a director of the institution at which he had formerly dealt called on him, and urged him to restore his business to the bank, assuring him that in future it would readily grant him any accommodation he might desire.

"No," he replied; "I will deal with no institution which, having had the opportunity of knowing me, suspects my responsibility."

Again having need of accommodation, he sent his notes for a large sum to one of the city banks for discount. The president said an indorser would be required.

"I shall indorse them myself," said Mr. Chickering.

"That will never do," replied the president.

"Very well," was the simple answer, and, without further words, he took the notes to another bank, which promptly loaned him the money on them.

He tolerated no irregularity in his own business. He was

true to the spirit as well as to the letter of a contract, and never, during the whole course of his long life, was he guilty of a transaction in which the most rigid moralist could find a taint of sharp practice. What a refutation of the theories of those who hold that cunning and trickery are unavoidable some time in the course of a long and successful mercantile career lies in the story of this man, who, beginning life penniless, filled with a burning ambition to be rich and famous, never swerved from the straight path of integrity, and by the exercise of only the highest traits of his nature more than realized his boyish dreams! Ponder it well, young man, and learn from it that honesty is indeed the best policy in any calling.

Mr. Chickering had married early in life, and now had three sons just entering upon manhood. These were carefully educated at the public schools for which Boston is so justly famed, and then put into their father's factory to learn the mechanical part of the business. It was the father's ambition to be succeeded by his sons, but he was not willing to trust the labor of his life to ignorant or incompetent hands. At the age of seventeen, Thomas Chickering, the eldest son, was taken from school, and, under his father's eye, taught every detail of the mechanical branch of the business, until he understood it as well as the senior Chickering himself. George, the second son, in due time passed through the same course of training; while Francis, the youngest, was brought up in the warehouse. The father thoroughly imbued his sons with his own system and energy, and to-day we see the result. The firm of Chickering & Sons is still the most prominent in America. Thomas is now the acting head of the house, and has led it on to continued success; Francis is the presiding genius of the mechanical department, and has made many important improvements in the field in which his father won success; and George exercises a general supervision at the immense factory in Boston. The mantle of the father has fallen upon the sons, and his labors have found their highest reward in their success.

Mr. Chickering's good fortune was not entirely uninterrupted. On the 1st of December, 1852, his factory was burned to the ground, with all its valuable patterns, stock, etc., involving a loss to him of two hundred thousand dollars. The interruption to his business was very serious, apart from the loss of his property. Expressions of sympathy poured in upon him from his friends, coupled with offers of pecuniary assistance in his efforts to reëstablish his business. His disaster seemed merely to inspire him with fresh energy, but the kindness of his friends entirely overcame him.

He wasted no time in vain regrets, but at once went to work. He was fifty-four years old, but he showed an energy and determination which more than rivaled the fire of his young manhood. The loss of his factory was not only a severe blow

"MY MEN SHALL NOT SUFFER."

to him, but to the three hundred workmen who had been employed in it, and who were dependent upon their wages for their support. His first care was to assure them that they should not suffer, but that they should continue to receive their wages as regularly as though nothing had happened to interrupt their labor. He had always been kind and generous to his employés, paying liberal wages, and rewarding especial merit, but this act of kindness did more to endear him to them than any previous benefaction. Having provided for his men, he set to work to prepare temporary accommodations for his business, and then began his arrangements for the construction of a new factory. He took a great degree of interest in the plans for the new building, the architect being almost entirely guided by his suggestions, and the result of his labors is the magnificent building to which reference was made at the opening of this chapter. He did not live to see it completed, however. He died at the house of a friend from the rupture of a blood-vessel, produced, it is believed, by severe mental labor, on the 8th of December, 1853. His fortune at the time of his death was estimated at a quarter of a million of dollars. His sons assumed the charge of the business, which they still conduct.

The loss of Mr. Chickering was felt by all classes of his fellow-citizens—especially by the poor. To them he had been a kind and generous friend. Distress never appealed to him in vain, and he proved a faithful steward of the riches committed to his care. Yet he performed his charities with such a modesty and reticence that few beside the grateful recipients were aware of them. Indeed, it was his custom to enjoin secrecy upon those whom he assisted; but they would not remain quiet. His liberality is in striking contrast with the closeness of many who were worth more than twenty times his wealth, but who lacked his warm and sympathizing nature.

CHAPTER VII.

NICHOLAS LONGWORTH.

THE grape culture of the United States is yet in its infancy. Although the annual wine product is estimated at nearly three millions of gallons, there can be no doubt that ere many years shall have elapsed America will rank as one of the most important wine countries of the world. California is already extending her vineyards for miles along her smiling valleys, where the clear sky and the balmy air, which are unchangeable at the season of the grape harvest, permit a degree of perfection in the fruit unattainable in any European country. Already her wines are commanding an enviable place in the markets of the world, with no apparent limits to the growing demand for them. The hillsides of the lower Ohio Valley are lined with thriving vineyards, whose rich clusters of Catawba and Isabella grapes delight the eye on every hand, and thousands of acres are now given to successful grape culture, where formerly only a few straggling vines were seen. More than five hundred thousand gallons of wine are now annually produced in the neighborhood of Cincinnati alone, and find a market in that city, and what was but a few years ago a mere experiment is now one of the chief sources of the wonderful prosperity of the Ohio Valley, and one of the most important features in the commerce of the Queen City of the West. The success which has attended this branch of our industry must be a matter of congratulation to the whole country, and the man to whose courage, energy, and liberality it is mainly due must be regarded as a public benefactor.

This man, NICHOLAS LONGWORTH by name, was born at Newark, New Jersey, on the 16th of January, 1782. His father had been a man of large property, but in consequence of being a Tory during the Revolution, his possessions were confiscated, and he and his family impoverished. Young Nicholas's childhood was passed in indigence, and it is said that he was apprenticed to a shoemaker, when a mere lad, to learn the trade as a means of livelihood. However this may be, it is certain that when very young he went to South Carolina as a clerk for his elder brother. The climate of the South, however, did not suit his health, and he returned to Newark, and began the study of the law.

He was poor, and the East was overcrowded, even at that early day, and offered but few inducements to a young man entirely dependent upon his own efforts. Ohio was then the "Far West," and emigration was setting in toward it rapidly. Those who had seen the country related what then seemed marvelous tales of its wonderful fertility and progress. Few professional men were seeking the distant land, and Longworth felt convinced that the services of such as did go would assuredly be in demand, and he resolved to cast his lot with the West.

In 1803, at the age of twenty-one, he removed to the little village of Cincinnati, and, having fixed upon this place as his future home, entered the law office of Judge Jacob Burnet, long the ablest jurist in Ohio. He soon won the confidence and esteem of his instructor, and succeeded so well in his studies that in an unusually short time he was admitted to the bar.

He entered upon the practice of his profession with energy, and soon acquired a profitable business, which increased rapidly. He was a man of simple habits, and lived economically. His savings were considerable, and were regularly invested by him in real estate in the suburbs of the town. Land was cheap at that time, some of his lots costing him but ten dollars each. Long before his death they were worth more than as many thousands. He had a firm conviction that Cincinnati was destined to become one of the largest and most flourishing cities in the Union, and that his real estate would increase in value at a rate which would render him wealthy in a very few years.

His first client was a man accused of horse-stealing, in those days the most heinous offense known to Western law. Longworth secured his acquittal, but the fellow had no money to pay his counsel, and in the absence of funds gave Longworth two second-hand copper stills, which were his property. These the lawyer accepted, thinking that he could easily dispose of them for cash, as they were rare and valuable there in those days. They were in the keeping of Mr. Joel Williams, who carried on a tavern adjacent to the river, and who was afterward one of the largest property-holders in Cincinnati. Mr. Williams was building a distillery at the time, and, as he had confidently reckoned upon using the two stills in his possession, was considerably nonplused when Longworth presented his order for them. In his extremity he offered to purchase them from the lawyer for a lot of thirty-three acres of barren land in the town, which was then worth little or nothing. Longworth hesitated, for although he had an almost prophetic belief in the future value of the land, he was sorely in need of ready money; but at length he accepted the offer. The deed for the land was made out in his name, and the stills became the property of Mr. Williams. The distillery was built, and its owner realized a fortune; but Longworth did more. His thirty-three acres of barren land were soon in the very heart of Cincinnati, and long before his death were valued at two millions of dollars.

The foresight of Mr. Longworth was fully justified by the course of events. The growth of Cincinnati was almost marvelous in its rapidity. In 1802, it contained about 800 inhabitants; in 1810, 2,540; in 1820, 9,060; in 1830, 24,831; in 1840, 46,338; in 1850, 118,761; and in 1860, just three years before Mr. Longworth's death, 171,293 inhabitants. The reader can easily imagine the immense profits which a half century's increase placed in the hands of the far-seeing lawyer. It seems almost like reading some old fairy tale to peruse the accounts of successful ventures in real estate in American cities. They have sprung up as if by magic, and it is impossible to say where their development will end. Said a gentleman of less than thirty-five years of age to the writer of these pages, "I am the oldest native-born citizen of Chicago. When I first saw the light, my native place could not boast even the dignity of a village; and young as I am, I have witnessed all this wonderful growth." The prosperity of Cincinnati was scarcely less marked, as the career of Mr. Longworth shows. The investment of a comparatively insignificant sum laid the foundation of his fortune, and the first counsel fee he ever earned, a sum trifling in itself, placed him in possession of millions.

Mr. Longworth continued carefully to invest his gains in real estate. The prices paid by him increased, of course, with the rise in the value of property, but as he was persuaded that the limit had not yet been reached, he extended his operations without fear of loss. He sold many of his original purchases, but continued until the day of his death the largest land-owner in the city. In 1850 his taxes were over $17,000, and in the same year the taxes of William B. Astor amounted to $23,116. At the time of his death Mr. Longworth's estate was valued at fifteen millions of dollars, and is doubtless worth fully one-third more at the present day.

Mr. Longworth retired from the practice of the law in 1819, to devote himself to the management of his property, which was already sufficiently important to require his undivided attention. He had always been an enthusiast in horticultural matters, and believing that the climate of the Ohio Valley was admirably adapted to the production of grapes, had for some time been making experiments in that direction; but he fell into the error of believing that only the foreign vines were worth cultivating, and his experiments were unsuccessful. The foreign grape did not mature well, and the wine produced from it was not good. In 1828 his friend Major Adlum sent him some specimens of the Catawba grape, which he had procured from the garden of a German living near Washington City, and he began to experiment with it in his own vineyard.

The Catawba grape, now so popular and well-known throughout the country, was then a comparative stranger to our people, and was regarded even by many who were acquainted with it as unfit for vintage purposes. It was first discovered in a wild condition about 1801, near Asheville, Buncombe County, North Carolina, near the source of the Catawba River. General Davy, of Rocky Mount, on that river, afterward Senator from North Carolina, is supposed to have given the German in whose garden Major Adlum found the grape a few of the vines to experiment upon. General Davy always regarded the bringing of this grape into notice as the greatest act of his life. "I have done my country a greater benefit in introducing this grape into public notice," said he, in after years, "than I would have done if I had paid the national debt."

Mr. Longworth's experiments with the Catawba were highly successful, and induced him to abandon all his efforts with foreign vines, and undertake only the Catawba, to which he afterward added the Isabella. He now entered systematically upon grape-growing. He established a large vineyard upon a hillside sloping down to the river, about four miles above the city, and employed German laborers, whose knowledge of vine-dressing, acquired in the Fatherland, made them the best workmen he could have. He caused it to be announced that all the grape juice produced by the small growers in the vicinity would find a cash purchaser in him, no matter in what quantities offered. At the same time he offered a reward of five hundred dollars for any improvement in the quality of the Catawba grape.

The enthusiasm which he manifested, as well as the liberality of his offer, had a decidedly beneficial effect upon the small growers in the neighborhood. "It proved a great stimulus to the growth of the Catawba vine in the country around Cincinnati," to know that a man of Mr. Longworth's means stood ready to pay cash, at the rate of from a dollar to a dollar and a quarter a gallon, for all the grape-juice that might be brought to him, without reference to the quantity. It was in this way, and by urgent popular appeals through the columns of the newspapers, that he succeeded, after many failures, and against the depressing influence of much doubt and indifference, in bringing the enterprise up to its present high and stable position. When he took the matter in hand there was much to discourage any one not possessed of the traits of constancy of purpose and perseverance peculiar to Mr. Longworth. Many had tried the manufacture of wine, and had failed to give it any economical or commercial importance. It was not believed, until Mr. Longworth practically demonstrated it, that a native grape was the only one upon which any hope could be placed, and that the Catawba offered the most assured promise of success, and was the one upon which all vine-growers might with confidence depend. It took years of unremitted care, multiplied and wide-spread investigations, and the expenditure of large sums of money, to establish this fact, and bring the agricultural community to accept it and act under its guidance. The success attained by Mr. Longworth soon induced other gentlemen resident in the vicinity of Cincinnati, and favorably situated for the purpose, to undertake the culture of the Catawba, and several of them are now regularly and extensively engaged in the manufacture of wine. The impetus and encouragement thus given to the business soon led the German citizens of Hamilton County to perceive its advantages, and, under their thrifty management, thousands of acres, stretching up from the banks of the Ohio, are now covered with luxuriant and profitable vineyards, rivaling in profusion and beauty the vine-clad hills of Italy and France. The oldest vineyard in the county of Hamilton is of Mr. Longworth's planting."

Mr. Longworth subsequently increased the size of his vineyard to two hundred acres, and toward the close of his life his wine houses annually produced one hundred and fifty thousand bottles of wine. His vaults usually contained a stock of three hundred thousand bottles in course of thorough ripening.

His cellars were situated on the declivity of East Sixth Street, on the road to Observatory Hill. They occupied a space ninety feet by one hundred and twenty-five in size, and consisted of two tiers of massive stone vaults, the lower of which was twenty-five feet below the surface of the ground. The manufacture of the wine was placed under the charge of a celebrated chemist from Rheims, and the mode of preparation was as follows:

After the pressing of the grape, the juice is subjected to the vinous fermentation, by which ten or eleven per cent. of alcohol is developed. In the following spring, it is mixed with a small quantity of sugar, and put into strong bottles, the corks of which are secured with twine and wire. The sugar accelerates a second fermentation, which always takes place about this time, and thus a strong movement is produced inside the glass, which generates gas enough to burst the vessels briskly, adding thereby considerably to the cost. This is known as the gaseous fermentation, and the effect of it is to render the wine more enlivening, more stinging to the taste, and more fruity. "This last effect results from this, that the flavor of the fruit mostly passes off with the carbonic acid gas, which is largely generated in the first or vinous fermentation, and in a less degree in this second or gaseous fermentation." It is impossible to avoid the loss of the flavor in the first fermentation, but the strong bottles and securely-fastened corks preserve it in the second. The liquid, which is muddy at first, becomes clear in about a year, a thick sediment having collected at the bottom of the bottle. The bottles are then placed in racks, with their necks downward, and are shaken vigorously every day for about three weeks. This forces the sediment to settle down in the neck against the cork. When it is all in the neck, the wires are cut, and the cork blown out by the gas, carrying the sediment with it. Fresh sugar, for sweetness, is now added, new corks are driven in and secured, and in a few weeks the wine is ready for the market.

Mr. Longworth continued his wine trade with great success for about twenty-five years, and though for some time his expenditures were largely in excess of his income from this source, he at length reaped a steady and increasing profit from it, which more than reimbursed him for his former losses. He was very fond of the strawberry, and succeeded, by careful and expensive cultivation, in making several very important improvements in that delicious fruit. His experiments in the sexual character of the strawberry are highly interesting, but must be passed by here. He manifested no selfishness with respect to his fruits. He was anxious that their cultivation should become general, and his discoveries and improvements were always at the service of any and every one who desired to make use of them.

He was thoroughly devoted to his adopted home, and anxious to secure its steady improvement. When it was proposed to establish an observatory, the Mount Adams property, then owned by him, was regarded as the most fitting site for it. He was asked to name the price for which he would sell the property. To the astonishment of the parties in charge of the enterprise, he made a free gift of the land—four acres in extent—to the trustees. A gentleman who had hoped to dispose of some of his own property for this purpose charged Mr. Longworth, through the press, with being influenced by a desire to improve his adjoining property by the erection of the observatory on Mount Adams. Longworth promptly replied that if the writer of the article in question would donate four acres of his own property for an observatory, he (Longworth) would put up, at his own expense, a building on it equal to that which had been erected on Mount Adams, and transfer the latter place to the city as a permanent pleasure ground. He quietly added that in this way his accuser might himself receive, for his adjacent property, all the benefits of such an improvement, and at the same time win for himself the lasting gratitude of the people of Cincinnati. This settled the matter, and no more was heard from the other side.

"Longworth," says one who knew him, "is a problem and a riddle—a problem worthy of the study of those who delight in exploring that labyrinth of all that is hidden and mysterious, the human heart; and a riddle to himself and others. He is a wit and a humorist of a high order; of keen sagacity and shrewdness in many other respects than in money matters; one who can be exact to a dollar, and liberal, when he chooses, with thousands; of marked peculiarity and tenacity in his own opinions, yet of abundant tolerance to the opinions, however extravagant, of others—a man of great public spirit and sound general judgment.

"In addition to all this, it would be difficult to find an individual of his position and standing so perfectly free from pride, in the ordinary sense. He has absolutely none, unless it be the pride of eccentricity. It is no uncommon circumstance for men to become rich by the concentration of time, and labor, and attention to some one object of profitable employment. This is the ordinary phase of money-getting, as closing the ear and pocket to applications for aid is that of money-saving. Longworth has become a rich man on a different principle. He appears to have started upon the calculation that if he could put any individual in the way of making a dollar for Longworth, and a dollar for himself at the same time, by aiding him with ground for a lot, or in building him a house on it; and if, moreover, he could multiply cases of the kind by hundreds, or perhaps thousands, he would promote his own interests just in the same measure as he was advancing those of others. At the same time he could not be unconscious that, while their half was subdivided into small possessions, owned by a thousand or more individuals, his half was a vast, boundless aggregate, since it was the property of one man alone. The event has done justice to his sagacity. Hundreds, if not thousands, in and adjacent to Cincinnati, now own houses and lots, and many have become wealthy, who would, in all probability, have lived and died as tenants under a different state of case. Had not Mr. Longworth adopted this course, he would have occupied that relation to society which many wealthy men now sustain, that of getting all they can and keeping all they get."

In politics, Mr. Longworth was a Whig, and afterward a Republican. During the famous Clay campaign he was asked to give one hundred dollars to help defray the expenses of the party..

"I never give something for nothing," said he. "We might fail to elect Clay, as we did before, and I should fling away the hundred dollars."

The applicant, who was himself a man of wealth, assured him that there was no doubt of Clay's election.

"There can be no chance of your losing," he said.

"Well," replied Longworth, "I'll tell you what I will do. I will give you the hundred dollars, but mind, you shall be personally responsible to me for its return if Clay is not elected."

The offer was accepted; and when the campaign resulted in the defeat of Clay, Longworth demanded his money from the politician, who was compelled to return it out of his own pocket.

In his own way—and a quaint, singular way it was—Mr. Longworth was exceedingly charitable. Long after he was worth millions, and when every moment of his time was valuable, he was supernumerary township trustee. This was an office which required the expenditure of a considerable portion of his time, and brought him in constant contact with some of the most wretched of the lowest class of the poor. He was always in his office, at stated times, and with a patience and kindness worthy of all admiration, the millionaire listened to their sad tales, and provided such aid as was necessary, oftentimes giving it out of his own purse when the public funds failed.

He was a bitter foe to vagabondage and mendicity. If people in need were willing to work, he would place them in the way of doing so. He was the owner of a stone quarry on Deer Creek, the traces of which may still be seen in the lines of the new Gilbert Avenue; and he kept in his office a supply of picks and shovels. When a stout beggar asked him for alms, he would inquire if he was willing to go to work. If answered affirmatively, he would give him a pick and shovel, and start him for the quarry, where the wages were promptly paid out every night. Many availed themselves of the opportunity, and worked for him faithfully; but others gave the quarry "a wide berth," and sold the pick and shovel for money or liquor. It was his custom to buy large quantities of bread tickets from the bakers, and to distribute them to those whom he considered worthy; and he would also keep on hand large quantities of shoes, dry goods, etc., which he gave away in the same manner.

Mr. Frank Pentland, who was once in his employ, relates the following incident:

"One morning, just after Mr. Longworth had gone to his office, near the Third-Street entrance, where he was accustomed to receive applicants for charity, he was accosted by a man who craved assistance. In answer to a question as to his needs, he replied that his main want was a pair of shoes, and a glance at his feet showed that he spoke truthfully. Mr. Longworth appeared 'to take his measure' at a glance, and impulsively shaking his right foot (he seldom wore his shoes tied), kicked the shoe over to the applicant, saying:

"'Try that on, my man. How does it fit?'

"'Illigant, yer honor.'

"'Well, try that, now,' said he, kicking off the other. 'How will they do?'

"'Illigant, yer honor; illigant! May many a blessing'—

"'Well, well, go now—that'll do,' and turning to Pentland, who was then a young boy in his service, ordered him to the house to get another pair. Frank obeyed, but was told by Mrs. Longworth that those he wore away from the house were all that he had. The result was that Frank was hurried off to William Hart's shoe store, on Fifth Street, for new ones, with instructions to 'Ask Mr. Hart for the kind I always buy, and don't pay over a dollar and a half for them.'"

Yet many persons charged this man with stinginess—a charge to which every rich man lays himself open who does not give to all who ask him. Even the rich must refuse sometimes, for there is no reason why they should answer *all* the calls made upon them—a course which would soon impoverish them. They must discriminate somewhere, and how this shall be done is a question which each must decide for himself. Longworth exercised this discrimination in an eccentric manner, eminently characteristic of him. He invariably refused cases that commended themselves to others. A gentleman once applied to him for assistance for a widow in destitute circumstances.

"Who is she?" asked the millionaire. "Do you know her? Is she a deserving object?"

"She is not only a woman of excellent character," answered his friend, "but she is doing all in her power to support a large family of children."

"Very well, then," said Mr. Longworth, "I sha'n't give a cent. Such persons will always find a plenty to relieve them."

He was firm, and turned coldly from the entreaties of his friend. Yet he opened his purse liberally to those whom others refused. Vagabonds, drunkards, fallen women, those who had gone down far into the depths of misery and wretchedness, and from whom respectable people shrank in disgust, never appealed to him in vain. "The devil's poor," he whimsically called them. He would listen to them patiently, moved to the depths of his soul by their sad stories, and would send them away rejoicing that they were not utterly friendless. "Decent paupers will always find a plenty to help them," he would say, "but no one cares for these poor wretches. Every body damns them, and as no one else will help them, I must." Yet he aided them in such a manner as to encourage them to rise above their wretchedness.

In his personal appearance Mr. Longworth was not prepossessing. He was dry and caustic in his remarks, and rarely spared the object of his satire. He was plain and careless in his dress, looking more like a beggar than a millionaire. He cared nothing for dress, except, perhaps, that he preferred common clothes to fine ones. One of his acquaintances relates the following story in illustration of this phase of his character:

"Many winters ago, it will be remembered that a style of striped goods was quite popular with poor people on account of its cheapness, and that it acquired the name of 'Hard Times.' Every body with scant purses wore coats or pants of it, for the reason that they could not very well buy any other kind. As the story goes, it appears that 'Old Nick,' as he was familiarly called, invested in an overcoat of this material, and took great pride in wearing it, much to the annoyance of the women folks. It happened that one cold, stormy night the faithful family coachman was at the house without an overcoat, and

Mrs. Longworth, after very feelingly depicting his forlorn condition to her husband, solicited the privilege of giving him the aforesaid overcoat. Much to her gratification, Mr. Longworth assented, and the coachman wore off the 'Hard Times,' the good wife replacing it by an elegant broadcloth that she had quietly provided for the occasion. The next morning 'Old Nick' very innocently (?) overlooked the new coat, and went off to make his usual morning rounds without one; but it would be impossible to portray the annoyance of the household when they saw him returning to dinner wearing a duplicate of the veritable 'Hard Times,' and for weeks afterward it was no uncommon occurrence to see the 'master and man' flitting about the old homestead dressed in their gray stripes."

The shabbiness of his dress once led to an amusing adventure, which he enjoyed very much. Climbing one of the hilly streets of the city one broiling summer day, he sat down on a pile of bricks, under the cool shade of a tree, to rest. Taking off his well-worn hat, he laid it on his knee, and closing his eyes, sat enjoying the breeze which had just then sprung up. He was very tired, and his whole figure expressed his weariness. As he sat there in his shabby dress, with his eyes closed, and his hat resting on his knees, he looked the very picture of a blind beggar soliciting charity. For such, indeed, he was mistaken by a working man who passed by a few minutes later, and who, pitying the supposed unfortunate, tossed a few pennies into his hat. The noise of the coppers made the old man open his eyes and look up; and to his amazement the workman recognized in the object of his charity Nicholas Longworth, the millionaire. Mr. Longworth looked at him a moment in his dry, quizzical way, and then, thanking him politely, put the coins in his pocket, and, closing his eyes, once more resumed his former position.

Mr. Longworth had erected a magnificent mansion in the midst of his vineyard. He gathered there a fine library, and a collection of paintings, statuary, and other art treasures, which were his pride. He died there on the 10th of February, 1863, at the age of eighty-one. His loss was severely felt by the community, especially by his "devil's poor," for whom he had cared so tenderly.

CHAPTER VIII.

GEORGE PEABODY.

IT is not often that men who pass their lives in the acquisition of money are able to retain the desire to give it to others who have had no share in the earning of it. In European countries, the wealthy merchant commonly uses his fortune for the purpose of founding a family, and securing sometimes a title of nobility. His wealth is entailed, that it may remain in his family and benefit remote generations; but few save those of his own blood enjoy any benefit from it, and the world is no better off for his life and success than if he had never been born. In America, instances of personal generosity and benevolence on a large scale are of more common occurrence than in the Old World. We have already borne witness to the munificence of Girard, Astor, Lawrence, Longworth, and Stewart, and shall yet present to the reader other instances of this kind in the remaining pages of this work. We have now to trace the career of one who far exceeded any of these in the extent and magnitude of his liberality, and who, while neglecting none connected with him by ties of blood, took the whole English-speaking race for his family, and by scattering his blessings far and wide on both sides of the Atlantic, has won a proud name

"As one who loved his fellow-men."

George Peabody came of an old English family, which

GEORGE PEABODY.

traced its descent back to the year of our Lord 61, the days of the heroic Boadicea, down through the brilliant circle of the Knights of the Round Table, to Francis Peabody, who in 1635 went from St. Albans, in Hertfordshire, to the New World, and settled in Danvers, Massachusetts, where the subject of this memoir was born one hundred and sixty years later, on the 18th of February, 1795. The parents of George Peabody were poor, and hard work was the lot to which he was born, a lot necessary to develop his sterling qualities of mind and heart. He was possessed of a strong, vigorous constitution, and a quick, penetrating intellect. His education was limited, for he was taken from school at the age of eleven, and set to earning his living. Upon leaving school, he was apprenticed to a Mr. Sylvester Proctor, who kept a "country store" in Danvers. Here he worked hard and faithfully for four or five years, devoting himself, with an energy and determination surprising in one so young, to learn the first principles of business. His mind matured more rapidly than his body, and he was a man in intellect long before he was out of his teens. Having gained all the information it was possible to acquire in so small an establishment, he began to wish for a wider field for the exercise of his abilities. A retail grocery store was no longer the place for one possessed of such talents, and thoroughly conscious of them at such an early age, and it was natural that he should desire some more important and responsible position.

Accordingly, he left Mr. Proctor's employment, and spent a year with his maternal grandfather at Post Mills village, Thetford, Vermont. "George Peabody's year at Post Mills," says a writer who knew him, "must have been a year of intense quiet, with good examples always before him, and good advice whenever occasion called for it; for Mr. Dodge and his wife were both too shrewd to bore him with it needlessly.

"It was on his return from this visit that he spent a night at a tavern in Concord, N. H., and paid for his entertainment by sawing wood the next morning. That, however, must have been a piece of George's own voluntary economy, for Jeremiah Dodge would never have sent his grandson home to Danvers without the means of procuring the necessaries of life on the way, and still less, if possible, would Mrs. Dodge. . . .

PEABODY PAYING FOR A NIGHT'S LODGING.

"The interest with which Mr. Peabody remembered this visit to Post Mills is shown by his second visit so late in life, and his gift of a library—as large a library as that place needs. Of its influence on his subsequent career, of course, there is no record. Perhaps it was not much. But, at least, it gave him a good chance for quiet thinking, at an age when he needed it; and the labors of the farm may have been useful both to mind and body."

At the age of sixteen, in the year 1811, he went to Newburyport, and became a clerk in the store of his elder brother, David Peabody, who was engaged in the dry goods business at that place. He exhibited unusual capacity and promise in his calling, and soon drew upon himself the favorable attention of the merchants of the place. He was prompt, reliable, and energetic, and from the first established an enviable reputation for personal and professional integrity. It is said that he earned here the first money he ever made outside of his business. This was by writing ballots for the Federal party in Newburyport. Printed ballots had not then come into use.

He did not stay long in Newburyport, as a great fire, which burned up a considerable part of the town, destroyed his brother's store, and obliged him to seek employment elsewhere. He always retained a warm attachment to the place, however, an attachment which a resident of the town explains as follows:

"The cause of Mr. George Peabody's interest in Newburyport was not alone that he had lived here for a brief period, or that his relatives had lived here; but rather it was the warm friendship that had been shown him, which was, in fact, the basis of his subsequent prosperity. He left here in 1811, and returned in 1857. The forty-six intervening years had borne to the grave most of the persons with whom he had formed acquaintance. Among those he recognized were several who were in business, or clerks, on State Street in 1811,—Messrs. John Porter, Moses Kimball, Prescott Spaulding, and a few others. Mr. Spaulding was fourteen years older than Mr. Peabody, and in business when the latter was a clerk with his uncle, Colonel John Peabody. Mr. Peabody was here in 1857, on the day of the Agricultural Fair, and was walking in the procession with the late Mayor Davenport, when he saw Mr. Spaulding on the sidewalk, and at once left the procession to greet him.

"Mr. Spaulding had rendered him the greatest of services.

When Mr. Peabody left Newburyport, he was under age, and not worth a dollar. Mr. Spaulding gave him letters of credit in Boston, through which he obtained two thousand dollars' worth of merchandise of Mr. James Reed, who was so favorably impressed with his appearance, that he subsequently gave him credit for a larger amount. This was his start in life, as he afterward acknowledged; for at a public entertainment in Boston, when his credit was good for any amount, and in any part of the world, Mr. Peabody laid his hand on Mr. Reed's shoulder, and said to those present, 'My friends, here is my first patron; and he is the man who sold me my first bill of goods.' After he was established in Georgetown, D. C., the first consignment made to him was by the late Francis Todd, of Newburyport. It was from these facts that Newburyport was always pleasant in his memory; and the donation he made to the Public Library was on his own suggestion, that he desired to do something of a public nature for our town."

From New England, George Peabody turned his face southward, and entered the employment of his uncle, Mr. John Peabody, who was engaged in the dry goods business in Georgetown, in the District of Columbia. He reached that place in the spring of 1812; but, as the second war with England broke out about the same time, was not able to give his immediate attention to business. He became a member of a volunteer company of artillery, which was stationed at Fort Warburton, but as no active duty was required of the company, he soon went back to his uncle's store. His uncle was a poor man and a bad manager, and for two years the business was conducted by George Peabody, and in his own name; but at the end of that time, seeing the business threatened with ruin by his uncle's incapacity, he resigned his situation, and entered the service of Mr. Elisha Riggs, who had just established a wholesale dry goods house in Georgetown. Mr. Riggs furnished the capital for the concern, and Mr. Peabody was given the management of it. Soon after this, the latter became a partner in the house. It is said that when Mr. Riggs invited Mr. Peabody to become his partner, the latter informed him that he could not legally assume the responsibilities of the business, as he was only nineteen years old. This was no objection in the mind of the merchant, as he wanted a young and active assistant, and had discerned in his boy-manager the qualities which never fail to win success.

The new business in which he was engaged consisted chiefly in the importation and sale of European goods, and consignments of dry goods from the northern cities. It extended over a wide field, and gave Mr. Peabody a fine opportunity for the display of his abilities. Mr. Riggs' friends blamed him very much for leaving his business so entirely in the hands of a boy of nineteen; but he had better proof than they that his affairs were not only in good but in the best hands, and he answered them all by telling them that time would justify his course. Mr. Peabody traveled extensively in establishing his business, often journeying into the wild and unsettled regions of the border States on horseback. He worked with energy and intelligence, and in 1815 the business was found to be so extensive that a removal to Baltimore became necessary. About this time a sort of irregular banking business was added to the operations of the house. This was chiefly the suggestion of Mr. Peabody, and proved a source of great profit.

Mr. Peabody quickly took a prominent rank among the merchants of Baltimore. His manner was frank and engaging, and won him many friends. He was noted for "a judgment quick and cautious, clear and sound, a decided purpose, a firm will, energetic and persevering industry, punctuality and fidelity in every engagement, justice and honor controlling every transaction, and courtesy—that true courtesy which springs from genuine kindness—presiding over the intercourse of life." His business continued to increase, and in 1822 it became necessary to establish branches in Philadelphia and New York, over which Mr. Peabody exercised a careful supervision. He was thoroughly familiar with every detail of his business, and never suffered his vigilance to relax, however competent might be the subordinates in the immediate charge of those details. In 1827 he went to England on business for his firm, and during the next ten years made frequent voyages between New York and London.

In 1829 Mr. Riggs withdrew from the firm, and Mr. Peabody become the actual head of the house, the style of the firm, which had previously been "Riggs & Peabody," being changed to "Peabody, Riggs & Co." The firm had for some time been the financial agents of the State of Maryland, and had managed the negotiations confided to them with great skill and success; and every year their banking department became more important and more profitable.

In 1836 Mr. Peabody determined to extend his business, which was already very large, to England, and to open a branch house in London. In 1837 he removed to that city for the purpose of taking charge of his house there, and from that time London became his home.

The summer of this year was marked by one of the most terrible commercial crises the United States has ever known. A large number of the banks suspended specie payment, and the majority of the mercantile houses were either ruined or in the greatest distress. Thousands of merchants, until then prosperous, were hopelessly ruined. "That great sympathetic nerve of the commercial world, credit," said Edward Everett, "as far as the United States was concerned, was for the time paralyzed. At that moment Mr. Peabody not only stood firm himself, but was the cause of firmness in others. There were not at that time, probably, half a dozen other men in Europe who, upon the subject of American securities, would have been listened to for a moment in the parlor of the Bank of England. But his judgment commanded respect; his integrity won back the reliance which men had been accustomed to place in American securities. The reproach in which they were all involved was gradually wiped away from those of a substantial character; and if, on this solid basis of unsuspected good faith, he reared his own prosperity, let it be remembered that at the same time he retrieved the credit of the State of Maryland, of which he was agent—performing that miracle by which the word of an honest man turns paper into gold."

The conduct of Mr. Peabody, as well as the evidences which he gave of his remarkable capacity for business, in this crisis, placed him among the foremost merchants of London. He carried on his business upon a large scale from his base of operations in that city. He bought British manufactures in all parts of England and shipped them to the United States. His vessels brought back in return all kinds of American produce which would command a ready sale in England. Profitable as these ventures were, there was another branch of his business much more remunerative to him. The merchants and manufacturers on both sides of the Atlantic who consigned their goods to him frequently procured from him advances upon the goods long before they were sold. At other times they would leave large sums in his hands long after the goods were disposed of, knowing that they could draw whenever they needed, and that in the meanwhile their money was being so profitably invested that they were certain of a proper interest for their loans. Thus Mr. Peabody gradually became a banker, in which pursuit he was as successful as he had been as a merchant. In 1843 he withdrew from the house of Peabody, Riggs & Co., and established the house of "George Peabody & Company, of Warnford Court, City."

His dealings were chiefly with America, and in American securities, and he was always regarded as one of the best specimens of the American merchant ever seen in London. He was very proud of his country; and though he passed so many years of his life abroad, he never forgot that he was an American. In speaking of the manner in which he organized his business establishment, he once said: "I have endeavored, in the constitution of its members and the character of its business, to make it an American house, and to give it an American atmosphere; to furnish it with American journals; to make it a center of American news, and an agreeable place for my American friends visiting London."

It was his custom, from his first settlement in England, to celebrate the anniversary of the independence of his country by an entertainment at one of the public houses in the city, to which the most distinguished Americans in London were always invited, as were also many of the prominent men of Great Britain; and this dinner was only discontinued in deference to the general celebration of the day which was afterward instituted by the whole body of Americans resident in the British metropolis. In the year 1851, when it was thought that there would be no representation of the achievements of American skill and industry in the Great Exhibition of that year, from a lack of funds, Mr. Peabody generously supplied the sum of fifteen thousand dollars, which enabled the Commissioners to make a suitable display of the American contributions. Said the Hon. Edward Everett, alluding to this act:

"In most, perhaps in all other countries, this exhibition had been a government affair. Commissioners were appointed by authority to protect the interests of the exhibitors; and, what was more important, appropriations of money had been made to defray their expenses. No appropriations were made by Congress. Our exhibitors arrived friendless, some of them penniless, in the great commercial Babel of the world. They found the portion of the Crystal Palace assigned to our country unprepared for the specimens of art and industry which they had brought with them; naked and unadorned by the side of the neighboring arcades and galleries fitted up with elegance and splendor by the richest governments in Europe. The English press began to launch its too ready sarcasms at the sorry appearance which Brother Jonathan seemed likely to make; and all the exhibitors from this country, as well as those who felt an interest in their success, were disheartened. At this critical moment, our friend stepped forward. He did what Congress should have done. By liberal advances on his part, the American department was fitted up; and day after day, as some new product of American ingenuity and taste was added to the list,—McCormick's reaper, Colt's revolver, Powers's Greek Slave, Hobbs's unpickable lock, Hoe's wonderful printing presses, and Bond's more wonderful spring governor,—it began to be suspected that Brother Jonathan was not quite so much of a simpleton as had been thought. He had contributed his full share, if not to the splendor, at least to the utilities of the exhibition. In fact, the leading journal at London, with a magnanimity which did it honor, admitted that England had derived more real benefit from the contributions of the United States than from those of any other country."

As has been said, Mr. Peabody made the bulk of his colossal fortune in the banking business. He had a firm faith in American securities, and dealt in them largely, and with confidence. His business instinct was remarkable, his judgment in mercantile and financial matters almost infallible, and he made few mistakes. His course was now onward and upward, and each year marked an increase of his wealth. His business operations were conducted in pursuance of a rigid system which was never relaxed. To the very close of his life he never abandoned the exact or business-like manner in which he sought to make money. He gave away millions with a generosity never excelled, yet he could be exacting to a penny in the fulfillment of a contract.

In his youth he contracted habits of economy, and these he retained to the last. Being unmarried, he did not subject himself to the expense of a complete domestic establishment, but lived in chambers, and entertained his friends at his club or at a coffee-house. His habits were simple in every respect, and he was often seen making his dinner on a mutton-chop at a table laden (at his cost) with the most sumptuous and tempting viands. His personal expenses for ten years did not average three thousand dollars per annum.

The conductor on an English railway once overcharged him a shilling for fare. He promptly complained to the directors, and had the man discharged. "Not," said he, "that I could not afford to pay the shilling, but the man was cheating many travelers to whom the swindle would be offensive."

Several years ago he chanced to ride in a hack in Salem, Massachusetts, and upon reaching his destination tendered the driver his usual fee of fifty cents.

"Here 's your change, sir," said the man, handing him back fifteen cents.

"Change!" exclaimed Mr. Peabody; "why, I 'm not entitled to any."

"Yes, you are; I don't charge but thirty-five cents for a ride in my hack."

"How do you live, then?"

"By fair dealing, sir. I don't believe in making a man pay more than a thing is worth just because I have an opportunity."

Mr. Peabody was so much pleased with this reply, that as long as he remained in Salem he sought this man out and gave him his custom.

In his dress Mr. Peabody was simple and unostentatious. He was scrupulously neat and tasteful, but there was nothing about him to indicate his vast wealth. He seldom wore any jewelry, using merely a black band for his watch-guard. Display of all kinds he abominated.

He made several visits to his native country during his last residence in London, and commemorated each one of them by acts of princely munificence. He gave large sums to the cause of education, and to religious and charitable objects, and made each one of his near kindred wealthy. None of his relatives received less than one hundred thousand dollars, and some were given as much as three times that sum. He gave immense sums to the poor of London, and became their benefactor to such an extent that Queen Victoria sent him her portrait, which she had caused to be executed for him at a cost of over forty thousand dollars, in token of her appreciation of his services in behalf of the poor of her realm.

Mr. Peabody made another visit to the United States in 1866, and upon this occasion added large sums to many of the donations he had already made in this country. He remained here until May, 1867, when he returned to England. He came back in June, 1869, but soon sailed again for England. His health had become very feeble, and it was his belief that it would be better in the atmosphere of London, to which he had been so long accustomed. His hope of recovery was vain. He failed to rally upon reaching London, and died in that city on the 4th of November, 1869.

The news of his death created a profound sadness on both sides of the Atlantic, for his native and his adopted country alike revered him as a benefactor. The Queen caused his body to be placed in a vault in Westminster Abbey, amidst the greatest and noblest of her kingdom, until all was in readiness for its transportation to the United States in a royal man-of-war. The Congress of the United States authorized the President to make such arrangements for the reception of the body as he should deem necessary. Sovereigns, statesmen, and warriors united to do homage to the mortal remains of this plain, simple man, who, beginning life a poor boy, and never departing from the character of an unassuming citizen, had made humanity his debtor by his generosity and goodness. He was borne across the ocean with kingly honors, two great nations acting as chief mourners, and then, when the pomp and the splendor of the occasion were ended, they laid him down in his native earth by the side of the mother from whom he had imbibed those principles of integrity and goodness which were the foundation of his fame and fortune.

It is impossible to obtain an accurate statement of the donations made by Mr. Peabody to the objects which enlisted his sympathy. In addition to those mentioned in the list below, he gave away for various public purposes sums ranging from two hundred and fifty to one thousand dollars, and extending back as far as the year 1835. He divided among his relatives the sum of about three millions of dollars, giving them a portion during his last visit to this country, and leaving them the remainder at his death.

The following is a statement of his more important donations during his life, including the bequests contained in his last will and testament:

To the State of Maryland, for negotiating the loan of $8,000,000	$60,000
To the Peabody Institute, Baltimore, Md., including accrued interest	1,500,000
To the Southern Education Fund	3,000,000
To Yale College	150,000
To Harvard College	150,000
To Peabody Academy, Massachusetts	140,000
To Phillips Academy, Massachusetts	25,000
To Peabody Institute, etc., at Peabody, Mass.	250,000
To Kenyon College, Ohio	25,000
To Memorial Church, in Georgetown, Mass.	100,000
To Homes for the Poor in London	3,000,000
To Libraries in Georgetown, Massachusetts, and Thetford, Vermont	10,000
To Kane's Arctic Expedition	10,000
To different Sanitary Fairs	10,000
To unpaid moneys advanced to uphold the credit of States	40,000
Total	$8,470,000

The life of such a man affords lessons full of hope and encouragement to others. In 1856, when on a visit to Danvers, now named Peabody, in honor of him, its most distinguished son and greatest benefactor, he said:

"Though Providence has granted me an unvaried and unusual success in the pursuit of fortune in other lands, I am still in heart the humble boy who left yonder unpretending dwelling. There is not a youth within the sound of my voice whose early opportunities and advantages are not very much greater than were my own, and I have since achieved nothing that is impossible to the most humble boy among you."

CORNELIUS VANDERBILT.

II.

CAPITALISTS.

CHAPTER IX.

CORNELIUS VANDERBILT.

STATEN ISLAND lies in the beautiful bay of New York, seven miles distant from the great city. Its lofty heights shut in the snug anchorage of the inner bay, and protect it from the rude storms which howl along the coast. It lies full in sight of the city, and is one of the most beautiful and attractive of its suburbs. The commanding heights and embowered shores are covered with villas and cottages, and afford a pleasant and convenient summer resort for the people of New York. It now contains a large and flourishing population, and maintains a speedy and constant communication with the metropolis by means of steam ferry-boats, the total travel on which sometimes reaches as many as ten or twelve thousand passengers per day.

Seventy-six years ago, Staten Island was a mere country settlement, and its communications with the city were maintained by means of a few sail-boats, which made one trip each way per day.

One of these boats was owned and navigated by Cornelius

Vanderbilt, a thriving farmer, who owned a small but well cultivated estate on Staten Island, near the present Quarantine Grounds. He was a man of exemplary character, great industry, and was generally regarded as one of the most prudent and reliable men on the island. Having a considerable amount of produce to sell in the city, he purchased a boat of his own for the purpose of transporting it thither. Frequently, residents of the island would secure passage in this boat to the city in the morning, and return with it in the evening. He realized a considerable sum of money in this way, and finally ran his boat regularly between the island and the city. This was the beginning of the New York and Staten Island Ferry. Mr. Vanderbilt, by close application to his farm and boat, soon acquired a property, which, though small, was sufficient to enable him to maintain his family independently. His wife was a woman of more than usual character, and aided him nobly in making his way in the world.

This admirable couple were blessed with nine children. The oldest of these, CORNELIUS, the subject of this sketch, was born at the old farm-house on Staten Island, on the 27th of May, 1794. He was a healthy, active boy, fond of all manner of out-door sports, and manifesting an unusual repugnance to the confinement and labors of the school-room. He has since declared that the only books he remembers using at school were the New Testament and the spelling-book. The result was, that he merely learned to read, write, and cipher, and that imperfectly. He was passionately fond of the water, and was never so well pleased as when his father allowed him to assist in sailing his boat. He was also a famous horseman from his earliest childhood, and even now recalls with evident pride the fact that when but six years old he rode a race-horse at full speed. When he set himself to accomplish any thing, he was not, like most boys, deterred by the difficulties of his undertaking, but persevered until success crowned his efforts. So early did he establish his reputation for overcoming obstacles, that his boyish friends learned to regard any task which he undertook as already virtually performed.

When he was only twelve years old his father contracted to remove the cargo from a ship which had gone ashore near Sandy Hook, and to convey it to New York. The lighters which were to carry the goods to the city could not reach the ship, and it was necessary to haul the cargo, transported in wagons, across the sands from the vessel to them. In spite of his tender age, little Cornelius was placed by his father in charge of the undertaking, which he accomplished promptly and successfully. He loaded his lighters, sent them up to New York, and then started for home with his wagons. Upon reaching South Amboy, where he was to cross over to Staten Island, he found himself, with his wagons, horses, and men, without any money to pay his ferriage across to the island. The ferriage would amount to six dollars, and how he was to raise this sum he was, for a time, at a loss to determine. Finally, he went to the keeper of the tavern, to whom he was a stranger, and asked for the loan of six dollars, offering to leave one of his horses as a pledge for the money, which he promised to return within two days. The tavern-keeper was so well pleased with the boy's energy, that he loaned him the money, and the party crossed over to Staten Island. The pawned horse was promptly redeemed.

Young Vanderbilt was always anxious to become a sailor, and, as he approached his seventeenth year, he determined to begin life as a boatman in the harbor of New York. On the 1st of May, 1810, he informed his mother of his determination, and asked her to lend him one hundred dollars to buy a boat.

The good lady had always opposed her son's wish to go to sea, and regarded this new scheme as equally hair-brained. As a means of discouraging him, she told him if he would plow, harrow, and plant with corn a certain ten-acre lot belonging to the farm, by the twenty-seventh of that month, on which day he would be seventeen years old, she would lend him the money. The field was the worst in the whole farm; it was rough, hard, and stony; but by the appointed time the work was done, and well done, and the boy claimed and received his money. He

VANDERBILT EARNING HIS FIRST HUNDRED DOLLARS.

hurried off to a neighboring village, and bought his boat, in which he set out for home. He had not gone far, however, when the boat struck a sunken wreck, and filled so rapidly that the boy had barely time to get into shoal water before it sank.

"Undismayed at this mishap," says Mr. Parton, from whose graphic memoir the leading incidents of this sketch are taken, "he began his new career. His success, as we have intimated, was speedy and great. He made a thousand dollars during each of the next three summers. Often he worked all night;

but he was never absent from his post by day, and he soon had the cream of the boating business of the port.

"At that day parents claimed the services and earnings of their children till they were twenty-one. In other words, families made common cause against the common enemy, Want. The arrangement between this young boatman and his parents was, that he should give them all his day earnings and half his night earnings. He fulfilled his engagement faithfully until his parents released him from it, and with his own half of his earnings by night, he bought all his clothes. He had forty competitors in the business, who, being all grown men, could dispose of their gains as they chose; but of all the forty, he alone has emerged to prosperity and distinction. Why was this? There were several reasons. He soon became the best boatman in the port. He attended to his business more regularly and strictly than any other. He had no vices. His comrades spent at night much of what they earned by day, and when the winter suspended their business, instead of living on their last summer's savings, they were obliged to lay up debts for the next summer's gains to discharge. In those three years of willing servitude to his parents, Cornelius Vanderbilt added to the family's common stock of wealth, and gained for himself three things—a perfect knowledge of his business, habits of industry and self-control, and the best boat in the harbor."

During the War of 1812, young Vanderbilt was kept very busy. All the harbor defenses were fully manned, and a number of war vesssls were in port all the time. The travel between these and the city was very great, and boatmen were in demand.

In September, 1813, a British fleet attempted to run past Fort Richmond, during a heavy gale. The commanding officer was anxious to send to New York for reënforcements, but it was blowing so hard that none of the old boatmen were willing to venture upon the bay. They all declared that if the voyage could be made at all, Cornelius Vanderbilt was the only man who could make it. The commandant at once sent for the young man, who, upon learning the urgency of the case, expressed his belief that he could carry the messengers to the city. "But," said he, "I shall have to carry them part of the way under water." He set out with the messengers, and in an hour landed them safe, but drenched through, at the foot of Whitehall Street, which was then the landing place of all the boatmen of the harbor.

He was now so prosperous in his calling that he determined to marry. He had wooed and won the heart of Sophia Johnson, the daughter of a neighbor, and he now asked his parents' consent to his marriage, and also requested them to allow him to retain his own earnings, in order that he might be able to support a wife. Both of his petitions received the approval of his parents, and in the winter of 1813 he was married. His wife was a woman of unusual personal beauty and strength of character, and proved the best of partners. He has often declared since that he owed his success in life as much to her counsel and assistance as to his own efforts.

In the spring of 1814, it became known in America that the British were fitting out a formidable military and naval expedition for the purpose of attacking one of the Atlantic ports of the United States. The whole coast was on the lookout, and, as it was feared that the blow would be struck at New York, every precaution was taken to be ready. The militia were called into service for three months, under a heavy penalty for refusing to obey the call. The term of service thus marked out covered the most prosperous season of the boatmen, and made the call fall particularly hard upon them. About this time, an advertisement was inserted in the city journals by the Commissary-General of the army, calling for bids from boatmen for the purpose of conveying provisions from New York to the various military posts in the vicinity. The labor was to be performed during the three months for which the militia were called out, and the contractor was to be exempted from all military duty during that time. Bids poured in from the boatmen, who offered to do the work at ridiculously low figures—the chief object of each one being to secure the exemption.

Young Vanderbilt, knowing that the work could not be done at the rates at which his comrades offered to perform it, at first decided not to bid for it, but at length—and more to please his father than because he expected to succeed—offered to transport the provisions at a price which would enable him to be sure of doing it well and thoroughly. He felt so little hope of success that he did not even trouble himself to go to the office of the Commissary on the day of the awarding of the contract, until he learned from his companions that all their efforts to secure it had been ineffectual. Then he called on the Commissary, merely through curiosity, to learn the name of the fortunate man, and to his utter astonishment was told that the contract had been awarded to himself. The Government was satisfied, from his sensible offer, that he would do the business thoroughly, and this the Commissary assured him was the reason why they had selected him.

There were six posts to be supplied—Harlem, Hell Gate, Ward's Island, the Narrows, and one other in the harbor, each of which was to be furnished with one load per week. The young contractor made arrangements to have a daily load of stores ready for him each evening at six o'clock, and thus performed all the duties of his contract at night, which left him free to attend to his boating during the day. He never failed to make a single delivery of stores, or to be absent from his post on the beach at Whitehall one single day during the whole three months. He was often without sleep, and performed an immense amount of labor during this period; but his indomitable energy and powerful physical organization carried him safely through it all.

He made a great deal of money that summer, and with his earnings built a splendid little schooner, which he named the "Dread." In 1815, in connection with his brother-in-law, Captain De Forrest, he built a fine schooner, called the "Charlotte," for the coasting service. She was celebrated for the beauty of her model and her great speed. He continued to ply his boat in the harbor during the summer, but in the fall and winter made voyages along the coast, often as far south as Charleston. During the three years succeeding the termination of the war he saved nine thousand dollars in cash, and built two or three small vessels. This was his condition in 1818.

By this time it had become demonstrated to his satisfaction that the new system of steamboats was a success, and was destined to come into general use at no very distant day. He therefore determined to identify himself with it at once, and thereby secure the benefits which he felt sure would result from a prompt connection with it. Accordingly, in 1818, to the surprise and dismay of his friends, he gave up his flourishing business, in order to accept the captaincy of a steamboat which was offered him by Mr. Thomas Gibbons. The salary attached to this position was one thousand dollars, and Captain Vanderbilt's friends frankly told him that he was very foolish in abandoning a lucrative business for so insignificant a sum. Turning a deaf ear to their remonstrances, however, he entered promptly upon the duties of his new career, and was given command of a steamboat plying between New York and New Brunswick.

Passengers to Philadelphia, at that day, were transported by steamer from New York to New Brunswick, where they remained all night The next morning they took the stage for Trenton, from which they were conveyed by steamer to Philadelphia. The hotel at New Brunswick was a miserable affair, and had never paid expenses. When Captain Vanderbilt took command of the steamer, he was offered the hotel rent free, and accepted the offer. He placed the house in charge of his wife, under whose vigorous administration it soon acquired a popularity which was of the greatest benefit to the line.

For seven years he was harassed and hampered by the hostility of the State of New York, which had granted to Fulton and Livingston the sole right to navigate New York waters by steam. Thomas Gibbons believed this law to be unconstitutional, and ran his boats in defiance of it. The authorities of the State resented his disregard of their monopoly, and a long and vexatious warfare sprang up between them, which was ended only in 1824, by the decision of the Supreme Court of the United States in favor of Mr. Gibbons.

As a means of crippling Gibbons, the New York authorities at one time determined to arrest Vanderbilt and his crew; but the wary captain was too cunning for them. He would land his crew in Jersey City, and take charge of the engine himself, while a lady managed the helm. In this way he approached the wharf at New York, landed his passengers, and took on more. As soon as he had made his boat fast, he concealed himself in the hold until the moment of his departure. As soon as he appeared on deck, the Sheriff's officer (who was changed every day to avoid recognition) would approach him with a warrant for his arrest. His reply was an order to let go the line. The officer, unwilling to be carried off to New Jersey, where he was threatened with imprisonment in the penitentiary for interfering with the steamer, would at once jump ashore, or beg to be landed. This was kept up for two months, but the captain successfully baffled his enemies during the whole of that period. The opponents of Mr. Gibbons offered a larger and better boat than the one he commanded if he would enter their service, but he firmly declined all their offers, avowing his determination to remain with Mr. Gibbons until the difficulty was settled.

After the decision of the Supreme Court placed Mr. Gibbons in the full enjoyment of his rights, Captain Vanderbilt was allowed to manage the line in his own way, and conducted it with so much skill and vigor that it paid its owner an annual profit of forty thousand dollars. Mr. Gibbons offered to increase his salary to five thousand dollars, but he refused to accept the offer.

"I did it on principle," he said, afterward. "The other captains had but one thousand, and they were already jealous enough of me. Besides, I never cared for money. All I ever cared for was to carry my point."

In 1829 he determined to leave the service of Mr. Gibbons, with whom he had been connected for eleven years. He was thirty-five years old, and had saved thirty thousand dollars. He resolved to build a steamer of his own, and command her himself, and accordingly made known his intention to his employer. Mr. Gibbons at once declared that he could not carry on the line without his assistance, and told him he might make his own terms if he would stay with him. Captain Vanderbilt had formed his decision after much thought, and being satisfied that he was doing right, he persisted in his determination to set

VANDERBILT CARRYING OFF THE SHERIFF.

up for himself. Mr. Gibbons then offered to sell him the line on the spot, and to take his pay as the money should be earned. It was a splendid offer, but it was firmly and gratefully refused. The captain knew the men among whom he would be thrown, and that they could never act together harmoniously. He believed his own ideas to be the best, and wished to be free to carry them out.

After leaving Mr. Gibbons he built a small steamer, called the "Caroline," which he commanded himself. In a few years he was the owner of several other small steamers plying between New York and the neighboring towns. He made slow progress at first, for he had strong opposition to overcome. The steamboat interest was in the hands of powerful companies, backed by immense capital, and these companies were not disposed to tolerate the interference of any new-comer. They met their match in all cases, however, for Vanderbilt inaugurated so sharp a business opposition that the best of them were forced to compromise with him. These troubles were very annoying to him, and cost him nearly every dollar he was worth, but he persevered, and at length "carried his point."

From that time he made his way gradually in his business, until he rose to the head of the steamboat interest of the United States. He has owned or been interested in one hundred steam vessels, and has been instrumental in a greater degree than any other man in bringing down the tariff of steamboat fares. He never builds a vessel without giving his personal superintendence to every detail, so that all his various craft have been models of their kind. He selects his officers with the greatest care, pays them liberal salaries, and, as long as they do their duty, sustains them against all outside interference or intrigue. In this way he inspires them with zeal, and the result is that he has never lost a vessel by fire, explosion, or wreck.

He built the famous steamer "North Star," and made a triumphal cruise in her to the Old World. It is said that he was at one time very anxious to divide the business of the ocean with the Collins Line of steamers. When the "Arctic" was lost he applied to Mr. Collins to allow his steamer to run in her place. He promised to make no claim for the mail subsidy which Collins received, and to take the vessel off as soon as Collins could build another to take her place. Mr. Collins was afraid to let Mr. Vanderbilt get any hold on the foreign trade of the country, and not only refused his request, but did so in a manner which roused the anger of the veteran, who thereupon told Mr. Collins that he would run his line off the ocean if it took his whole life and entire fortune to do it. He kept his word. He at once offered the Government to carry the mails more promptly and regularly than had ever been done before, and to do this for a term of years without asking one single cent as subsidy. It was well known that he was perfectly able to do what he promised, and he pressed the matter upon the Government so vigorously that he was successful. The subsidy to Collins was withdrawn, and the magnificent line soon fell to pieces in consequence of the bankruptcy of its owner, who might have averted his fate by the exercise of a little liberality.

Of late years, Mr. Vanderbilt has been withdrawing his money from ships and steamers, and investing it in railroads and iron works. Success has attended him in all his ventures, and he is to-day worth over thirty millions of dollars. He controls the Hudson River, Harlem, and New York Central Roads, and is largely interested in many others. He is all powerful in the stock market, and can move it as he will.

A few years ago he wished to consolidate the Hudson River and Harlem Railroads, and when the scheme was presented before the Legislature of New York, secured a sufficient number of votes to insure the passage of the bill authorizing the consolidation. Before the bill was called up on its final passage, however, he learned from a trustworthy source that the members of the Legislature who had promised to vote for the bill were determined to vote against it, with the hope of ruining him. The stock of Harlem Road was then selling very high, in consequence of the expected consolidation. The defeat of the bill would, of course, cause it to fall immediately. The unprincipled legislators at once commenced a shrewd game. They sold Harlem right and left, to be delivered at a future day, and found plenty of purchasers. They let their friends into the secret, and there was soon a great deal of "selling 'short'" in this stock.* Commodore Vanderbilt, although indignant at the treachery of which he was to be made the victim, held his peace. He went into the market quietly, with all the funds he could raise, purchased every dollar's worth of Harlem stock he could lay his hands on, and locked it up in his safe. When the bill came before the Legislature on its final passage, the members who had pledged themselves to vote for it voted against it, and it was rejected.

The speculators were jubilant. They were sure that the defeat of the bill would bring down "Harlem" with a rush. To their astonishment, however, "Harlem" did not fall. It remained stationary the first day, and then, to their dismay,

* For the benefit of the uninitiated reader, we will explain the "game" more clearly. Harlem stock was selling at a high price, in consequence of the expected consolidation. Those who sold "short" at this time sold at the market price, which, as we have said, was high. By engaging to deliver at some future day, they expected to be able to buy the stock for little or nothing after the defeat of the bill, and then to demand for it the price for which they had sold it in the first place. Such a transaction was infamous, but would have enabled those engaged in it to realize immense sums by the difference in the price of the stock.

began to rise steadily. Those to whom they had sold demanded the delivery of the stock, but the speculators found it impossible to buy it. There was none in the market at any price. Being unable to deliver stock, they were forced to pay its equivalent in money, and the result was, that all who were engaged in the infamous scheme were ruined. One of the shrewdest operators in New York lost over two hundred thousand dollars. He refused to pay, but his name was at once stricken from the list of stock-brokers. This brought him to terms, and he made good his contracts. Vanderbilt made enough money out of this effort to crush him to pay for all the stock he owned in the Harlem Road.

During the rebellion, Commodore Vanderbilt was one of the stanchest supporters of the Government. Early in the struggle he equipped his splendid steamer, the "Vanderbilt," as a man-of-war, and offered her to the Navy Department at a fair price. He found that, in order to sell the vessel, he would have to pay a percentage of the price received for her to certain parties who stood between the Government and the purchase, and levied black mail upon every ship the Government bought. Indignant and disgusted, he withdrew his ship, and declared she was not for sale. Then, satisfying himself that she was in perfect condition, he presented her to the Navy Department *as a free gift to the nation.*

Says a recent writer, whose fondness for courtly similes the reader must pardon, for the sake of the information he imparts: "No man is felt in Wall Street more than Commodore Vanderbilt, yet he is seldom seen there. All of his business is done in his office in Fourth Street. Here his brokers meet him, receive their orders, and give reports. Here the plans are laid that shake the street, and Wall Street trembles at the foot of an invisible autocrat. If the reader would care to visit the court of that great railroad king, whose name has become the terror of Wall Street, he may accompany us to a plain brick residence in Fourth Street, near Broadway, and distant from Wall Street nearly two miles. No sign indicates its imperial occupant, except that the upper story being occupied as a millinery establishment bears a legend of that character. However, as we enter the hall, we notice the word 'office,' and open the door thus inscribed. Here we see a table, a few chairs, and a desk, at which a solitary clerk of middle age is standing at work.

"The walls are bare, with the exception of a few pictures of those steamships which originated the title of 'Commodore.' This is the ante-chamber, and a pair of folding doors screen the king from vulgar gaze. He is closeted with his marshals, and this privy council will last an hour or so. One after the other they depart, and before three o'clock the effect of this council will not only be felt in Wall Street, but will be flashed over the Union. At length you are permitted to enter. The folding door is opened, and you behold an office as plain in appearance as the one just described. It contains a few arm-chairs and a long business-table, thrown flush before you, on the opposite side of which sits a large man, with his face fronting you. He is writing, and his eyes are fixed on the paper, so that you have a moment to note the dignity of frame and the vast development of brain. In a few minutes the countenance raises, and you meet its expansive and penetrating glance.

"You face the king. He smiles in a pleasant and whole-souled manner, and in a moment puts you at ease. No stiffness nor formality here. His kingship is in himself, not in etiquette. He is ready for a pleasantry, and will initiate one if it comes in the line of conversation. You note those wonderful eyes, bright and piercing, and so large and rich that one is fascinated, and does not know how to stop gazing into them. Such is the appearance of the railway king, and you take your leave, conscious that some men, as Shakespeare says, 'are born great.' Indeed, we know a man who would rather give five dollars to sit and look at Commodore Vanderbilt for an hour than to see any other sight in this city. Next door to the office is a building of brown stone, with spacious doors and a roadway. This is the Commodore's stable, where are some of the finest horses in the country.

"Every afternoon he is wont to take an airing, and after tea a game of whist affords an evening amusement. The Commodore is simple in his manners and habits. He is a representative of a former age, when men lived less artificially than at the present time, and when there was more happiness and less show. As for business, it is his nature. He can not help being king. He is but developing himself, and any other mode of life would be painful. He has in the Central afforded a third wonder, the Harlem and the Hudson River being the first and second, and if he gets the Erie he will soon show the world another wonder. On Sundays the Commodore attends Dr. Hutton's church on Washington Square, and here his tall and dignified form may be seen, head and shoulders above the rest of the congregation. He is a friend of the pastor, who takes a deep interest in his welfare, and we hope will meet him in a better world. He stood by the Commodore's side when his wife was laid in the tomb, and cheered him in that dark and trying hour. Among his more recent works is the completing of a tomb in the old Moravian burial-ground in Staten Island. The subterranean chamber is about thirty feet square, and is surmounted by a lofty shaft, and a statue of grief adds a peculiar finish to the spot. The cemetery is on an eminence, from which one gets a fine view of the ocean, dotted with ships."

Commodore Vanderbilt's early passion for horses still survives, and his stable contains some of the finest in the world. Nothing pleases him so well as to sit behind a fast team, with the reins in his hands, and fly along the road with almost the speed of the wind.

He is extremely generous to his friends, and gives liberally to charitable objects. He never puts his name to a subscription paper, but his donations are none the less liberal for that. His old acquaintances—especially those of his boyhood—find him a tender friend, and many of them owe to his bounty the comforts which surround their age.*

He is the father of thirteen children—nine daughters and four sons—nearly all of whom are still living. A few years ago, at the celebration of his golden wedding, over one hundred and forty of his descendants and relatives assembled to congratulate him. He lost a promising son during the war, and his wife died two years ago. Not long since he married a second time. He is still one of the handsomest and most imposing men in New York, and will doubtless live to see his children's grandchildren.

* In July, 1870, Mr. Vanderbilt chanced to hear that the Rev. Dr. Deems, of New York, was in want of a church. Admiring the energy with which the reverend gentleman had built up his congregation in the short space of three years, Mr. Vanderbilt quietly made up his mind that he should not want in vain. Accordingly he bought the Mercer Street Presbyterian Church, and made the Doctor a present of it, keeping him in ignorance of his intention until he placed the title deeds in his hand.

CHAPTER X.

DANIEL DREW.

THE name of DANIEL DREW has so long been familiar in the financial circles of the country, that it is surprising that the history of his life is not more generally known.

He was born at Carmel, in Putnam County, New York, on the 29th of July, 1797. His father was a small farmer, with limited means, and had to work hard to provide his family with food and clothing. Young Daniel was brought up to work on the farm, and at such times as he could be spared from this work, was sent to the country school in the neighborhood, where he acquired but a meager stock of learning. When he was fifteen years old, his father died, leaving his family in an almost helpless condition. Young Daniel remained on the farm three years longer, and in 1815, being then eighteen years old, started out to try and earn a living for himself.

He came to New York in search of employment, but the country, just then, was in too depressed a condition to afford him a chance in any regular business. After looking around for awhile, he at length became a cattle drover. He spent five years in driving cattle from Putnam County to New York for sale, but failed to make any money at the business.

In 1820, he removed to New York, and established his head-quarters at the famous Bull's Head Tavern, in the Bowery, which was the great resort of the butchers and drovers doing business in the city. He kept this tavern a part of the time, and found it quite a profitable investment. He soon formed a partnership with two other drovers, and commenced buying

FOUNDING A GREAT FORTUNE.

cattle in the adjoining counties and bringing them to New York for sale. These ventures were so successful that the operations of the firm were extended into Pennsylvania, and finally into Ohio and the other States of the great West. Mr. Drew and his partners brought over the mountains the first drove of cattle that ever came from the West into New York city. The cattle, two thousand in number, were collected into droves of one hundred each, and were driven by experienced and careful men. The journey occupied two months, and the total cost of the purchase and trip was twenty-four dollars per head. The profit on the venture was very large.

Mr. Drew continued in this business for fourteen years,

slowly and carefully laying the foundations of that immense fortune which has made him so conspicuous an example to others who have entered upon the life-struggle since then.

In 1834, an event occurred which changed the whole tenor of his career. In that year, the steamer "General Jackson," owned by Jacob Vanderbilt (a brother of the famous Commodore), and plying between New York and Peekskill, blew up at Grassy Point. A friend of Mr. Drew at once put a boat called the "Water Witch" in her place, and Mr. Drew, to oblige his friend, advanced one thousand dollars toward the enterprise. Commodore Vanderbilt was not willing that any rival should contest the river trade with him, and built a steamer called the "Cinderella," with which he ran a sharp opposition to Mr. Drew. The contest was so sharp that fares and freights were lowered to a ridiculous figure, and both parties lost heavily. At the end of the season, the owner of the "Water Witch" found himself ten thousand dollars in debt, and sold his boat to Drew, Kelly & Richards for twenty thousand dollars.

Finding that Mr. Drew was not frightened off by his opposition, Commodore Vanderbilt urged him to withdraw from his attempt, telling him he knew nothing of the management of steamboats. Mr. Drew refused to be intimidated, however, and continued his efforts. Since then, there have been fifty attempts to run him off the river, but all alike have failed of success.

In 1836, the "Water Witch" was replaced by a fine steamer called the "Westchester," which was subsequently run as a day boat to Hartford, Connecticut. The "Westchester" was run against the Hudson River Line, from New York to Albany. The Hudson River Line at that time owned the "De Witt Clinton," the "North America," and others—the finest steamboats then afloat—and it seemed at first foolhardiness for any one to attempt to oppose so popular a company. Mr. Drew and his partners bought the "Bright Emerald," for which they gave twenty-six thousand dollars, and ran her as a night boat between New York and Albany, reducing the fare from three dollars to one dollar. During the season, they bought the "Rochester" for fifty thousand dollars, and also bought out the Hudson River Line, after which they restored the fare to three dollars.

Several years later, Isaac Newton, who was largely interested in the towing business of the Hudson, built two splendid passenger steamers called the "North America" and the "South America." In 1840, Mr. Drew formed a partnership with Mr. Newton, and the celebrated "People's Line" was organized, which purchased all the passenger steamers owned by Drew and Newton. Mr. Drew was the largest stockholder in this company, which, to-day, after a lapse of nearly thirty years, still owns the most magnificent and popular steamers in the world. Soon after its organization, the company built the "Isaac Newton," the first of those floating palaces for which the Hudson is famed. Since then, it has built the "New World," the "St. John," the "Dean Richmond," and the "Drew," the last two of which cost over seven hundred thousand dollars each. Repeated efforts have been made to drive this line from the river, but it has been conducted so judiciously and energetically, that, for nearly thirty years, it has held the first place in the public favor.

In 1847, George Law and Daniel Drew formed a partnership, and established a line of steamers between New York and Stonington, for the purpose of connecting with the railroad from the latter place to Boston. The "Oregon" and the "Knickerbocker" were placed on the route, and the enterprise proved a success. Mr. Drew and Commodore Vanderbilt secured a sufficient amount of stock in the railroad to give them a controlling interest in it, and by the year 1850 the Stonington Steamboat Line was firmly established.

When the Hudson River Railroad was opened, in 1852, it was confidently expected that the steamboat trade on the river would be destroyed, and the friends and enemies of Mr. Drew alike declared that he might as well lay up his boats, as he would find it impossible to compete with the faster time of the railroad. He was not dismayed, however, for he was satisfied that the land route could not afford to carry freight and passengers as cheap as they could be transported by water. He knew that it would only be necessary to reduce his passenger and freight rates below those of the railroad, to continue in the enjoyment of his immense business, and his faith in the steady expansion of the trade of the city induced him to believe that the time was close at hand when railroad and steamers would all have as much as they could do to accommodate it. His views were well founded, and his hopes have been more than realized. The river trade has steadily increased, while the Hudson River Railroad is taxed to its utmost capacity to accommodate its immense traffic.

In 1849, Mr. Drew, in connection with other parties, bought out the Champlain Transportation Company. This corporation had a capital of one hundred and fifty thousand dollars, and ran a line of five steamers from White Hall to the Canada end of the lake. The new proprietors ran the line seven years, and in 1856 sold out to the Saratoga and White Hall Railroad Company.

As a steamboat manager, Daniel Drew has few equals and no superiors. His ventures on the water have all been crowned with success, a result due entirely to his judicious and liberal management. His employés are chosen with the greatest care, and generally remain with him during their lives. He is very liberal in his dealings with those who serve him faithfully, but will not tolerate a single careless or incompetent man, however unimportant may be his position. The steamers owned by him are almost entirely free from accidents, and such misfortunes as have befallen them have been those against which no skill or foresight could guard. He refuses to insure his boats, holding that care and prudence are the best safeguards against accidents, and thus saves half a million of dollars. When the "Dean Richmond" was run down by the "Vanderbilt," a year or two ago, he lost nearly three hundred thousand dollars. He paid every claim presented by shippers and passengers, as soon as made, without submitting one of them to the adjudication of the courts.

In 1836, Mr. Drew entered the banking business in Wall Street, and in 1840 established the widely-known firm of Drew, Robinson & Co. This house engaged largely in the financial operations of the day, and became known as one of the most uniformly successful in its dealings of any in the city. Mr. Drew remained at the head of it for thirteen years, but in 1855 withdrew to make room for his son-in-law, Mr. Kelley. This gentleman died soon after his connection with the firm, and Mr. Drew resumed his old place.

Having succeeded so well in all his ventures, Mr. Drew now determined to enter another field. Railroad stocks were very profitable, and might be made to yield him an immense return for his investments, and he decided to invest a considerable part of his fortune in them. In 1855, he indorsed the acceptances of the Erie Railroad Company for five hundred thousand dollars. This was the first decided evidence the public had received of his immense wealth, and in 1857 another was given by his indorsement of a fresh lot of Erie acceptances amounting to a million and a half of dollars. This last indorsement was made in the midst of the great financial panic of 1857, and occasioned no little comment. Men could admire, though they could not understand, the sublime confidence which enabled Mr. Drew to risk a million and a half of dollars in the midst of such a terrible crisis. Some one asked him if he could sleep quietly at night with such large interests at stake. "Sir," he replied, calmly, "I have never lost a night's rest on account of business in my life."

In 1857, Mr. Drew was elected a director of the Erie Railroad Company, a position he held until recently. He was subsequently elected treasurer of the company, and is one of the principal holders of Erie stock. He is also one of the principal creditors of the company. The recent proceedings in the New York courts to prevent the Erie Road from issuing the new stock necessary to complete its broad-gauge connections with the West, are too fresh in the mind of the reader to need a recital of them here. It was proposed to issue ten millions of dollars worth of new stock, and Mr. Drew was to guarantee the bonds. After a tedious and costly suit, in which the New York Central Road endeavored to prevent the issue of the stock, in the hope of keeping the Erie Road from forming through connections with the West, the New York Legislature legalized the new issue, and a compromise was effected between Mr. Drew, in behalf of the Erie Road, and Commodore Vanderbilt, who represented the New York Central.

Mr. Drew still continues his operations in Wall Street, where he is known as one of the boldest and most extensive, as well as one of the most successful, of all the operators in railroad stocks. Though losing heavily at times, he has nevertheless been one of fortune's favorites. His efforts have not been confined to the Erie Road. He owns stock in other roads, and, together with Commodore Vanderbilt, took up the floating debt of over half a million of dollars which weighed down the Harlem Road, and placed it in its present prosperous condition.

He owns a fine grazing farm on the Harlem Railroad, about fifty miles from New York. It is situated in Carmel, in Putnam County; is nearly one thousand acres in extent, and includes the old farm on which he was born. He has made it one of the finest and most profitable in the State, and, it is said, values it above all his other possessions. He has improved and beautified it upon an extensive scale, and near the old grave-yard, where his parents lie sleeping, he has built one of the most beautiful churches in the land.

In 1811, Mr. Drew became a member of the Methodist Church, but for twenty-five years this connection was merely nominal. During all the years of his drover's life he kept himself free from the sins of intemperance and swearing. Once while riding out in a buggy with a friend, to look at some cattle, a thunder-storm came on, and his horse was killed in the shafts by lightning. This narrow escape from death made a deep impression on his mind, and in 1841 he united with the Mulberry Street Methodist Church, of which he became an active member and a trustee. The elegant marble structure now standing at the corner of Fourth Avenue and Twenty-second Street attests his liberality to this congregation. He is a trustee in the Wesleyan University, and has largely endowed that institution; and within the past few years has contributed several hundred thousand dollars for the endowment of the Drew Theological Seminary, which has been established at Madison, New Jersey, for the education of candidates for the Methodist ministry. He gives largely in aid of missionary work, and is one of the most liberal men in his denomination. It is said that he gives away at least one hundred thousand dollars annually in private charities, besides the large donations with which the public are familiar. He selects his own charities, and refuses promptly to aid those which do not commend themselves to him.

His property is estimated at twenty millions of dollars, and he is said to earn at least half a million of dollars every year. He has two children, a son and a daughter, the latter of whom is the wife of a clergyman of the Baptist Church.

Mr. Drew is about five feet ten inches high, and slenderly made. He is very active and vigorous for his age, and looks a much younger man than he is. His expression is firm, but withal pleasant. His features are regular, but dark and deeply marked, while his black hair is still unstreaked with gray. He is courteous and friendly in his intercourse, and is very much liked by his acquaintances.

CHAPTER XI.

JAMES B. EADS.

JAMES B. EADS was born in Lawrenceburg, Indiana, in the year 1820. His father was a man of moderate means, and was able to give him a fair English education. From his earliest childhood he evinced a remarkable fondness for all sorts of machinery and mechanical arrangements. This fondness became at length a passion, and excited the surprise of his friends, who could not imagine why a mere child should be so much interested in such things. His greatest delight was to go to the machine shops in his neighborhood, in which he had many friends, and watch the workings of the various inventions employed therein.

When he was nine years old his father removed to Louisville, Kentucky. During the voyage down the Ohio, young Eads passed the most of his time in watching the engines of the steamer. The engineer was so much pleased to see his interest in the machinery that he explained the whole system of the steam-engine to him. The boy listened eagerly, and every word remained fixed in his mind. Two years later, with no further instruction on the subject, he constructed a miniature engine, which was worked by steam. This, for a boy of eleven years, was no insignificant triumph of genius. His father, anxious to encourage such unmistakable talent, now fitted up a small workshop for him, in which he constructed models of saw mills, fire engines, steamboats, and electrifying machines. When he was only twelve years old he was able to take to pieces and reset the family clock and a patent lever watch, using no tool for this purpose but his pocket-knife.

At the age of thirteen his pleasant employment was brought to a sudden end. His father lost all his property by the failure of some commercial transactions, and the family was brought to the verge of ruin. It now became necessary for young Eads to labor for his own support, and for that of his mother and sisters. Boy as he was, he faced the crisis bravely. Having in vain sought employment in Louisville, he resolved to go to St. Louis. He engaged his passage there on a river steamer, and landed in that city so poor that he had neither shoes to his feet nor a coat to his back. He found it as difficult to procure work here as it had been in Louisville, and was at length compelled to resort to peddling apples on the street in order to secure a living. He did this for some time, never relaxing his efforts to obtain more desirable employment.

After many attempts he succeeded in getting a situation in a mercantile house, at a fair salary. One of his employers was a man of wealth and culture, and was possessed of one of the finest private libraries in the West. Learning the extraordinary mechanical talent possessed by his young clerk, this gentleman placed his library at his disposal. The offer was promptly and gratefully accepted, and young Eads devoted almost all his leisure time to the study of mechanics, machinery, and civil engineering. He remained with this house for several years, and then obtained a clerkship on one of the Mississippi River steamers, where he passed several years more. During this time he became intimately acquainted with the great river and its tributaries, and acquired an extensive knowledge of all subjects appertaining to western navigation, which proved of great service to him in his after life.

In 1842, being then twenty-two years old, and having saved a moderate sum of money, he formed a copartnership with Messrs. Case & Nelson, boat builders, of St. Louis, for the purpose of recovering steamboats and their cargoes which had been sunk or wrecked in the Mississippi. Accidents of this kind were then very common in those waters, and the business bade fair to be very profitable. The enterprise succeeded better than had been expected, and the operations of the wrecking company extended from Galena, Illinois, to the Balize, and into many of the tributaries of the great river. The parties interested in the scheme realized a handsome profit on their investments. Mr. Eads was the practical man of the concern, and worked hard to establish it upon a successful footing. In 1845 he sold out his interest in the company, and established a glass manufactory in St. Louis. This was the first enterprise of the kind ever attempted west of the Mississippi. Two years later, in 1847, he organized a new company for the purpose of recovering boats and cargoes lost in the Mississippi and its tributaries. This company started with a capital of fifteen hundred dollars. It was slow work at first, but a steady improvement was made every year, and in 1857, just ten years from the date of their organization, the property of the firm was valued at more than half a million of dollars. During the winter of 1856–'57, Mr. Eads laid before Congress a formal proposition to remove the obstructions from the western rivers and keep them open for a term of years, upon payment of a reasonable sum by the General Government. Had this proposition been accepted, the benefits thereby secured to all who were engaged in the navigation of those rivers would have been very great. A bill was reported in Congress authorizing the acceptance of Mr. Eads' offer, but was defeated through the influence of the Senators from Mississippi (Jefferson Davis) and Louisiana (J. P. Benjamin).

In 1857, Mr. Eads was compelled, on account of ill-health, to retire from business. He had earned a handsome fortune by his industry and enterprise, and could well afford to rest for a short time, preparatory, as it afterward proved, to the most important part of his whole career.

When the secession troubles began to agitate the country, toward the close of the year 1860, Mr. Eads cast the weight of his private and public influence on the side of the Union. He felt that the war, if it should come, would be a very serious affair for the West, as the prosperity of that section depends largely upon the absolute freedom of the navigation of the Mississippi. The Confederates well understood this, and prepared from the first to close the great river until their independence should be acknowledged by the General Government. Dr. Boynton, in his "History of the United States Navy During the Rebellion," thus describes the condition of affairs in the West, a proper understanding of which will show the reader the importance of the services subsequently rendered by Mr. Eads:

The main features of the rebel plan of war in the West were to seize and hold Missouri, and, as a consequence, Kansas and Nebraska, and thus threaten or invade the free States of the North-west from that point; to hold Kentucky and Tennessee, and, if possible, to cross the Ohio, and make the Northern States the theater of the war; or, in case they should be unable to invade the North, to maintain their battle line unbroken along the Ohio and through Missouri; to keep the great rivers closed, and thus holding back the North, and being secure within their own territory, at length compel the recognition of their independence. They certainly presented to the North a most formidable front, a line of defenses which was indeed impregnable to any means of assault which the

Government at first possessed. No army could be moved into Tennessee by land alone, because the line of communication with a Northern base could not be held secure, and a defeat far from the Ohio would be the destruction of an army, and open the road for an invasion of Illinois, Indiana, and Ohio, and the destruction of their cities.

It was quite evident that no impression could be made upon the power of the rebellion in the West, until a firm foothold could be gained in Kentucky and Tennessee, and until the Mississippi could be wrested from the conspirators' control. It was clear that the whole seaboard might be regained, even to Florida, and yet the rebellion remain as dangerous as ever, if the rebels could hold the Mississippi River and the valley up to or near the Ohio.

France was looking with eager eyes toward Texas, in the hope of securing and extending her Mexican usurpation. England was ready to give all the assistance in her power to any step which would weaken the North; and had the rebels been pressed back from the seaports and the Northern Atlantic slope, they would have had it in their power, if still holding the Mississippi, the South-west, including Tennessee, and the great natural fortresses of the mountains, to have so connected themselves with Mexico and France as to have caused the most serious embarrassment. It became absolutely necessary to the success of the Government that the rebels' northern line of defenses should be broken through, and that the Mississippi should be opened to its mouth.

At first, and before the nature of the work was fully understood, the whole was placed under the direction of the War Department, as it was thought the few armed transports which would be needed would be a mere appendage of the army. The idea of a formidable river navy of a hundred powerful steamers did not in the beginning enter into the minds of any.

It was soon seen, however, that an entirely new description of craft was needed for this work. It was clear that the river boats, which had been built for the common purposes of freight and passage, were not capable of resisting the fire of heavy artillery, and that the batteries of the rebels could not be captured nor even passed by them. They could not even be safely employed alone in the transportation of troops, for they could be sunk or crippled by the field batteries that could be moved from point to point. The question of iron-clads was proposed, but with only the ocean iron-clads as a guide, who should conceive the proper form of an armored boat which could navigate our rivers and compete successfully with the heavy guns, rifled as well as smooth-bore, of the fortifications. It was by no means easy to solve this problem, but it was absolutely necessary that the attempt should be made. These forts could only be reduced by the aid of gunboats, and these were almost literally to be created.

There was in the Cabinet of President Lincoln at this time a western man, intimately acquainted with the steamboat interest of the Mississippi. This was Edward Bates, the Attorney-General of the United States. He was an old friend of Mr. Eads, and felt assured that in case of war the services of that gentleman would be of the greatest value to the country. When it was found that hostilities could not be avoided, he mentioned the name of Mr. Eads to the Cabinet, and strongly urged that his services should be secured at the earliest possible moment. On the 17th of April, 1861, three days after Fort Sumter had fallen, he wrote to Mr. Eads, who was living in comfortable retirement, at St. Louis: "Be not surprised if you are called here suddenly by telegram. If called, come instantly. In a certain contingency it will be necessary to have the aid of the most thorough knowledge of our western rivers, and the use of steam on them, and in that event I have advised that you should be consulted."

A few days later Mr. Eads was summoned to Washington. Mr. Bates there explained to him in full a plan he had conceived for occupying Cairo, and endeavoring to hold the Mississippi by means of gunboats. Mr. Eads warmly indorsed the plan, and was introduced by Mr. Bates to the President and members of the Cabinet. When the plan was proposed to the Cabinet, the Secretary of War pronounced it unnecessary and impracticable, but the Secretary of the Navy was much impressed with it, and requested Mr. Eads to submit his views in writing, which was done. The paper embodied Judge Bates's general plan in addition to Mr. Eads's own views, and contained suggestions as to the kind of boats best fitted for service on the western rivers, and also in regard to the best points on those streams for the erection of land batteries. This paper was submitted to the Navy Department on the 29th of April, 1861, and was referred by the Secretary to Commodore Paulding, who reported in favor of its adoption.

The Secretary of the Navy now detailed Captain John Rodgers to accompany Mr. Eads to the West, and purchase and fit out such steamers as should be found necessary for the service. Up to this time the Secretary of War had manifested the most supreme indifference in regard to the whole subject, but he now claimed entire jurisdiction in the matter, and this interference caused considerable vexation and delay. At length he issued an order to Mr. Eads and Captain Rodgers to proceed with their purchases. These gentlemen obtained the approval of General McClellan, in whose department the purchases were to be made, and began their operations.

Upon arriving at Cairo, they found one of the old snag-boat fleet, called the "Benton." Mr. Eads knew the boat well, as he had formerly owned her, and proposed to purchase and arm her, but Captain Rodgers did not approve the plan for converting her into a gunboat. Mr. Eads then proposed to purchase and arm several of the strong, swift boats used for the navigation of the Missouri River, and equip them at St. Louis, from which point there would always be water enough to get them below Cairo. Captain Rodgers disapproved this plan also, and went to Cincinnati, where he purchased and equipped the "Conestoga," "Tyler," and "Lexington," and started them down the river. They were not iron-clad, but were merely protected around the boilers with coal bunkers, and provided with bullet-proof oaken bulwarks. Mr. Eads had warned Captain Rodgers that he could not depend upon the Ohio to get his boats down to Cairo, and his predictions were realized. The boats were started from Cincinnati some time in July; they were detained on the bars of the Ohio for six or seven weeks, and did not reach Cairo until about the first of September; then the bottom of the "Tyler" was found to be so badly damaged by sand-bars that she had to be put on the marine railway for repairs.

In July, 1861, the War Department advertised for proposals to construct a number of iron-clad gunboats for service on the Mississippi River. On the 5th of August, when the bids were opened, it was found that Mr. Eads proposed to build these boats in a shorter time and upon more favorable terms than any one else. His offer was accepted, and on the 7th of August he signed a contract with Quartermaster-General Meigs to have ready for their crews and armaments, *in sixty-five days*, seven vessels, of about six hundred tons each, each to draw six feet of water, to carry thirteen heavy guns, to be plated with iron two and a half inches thick, and to steam nine miles per hour. "They were one hundred and seventy-five feet long, and fifty-one and a half feet wide; the hulls of wood; their sides placed out from the bottom of the boat to the water line at an angle of about thirty-five degrees, and from the water line the sides fell back at about the same angle, to form a slanting casemate, the gun-deck being but a foot above water. This slanting casemate extended across the hull, near the bow and stern, forming a quadrilateral gun-deck. Three nine or ten-inch guns were placed in the bow, four similar ones on each side, and two smaller ones astern. The casemate inclosed the wheel, which was placed in a recess at the stern of the vessel. The plating was two and a half inches thick, thirteen inches wide, and was rabbeted on the edges to make a more perfect joint."

In undertaking to complete these vessels in sixty-five days, Mr. Eads had assumed a heavy responsibility. The manufacturing interests of the West were sadly crippled by the sudden commencement of hostilities, and doubt and distrust prevailed every-where. The worst feature of all was, that skilled workmen were either enlisting in the army or seeking employment in States more remote from the scene of war. Every thing needed for the gunboats was to be made. Even the timber for their hulls was still standing in the forest, and the huge machinery which was to roll out and harden their iron plates had yet to be constructed. No single city, no two cities, however great in resources, could possibly supply every thing needed within the stipulated time, and it was necessary to employ help wherever it could be obtained.

The very day the contract was signed, the telegraph was kept busy sending instructions all over the West for the commencement of the various parts of the work. The saw-mills in Kentucky, Tennessee, Illinois, Indiana, Ohio, Minnesota, and Missouri were set to getting out the timber, which was hurried to St. Louis by railroad and steamboat as fast as it was ready. There were twenty-one steam engines and thirty-five boilers to be made, and the machine-shops in St. Louis, Cincinnati, and Pittsburgh were put to work upon them. The huge rolling-mills of Cincinnati and Portsmouth, Ohio, Newport, Kentucky, and St. Louis were engaged in making the iron plates, and employed for this purpose no less than four thousand men. Night and day, Sundays included, the work went on with an almost superhuman swiftness. Mr. Eads paid the workmen on the hulls large sums from his own pocket, in addition to their wages, to induce them to continue steadily at their work.

On the 12th of October, 1861, just forty-five days from the time of laying her keel, the first iron-clad, belonging to the United States, was launched, with her engines and boilers on board. Rear Admiral Foote (then a flag officer), appointed to command the Mississippi squadron, named her the "St. Louis," but upon being transferred to the Navy Department her name was changed to the "Baron de Kalb." She was followed by the other vessels in rapid succession, all being completed within the stipulated time.

In September, 1861, General Fremont ordered the purchase of the snag boat "Benton," which had been proposed by Mr. Eads and rejected by Captain Rodgers, and sent her to Mr. Eads to be armored and equipped as a gunboat. Work was at once begun on her, and pushed forward with the same energy that had been displayed in the construction of the other iron-clads. Her performances during the war fully sustained the high esteem in which she was held by the officers of the navy. Admirals Foote and Davis pronounced her the "best iron-clad in the world."

By dint of such skill and energy as we have described, Mr. Eads, in the brief period of one hundred days, built and had ready for service a powerful iron-clad fleet of eight steamers, carrying one hundred and seven heavy guns, and having an aggregate capacity of five thousand tons. Such a work was one of the greatest in magnitude ever performed, and, as may be supposed, required a heavy capital to carry it to perfection. Mr. Eads soon exhausted his own means, and but for the assistance of friends, whose confidence in his integrity and capacity induced them to advance him large sums, would have been compelled to abandon the undertaking; for the Government, upon various pretexts, delayed for months the stipulated payments, and by its criminal negligence came near bringing the iron-clad fleet, so necessary to its success, to an untimely end. It was prompt enough, however, to commission the vessels as soon as they were ready. At the time they rendered such good service in the conquest of Forts Henry and Donelson, and compelled the fall of Island No. 10, they were still unpaid for, and the private property of Mr. Eads.

In the spring of 1862, Mr. Eads, in accordance with the desire of the Navy Department, submitted plans for light-draught armored vessels for service on the western rivers. He proposed an ingenious revolving turret to be used on these vessels, the performance of which he agreed to guarantee to the satisfaction of the Department; but the Government decided to use the Ericsson turret, which the recent encounter between the Monitor and Merrimac had proved to be a success. Mr. Eads was allowed, however, to modify the Ericsson turret considerably, in order to avoid making the draft of his steamers greater than was desired. He built the "Osage" and "Neosho," and when these vessels were launched, with all their weight on board, it was found that they were really lighter than the contract called for, a circumstance which permitted the thickness of their armor to be afterward increased half an inch without injuring their draught or speed.

In May, 1862, at the request of the Navy Department, Mr. Eads submitted plans for four iron-clads, iron hull propellers, to carry two turrets each of eight inches thickness, four eleven inch guns, and three-quarters inch deck armor, to steam nine nautical miles per hour, to carry three days' coal, and not to exceed a draught of six feet of water. His plans were accepted, and he constructed the "Winnebago," "Kickapoo," "Milwaukee," and "Chickasaw." Like the "Osage" and "Neosho," these vessels were found to be of lighter draught than had been agreed upon, and the Department ordered all four to have an extra plating of three-quarters inch armor, which was done.

Whatever may be the distinction awarded to others, to him belongs the credit of having been the first to provide the Government with the means of securing that firm hold upon the great river of the West which, once gained, was never relaxed.

The great cast-steel arched bridge now building at St. Louis, by Mr. Eads, furnishes one of those remarkable instances where bold and original ideas, supported by arguments logically based on physical laws, have signally triumphed over groundless prejudice and professional egotism. His plans for that structure were assailed and unanimously condemned by a grave convention of twenty-seven distinguished engineers specially convoked in 1867, to consider the question of bridging the river at St. Louis. In his report (May 1868), Mr. Eads patiently reviewed the objections of the convention; published in detail the most minute data involved in the questions of strength and cost of his bridge, and challenged the profession throughout the world to disprove his conclusions, or to produce a design more safe and economical than his own. His appeal from the convention to the profession at large was triumphantly sustained, and the confidence of his company in their chief engineer never faltered. His arguments were so conclusive, in the opinion of English engineers, that the bonds of his company ($4,000,000) were afterwards sold in London. The massive piers of the bridge are already safely resting on the bed-rock of the Mississippi, and soon the completed structure will stand a proud monument of the energy and talent of its builder, the bare-footed apple-boy of 1833.

CHAPTER XII.

CYRUS W. FIELD.

THUS far we have been considering the struggles of men who have risen from obscure positions in life, by the aid of their own genius, industry, and courage, to the front rank of their respective callings. We shall now relate the story of one who having already won fortune, periled it all upon an enterprise in which his own genius had recognized the path to fame and to still greater success, but which the almost united voice of the people of his country condemned as visionary, and from which they coldly held aloof until its brilliant success compelled them to acknowledge the wisdom and foresight of its projector.

Fifteen years ago very few persons had heard of Cyrus W. Field. Ten years ago he had achieved considerable notoriety as a visionary who was bent on sinking his handsome fortune in the sea. To-day, the world is full of his fame, as the man to whom, above all others, it is indebted for the successful completion of the Atlantic Telegraph; and those who were formerly loudest in ridiculing him are now foremost in his praise. "Nothing succeeds like success," and what was once in their eyes mere folly, and worthy only of ridicule, they now hail as the evidences of his courage, foresight, and profound wisdom, and wonder that they never could see them in their true light before.

Cyrus West Field was born at Stockbridge, Massachusetts, on the 30th day of November, 1819, and is the son of the Rev. David Dudley Field, a distinguished clergyman of that State. He was carefully educated in the primary and grammar schools of his native county, and at the age of fifteen went to New York to seek his fortune. He had no difficulty in obtaining a clerkship in an enterprising mercantile house in that city, and, from the first, gave evidence of unusual business capacity. His employers, pleased with his promise, advanced him rapidly, and in a few years he became a partner in the house. His success as a merchant was uniform and marked—so marked, indeed, that in 1853, when only thirty-four years old, he was able to partially retire from business with a large fortune as the substantial reward of his mercantile career.

Mr. Field had devoted himself so closely to his business that, at his retirement, he resolved to seek recreation and change of scene in foreign travel, and accordingly he left New York, and passed the next six months in journeying through the mountains of South America. Upon his return home, at the close of the year 1853, he declared his intention to withdraw entirely from active participation in business, and to engage in no new schemes.

He had scarcely returned home, however, when his brother, Mr. Matthew D. Field, a successful and well-known civil engineer, informed him that he had just become acquainted with a Mr. Frederick N. Gisborne, of Newfoundland, who had come to New York for the purpose of interesting some American capitalists in a company which had been organized in Newfoundland for the purpose of procuring news in America and Europe, and transmitting it between the two continents with greater dispatch than was possible in the then existing mode of communication between the two countries. The scheme of Mr. Gisborne had commended itself to Mr. Matthew Field, and he urged his brother to meet that gentleman and hear his statements. Mr. Cyrus Field at once declined to undertake any share in the enterprise, and said that it would be useless for him to meet Mr. Gisborne; but his brother was so urgent that he at last consented to grant Mr. Gisborne an interview, and at least hear what he had to say. At the appointed time, Mr. Field received Mr. Gisborne at his house, and was there made acquainted with the proposed plan of operations of the "Electric Telegraph Company of Newfoundland." This company had gone into bankruptcy a short time previous, but Mr. Gisborne hoped to be able to revive it by the aid of American capital. The scheme which he laid before Mr. Field, can not be better stated than by quoting the following extract from the charter which the Legislature of Newfoundland had granted the bankruptcy company:

"The telegraph line of this company is designed to be strictly an 'Inter-Continental Telegraph.' Its termini will be New York, in the United States, and London, in the Kingdom of Great Britain; these points are to be connected by a line of electric telegraph from New York to St. John's, Newfoundland, partly on poles, partly laid in the ground, and partly through the water, and a line of the swiftest steamships ever built, from that point to Ireland. The trips of these steamships, it is expected, will not exceed five days, and as very little time will be occupied in transmitting messages between St. John's and New York, the communication between the latter city and London or Liverpool, will be effected in *six days*, or less. The company will have likewise stationed at St. John's a steam yacht, for the purpose of intercepting the

European and American steamships, so that no opportunity may be lost in forwarding intelligence in advance of the ordinary channels of communication."

Mr. Field listened attentively to his visitor, but declined to commit himself to more than an expression of sympathy with the enterprise. After the departure of his guest, he took the globe which stood in his library, and turning it over, began to examine the proposed route of the telegraph line and the distance to be traversed by the steamers. While engaged in this examination, the idea flashed across his mind that instead of undertaking such a complicated scheme, it would be better to attempt to stretch a telegraph wire entirely across the ocean, from the shores of Newfoundland to the coast of Ireland. The vastness of this scheme pleased him, and its usefulness to the entire world, if it could be carried out, was clear to his mind from the first.

He at once set to work to ascertain if such an undertaking as an Atlantic telegraph was practicable. He wrote to Lieutenant Maury, then the Chief of the National Observatory at Washington, and asked if the laying of such a wire was possible; and to Professor Morse, the inventor of the telegraph, to know if such a wire would be available for sending messages if it could be laid. Lieutenant Maury promptly replied, inclosing a copy of a report he had just made to the Secretary of the Navy on the subject, from which Mr. Field learned that the idea of laying a telegraph across the ocean was not original with himself. In this report Lieutenant Maury demonstrated the entire practicability of such an enterprise, and sustained his conclusions by a statement of the recent discoveries concerning the bed of the ocean, made by Lieutenant Berryman. Professor Morse came in person to visit Mr. Field, and assured him of his entire faith in the possibility of sending telegraphic messages across the ocean with rapidity and success.

The two highest authorities in the world thus having assured him of the entire practicability of the undertaking, Mr. Field declared his readiness, if he could procure the assistance of a sufficient number of capitalists in the United States, to undertake the laying of a telegraph across the Atlantic between Europe and America. Further deliberation only made him better satisfied with the undertaking, and he set to work to find ten capitalists, each of whom he proposed should contribute one hundred thousand dollars, making the capital of the proposed company one million of dollars. Mr. Field was convinced that the undertaking would be expensive, but he had then but a faint conception of its magnitude, and was very far from supposing that "he might yet be drawn on to stake upon its success the whole fortune he had accumulated; that he was to sacrifice for it all the peace and quiet he had hoped to enjoy, and that for twelve years he was to be almost without a home, crossing and recrossing the sea, urging his enterprise in Europe and America."

The scientific questions involved in the undertaking were so little understood at the time by the public, and the popular judgment regarded the attempt to stretch a cable across the deep, mysterious ocean with so much incredulity, that Mr. Field had considerable trouble in finding gentlemen willing or prepared to share his faith in the enterprise. His first effort was to induce Mr. Peter Cooper, of New York, his next door neighbor, to join him, and he succeeded so well that Mr. Cooper consented to do so if several others would unite with them. Encouraged by his success with Mr. Cooper, whose name was a tower of strength to his cause, Mr. Field renewed his efforts, and succeeded in winning over the following gentlemen, and in the order named: Moses Taylor, Marshall O. Roberts, and Chandler White. These gentlemen were very slow to accept the views of Mr. Field, but, once having done so, they never lost faith in the ultimate success of the undertaking. The more thoroughly they became acquainted with its magnitude and costliness, the stronger grew their confidence in it, for this increase of knowledge not only showed them more plainly its difficulties and dangers, but developed new grounds on which to base their hopes.

Mr. Field was about to continue his efforts to procure additional names, when Mr. Cooper proposed that the five gentlemen already pledged to the scheme should undertake its entire cost without waiting for the other four. The proposition was agreed to, and it was decided to take the necessary steps to procure a charter for their company from the Legislature of Newfoundland. Mr. Field consented to undertake this, and at once set off for St. John's, accompanied by his brother, Mr. David Dudley Field, who was made the legal adviser of the company. At St. John's they were greatly aided by Mr. Archibald, then the Attorney-General of the Colony, and afterward the British Consul at New York, and by the Governor of Newfoundland. They succeeded in obtaining a charter from the Legislature under the name of the "New York, Newfoundland, and London Telegraph Company," with liberal grants in land and money. This accomplished, they assumed and paid the liabilities of the old Telegraph Company which had been brought to Mr. Field's notice by Mr. Gisborne, and thus removed the last difficulty in their way. This much accomplished, Mr. Field hastened back to New York, and on the 6th of May, 1854, the Company was formally organized at the residence of Mr. David Dudley Field. Messrs. Cooper, Taylor, Field, Roberts, and White were the first directors. Mr. Cooper, was made President of the Company, Mr. White, Vice-President, and Mr. Taylor Secretary. A capital of one million and a half of dollars was subscribed on the spot, Mr. Field contributing about two hundred thousand dollars in cash.

Work was at once begun on the section between New York and St. John's. There was no road across the island of Newfoundland, and the Company had not only to build their telegraph line, but to construct a road by the side of it through an almost unbroken wilderness. It was a work which required the highest executive ability, and the services of an army of men. The distance across the island was four hundred miles, and there were numerous rocky gorges, morasses, and rivers in the way. The country was a desolation, and it was found that supplies would have to be transported from St. John's. The execution of the work was committed to Mr. White, the Vice-President, who went to St. John's to act as the general agent of the Company, and to Mr. Matthew D. Field, who was appointed constructing engineer. These gentlemen displayed such skill and energy in their respective positions that in two years the Company had not only built a telegraph line and a road of four hundred miles across the island, but had constructed another line of one hundred and forty miles in the island of Cape Breton, and had stretched a submarine cable across the Gulf of St. Lawrence.* The line was now in working order from New York to St. John's, Newfoundland, a distance of one thousand miles, and it had required about a million of dollars for its construction. It now remained to complete the great work by laying the cable between Newfoundland and Ireland.

It being desirable to examine still further the bed of the

* The first effort to lay a cable in the Gulf of St. Lawrence was made by this Company, in August, 1855. It was a failure, and the cable was lost. The second attempt was made in the summer of 1856, and was entirely successful.

ocean over which the cable was to be laid, Mr. Field requested the Government of the United States to send out an expedition over the route for the purpose of taking deep sea soundings. His request was promptly granted, and an expedition under Lieut. Berryman was dispatched, which proceeded to examine the ocean bed, with the most satisfactory results. This was accomplished in the summer of 1856, and the next year the same route was surveyed by Commander Daymon, with the British war steamer Cyclops—this survey being ordered by the Lords of the Admiralty, at Mr. Field's request. These surveys made it plain beyond question that a cable could lie safely on the bed of the sea, at a depth sufficient to protect it from vessels' anchors, from icebergs, and from submarine currents, and that it would receive sufficient support from that bed to free it from all undue tension. There was no doubt of the ultimate success of the enterprise in the minds of the directors, but it was necessary to convince the public in both Europe and America that it was not an impossibility, and also to enlist the sympathies of the Governments of Great Britain and the United States, and secure their assistance.

Mr. Field, who had made several voyages to England and to Newfoundland in behalf of the company, was elected Vice-President after the death of Mr. White, in 1856, and was charged with the duty of proceeding to England to obtain the assistance of the British Government, and to organize the company in London. Thus far the directors had borne the entire cost of the undertaking, and it was but fair that they should seek the means for completing their work in the country which was to be so much benefited by it. Mr. Field sailed for England in the summer of 1856, and upon reaching that country proceeded to consult some of its most eminent engineers and electricians. The English people were slow to believe that so long a cable could be successfully worked, even if laid intact, and to remove their doubts, the opinions of Professor Morse and Lieutenant Maury were published in their newspapers; and this publication brought out communications from many scientific men on the subject, a number of them advocating the undertaking. Thus, the attention of the English public was gained. Experiments were made by Professor Morse, Mr. Bright, and Dr. Whitehouse, which proved beyond all doubt the ease with which a continuous line of more than two thousand miles of wire could be worked; and Professor Morse was able, from these experiments, to declare his conviction that an electric current could pass between London and New York, on such a wire, in the space of one second.

Science had now done its utmost, and had in every thing sustained the great plan. It was now necessary to ask the aid of Her Majesty's Government. This effort was intrusted to Mr. Field, who carried it through successfully. The English Government agreed to furnish the ships necessary for making soundings and surveys, and to furnish vessels to assist in laying the cable. It also agreed to pay to the company an annual subsidy of fourteen thousand pounds for the transmission of the government messages until the net profits of the company were equal to a dividend of six pounds per cent., when the payment was to be reduced to ten thousand pounds per annum, for a period of twenty-five years. Provision was made for extra payment, in case the government messages exceeded a certain amount; and it was provided that the messages of the Governments of Great Britain and the United States should be placed upon an equal footing, and should have priority in the order in which they arrived at the stations. This last provision exhibited a decided liberality on the part of the English Government, since both ends of the proposed cable would be in British territory. Indeed, throughout the whole negotiation, Great Britain cheerfully accorded to the United States every privilege which she claimed for herself.

Having secured the aid of the Queen's Government on such liberal terms, Mr. Field now undertook the organization of the company, in addition to the task of raising a capital of three hundred and fifty thousand pounds. In both efforts he was effectively assisted by Mr. John W. Brett, who had laid the first cable across the English Channel, and by Mr. Charles T. Bright and Dr. Edward O. W. Whitehouse. The efforts of these gentlemen were successful. In a few weeks the whole capital was subscribed. It had been divided into three hundred and fifty shares of a thousand pounds each. One hundred and one of these were taken up in London, eighty-six in Liverpool, thirty-seven in Glasgow, twenty-eight in Manchester, and a few in other parts of England. Mr. Field, at the final division of shares, took eighty-eight. He did not design making this investment on his own account, but thinking it but fair that at least one-fourth of the stock should be held in America, he made this subscription with the intention of disposing of his shares after his return home. Owing to his continued absence from New York, and the straitened condition of the money market, it was nearly a year before he could succeed in selling as much as twenty-seven shares. The company was organized in December, 1856, a Board of Directors elected, and a contract made for the cable, half of which was to be made in London and the other half in Liverpool.

The day after the organization of the company, Mr. Field sailed for New York, from which place he at once made a voyage to Newfoundland, to look after some matters which required his presence. Returning home, he hurried to Washington, to secure the aid of the General Government. He met with more opposition here than he had encountered in England. A powerful lobby opposed him, and a spirit of hostility to his bill exhibited itself in Congress, and to such a degree that the measure passed the Senate by a majority of only one vote. It came very near failing in the House, but at length got through, and received the President's signature on the 3d of March, 1857.

In the summer of 1857, Mr. Field having returned to England, the cable was declared to be in readiness for laying. The United States Government now placed at the disposal of the Telegraph Company the magnificent new steam frigate "Niagara," as the most suitable vessel for laying the cable, and ordered the "Susquehanna," the largest side-wheel frigate in the service, to accompany her in the expedition. The British Government provided the steam frigate "Agamemnon," a splendid vessel, which had been the flagship of the English fleet at the bombardment of Sebastopol, and ordered the "Leopard" to accompany her as an escort. The "Niagara" was commanded by Captain W. L. Hudson, of the United States Navy, and the "Agamemnon" by Captain Noddal, of the Royal Navy. The "Niagara" took on her share of the cable at Liverpool, and the "Agamemnon" received hers at London. It was agreed that the "Niagara" should begin the laying of the cable, and continue it until her portion of it should be exhausted in mid-ocean, when her end of it should be united with the cable on board the "Agamemnon," which ship should continue laying the line until the shores of Newfoundland were reached. After taking on the cable, the ships were ordered to Queenstown.

The vessels left England in the midst of general rejoicings, and arrived at the rendezvous at the proper time. Thence they sailed for the harbor of Valentia, which was to be the eastern terminus of the line and the starting point of the expedition. They were greeted every-where with enthusiasm, and the greatest confidence in the success of the enterprise was manifested by those on board. Mr. Field, Professor Morse, and several other officers of the company were on board the "Niagara," as that ship was to conduct the first part of the sinking of the cable.

At length all was in readiness. The shore end of the cable was landed and made fast on Wednesday afternoon, the 5th of August, and the next morning the fleet stood out to sea. "Before they had gone five miles the heavy shore end of the cable caught in the machinery and parted. The 'Niagara' put back, and the cable was 'underrun' the whole distance. At length the end was lifted out of the water and spliced to the gigantic coil, and as it dropped safely to the bottom of the sea, the mighty ship began to stir. At first she moved very slowly, not more than two miles an hour, to avoid the danger of accident; but the feeling that they are at last away is itself a relief. The ships are all in sight, and so near that they can hear each other's bells. The 'Niagara,' as if knowing that she is bound for the land out of whose forests she came, bends her head to the waves, as her prow is turned toward her native shores.

"Slowly passed the hours of that day. But all went well, and the ships were moving out into the broad Atlantic. At length the sun went down in the west, and stars came out on the face of the deep. But no man slept. A thousand eyes were watching a great experiment, as those who have a personal interest in the issue. All through that night, and through the anxious days and nights that followed, there was a feeling in every soul on board as if a friend in the cabin were at the turning-point of life or death, and they were watching beside him. There was a strange, unnatural silence in the ship. Men paced the deck with soft and muffled tread, speaking only in whispers, as if a loud voice or a heavy footfall might snap the vital cord. So much had they grown to feel for the enterprise, that the cable seemed to them like a human creature, on whose fate they hung, as if it were to decide their own destiny.

"There are some who will never forget that first night at sea. Perhaps the reaction from the excitement on shore made the impression the deeper. What strange thoughts came to them as they stood on the deck and watched that mysterious cord disappearing in the darkness, and gliding to its ocean bed! There are certain moments in life when every thing comes back upon us—when the events of years seem crowded into an hour. What memories came up in those long night hours! How many on board that ship thought of homes beyond the sea, of absent ones, of the distant and the dead! Such thoughts, mingling with those suggested by the scene around, added to the solemnity of the hour, had left an impression which can never be forgotten.

"But with the work in hand all is going on well. There are vigilant eyes on deck. Mr. Bright, the engineer of the company, is there, and Mr. Everett, Mr. De Sauty, the electrician, and Professor Morse. The paying-out machinery does its work, and though it makes a constant rumble in the ship, that dull, heavy sound is music to their ears, as it tells them that all is well. If one should drop to sleep, and wake up at night, he has only to hear the sound of 'the old coffee-mill,' and his fears are relieved, and he goes to sleep again."

Saturday and Sunday passed away without accident, but on Monday, when two hundred miles at sea, in deep water, and safely beyond the great submarine mountain, the electrical continuity was suddenly lost. This interruption amazed and perplexed all on board, but no one was able to remedy it, or to account for it satisfactorily. It lasted for two hours, and then, just as the order was about to be given to cut the cable and endeavor to wind it in, it came back as suddenly and mysteriously as it had disappeared. The greatest delight was now manifested by all on board. "You could see," says the correspondent of the London *Times*, "the tears of joy standing in the eyes of some as they almost cried for joy, and told their messmates that it was all right."

That night, however, the expedition came to grief. The cable was running out freely at the rate of six miles per hour, while the ship was making only four. This was supposed to be owing to a powerful undercurrent. To check this waste of the cable the engineer applied the brakes firmly, which at once stopped the machine. The effect was to bring a heavy strain on the cable that was in the water. The stern of the ship was down in the trough of the sea, and as it rose upward on the swell, the pressure was too great, and the cable parted. The alarm was at once given, and the greatest consternation and grief prevailed on board. "It made all hands of us through the day," says Captain Hudson, "like a household or family which had lost their dearest friend, for officers and men had been deeply interested in the success of the enterprise."

The fleet immediately put about and returned to England, where Mr. Field at once informed the directors of the extent of the disaster. The remaining portions of the cable were landed and stored safely away, and the vessels were returned to their respective Governments. Orders were given for the manufacture of seven hundred miles of cable to replace the portion which had been lost, and to allow for waste in paying it out, and the most energetic preparations were made for another attempt.

Being satisfied that the machine used for paying out the cable was defective, Mr. Field went to Washington and procured from the Navy Department the services of Mr. Wm. E. Everett, the chief engineer of the "Niagara," stating to that gentleman the necessity for a new machine, and urging him to invent it. This Mr. Everett succeeded in doing during the winter. His machine was regarded as a great improvement on that which had been used on the "Niagara." "It was much smaller and lighter. It would take up only about one third as much room on the deck, and had only one fourth the weight of the old machine. Its construction was much more simple. Instead of four heavy wheels, it had but two, and these were made to revolve with ease, and without danger of sudden check, by the application of what were known as self-releasing brakes. These were the invention of Mr. Appold, of London, a gentleman of fortune, but with a strong taste for mechanics, which led him to spend his time and wealth in exercising his mechanical ingenuity. These brakes were so adjusted as to bear only a certain strain, when they released themselves. This ingenious contrivance was applied by Mr. Everett to the paying-out machinery. The strength of the cable was such that it would not break except under a pressure of a little over three tons. The machinery was so adjusted that not more than half that strain could possibly come upon the cable, when the brakes would relax their grasp, the wheels revolve easily, and the cable run out into the sea 'at its own sweet will.' The paying-out machine, therefore, we are far from claiming as wholly an American invention. This part of the mechanism was English. The merit of Mr. Everett lay in the skill with which he adapted it to the laying of the Atlantic cable, and in his great improvements of other parts of the machinery. The whole construction, as it afterward stood upon the decks of the "Niagara" and the "Agamemnon," was the combined product of English and American invention."

In January, 1858, the Board of Directors offered Mr. Field the sum of five thousand dollars per annum if he would assume the post of general manager of the company. He at once undertook the duties of the position, but declined all compensation.

Every thing being in readiness for the second attempt at laying the cable, the "Niagara" sailed from New York in March, 1858, to take on her portion of the cable at Plymouth. The "Agamemnon" was again ordered to assist in the undertaking, and the "Gorgon" was made her consort. Mr. Field had hoped that the "Susquehanna" would again be the consort of the "Niagara," but a few days before the sailing of the fleet he was officially informed that he could not have the ship, as she was then in the West Indies, with the greater part of her crew down with the yellow fever. This was a keen disappointment, as every arrangement had been made with the expectation of having the assistance of the "Susquehanna." It was too late to ask the Government at Washington for another ship, and it was by no means certain that the request would be granted if made. In this dilemma Mr. Field frankly stated his disappointment to the Lords of the Admiralty of England, and asked for a ship to accompany the "Niagara." He was informed that the English Government was at that moment chartering vessels to convey troops to Malta, as it had not ships enough of its own, and that it was doubtful whether it could contribute a third ship to the expedition. Still, so greatly did the government desire the success of the enterprise, that a little later on the same day the "Valorous" was ordered to take the place of the "Susquehanna" in the telegraph fleet. This generous assistance was all the more praiseworthy, as it was given at a time when the need of England for ships was very urgent.

After shipping the cable, the squadron sailed from Plymouth on the 29th of May, 1868, for the Bay of Biscay, where the cable was subjected to numerous and thorough tests, which demonstrated its strength and its sensitiveness to the electric current. This accomplished, the vessels returned to Plymouth.

"Among the matters of *personal* solicitude and anxiety at this time, next to the success of the expedition, was Mr. Field himself. He was working with an activity which was unnatural—which could only be kept up by great excitement, and which involved the most serious danger. The strain on the man was more than the strain on the cable, and we were in fear that both would break together. Often he had no sleep, except such as he caught flying on the railway. Indeed, when we remonstrated, he said he could rest better there than anywhere else, for then he was not tormented with the thought of any thing undone. For the time being he could do no more; and then, putting his head in the cushioned corner of the carriage, he got an hour or two of broken sleep.

"Of this activity we had an instance while in Plymouth. The ships were then lying in the Sound, only waiting orders from the Admiralty to go to sea; but some business required one of the directors to go to Paris, and, as usual, it fell upon him. He left on Sunday night, and went to Bristol, and thence, by the first morning train, to London. Monday he was busy all day, and that night went to Paris. Tuesday, another busy day, and that night back to London. Wednesday, occupied every minute till the departure of the Great Western train. That night back to Plymouth. Thursday morning on board the 'Niagara,' and immediately the squadron sailed."

The plan of operations this time was for the vessels to proceed to a given point in mid-ocean, and there unite the two ends of the cable, after which the "Niagara" should proceed toward Newfoundland and the "Agamemnon" toward Ireland, and it was supposed that each vessel would make land about the same time. This was believed to be a better plan than the one pursued in the first expedition.

The squadron sailed from Plymouth on the 10th of June. The weather was favorable for the first two or three days of the voyage, but on the 13th a severe gale set in, which lasted for over a week, and came near causing the "Agamemnon" to founder beneath her immense load, a portion of which broke loose in her hold. All the vessels succeeded in weathering the storm, however, and on the 25th reached the rendezvous in mid-ocean. The next day the splice was made, and the ships set out for their respective destinations. Before they had gone three miles the machinery of the "Niagara" caught the cable and broke it. A second splice was made, but when each ship had paid out about forty miles, the electric current suddenly ceased. The cable was cut promptly, and the two vessels at once returned to the rendezvous, where they rejoined each other on the 28th. A comparison of the logs of the two ships "showed the painful and mysterious fact that at the same second of time each vessel discovered that a total fracture had taken place, at a distance of certainly not less than ten miles from each ship, in fact, as well as can be judged, at the bottom of the ocean." A third splice was made without delay, and the two ships again set out for the opposite shores of the Atlantic. This time about two hundred miles of the cable were successfully laid, when it parted about twenty feet from the stern of the "Agamemnon." The "Niagara," being unable to communicate with the English frigate, bore away for Queenstown, where she was joined a few days later by the "Agamemnon."

This second failure greatly disheartened the directors, and it required all Mr. Field's persuasiveness to induce them to sanction another attempt. Yet he prevailed, and, hastening from London to Queenstown, sailed with the telegraph fleet on the third attempt to lay the cable, leaving Queenstown on the 17th of July. The rendezvous was reached on the 28th, and on the 29th the splice was made, and the "Niagara" and "Agamemnon" parted company. This time the undertaking was successful. The cable was laid across the Atlantic, the "Niagara" reaching Trinity Bay, Newfoundland, on the 5th of August, and the "Agamemnon" arriving at Valentia, Ireland, a few hours later on the same day. Signals were sent across the entire length of the line, from shore to shore, with ease and rapidity, and nothing occurred to mar the success of the mighty undertaking.

The successful laying of the cable was hailed with the liveliest joy on both sides of the Atlantic, and those who had participated in it were regarded as heroes. But great as was the achievement, it was not destined to be a lasting success. After working for four weeks, the electric current suddenly ceased on the 1st of September. It never worked *perfectly* at any period of its existence, but it did transmit a number of messages with intelligibleness, and thus put an end to all doubt in the minds of the scientific men of the expedition of the feasibility of laying a successful line across the ocean.

The public generally and the directors of the company were greatly disappointed, and many of the latter and nearly all of the former declared that all such attempts must of necessity fail. Some persons even went so far as to avow their belief that the statements as to the successful transmission of signals over the wire were false; but the proofs that the wire did work properly for awhile are too strong to allow us to accord the slightest weight to this disbelief. But whether signals had passed over the wire or not, there could be no doubt that the cable had ceased to respond to the efforts of the electricians, and was a total failure, and the discouragement of nearly every one connected with it was most profound.

Mr. Field and one or two others were the only persons who retained the slightest confidence in the enterprise, and it was clear to them that any further effort to secure the aid of private capital would be useless just then. An appeal was made to the British Government. It was urged that the work was too great to be undertaken by private capital alone, and that, since it was to be more of a public than a private nature, it was but just that the Government should undertake it. The company asked the Government to guarantee the interest on a certain amount of stock, even if the second attempt should not prove a complete success. The failure of the Red Sea cable, to which the British Government had given an unconditional guarantee, had just occurred, and had caused a considerable loss to the treasury, and the Government was not willing to assume another such risk. Anxious, however, for the success of the Atlantic telegraph, it increased its subsidy from fourteen thousand to twenty thousand pounds, and agreed to guarantee eight per cent. on six hundred thousand pounds of new capital for twenty-five years, upon the single condition that the cable should be made to work successfully.

This was not all, however. The Government caused further soundings to be made off the coast of Ireland, which effectually dispelled all the fears which had been entertained of a submarine mountain which would prove an impassable barrier in the path of an ocean telegraph. In addition to this, it caused the organization of a board of distinguished scientific men for the purpose of determining all the difficult problems of submarine telegraphy. This board met in 1859, and sat two years. The result of its experiments and investigations was a declaration, signed by the members, that a cable properly made, "and paid into the ocean with the most improved machinery, possesses every prospect of not only being successfully laid in the first instance, but may reasonably be relied upon to continue many years in an efficient state for the transmission of signals."

Meanwhile, Mr. Field labored energetically to revive the company. The war which had broken out in the United States brought home to our Government the urgent need of telegraphic communication with Europe, and Mr. Field had no difficulty in obtaining from the President an assurance that this Government would be most happy to join with Great Britain in promoting this great international work. He addressed meetings of merchants in various American cities, and displayed the greatest energy in his efforts to enlist the aid of American capital. Very little was accomplished, however, until 1863. By this time the success of the lines in the Mediterranean and in the Persian Gulf had demonstrated the practicability of long submarine telegraphs, and the public confidence in the attempt had been revived to such an extent that the directors ventured to call for proposals for the manufacture of a cable. Seventeen offers were made, from which that of Messrs. Glass, Elliott & Co., of London, was selected. Mr. Field now renewed his indomitable efforts, and in a few months the new capital of six hundred thousand pounds was subscribed, Messrs. Glass, Elliott & Co. taking three hundred and fifteen thousand pounds, besides one hundred thousand pounds in bonds. This was accomplished in 1864, and work on the cable was immediately begun. The cable now adopted was very different from, and much more sensitive than, those which had been used before. It was heavier, and less liable to be injured by the water.

The "Great Eastern" steamship, the greatest wonder of naval architecture, was at this time advertised for sale, and it occurred to several of the gentlemen interested in the telegraph company that she was the best vessel for laying the cable that could be found. They at once organized themselves into a company, purchased the ship, and fitted her up for that service. They were fortunate in securing the services of Captain James Anderson, and placing him in charge of her, sent her to Sheerness, where the cable was sent down to her in lighters from the factory at Greenwich. When the cable was on board, and all the other arrangements had been completed, the big ship left the Thames and sailed for Valentia harbor.

The point of landing had been changed from Valentia harbor, five or six miles, to Foilhommerum Bay. On the 23d of July, 1865, the shore end was connected with the cable on board the ship, and the voyage was begun. It would be interesting to follow the huge steamer on this remarkable voyage, and to relate to the reader the almost marvelous manner in which faults were detected in the line hundreds of miles from the shore, and how the cable was successfully hauled in and the damage repaired. All went well until twelve hundred miles of cable had been paid out, and the ship was but six hundred miles from the shores of Newfoundland, when the cable broke again and plunged into the sea.

Mr. Canning, the engineer in charge, was dismayed, but not disheartened. For nine days the ship hung around the spot grappling for the cable, in the hope of raising it, and sinking its grapnels for this purpose to a depth of two miles. The cable was caught several times, but the rope which held the grapnel broke each time, and the precious coil fell back again into the deep. At length, having marked the place where the cable was lost with buoys, the ship put back for England, and the enterprise was abandoned for that year.

Though unsuccessful in carrying the cable across the ocean, this expedition was by no means a failure. Its results are thus summed up by the officers in charge of it:

1. It was proved by the expedition of 1858 that a submarine telegraph cable could be laid between Ireland and Newfoundland, and messages transmitted through the same.

By the expedition of 1865 it has been fully demonstrated:

2. That the insulation of a cable improves very much after its submersion in the cold deep water of the Atlantic, and that its conducting power is considerably increased thereby.

3. That the steamship "Great Eastern," from her size and constant steadiness, and from the control over her afforded by the joint use of paddles and screw, renders it safe to lay an Atlantic cable in any weather.

4. That in a depth of over two miles four attempts were made to grapple the cable. In three of them the cable was caught by the grapnel, and in the other the grapnel was fouled by the chain attached to it.

5. That the paying-out machinery used on board the Great Eastern worked perfectly, and can be confidently relied on for laying cables across the Atlantic.

6. That with the improved telegraphic instruments for long submarine lines, a speed of more than eight words per minute can be obtained through such a cable as the present Atlantic one between Ireland and Newfoundland, as the amount of slack actually paid out did not exceed fourteen per cent., which would have made the total cable laid between Valentia and Heart's Content nineteen hundred miles.

7. That the present Atlantic cable, though capable of bearing a strain of seven tons, did not experience more than fourteen hundredweight in being paid out into the deepest water of the Atlantic between Ireland and Newfoundland.

8. That there is no difficulty in mooring buoys in the deep water of the Atlantic between Ireland and Newfoundland, and that two buoys even when moored by a piece of the Atlantic cable itself, which had been previously lifted from the bottom, have ridden out a gale.

9. That more than four nautical miles of the Atlantic cable have been recovered from a depth of over two miles, and that the insulation of the gutta-percha covered wire was in no way whatever impaired by the depth of water or the strains to which it had been subjected by lifting and passing through the hauling-in apparatus.

10. That the cable of 1865, owing to the improvements introduced

into the manufacture of the gutta-percha core, was more than one hundred times better insulated than cables made in 1858, then considered perfect and still working.

11. That the electrical testing can be conducted with such unerring accuracy as to enable the electricians to discover the existence of a fault immediately after its production or development, and very quickly to ascertain its position in the cable.

12. That with a steam-engine attached to the paying-out machinery, should a fault be discovered on board whilst laying the cable, it is possible that it might be recovered before it had reached the bottom of the Atlantic, and repaired at once.

It was now placed beyond the possibility of a doubt that the cable would be laid within the next year. More than this, it was determined not only to lay a new cable between the two continents, but to fish up the cable of 1865, splice it and continue it to Newfoundland, thus giving the company two working lines.

It was necessary, however, to raise more capital, and in this effort Mr. Field again put forth his restless and indomitable energies. As the public confidence in the scheme had been effectually restored, it was resolved to raise six hundred thousand pounds of new capital by the issue of one hundred and twenty thousand shares of five pounds each, which should be preferential shares, entitled to a dividend of twelve per cent. before the eight per cent. dividend to be paid on the former preference shares, and the four per cent. on the ordinary stock. They at once proceeded to issue these bonds, when they were informed by the Attorney-General that the proceeding was contrary to law.

In this dilemma work on the new cable was at once stopped, and the money which had been paid in returned to the subscribers. As Parliament was not in session, and a new issue of stock could not be made by the company without its authorization, and as to wait for this would be to postpone the laying of the cable for another year, Mr. Field was now advised by Mr. Daniel Gooch, M. P., that the only way out of the difficulty was to organize a new company at once, which should assume the work, issue its own shares, and raise its own capital. Eminent legal gentlemen sustained Mr. Gooch in this opinion, and Mr. Field again set to work to organize a new company, under the name of the "Anglo-American Telegraph Company." The capital was fixed at six hundred thousand pounds, Mr. Field taking ten thousand pounds. The whole amount was raised in a short time, and the company "contracted with the Atlantic Cable Company to manufacture and lay down a cable in the summer of 1866, for doing which it is to be entitled to what virtually amounts to a preference dividend of twenty-five per cent., as a first claim is secured to them by the Atlantic Telegraph Company upon the revenue of the cable or cables (after the working expenses have been provided for) to the extent of one hundred and twenty-five thousand pounds per annum, and the New York, Newfoundland, and London Telegraph Company undertake to contribute from their revenue a further annual sum of twenty-five thousand pounds, on condition that a cable shall be working during 1866."

Once more the furnaces glowed and the hammers rang in the manufacture of the cable. Great improvements were made in the cable itself and in the machinery for laying it, and the "Great Eastern" was thoroughly overhauled. The cable was completed and put on board in June, and the big ship left the Medway on the last of the month and proceeded to Berehaven, in Ireland, where she took on her final stores of coal. This done, she proceeded to Valentia, where she arrived on the seventh of July.

The shore end was successfully laid and made fast to the cable on board the "Great Eastern," and on Friday morning, the 13th of July, 1866, the huge ship set sail for Newfoundland, accompanied by her consorts of the telegraph fleet. The voyage occupied fourteen days, the ship making an average run of about one hundred and eighteen miles per day, and paying out about one hundred and thirty-one miles of cable in the same period of time. The weather was fair during the whole voyage, but the anxiety of the officers in charge was none the less on that account. There were accidents to be dreaded more than unfavorable weather. The ship was run at moderate speed all the way, as it was thought she had once or twice run too fast on the last voyage, and exposed the cable to danger. "The total slack of the cable was less than twelve per cent., showing that the cable was laid almost in a straight line, allowing for the swells and hollows in the bottom of the sea.

"As the next week drew toward its close, it was evident that they were approaching the end of their voyage. By Thursday they had passed the great depths of the Atlantic, and were off soundings. Besides, their daily observations, there were many signs well known to mariners that they were near the coast. There were the sea-birds, and even the smell of the land, such as once greeted the sharp senses of Columbus, and made him sure that he was floating to some undiscovered shore. Captain Anderson had timed his departure so that he should approach the American coast at the full moon; and so, for the last two or three nights, as they drew near the Western shore, the round orb rose behind them, casting its soft light over sea and sky; and these happy men seemed like heavenly voyagers, floating gently on to a haven of rest.

"In England the progress of the expedition was known from day to day, but on this side of the ocean all was uncertainty. Some had gone to Heart's Content, hoping to witness the arrival of the fleet, but not so many as the last year, for the memory of their disappointment was too fresh, and they feared the same result again. But still a faithful few were there, who kept their daily watch. Two weeks have passed. It is Friday morning, the 27th of July. They are up early, and looking eastward to see the day break, when a ship is seen in the offing. She is far down on the horizon. Spy-glasses are turned toward her. She comes nearer; and look, there is another, and another! And now the hull of the 'Great Eastern' looms up all glorious in that morning sky. They are coming! Instantly all is wild excitement on shore. Boats put off to row toward the fleet. The 'Albany' is the first to round the point and enter the bay. The 'Terrible' is close behind; the 'Medway' stops an hour or two to join on the heavy shore end, while the 'Great Eastern,' gliding calmly in as if she had done nothing remarkable, drops her anchor in front of the telegraph house, having trailed behind her a chain of two thousand miles, to bind the old world to the new.

"Although the expedition reached Newfoundland on Friday, the 27th, yet, as the cable across the Gulf of St. Lawrence was broken, the news was not received in New York till the 29th. It was early Sunday morning, before the Sabbath bells had rung their call to prayer, that the tidings came. The first announcement was brief: 'Heart's Content, July 27th. We arrived here at nine o'clock this morning. All well. Thank God, the cable is laid, and is in perfect working order. Cyrus W. Field.'"

There was no failure in the communication this time. The electric current has continued to flow strongly and uninterruptedly from that day until the present, and experience has demonstrated for the wonderful wire a capacity far beyond the hopes of its projectors.

Having laid the cable, the "Great Eastern" proceeded with

surprising accuracy to where the line had been lost the year before, and succeeded in grappling and raising it to the surface. It was tested, and found to be in perfect order, messages being sent with ease from the ship to Valentia, and from that point back again. A splice was then made, and the line was continued to Newfoundland. Both cables are still working, and bid fair to be serviceable for many years to come.

Many persons had contributed to this great success, but to Cyrus W. Field must be assigned the chief praise. His energy and perseverance kept the subject constantly before the public. His courage inspired others, and his faith in its ultimate success alone kept its best friends from abandoning it in its darkest hours. In its behalf he spent twelve years of constant toil, and made over fifty voyages, more than thirty of which were across the Atlantic. He devoted his entire fortune to the undertaking, of which he was the projector, and cheerfully incurred the risk of poverty rather than abandon it. Therefore, it is but just that he, who was the chief instrument in obtaining for the world this great benefit, should receive the chief measure of the praise which it has brought to all connected with it.

ROBERT FULTON.

III.

INVENTORS.

CHAPTER XIII.

ROBERT FULTON.

ONE of the pleasantest as well as one of the most prominent places in the city of New York is the grave-yard of old Trinity Church. A handsome iron railing separates it from Broadway, and the thick rows of grave-stones, all crumbling and stained with age, present a strange contrast to the bustle, vitality, and splendor with which they are surrounded. They stare solemnly down into Wall Street, and offer a bitter commentary upon the struggles and anxiety of the money kings of the great city. Work, toil, plan, combine as you may, they seem to say, and yet it must all come to this.

Not far from the south door of the church, and shaded by a venerable tree, is a plain brown stone slab, bearing this inscription: "The vault of Walter and Robert C. Livingston, sons of Robert Livingston, of the manor of Livingston." A stranger would pass it by without a second glance; yet it is one of the Meccas of the world of science, for the mortal part of Robert Fulton sleeps in the vault below, without monument or legendary stone to his memory, but in sight of the mighty steam fleets which his genius called forth. Very few visitors ever see this part of the churchyard, and the grave of Fulton is unknown to nine out of ten of his countrymen. Yet this man, sleeping so obscurely in his grave without a name, did far more for the world than either Napoleon or Wellington. He revolutionized commerce and manufactures, changed the entire system of navigation, triumphed over the winds and the waves, and compelled the adoption of a new system of modern warfare. Now he lies in a grave not his own, with no monument or statue erected to his memory in all this broad land.

ROBERT FULTON was born in the township of Little Britain (now called Fulton), in Lancaster County, Pennsylvania, in 1765. He was of Irish descent, and his father was a farmer in moderate circumstances. He was the eldest son and third child of a family of five children. The farm upon which he was born was conveyed by his father in 1766 to Joseph Swift, in whose family it still remains. It contains three hundred and sixty-four acres, and is one of the handsomest farms in Lancaster County.

After disposing of his farm, Mr. Fulton, senior, removed to the town of Lancaster, where he died in 1768, and there young Robert grew up under the care of his mother. He learned to read and write quickly, but did not manifest much fondness for his books after mastering his elementary studies. He early exhibited an unusual talent for drawing, however, greatly preferring the employment of his pencil to the more serious duties of the school. His instructors and companions considered him a dull boy, though all admitted that he showed no disposition to be idle. All his leisure time was spent either in drawing, or in visiting the shops of the mechanics in the place and eagerly watching their operations. He displayed a remarkable talent for mechanism, which was greatly assisted by his skill in drawing, and his visits to the machine shops were always welcomed by both the apprentices and their employers, who recognized the unusual genius of the boy, and predicted great things for him in the future. But to his teacher, who seems to have been rather more belligerent than is usual with Quakers, Robert's neglect of his studies and visits to the machine shops were so many indications of growing worthlessness. The indignant pedagogue once took occasion to remonstrate with him upon his course, and, failing to convince him by argument, rapped him sharply over the knuckles with a ruler, telling him he would make him do something. Robert at once placed his arms akimbo, and, looking his tutor sternly in the face, replied: "Sir, I came here to have something beat into my brains, not into my knuckles."

Some time after this Mrs. Fulton, in conversation with the teacher, expressed her solicitude lest her son should "turn out nothing," since he neglected his books so entirely. The teacher frankly confessed that he had done all in his power for the boy, but that he was discouraged, and added: "Only yesterday, madam, Robert pertinaciously declared to me that his head was so full of original notions that there was no vacant chamber to store away the contents of any dusty books." The lad was only ten years of age at the time, and, as may be supposed, the good Quaker who directed his education was not a little dismayed by such a remark.

The boyhood of Fulton was passed during the stormy period of the Revolution, and in a section so close to the theater of war that he was in the midst of all the excitement engendered by the conflict. He was an ardent patriot from the first, and used his pencil freely to caricature all who showed the slightest leaning to the cause of the enemy.

In 1778 the supply of candles was so low in Lancaster that

the town authorities advised the people to refrain from illuminating their houses on the 4th of July of that year, in order to save their candles. Robert, at this time but thirteen years old, was determined not to forego a patriotic display of some sort. He had prepared a quantity of candles for the occasion, and after the proclamation of the Town Council was issued, he took them to a Mr. John Fisher, who kept a store in the place, and sold powder and shot. Mr. Fisher was somewhat astonished at Robert's desire to part with the candles, which were at that time scarce articles, and asked his reason for so doing. The boy replied: "Our rulers have requested the citizens to refrain from illuminating their windows and streets; as good citizens we should comply with their request, and I prefer illuminating the heavens with sky-rockets." Having procured the powder, he left Mr. Fisher's, and entered a small variety store kept by a Mr. Cossart, where he purchased several sheets of large-sized pasteboard. As Mr. Cossart was about to roll them, the boy stopped him, saying he wished to carry them open. Mr. Cossart, knowing Robert's mechanical genius, asked him what he was about to invent.

"Why," said the boy, "we are prohibited from illuminating our windows with candles, and I 'm going to shoot my candles through the air."

"Tut, tut, tut," said Mr. Cossart, laughingly; "that 's an impossibility."

"No, sir," said Robert, "there is nothing impossible."*

"Robert was known," says one of his biographers, "to purchase small quantities of quicksilver from Dr. Adam Simon Kuhn, druggist, residing opposite the market-house. He was trying some experiments that he did not wish to make public,

* He proved that this was not impossible, for he had his display, making his rockets himself, and after his own model.

and which the workmen in Mr. Fenno's and Mr. Christian Isch's shops were anxious to find out, but could not. He was in the habit almost daily of visiting those shops, and was a favorite among the workmen, who took advantage of his talent for drawing by getting him to make ornamental designs for guns, and sketches of the size and shape of guns, and then giving the calculations of the force, size of the bore and balls, and the distances they would fire; and he would accompany them to the open commons near by potter's field, to prove his calculations by shooting at a mark. On account of his expertness in his calculations, and of their ineffectual efforts to discover the use he was making of quicksilver, the shop-hands nicknamed him 'quicksilver Bob.'

"Mr. Messersmith and Mr. Christian Isch were employed by the Government to make and repair the arms for the troops; and on several occasions guards were stationed at their shops to watch and see that the workmen were constantly employed during whole nights and on Sunday, to prevent any delay. The workmen had so much reliance and confidence in 'quicksilver Bob's' judgment and mechanical skill, that every suggestion he would make as to the alteration of a gun, or any additional ornament that he would design, was invariably adopted by common consent.

"In the summer of 1779, Robert Fulton evinced an extraordinary fondness for inventions. He was a frequent visitor at Mr. Messersmith's and Mr. Fenno's gunsmith shops, almost daily, and endeavored to manufacture a small air-gun."

Among the acquaintances of Robert Fulton at this time was a young man, about eighteen years of age, named Christopher Gumpf, who used frequently to accompany his father in his fishing excursions on the Conestoga. Mr. Gumpf, Sen., being an experienced angler, readily consented to allow Robert to join himself and his son in these expeditions, and made the two boys earn their pleasure by pushing the boat about the stream, as he desired to move from point to point. As the means of propulsion was simply a pole, the labor was very severe, and Robert soon became tired of it. Not wishing, however, to give up his pleasant fishing trips, he determined to devise some means of lightening the labor.

"He absented himself a week, having gone to Little Britain township to spend a few days at his aunt's; and while there he planned and completed a small working model of a fishing boat, with paddle-wheels. On leaving his aunt's, he placed the model in the garret, with a request that it should not be destroyed. Many years afterward, that simple model was the attraction of friends, and became, instead of lumber in the garret, an ornament in the aunt's parlor, who prized it highly. That model was the result of Robert's fishing excursions with Christopher Gumpf; and when he returned from his aunt's he told Christopher that he must make a set of paddles to work at the sides of the boat, to be operated by a double crank, and then they could propel the old gentleman's fishing-boat with greater ease. Two arms or pieces of timber were then fastened together at right angles, with a paddle at each end, and the crank was attached to the boat across it near the stern, with a paddle operating on a pivot as a rudder; and Fulton's first invention was tried on the Conestoga River, opposite Rockford, in the presence of Peter and Christopher Gumpf. The boys were so pleased with the experiment, that they hid the paddles in the bushes on the shore, lest others might use and break them, and attached them to the boat whenever they chose; and thus did they enjoy very many fishing excursions."

This was the first experiment in the science of navigation

attempted by the man who afterward became the author of a new system.

Having chosen the profession of an artist and portrait painter, young Fulton removed to Philadelphia at the age of seventeen, and remained there, pursuing his vocation, until the completion of his twenty-first year. He formed there the acquaintance of Benjamin Franklin, by whom he was much noticed. His success was rapid, and upon attaining his majority he was enabled to purchase and stock a farm of eighty-four acres in Washington County, Pennsylvania, which he gave to his mother for a home as long as she should live. Having thus insured her comfort, he went to England for the purpose of completing his studies in his profession. He took with him letters to Benjamin West, then at the height of his fame, and living in London. He was cordially received by Mr. West, who was also a native of Pennsylvania, and remained an inmate of his family for several years. West was then the President of the Royal Academy of Great Britain, and was thus enabled to extend to Fulton, to whom he became deeply attached, many advantages, both social and professional, of which the young artist was prompt to avail himself.

Upon leaving the family of Mr. West, Fulton commenced a tour for the purpose of examining the treasures of art contained in the residences of the English nobility, and remained for two years in Devonshire. There he became acqainted with the Duke of Bridgewater, to whom England is indebted for the introduction of the canal system within her limits; and it is said that he was induced by this nobleman to abandon the profession of an artist, and enter upon that of a civil engineer. This nobleman being devoted to mechanical investigations, proved a very congenial acquaintance to Fulton. He was engaged at the time on a scheme of steam navigation by a propeller, modeled after the foot of a water fowl. His plan did not commend itself to Fulton's judgment, and he addressed him a letter, setting forth its defects, and advancing some of the views upon which he acted himself in after life. Here he also met with Watt, who had just produced the steam-engine, which Fulton studied enthusiastically. His own inventive genius was not idle, and while living in Devonshire, he produced an improved mill for sawing marble, which won him the thanks and medal of the British Society for the Promotion of the Arts and Commerce; a machine for spinning flax and making ropes; and an excavator for scooping out the channels of canals and aqueducts, all of which were patented. He published a number of communications on the subject of canals in one of the leading London journals, and a treatise upon the same subject. Having obtained a patent in England for canal improvements, he went to France in 1797, with the design of introducing them in that country.

Upon reaching Paris, he took up his residence with Mr. Joel Barlow, and thus was laid the foundation of a friendship between these two gentlemen which lasted during their lives. He remained in Paris seven years, residing during that time with Mr. Barlow, and devoting himself to the study of modern languages, and engineering and its kindred sciences.

His work was continuous and severe in Paris. He invented and painted the first panorama ever exhibited in that city, which he sold for the purpose of raising money for his experiments in steam navigation; he also designed a series of splendid colored illustrations for *The Columbiad,* the famous poem of his friend Mr. Barlow. Besides these, he invented a number of improvements in canals, aqueducts, inclined planes, boats, and guns, which yielded him considerable credit, but very little profit.

In 1801, he invented a submarine boat which he called the

"Nautilus," which is thus described by M. de St. Aubin, a member of the Tribunate:

"The diving-boat, in the construction of which he is now employed, will be capacious enough to contain eight men and provision for twenty days, and will be of sufficient strength and power to enable him to plunge one hundred feet under water, if necessary. He has contrived a reservoir of air, which will enable eight men to remain under water eight hours. When the boat is above water, it has two sails, and looks just like a common boat; when it is to dive, the mast and sails are struck.

"In making his experiments, Mr. Fulton not only remained a whole hour under water, with three of his companions, but had the boat parallel to the horizon at any given distance. He proved that the compass points as correctly under water as on the surface, and that while under water the boat made way at the rate of half a league an hour, by means contrived for that purpose.

"It is not twenty years since all Europe was astonished at the first ascension of men in balloons: perhaps in a few years they will not be less surprised to see a flotilla of diving-boats, which, on a given signal, shall, to avoid the pursuit of an enemy, plunge under water, and rise again several leagues from the place where they descended!

"But if we have not succeeded in steering the balloon, and even were it impossible to attain that object, the case is different with the diving-boat, which can be conducted under water in the same manner as upon the surface. It has the advantage of sailing like the common boat, and also of diving when it is pursued. With these qualities, it is fit for carrying secret orders, to succor a blockaded fort, and to examine the force and position of an enemy in their harbors."

In connection with this boat, Fulton invented a torpedo, or infernal machine, for the purpose of destroying vessels of war by approaching them under water and breaking up their hulls by the explosion. He offered his invention several times to the French Government, and once to the Ambassador of Holland at Paris, without being able to induce them to consider it. Somewhat later, he visited London, at the request of the British Ministry, and explained his invention to them. Although he succeeded in blowing up a vessel of two hundred tons with one hundred and seventy pounds of powder, and in extorting from Mr. Pitt the acknowledgment that, if introduced into practice, the torpedo would annihilate all navies, his invention was rejected, through the influence of Lord Melville, who feared that its adoption might injure England more than it would benefit her. At the first, when it was thought that England would purchase Fulton's invention, it was intimated to him that he would be required to pledge himself not to dispose of it to any other power. He replied promptly:

"Whatever may be your award, I never will consent to let these inventions lie dormant should my country at any time have need of them. Were you to grant me an annuity of twenty thousand pounds, I would sacrifice all to the safety and independence of my country."

In 1806, Mr. Fulton returned to New York, and in the same year he married Miss Harriet Livingston, a niece of Chancellor Livingston, by whom he had four children. He offered his torpedo to the General Government, but the trial to which it was subjected by the Navy Department was unsuccessful for him, and the Government declined to purchase the invention.

But it was not as the inventor of engines of destruction that Robert Fulton was to achieve fame. A still nobler triumph was reserved for him—one which was to bring joy instead of sorrow to the world. From the time that Fulton had designed the paddle-wheels for his fishing-boat, he had never ceased to give his attention to the subject of propelling vessels by machinery, and after his acquaintance with Watt, he was more than ever convinced that the steam-engine could, under proper circumstances, be made to furnish the motive power.

Several eminent and ingenious men, previous to this, had proposed to propel vessels by steam power, among whom were Dr. Papin, of France, Savery, the Marquis of Worcester, and Dr. John Allen, of London, in 1726. In 1786, Oliver Evans, of Philadelphia, and about the same time Dr. Franklin, proposed to accomplish this result by forcing a quantity of water, by means of steam power, through an opening made for that purpose in the stern of the hull of the boat.

In 1737, Jonathan Hulls issued a pamphlet proposing to construct a boat to be moved by steam power, for the purpose of towing vessels out of harbors against tide and winds. In his plan the paddle-wheel was used, and was secured to a frame placed far out over the stern of the boat. It was given this position by the inventor because water fowls propelled themselves by pushing their feet behind them.

In 1787, Mr. James Rumsey, of Shepherdstown, Virginia, constructed and navigated the first steamboat in actual use. His boat was eighty feet in length, and was propelled by means of a vertical pump in the middle of the vessel, by which the water was drawn in at the bow and expelled at the stern through a horizontal trough in her hull. The engine weighed about one third of a ton, and the boat had a capacity of about three tons burthen. When thus laden, a speed of about four miles an hour could be attained. The boiler held only five gallons of water, and needed but a pint at a time. Rumsey went to England to exhibit his plan on the Thames, and died there in 1793.

About the same time the Marquis de Joffrey launched a steamer one hundred feet long on the Loire, at Lyons, using paddles revolving on an endless chain, but only to find his experiment a failure.

In December, 1786, John Fitch published the following account of a steamer with which he had made several experiments on the Delaware, at Philadelphia, and which came nearer to success than any thing that had at that time been invented:

"The cylinder is to be horizontal, and the steam to work with equal force at each end. The mode by which we obtain what I term a vacuum is, it is believed, entirely new, as is also the method of letting the water into it, and throwing it off against the atmosphere without any friction. It is expected that the cylinder, which is of twelve inches diameter, will move a clear force of eleven or twelve cwt. after the frictions are deducted: this force is to be directed against a wheel of eighteen inches diameter. The piston moves about three feet, and each vibration of it gives the axis about forty revolutions. Each revolution of the axis moves twelve oars or paddles five and a half feet: they work perpendicularly, and are represented by the strokes of a paddle of a canoe. As six of the paddles are raised from the water, six more are entered, and the two sets of paddles make their strokes of about eleven feet in each revolution. The crank of the axis acts upon the paddles about one-third of their length from their lower ends, on which part of the oar the whole force of the axis is applied. The engine is placed in the bottom of the boat, about one-third from the stern, and both the action and reaction turn the wheel the same way."

Fitch was unfortunate in his affairs, and became so disheartened that he ceased to attempt to improve his invention, and finally committed suicide by drowning himself in the Alleghany River at Pittsburgh.

In 1787, Mr. Patrick Miller, of Dalwinston, Scotland, designed a double vessel, propelled by a wheel placed in the stern between the two keels. This boat is said to have been very successful, but it was very small, the cylinder being only four inches in diameter. In 1789, Mr. Miller produced a larger vessel on the same plan, which made seven miles per hour in the still water of the Forth and Clyde Canal, but it proved too weak for its machinery, which had to be taken out.

It was in the face of these failures that Fulton applied himself to the task of designing a successful steamboat. During his residence in Paris he had made the acquaintance of Mr. Robert R. Livingston, then the American minister in France, who had previously been connected with some unsuccessful steamboat experiments at home. Mr. Livingston was delighted to find a man of Fulton's mechanical genius so well satisfied of the practicability of steam navigation, and joined heartily with him in his efforts to prove his theories by experiments. Several small working models made by Fulton convinced Mr. Livingston that the former had discovered and had overcome the cause of the failure of the experiments of other inventors, and it was finally agreed between them to build a large boat for trial on the Seine. This experimental steamer was furnished with paddle wheels, and was completed and launched early in the spring of 1803. On the very morning appointed for the trial, Fulton was aroused from his sleep by a messenger from the boat, who rushed into his chamber, pale and breathless, exclaiming, "Oh, sir, the boat has broken in pieces and gone to the bottom!" Hastily dressing and hurrying to the spot, he found that the weight of the machinery had broken the boat in half and carried the whole structure to the bottom of the river. He at once set to work to raise the machinery, devoting twenty-four hours, withont resting or eating, to the undertaking, and succeeded in doing so, but inflicted upon his constitution a strain from which he never entirely recovered. The machinery was very slightly damaged, but it was necessary to rebuild the boat entirely. This was accomplished by July of the same year, and the boat was tried in August with triumphant success, in the presence of the French National Institute and a vast crowd of the citizens of Paris.

This steamer was very defective, but still so great an improvement upon all that had preceded it, that Messrs. Fulton and Livingston determined to build one on a larger scale in the waters of New York, the right of navigating which by steam vessels had been secured by the latter as far back as 1798. The law which granted this right had been continued from time to time through Mr. Livingston's influence, and was finally amended so as to include Fulton within its provisions. Having resolved to return home, Fulton set out as soon as possible, stopping in England on his return, to order an engine for his boat from Watt and Boulton. He gave an exact description of the engine, which was built in strict accordance with his plan, but declined to state the use to which he intended putting it.

Very soon after his arrival in New York, he commenced building his first American boat, and finding that her cost would greatly exceed his estimate, he offered for sale a third interest in the monopoly of the navigation of the waters of New York, held by Livingston and himself, in order to raise money to build the boat, and thus lighten the burdens of himself and his partner, but he could find no one willing to risk money in such a scheme. Indeed, steam navigation was universally regarded in America as a mere chimera, and Fulton and Livingston were ridiculed for their faith in it. The bill granting the monopoly held by Livingston was regarded as so utterly absurd by the Legislature of New York, that that wise body could with difficulty be induced to consider it seriously. Even among scientific men the project was considered impracticable. A society in Rotterdam had, several years before Fulton's return home, applied to the American Philosophical Society to be informed whether any and what improvements had been made in the construction of steam-engines in America. A reply to this inquiry was prepared, at the request of the Society, by Mr. Benjamin H. Latrobe, a distinguished engineer. The following extracts from this paper will show the reader how Fulton's scheme was regarded by one who was confessedly one of the most brilliant engineers of his day, and who has since accomplished so much for the improvement of steam travel:

During the general lassitude of mechanical exertion which succeeded the American Revolution, the utility of steam-engines appears to have been forgotten; but the subject afterward started into very general notice in a form in which it could not possibly be attended with success. A sort of mania began to prevail, which, indeed, has not yet entirely subsided, for impelling boats by steam-engines. Dr. Franklin proposed to force forward the boat by the immediate application of the steam upon the water. Many attempts to simplify the working of the engine, and more to employ a means of dispensing with the beam in converting the *libratory* into a rotatory motion, were made. For a short time, a passage-boat, rowed by a steam-engine, was established between Bordentown and Philadelphia, but it was soon laid aside. The best and most powerful steam-engine which has been employed for this purpose—excepting, perhaps, one constructed by Dr. Kinsey, with the performance of which I am not sufficiently acquainted—belonged to a gentleman of New York. It was made to act, by way of experiment, upon oars, upon paddles, and upon flutter-wheels. Nothing in the success of any of these experiments appeared to be sufficient compensation for the expense and the extreme inconvenience of the steam-engine in the vessel.

There are, indeed, general objections to the use of the steam-engine for impelling boats, from which no particular mode of application can be free. These are:

First. The weight of the engine and of the fuel.

Second. The large space it occupies.

Third. The tendency of its action to rack the vessel, and render it leaky.

Fourth. The expense of maintenance.

Fifth. The irregularity of its motion, and the motion of the water in the boiler and cistern, and of the fuel-vessel in rough water.

Sixth. The difficulty arising from the liability of the paddles and oars to break, if light, and from the weight, if made strong.

Nor have I ever heard of an instance, verified by other testimony than that of the inventor, of a speedy and agreeable voyage having been performed in a steamboat of any construction.

I am well aware that there are still many very respectable and ingenious men who consider the application of the steam-engine to the purpose of navigation as highly important, and as very practicable, especially on the rapid waters of the Mississippi, and who would feel themselves almost offended at the expression of an opposite opinion. And, perhaps, some of the objections against it may be avoided. That founded on the expense and weight of the fuel may not, for some years, exist on the Mississippi, where there is a redundance of wood on the banks; but the cutting and loading will be almost as great an evil.

Scientific men and amateurs all agreed in pronouncing Fulton's scheme impracticable; but he went on with his work, his boat attracting no less attention and exciting no less ridicule than the ark had received from the scoffers in the days of Noah. The steam-engine ordered from Boulton and Watt was received in the latter part of 1806; and in the following spring the boat was launched from the ship-yard of Charles Brown, on the East River. Fulton named her the "Clermont," after the country-seat of his friend and partner, Chancellor Livingston. She was one hundred and sixty tons burthen, one hundred and thirty feet long, eighteen feet wide, and seven feet deep. Her engine was made with a single cylinder, two feet in diameter, and of four feet stroke; and her boiler was twenty feet long, seven feet deep, and eight feet broad. The diameter of the paddle-wheels was fifteen feet, the boards four feet long, and dipping two feet in the water. The boat was completed about the last of August, and she was moved by her machinery from the East River into the Hudson, and over to the Jersey shore. This trial, brief as it was, satisfied Fulton of its success, and he announced that in a few days the steamer would sail from New York for Albany. A few friends, including several scientific men and mechanics, were invited to take passage in the boat, to witness her performance; and they accepted the invitation with a general conviction that they were to do but little more than witness another failure.

Monday, September 10, 1807, came at length, and a vast crowd assembled along the shore of the North River to witness the starting. As the hour for sailing drew near, the crowd increased, and jokes were passed on all sides at the expense of the inventor, who paid little attention to them, however, but busied himself in making a final and close inspection of the machinery. Says Fulton, "The morning I left New York, there were not, perhaps, thirty persons in the city who believed that the boat would ever move one mile per hour, or be of the least utility; and while we were putting off from the wharf, which was crowded with spectators, I heard a number of sarcastic remarks."

One o'clock, the hour for sailing, came, and expectation was at its highest. The friends of the inventor were in a state of feverish anxiety lest the enterprise should come to grief, and the scoffers on the wharf were all ready to give vent to their shouts of derision. Precisely as the hour struck, the moorings were thrown off, and the "Clermont" moved slowly out into the stream. Volumes of smoke and sparks from her furnaces, which were fed with pine wood, rushed forth from her chimney, and her wheels, which were uncovered, scattered the spray far behind her. The spectacle she presented as she moved out gradually from her dock was certainly novel to the people of those days, and the crowd on the wharf broke into shouts of ridicule. Soon, however, the jeers grew silent, for it was seen that the steamer was by degrees increasing her speed. In a little while she was fairly under weigh, and making a steady progress up the stream at the rate of five miles per hour. The incredulity of the spectators had been succeeded by astonishment, and now this feeling gave way to undisguised delight, and cheer after cheer went up from the vast throng. Many people followed the boat for some distance up the river shore. In a little while, however, the boat was observed to stop, and the enthusiasm of the people on the shore at once subsided. The scoffers were again in their glory, and unhesitatingly pronounced the boat a failure. Their chagrin may be imagined when, after a short delay, the steamer once more proceeded on her way, and this time even more rapidly than before. Fulton had discovered that the paddles were too long, and took too deep a hold on the water, and had stopped the boat for the purpose of shortening them.

Having remedied this defect, the "Clermont" continued her voyage during the rest of the day and all night, without stopping, and at one o'clock the next day ran alongside the landing at Clermont, the seat of Chancellor Livingston. She lay there until nine the next morning, when she continued her voyage toward Albany, reaching that city at five in the afternoon, having made the entire distance between New York and Albany (one hundred and fifty miles) in thirty-two hours of actual running time, an average speed of nearly five miles per hour. On her return trip, she reached New York in thirty hours running time—exactly five miles per hour. Fulton states that during both trips he encountered a head wind.

The river was at this time navigated entirely with sailing vessels, and large numbers of these were encountered by the "Clermont" during her up and down trips. The surprise and dismay excited among the crews of these vessels by the appearance of the steamer was extreme. These simple people, the majority of whom had heard nothing of Fulton's experiments, beheld what they supposed to be a huge monster, vomiting fire and smoke from its throat, lashing the water with its fins, and shaking the river with its roar, approaching rapidly in the very face of both wind and tide. Some threw themselves flat on the deck of their vessels, where they remained in an agony of terror until the monster had passed, while others took to their boats and made for the shore in dismay, leaving their vessels to drift helplessly down the stream. Nor was this terror confined to the sailors. The people dwelling along the shore crowded the banks to gaze upon the steamer as she passed by. A former resident of the neighborhood of Poughkeepsie thus describes the scene at that place, which will serve as a specimen of the conduct of the people along the entire river below Albany:

"It was in the early autumn of the year 1807 that a knot of villagers was gathered on a high bluff just opposite Poughkeepsie, on the west bank of the Hudson, attracted by the appearance of a strange, dark-looking craft, which was slowly making its way up the river. Some imagined it to be a sea-monster, while others did not hesitate to express their belief that it was a sign of the approaching judgment. What seemed strange in the vessel was the substitution of lofty and straight black smoke-pipes, rising from the deck, instead of the gracefully tapered masts that commonly stood on the vessels navigating the stream, and, in place of the spars and rigging, the curious play of the working-beam and pistons, and the slow turning and splashing of the huge and naked paddle-wheels, met the astonished gaze. The dense clouds of smoke, as they rose wave upon wave, added still more to the wonderment of the rustics.

"This strange-looking craft was the 'Clermont,' on her trial trip to Albany; and of the little knot of villagers mentioned above, the writer, then a boy in his eighth year, with his parents, formed a part. I well remember the scene, one so well fitted to impress a lasting picture upon the mind of a child accustomed to watch the vessels that passed up and down the river.

"The forms of four persons were distinctly visible on the deck as she passed the bluff—one of whom, doubtless, was Robert Fulton, who had on board with him all the cherished hopes of years, the most precious cargo the wonderful boat could carry.

"On her return trip, the curiosity she excited was scarcely less intense. The whole country talked of nothing but the sea-monster, belching forth fire and smoke. The fishermen became terrified, and rowed homewards, and they saw nothing but destruction devastating their fishing-grounds; while the wreaths of black vapor, and rushing noise of the paddle-wheels, foaming with the stirred-up waters, produced great excitement among the boatmen, which continued without abatement, until the character of that curious boat, and the nature of the enterprise which she was pioneering, had been understood."

The alarm of the sailors and dwellers on the river shore disappeared as the character of the steamer became better known; but when it was found that the "Clermont" was to run regularly between New York and Albany, as a packet-boat, she became the object of the most intense hatred on the part of the boatmen on the river, who feared that she would entirely destroy their business. In many quarters Fulton and his invention were denounced as baneful to society, and frequent attempts were made by captains of sailing vessels to sink the "Clermont" by running into her. She was several times damaged in this way, and the hostility of the boatmen became so great that it was necessary for the Legislature of New York to pass a law declaring combinations to destroy her, or willful attempts to injure her, public offenses punishable by fine and imprisonment.

It had been supposed that Fulton's object was to produce a steamer capable of navigating the Mississippi River, and much surprise was occasioned by the announcement that the "Clermont" was to be permanently employed upon the Hudson. She continued to ply regularly between New York and Albany until the close of navigation for that season, always carrying a full complement of passengers, and more or less freight. During the winter she was overhauled and enlarged, and her speed improved. In the spring of 1808 she resumed her regular trips, and since then steam navigation on the Hudson has not ceased for a single day, except during the closing of the river by ice.

In 1811 and 1812, Fulton built two steam ferry-boats for the North River, and soon after added a third for the East River. These boats were the beginning of the magnificent steam ferry system which is to-day one of the chief wonders of New York. They were what are called twin-boats, each of them consisting of two complete hulls, united by a deck or bridge. They were sharp at both ends, and moved equally well with either end foremost, so that they could cross and recross without being turned around. These boats were given engines of sufficient power to enable them to overcome the force of strong ebb tides; and in order to facilitate their landing, Fulton contrived a species of floating dock, and a means of decreasing the shock caused by the striking of the boat against the dock. These boats could accommodate eight four-wheel carriages, twenty-nine horses, and four hundred passengers. Their average time across the North River, a mile and a half wide, was twenty minutes.

The introduction of the steamboat gave a powerful impetus to the internal commerce of the Union. It opened to navigation many important rivers (whose swift currents had closed them to sailing craft), and made rapid and easy communication between the most distant parts of the country practicable. The public soon began to appreciate this, and orders came in rapidly for steamboats for various parts of the country. Fulton executed these as fast as possible, and among the number several for boats for the Ohio and Mississippi Rivers.

Early in 1814, the city of New York was seriously menaced with an attack from the British fleet, and Fulton was called on by a committee of citizens to furnish a plan for a means of defending the harbor. He exhibited to the committee his plans for a vessel of war to be propelled by steam, capable of carrying a strong battery, with furnaces for red-hot shot, and which, he represented, would move at the rate of four miles an hour. These plans were also submitted to a number of naval officials, among whom were Commodore Decatur, Captain Jones, Captain Evans, Captain Biddle, Commodore Perry, Captain Warrington, and Captain Lewis, all of whom warmly united in urging the Government to undertake the construction of the proposed steamer. The citizens of New York offered, if the Government would employ and pay for her after she was built, to advance the sum ($320,000) necessary for her construction. The subject was vigorously pressed, and in March, 1814, Congress authorized the building of one or more floating batteries after the plan presented by Fulton. Her keel was laid on the 20th of June, 1814, and on the 31st of October, of the same year, she was launched, amid great rejoicings, from the ship-yard of Adam and Noah Brown. In May, 1815, her engines were put on board, and on the 4th of July of that year she made a trial trip to Sandy Hook and back, accomplishing the round trip—a distance of fifty-three miles—in eight hours and twenty minutes, under steam alone. Before this, however, peace had been proclaimed, and Fulton had gone to rest from his labors.

The ship was a complete success, and was the first steam vessel of war ever built. She was called the "Fulton the First," and was for many years used as the receiving ship at the Brooklyn Navy Yard. She was an awkward and unwieldy mass, but was regarded as the most formidable vessel afloat; and as the pioneer of the splendid war steamers of to-day is still an object of great interest. The English regarded her with especial uneasiness, and put in circulation the most marvelous stories concerning her. One of these I take from a treatise on steam navigation published in Scotland at this period, the author of which assures his readers that he has taken the utmost pains to obtain full and accurate information respecting the American war steamer. His description is as follows:

"Length on deck three hundred feet, breadth two hundred feet, thickness of her sides, thirteen feet, of alternate oak plank and corkwood; carries forty-four guns, four of which are 100-pounders, quarter-deck and forcastle guns, 44-pounders; and further, to annoy an enemy attempting to board, can discharge one hundred gallons of boiling water in a minute, and by mechanism brandishes three hundred cutlasses, with the utmost regularity, over her gunwales; works also an equal number of heavy iron pikes of great length, darting them from her sides with prodigious force, and withdrawing them every quarter of a minute!"

Fulton followed up the "Clermont," in 1807, with a larger boat, called the "Car of Neptune," which was placed on the Albany route as soon as completed. The Legislature of New York had enacted a law, immediately upon his first success, giving to Livingston and himself the exclusive right to navigate the waters of the State by steam, for five years for every additional boat they should build in the State, provided the whole term should not exceed thirty years. "In the following year the Legislature passed another act, confirmatory of the prior grants, and giving new remedies to the grantees for any invasion of them, and subjecting to forfeiture any vessel propelled by steam which should enter the waters of the State without their license. In 1809 Fulton obtained his first patent from the United States; and in 1811 he took out a second patent for some improvement in his boats and machinery. His patents were limited to the simple means of adapting paddle wheels to the axle of the crank of Watt's engine.

"Meanwhile the power of the Legislature to grant the steamboat monopoly was denied, and a company was formed at Albany to establish another line of steam passage boats on the Hudson, between that city and New York. The State grantees filed a bill in equity, and prayed for an injunction, which was refused by Chancellor Lansing, on the ground that the act of the State Legislature was repugnant to the Constitution of the United States, and against common right. This decree was unanimously reversed by the Court of Errors, and a compromise was effected with the Albany company by an assignment to them of the right to employ steam on the waters of Lake Champlain.

"Legislative aid was again invoked, and an act was passed directing peremptorily the allowance of an injunction on the prayer of the State grantees, and the seizure of any hostile boat at the commencement of the suit. Litigation was thus effectually arrested in New York, though by an arbitrary and unconstitutional enactment, and the waters of the State remained in the exclusive possession of Fulton and his partner during the lifetime of the former. A similar controversy with Colonel Aaron Ogden, of New Jersey, was compromised by advantageous concessions, which converted the opponent of the monopoly into its firmest friend, and left him many years afterward the defeated party in the famous suit of Gibbons and Ogden, in the Supreme Court of the United States."

In January, 1815, Fulton was summoned to Trenton, New Jersey, as a witness in one of the numerous suits which grew out of the efforts to break down his monopoly. During his examination he was very much exposed, as the hall of the Legislature was uncommonly cold. In returning home, he crossed the Hudson in an open boat, and was detained on the river several hours. This severe exposure brought on an attack of sickness, which for a short time confined him to his bed. The steam frigate, then almost ready for her engines, occasioned him great anxiety at the time, and before he had fairly recovered his strength he went to the ship-yard to give some directions to the workmen employed on her, and thus exposed himself again to the inclemency of the weather. In a few days his indisposition prostrated him again, and, growing rapidly worse, he died on the 24th of February, 1815, at the age of fifty years. His death was universally regarded as a national calamity, and appropriate honors were paid to his memory by the General Government and by many of the State and municipal governments of the Union. He was buried from his residence, No. 1 State Street, on the 25th of February, and his body was placed in the vault of the Livingston family, in Trinity church-yard.

He left a widow and four children. By the terms of his will he bequeathed to his wife an income of nine thousand dollars a year, and five hundred dollars to each of his children until they were twelve years old, after which they were each to receive one thousand dollars a year until they should attain the age of twenty-one years.

In person, Fulton was tall and handsome. His manner was polished, cordial, and winning. He made friends rapidly, and never failed in his efforts to enlist capital and influence in support of his schemes. He was manly, fearless, and independent in character, and joined to a perfect integrity a patience and indomitable resolution which enabled him to bear up under every disappointment, and which won him in the end a glorious success. His name and fame will always be dear to his countrymen, for while we can not claim that he was (nor did he ever assume to be) the inventor of steam navigation, or even the inventor of the means of such navigation, we do claim for him the honor of being the first man to cross the gulf which lies between experiment and achievement, the man whose skill and perseverance first conquered the difficulties which had baffled so many others, and made steam navigation both practicable and profitable. The Committee of the London Exhibition of 1851 gave utterance in their report to a declaration which places his fame beyond assault, as follows:

"Many persons, in various countries, claim the honor of having first invented small boats propelled by steam, but it is to the undaunted perseverance and exertions of the American Fulton that is due the everlasting honor of having produced this revolution, both in naval architecture and navigation."

CHAPTER XIV.

CHARLES GOODYEAR.

IN the year 1735, a party of astronomers, sent by the French Government to Peru for purposes of scientific investigation, discovered a curious tree growing in that country, the like of which no European had ever seen before. It grew to a considerable size, and yielded a peculiar sap or gum. It was the custom of the natives to make several incisions in each tree with an ax, in the morning, and to place under each incision a cup or jar made of soft clay. Late in the afternoon, the fluid thus obtained was collected in a large clay vessel, each incision yielding about a gill of sap per day. This process was repeated for several days in succession, until the tree had been thoroughly drained. This sap was simply a species of liquid gum, which, though clear and colorless in its native state, had the property of becoming hard and tough when exposed to the sun or artificial heat. It was used by the natives for the manufacture of a few rude and simple articles, by a process similar to that by which the old-fashioned "tallow-dip" candles were made. It was poured over a pattern of clay or a wooden mold or last covered with clay, and successive coatings were applied as fast as the former ones dried, until the article had attained the desired thickness, the whole taking the shape of the mold over which the gum was poured. As the layers were applied, their drying was hastened by exposure to the heat and smoke of a fire, the latter giving to the gum a dark-black hue. Dried without exposure to the smoke, or by the sun alone, the gum became white within and yellowish-brown without. The drying process required several days, and during its progress the gum was ornamented with characters or lines made with a stick. When it was completed, the clay mold was broken to pieces and shaken out of the opening. The natives in this manner made a species of rough, clumsy shoe, and an equally rough bottle. In some parts of South America, the natives make it a rule to present their guests with one of these bottles, furnished with a hollow stem, which serves as a syringe for squirting water into the mouth in order to cleanse it after eating. The articles thus made were liable to become stiff and unmanageable in cold weather, and soft and sticky in warm. The French astronomers, upon their return to their own country, were quick to call attention to this remarkable gum, which was afterward discovered in Cayenne by Trismau, in 1751. At present it is found in large quantities in various parts of South America, but the chief supplies used in commerce are produced in the province of Para, which lies south of the equator, in Brazil. It is also grown largely in the East Indies, vast and inexhaustible forests of the trees which yield it being found in Assam, beyond the Ganges, although the quality can not compare with that of the South American article.

This substance, variously known as cachuchu, caoutchouc, gum elastic, and India-rubber, was first introduced into Europe in 1730, where it was regarded merely as a curiosity, useful for erasing pencil marks, but valueless for any practical use. Ships from South America brought it over as ballast, but it was not until ninety years after its first appearance in Europe that any effort was made to utilize it. About the year 1820 it began to be used in France in the manufacture of suspenders and garters, India-rubber threads being mixed with the materials used in weaving those articles. It was also used in blacking and varnish, and some years later, Mackintosh brought it into prominent notice by using it in his famous water-proof coats, which were made by spreading a layer of the gum between two pieces of cloth. The gum was thus protected from the air, and preserved from injury.

Up to this time, it was almost an unknown article in the United States, but in 1820 a pair of India-rubber shoes were exhibited in Boston. Even then they were regarded as merely a curiosity, and were covered with gilt foil to hide their natural ugliness. In 1823, a merchant, engaged in the South American trade, imported five hundred pairs from the Para district. He had no difficulty in disposing of them; and so great was the favor with which they were received, that in a few years the annual importation of India-rubber shoes amounted to five hundred thousand pairs. It had become a matter of fashion to wear these shoes, and no person's toilet was complete in wet weather unless the feet were incased in them; yet they were terribly rough and clumsy. They had scarcely any shape to them, and were not to be depended on in winter or summer. In the cold season they froze so hard that they could be used only after being thawed by the fire, and in summer they could be preserved only by keeping them on ice; and if, during the thawing process, they were placed too near the fire, there was danger that they would melt into a shapeless and useless mass. They cost from three to five dollars per pair, which was very high for an article so perishable in its nature.

The great popularity of India-rubber induced Mr. E. M.

Chaffee, of Boston, the foreman of a patent leather factory in that city, to attempt to apply the new substance to some of the uses to which patent leather was then put. His hope was that, by spreading the liquid gum upon cloth, he could produce an article which, while possessing the durability and flexibility of patent leather, would also be water-proof. His experiments extended over a period of several months, during which time he kept his plan a secret. He dissolved a pound of the gum in three quarts of spirits of turpentine, and added to the mixture enough lamp-black to produce a bright black color, and was so well satisfied with his compound, that he felt sure that the only thing necessary to his entire success was a machine for spreading it properly on the cloth. Like a true son of New England, he soon overcame this difficulty by inventing the desired machine. His compound was spread on the cloth, and dried in the sun, producing a hard, smooth surface, and one sufficiently flexible to be twisted into any shape without cracking. Mr. Chaffee was now sure that he had mastered the difficulty. Taking a few capitalists into his confidence, he succeeded so well in convincing them of the excellence of his invention, that in February, 1833, a company, called the "Roxbury India-rubber Company," was organized, with a capital of thirty thousand dollars. In three years this sum was increased to four hundred thousand dollars. The new company manufactured India-rubber cloth according to Mr. Chaffee's process, and from it made wagon-covers, piano-covers, caps, coats, and a few other articles, and, in a little while, added to their list of products shoes without fiber. They had no difficulty in disposing of their stock. Every body had taken the "India-rubber fever," as the excitement caused by Mr. Chaffee's discovery was called; and so high were the hopes of the public raised by it, that buyers were found in abundance whenever the bonds of the numerous India-rubber companies were offered for sale. The extraordinary success of the Roxbury Company led to the establishment of similar enterprises at Boston, Framingham, Salem, Lynn, Chelsea, Troy, and Staten Island. The Roxbury Company could not supply the demand for its articles, and the others appeared to have as much business as they could attend to. Apparently, they were all on the high road to wealth.

Their prosperity was only fictitious, however, and a day of fearful disaster was pending over them. The bulk of the goods produced in 1833 and 1834 had been manufactured in the cold weather, and the greater part of them had succumbed to the heat of the ensuing summer. The shoes had melted to a soft mass, and the caps, wagon-covers, and coats had become sticky and useless in summer, and rigid in the cold of winter. In some cases the articles had borne the test of one year's use, but the second summer had ruined them. To make the matter worse, they emitted an odor so offensive that it was necessary to bury them in the ground to get rid of the smell. Twenty thousand dollars' worth were thrown back on the hands of the Roxbury Company alone, and the directors were appalled by the ruin which threatened them. It was useless for them to go on manufacturing goods which might prove worthless at any moment; and, as their capital was already taxed to its utmost, it was plain that unless a better process should be speedily discovered, they must become involved in irretrievable disaster. Their efforts were unavailing, however. No better process was found, and the disgust of the public with their goods was soon general and unmitigable. India-rubber stock fell rapidly, and by the end of the year 1836 there was not a solvent company in the Union. The loss of the stockholders was complete, and amounted in the aggregate to two millions of dollars. People came to detest the very name of India-rubber, since it reminded them only of blighted hopes and heavy losses.

Before the final disaster, however, it chanced that a bankrupt merchant of Philadelphia, being one day in New York on business, was led by curiosity to visit the salesroom of the agency of the Roxbury Company in that city. His visit resulted in the purchase of a life-preserver, which he took home with him for the purpose of examining it. Subjecting it to a careful investigation, he discovered a defect in the valve used for inflating it, and promptly devised a simpler and better apparatus.

This man, afterward so famous in the history of India-rubber manufacture, was CHARLES GOODYEAR. He was born at New Haven, Connecticut, on the 29th of December, 1800. He attended a public school during his boyhood, thus acquiring a limited education. When quite a youth, he removed with his family to Philadelphia, where his father entered into the hardware business. Upon coming of age, he was admitted to partnership with his father and one of his brothers, the style of the firm being A. Goodyear & Sons. The house was extensively engaged in the manufacture of hardware, and among the other articles which they introduced was a light hay-fork, made of spring steel, which gradually took the place of the heavy wrought iron implement formerly in general use among the farmers. It required a large outlay and a great deal of time to introduce this fork, but, once in use, it rapidly drove the old one out of the market, and proved a source of considerable profit to its inventor. The prosperity of the house, however, soon began to wane, and it was brought to bankruptcy by the crisis of 1836.

Mr. Goodyear's attention had for some time been attracted to the wonderful apparent success of the India-rubber companies of the country, and he was hopeful that his improvement in the inflating apparatus of the life-preserver would bring him the means of partially extricating himself from his difficulties. Repairing to New York, he called on the agent of the Roxbury Company, and explaining his invention to him, offered to sell it to the company. The agent was struck with the skill displayed in the improvement of Mr. Goodyear, but, instead of offering to buy it, astounded the inventor by informing him of the real state of the India-rubber trade of the country. He urged Mr. Goodyear to exert his inventive skill to discover some means of imparting durability to India-rubber goods, and assured him that if he could discover a process which would secure that end, the various companies of the United States would eagerly buy it at his own price. He explained to him the process then in use, and pointed out its imperfections. Mr. Goodyear listened carefully to his statements, forgot all about his disappointment in failing to sell his improved inflating apparatus, and went home firmly convinced that he had found his true mission in life. In after years, when success had crowned his labors, he modestly referred to this period of his career in language the substance of which is thus recorded:

"From the time that his attention was first given to the subject, a strong and abiding impression was made upon his mind that an object so desirable and important, and so necessary to man's comfort, as the making of gum elastic available to his use was most certainly placed within his reach. Having this presentiment, of which he could not divest himself under the most trying adversity, he was stimulated with the hope of ultimately attaining this object. Beyond this, he would refer the whole to the great Creator, who directs the operations of the mind to the development of properties of matter, in his own way, at the time when they are specially needed, influencing some mind for every work or calling."

There was something sublime in the attitude of this one man, now feeble in health, the only dependence of a young family, a bankrupt in business, starting out to seek success in a field in which so many had found only ruin. He was convinced in his own mind that he would master the secret, while his friends were equally sure that he would but increase his difficulties. The firm of which he had been a member had surrendered all their property to their creditors; but they still owed thirty thousand dollars, and immediately upon his return from New York, after his visit to the agent of the Roxbury Company, he was arrested for debt, and though not actually thrown in jail, was compelled to take up his residence within prison limits.

Strong in the conviction before named, that he was the man of all others to discover the secret of controlling India-rubber, he at once began his experiments. This was in the winter of 1834–35. The gum had fallen in price to five cents per pound, and, poor as he was, he had no difficulty in procuring a sufficient quantity to begin with. By melting and working the gum thoroughly, and by rolling it upon a stone table with a rolling-pin, he succeeded in producing sheets of India-rubber which seemed to him to possess the properties which those of Mr. Chaffee had lacked. He explained his process to a friend, who, becoming interested in it, loaned him the money to manufacture a number of shoes, which at first seemed all that could be desired. Fearful, however, of meeting the fate which had befallen the Roxbury Company, Mr. Goodyear put his shoes away until the next summer, to ascertain whether they would bear the heat. His doubts were more than realized. The warm weather completely ruined them, reducing them to a mass of so offensive an odor that he was glad to throw them away.

The friend of the inventor was thoroughly disheartened by this failure, and refused to have any thing more to do with Goodyear's schemes; but the latter, though much disappointed, did not despair. He set to work to discover the cause of his failure, and traced it, as he supposed, to the mixing of the gum with the turpentine and lamp-black. Having procured some barrels of the gum in its native liquid state, he spread it on cloth without smoking it or mixing it with any thing else. He succeeded in producing a very handsome white rubber cloth, but it was one that became soft and sticky as quickly as the other had done.

It now occurred to him that there must be some mineral substance which, mixed with the gum, would render it durable, and he began to experiment with almost every substance that he could lay his hands on. All these proved total failures, with the exception of magnesia. By mixing half a pound of magnesia with a pound of the gum, he produced a compound much whiter than the pure gum, and one which was at first as firm and flexible as leather. He made book-covers and piano-covers out of it, and for a time it seemed that he had discovered the longed-for secret; but in a month his pretty product was ruined. The heat caused it to soften; then fermentation set in, and, finally, it became as hard and brittle as thin glass.

His friends, who had aided him at first, now turned from him coldly, regarding him as a dreamer; and his own stock of money was exhausted. In his extremity he was forced to pawn all his own valuables, and even some of the trinkets of his wife. In spite of this, he felt sure that he was on the road to success, and that he would very soon be enabled to rise above his present difficulties, and win both fame and fortune. He was obliged for the time, however, to remove his family to the country, depositing with his landlord, as security for the payment of the first quarter's rent, some linen which had been spun by his wife, and which he was never able to redeem. Having settled his family in the country, he set out for New York, where he hoped to find some one willing to aid him in extending his researches still further.

Arrived in the great city, he found two old acquaintances, to whom he stated his plans and his hopes. One of them offered him the use of a room in Gold Street, as a laboratory, and the other, who was a druggist, agreed to let him have such chemicals as he needed on credit. He now proceeded to boil the gum, mixed with magnesia, in quicklime and water, and, as the result, obtained sheets of his compound whose firmness and smoothness of surface won them a medal at the fair of the American Institute in 1835. He seemed now on the point of success, and readily disposed of all the sheets he could manufacture. The newspapers spoke highly of his invention, for which he obtained a patent; and he was about to endeavor to enlist some persons of means in its manufacture on a large scale, when, to his dismay, he discovered that a single drop of the weakest acid, such as the juice of an apple, or diluted vinegar, would utterly destroy the influence of the lime in the compound, and reduce it to the old sticky substance that had baffled him so often.

His next step was to mix quicklime with the gum. In order to work the compound thoroughly, he used to carry the vessel containing it, on his shoulder, to a place three miles distant from his laboratory, where he had the use of horse power. The lime, however, utterly destroyed the gum, and nothing came of this experiment.

The discovery which followed was the result of accident, and brought him on the very threshold of success, yet did not entirely conquer his difficulties. He was an ardent lover of the beautiful, and it was a constant effort with him to render his productions as attractive to the eye as possible. Upon one occasion, while bronzing a piece of rubber cloth, he applied aqua fortis to it for the purpose of removing the bronze from a certain part. It took away the bronze as he had designed, but it also discolored the cloth to such a degree that he supposed it ruined, and threw it away. A day or two later, he chanced to remember that he had not examined very closely into the effect of the aqua fortis upon the rubber, and thereupon instituted a search for it. He was fortunate enough to find it, and was overjoyed to discover that the rubber had undergone a remarkable change, and that the effect of the acid was to harden it to such an extent that it would now stand a degree of heat which would have melted it before. When the reader remembers that aqua fortis is a compound two-fifths of which is sulphuric acid, he will understand that Mr. Goodyear had almost mastered the secret of vulcanizing rubber. He does not appear, however, to have known the true nature of aqua fortis, and called his process the "curing" of India-rubber by the use of that acid.

The "cured" India-rubber was subjected to many tests, and passed through them successfully, thus demonstrating its adaptability to many important uses. Mr. Goodyear readily obtained a patent for his process, and a partner with a large capital was found ready to aid him. He hired the old India-rubber works on Staten Island, and opened a salesroom in Broadway. He was thrown back for six weeks at this important time by an accident, which happened to him while experimenting with his fabrics, and which came near causing his death. Just as he was recovering and preparing to commence the manufacture of his goods on a large scale, the terrible commercial crisis of 1836 swept over the country, and, by destroying his partner's fortune at one blow, reduced Goodyear to absolute beggary. His family had joined him in New York, and he was entirely without the means of supporting them. As the only resource at hand, he decided to pawn an article of value, one of the few which he possessed, in order to raise money enough to procure one day's supply of provisions. At the very door of the pawnbroker's shop he met one of his creditors, who kindly asked if he could be of any further assistance to him. Weak with hunger, and overcome by the generosity of his friend, the poor man burst into tears, and replied that, as his family was on the point of starvation, a loan of fifteen dollars would greatly oblige him. The money was given him on the spot, and the necessity for visiting the pawnbroker averted for several days longer. Still he was a frequent visitor to that individual during the year; and thus, one by one, the relics of his better days disappeared. Another friend loaned him one hundred dollars, which enabled him to remove his family to Staten Island, in the neighborhood of the abandoned rubber works, which the owners gave him permission to use as far as he could. He contrived in this way to manufacture enough of his "cured" cloth, which sold readily, to enable him to keep his family from starvation. He made repeated efforts to induce capitalists to come to the factory and see his samples and the process by which they were made, but no one would venture near him. There had been money enough lost in such experiments, they said, and they were determined to risk no more.

Indeed, in all the broad land there was but one man who had the slightest hope of accomplishing any thing with India-rubber, and that one was Charles Goodyear. His friends regarded him as a monomaniac. He not only manufactured his cloth, but even dressed in clothes made of it, wearing it for the purpose of testing its durability, as well as of advertising it. He was certainly an odd figure, and in his appearance justified the remark of one of his friends, who, upon being asked how Mr. Goodyear could be recognized, replied: "If you see a man with an India-rubber coat on, India-rubber shoes, an India-rubber cap, and in his pocket an India-rubber purse, with not a cent in it, that is Goodyear."

In September, 1836, a new gleam of hope lit up his pathway. A friend having loaned him a small sum of money, he went to Roxbury, taking with him some of his best specimens. Although the Roxbury Company had gone down with such a fearful crash, Mr. Chaffee, the inventor of the process in this country, was still firm in his faith that India-rubber would at some future time justify the expectations of its earliest friends. He welcomed Mr. Goodyear cordially, and allowed him to use the abandoned works of the company for his experiments. The result was that Goodyear succeeded in making shoes and cloths of India-rubber of a quality so much better than any that had yet been seen in America, that the hopes of the friends of India-rubber were raised to a high point. Offers to purchase rights for certain portions of the country came in rapidly, and by the sale of them Goodyear realized between four and five thousand dollars. He was now able to bring his family to Roxbury, and for the time fortune seemed to smile upon him.

His success was but temporary, however. He obtained an order from the General Government for one hundred and fifty India-rubber mail-bags, which he succeeded in producing, and as they came out smooth, highly polished, hard, well shaped, and entirely impervious to moisture, he was delighted, and summoned his friends to inspect and admire them. All who saw them pronounced them a perfect success; but, alas! in a single month they began to soften and ferment, and finally became useless. Poor Goodyear's hopes were dashed to the ground. It was found that the aqua fortis merely "cured" the surface of the material, and that only very thin cloth made in this way was durable. His other goods began to prove worthless, and his promising business came to a sudden and disastrous end. All his possessions were seized and sold for debt, and once more he was reduced to poverty. His position was even worse than before, for his family had increased in size, and his aged father also had become dependent upon him for support.

Friends, relatives, and even his wife, all demanded that he should abandon his empty dreams, and turn his attention to something that would yield a support to his family. Four years of constant failure, added to the unfortunate experience of those who had preceded him, ought to convince him, they said, that he was hoping against hope. Hitherto his conduct, they said, had been absurd, though they admitted that he was to some extent excused for it by his partial success; but to persist in it would now be criminal. The inventor was driven to despair, and being a man of tender feelings and ardently devoted to his family, might have yielded to them had he not felt that he was nearer than ever to the discovery of the secret that had eluded him so long.

Just before the failure of his mail-bags had brought ruin upon him, he had taken into his employ a man named Nathaniel Hayward, who had been the foreman of the old Roxbury works, and who was still in charge of them when Goodyear came to Roxbury, making a few rubber articles on his own account. He hardened his compound by mixing a little powdered sulphur with the gum, or by sprinkling sulphur on the rubber cloth, and drying it in the sun. He declared that the process had been revealed to him in a dream, but could give no further account of it. Goodyear was astonished to find that the sulphur cured the India-rubber as thoroughly as the aqua fortis, the principal objection being that the sulphurous odor of the goods was frightful in hot weather. Hayward's process was really the same as that employed by Goodyear, the "curing" of the India-rubber being due in each case to the agency of sulphur, the principal difference between them being that Hayward's goods were dried by the sun, and Goodyear's with nitric acid. Hayward set so small a value upon his discovery that he had readily sold it to his new employer.

Goodyear felt that he had now all but conquered his difficulties. It was plain that sulphur was the great controller of India-rubber, for he had proved that when applied to thin cloth it would render it available for most purposes. The problem that now remained was how to mix sulphur and the gum in a mass, so that every part of the rubber should be subjected to the agency of the sulphur. He experimented for weeks and months with the most intense eagerness, but the mystery completely baffled him. His friends urged him to go to work to do something for his family, but he could not turn back. The goal was almost in sight, and he felt that he would be false to his mission were he to abandon his labors now. To the world he seemed a crack-brained dreamer, and some there were who, seeing the distress of his family, did not hesitate to apply still harsher names to him; but to the Great Eye that reads all hearts, how different did this man appear! It saw the anguish that wrung the heart of Charles Goodyear, and knew the more than heroic firmness with which, in the midst of his poverty and suffering, he agonized for the great discovery. Had it been merely wealth that he was working for, doubtless he would have turned back and sought

AN AMAZING REVELATION

some other means of obtaining it; but he sought more. He was striving for the good of his fellow-men, and ambitious of becoming a benefactor of the race. He felt that he had a mission to fulfill, and no one else could perform it.

He was right. A still greater success was about to crown his labors, but in a manner far different from his expectations. His experiments had developed nothing; chance was to make the revelation. It was in the spring of 1839 that this revelation came to him, and in the following manner: Standing before a stove in a store at Woburn, Massachusetts, he was explaining to some acquaintances the properties of a piece of sulphur-cured India-rubber which he held in his hand. They listened to him good-naturedly, but with evident incredulity, when suddenly he dropped the rubber on the stove, which was red hot. His old cloths would have melted instantly from contact with such heat; but, to his surprise, this piece underwent no such change. In amazement, he examined it, and found that while it had charred or shriveled, like leather, it had not softened at all. The bystanders attached no importance to this phenomenon, but to him it was a revelation. He renewed his experiments with enthusiasm, and in a little while established the facts that India-rubber, when mixed with sulphur and exposed to a certain degree of heat for a certain time, would not melt or even soften at any degree of heat, that it would only char at two hundred and eighty degrees, and that it would not stiffen from exposure to any degree of cold. The difficulty now consisted in finding out the exact degree of heat necessary for the perfection of the rubber, and the exact length of time required for the heating.

He made this discovery in his darkest days; when, in fact, he was in constant danger of arrest for debt, having already been a frequent inmate of the debtor's prison. He was in the depths of bitter poverty, and in such feeble health that he was constantly haunted by the fear of dying before he had perfected his discovery—before he had fulfilled his mission. His poverty was a greater drawback to him than ever before. He needed an apparatus for producing a high and uniform heat for his experiments, and he was unable to obtain it. He used to bake his compound in his wife's bread oven, and steam it over the spout of her tea-kettle, and to press the kitchen fire into his service as far as it would go. When this failed, he would go to the shops in the vicinity of Woburn, and beg to be allowed to use the ovens and boilers after working hours were over. The workmen regarded him as a lunatic, but were too good-natured to deny him the request. Finally, he induced a bricklayer to make him an oven, and paid him in mason's aprons of India-rubber. The oven was a failure. Sometimes it would turn out pieces of perfectly vulcanized cloth, and again the goods would be charred and ruined. Goodyear was in despair.

All this time he lived on the charity of his friends. His neighbors pretended to lend him money, but in reality gave him the means of keeping his family from starvation. He has declared that all the while he felt sure he would, before long, be able to pay them back, but they declared with equal emphasis that, at that time, they never expected to witness his success. He was yellow and shriveled in face, with a gaunt, lean figure, and his habit of wearing an India-rubber coat, which was charred and blackened from his frequent experiments with it, gave him a wild and singular appearance. People shook their heads solemnly when they saw him, and said that the madhouse was the proper place for him.

The winter of 1839–40 was long and severe. At the opening of the season, Mr. Goodyear received a letter from a house in Paris, making him a handsome offer for the use of his process of curing India-rubber with aqua fortis. Here was a chance for him to rise out of his misery. A year before he would have closed with the offer, but since then he had discovered the effects of sulphur and heat on his compound, and had passed far beyond the aqua fortis stage. Disappointment and want had not warped his honesty, and he at once declined to enter into any arrangements with the French house, informing them that although the process they desired to purchase was a valuable one, it was about to be entirely replaced by another which he was then on the point of perfecting, and which he would gladly sell them as soon as he had completed it. His friends declared that he was mad to refuse such an offer; but he replied that nothing would induce him to sell a process which he knew was about to be rendered worthless by still greater discoveries.

A few weeks later, a terrible snow-storm passed over the land, one of the worst that New England has ever known, and in the midst of it Goodyear made the appalling discovery that he had not a particle of fuel or a mouthful of food in the house. He was ill enough to be in bed himself, and his purse was entirely empty. It was a terrible position, made worse, too, by the fact that his friends who had formerly aided him had turned from him, vexed with his pertinacity, and abandoned him to his fate. In his despair, he bethought him of a mere acquaintance who lived several miles from his cottage, and who but a few days before had spoken to him with more of kindness than he had received of late. This gentleman, he thought, would aid him in his distress, if he could but reach his house, but in such a snow the journey seemed hopeless to a man in his feeble health. Still the effort must be made. Nerved by despair, he set out, and pushed his way resolutely through the heavy drifts. The way was long, and it seemed to him that he would never accomplish it. Often he fell prostrate on the snow, almost fainting with fatigue and hunger, and again he would sit down wearily in the road, feeling that he would gladly die if his discovery were but completed. At length, however, he reached the end of his journey, and fortunately found his acquaintance at home. To this gentleman he told the story of his discovery, his hopes, his struggles, and his present sufferings, and implored him to aid him. Mr. Coolidge*—for such was the gentleman's name—listened to him kindly, and after expressing the warmest sympathy for him, loaned him money enough to support his family during the severe weather, and to enable him to continue his experiments.

"Seeing no prospect of success in Massachusetts, he now resolved to make a desperate effort to get to New York, feeling confident that the specimens he could take with him would convince some one of the superiority of his new method. He was beginning to understand the causes of his many failures, but he saw clearly that his compound could not be worked with certainty without expensive apparatus. It was a very delicate operation, requiring exactness and promptitude. The conditions upon which success depended were numerous, and the failure of one spoiled all. . . It cost him thousands of failures to learn that a little acid in his sulphur caused the blistering; that his compound must be heated almost immediately after being mixed, or it would never vulcanize; that a portion of white lead in the compound greatly facilitated the operation and improved the result; and when he had learned these facts, it still required costly and laborious experiments to devise the best methods of compounding his ingredients, the best proportions, the best mode of heating, the proper duration of the heating,

* O. B. Coolidge, of Woburn.

and the various useful effects that could be produced by varying the proportions and the degree of heat. He tells us that many times when, by exhausting every resource, he had prepared a quantity of his compound for heating, it was spoiled because he could not, with his inadequate apparatus, apply the heat soon enough.

"To New York, then, he directed his thoughts. Merely to get there cost him a severer and a longer effort than men in general are capable of making. First he walked to Boston, ten miles distant, where he hoped to borrow from an old acquaintance fifty dollars, with which to provide for his family and pay his fare to New York. He not only failed in this, but he was arrested for debt and thrown into prison. Even in prison, while his father was negotiating to procure his release, he labored to interest men of capital in his discovery, and made proposals for founding a factory in Boston. Having obtained his liberty, he went to a hotel, and spent a week in vain efforts to effect a small loan. Saturday night came, and with it his hotel bill, which he had no means of discharging. In an agony of shame and anxiety, he went to a friend and entreated the sum of five dollars to enable him to return home. He was met with a point blank refusal. In the deepest dejection, he walked the streets till late in the night, and strayed at length, almost beside himself, to Cambridge, where he ventured to call upon a friend and ask shelter for the night. He was hospitably entertained, and the next morning walked wearily home, penniless and despairing. At the door of his house a member of his family met him with the news that his youngest child, two years old, whom he had left in perfect health, was dying. In a few hours he had in his house a dead child, but not the means of burying it, and five living dependents without a morsel of food to give them. A storekeeper near by had promised to supply the family, but, discouraged by the unforeseen length of the father's absence, he had that day refused to trust them further. In these terrible circumstances, he applied to a friend upon whose generosity he knew he could rely, one who never failed him. He received in reply a letter of severe and cutting reproach, inclosing seven dollars, which his friend explained was given only out of pity for his innocent and suffering family. A stranger who chanced to be present when this letter arrived sent them a barrel of flour—a timely and blessed relief. The next day the family followed on foot the remains of the little child to the grave."

He had now reached the lowest ebb of his misery, and a brighter day was in store for him. Obtaining fifty dollars from a relative, he went to New York, where he succeeded in interesting in his discovery two brothers, William and Emory Rider. They agreed to advance him a certain sum to support his family and continue his experiments. By means of this aid he was enabled to keep his family from want in the future, and from that time his experiments never flagged. Before entire success crowned his efforts, the brothers Rider failed; but he had advanced his experiments so greatly that his brother-in-law, William De Forrest, a rich woolen manufacturer, came to his support, and supplied him with the means to go on with his labors. Mr. De Forrest's total advances amounted to forty-six thousand dollars, from which fact the reader may gain some idea of the obstacles overcome by Goodyear in this last stage of his invention.

The prize for which he had labored so long and so heroically was secured at last, and in 1844, ten years after the commencement of his experiments, he was able to produce perfectly vulcanized India-rubber with expedition and economy, and, above all, with certainty. He had won a success which added a new material to art and commerce, and one which could be applied in a thousand different ways, and all of them useful to man. But great as his success was, he was not satisfied with it. To the end of his life his constant effort was to improve his invention, and apply it to new uses. He had an unlimited faith in its adaptability, believing that there was scarcely any article of general use that could not be made of it. Upon one occasion he read in a newspaper that twenty persons perished every hour by drowning. The statement impressed him deeply, and his wife noticed that for several nights he scarcely slept at all. "Try to compose yourself, and sleep," she said to him. "Sleep!" he exclaimed, "how can I sleep when twenty human beings are drowning every hour, and I am the man that can save them?" And at this time it was his constant endeavor to invent some article of India-rubber which could be easily carried by travelers, and which would render it impossible for them to sink in water.

Having brought his process to a successful completion in this country, and obtained patents for it, he went to Europe to secure similar protections in the principal countries of the Old World. "The French laws require that the patentee shall put and keep his invention in public use in France within two years from its date. Goodyear had, at great inconvenience and expense, endeavored to comply with this and with all other requirements of the French laws, and thought he had effectually done so; but the courts of France decided that he had not in every particular complied with the strict requisitions of the law, and that, therefore, his patent in France had become void. In England he was still more unfortunate. Having sent specimens of vulcanized fabrics to Charles Mackintosh & Co., in 1842, and having opened with them a negotiation for the sale of the secret of the invention or discovery, one of the partners of that firm, named Thomas Hancock, availing himself, as he admits, of the hints and opportunities thus presented to him, rediscovered, as he affirms, the process of vulcanization, and described it in a patent for England, which was enrolled on May 21, 1844, *about five weeks after* the specification and publication of the discovery to the world by Goodyear's patent for vulcanization in France. And the patent of Hancock, held good according to a peculiarity of English law, thus superseded Goodyear's English patent for vulcanization, which bore date a few days later. Goodyear, however, obtained the great council medal of the exhibition of all nations at London, the grand medal of the world's exhibition at Paris, and the ribbon of the Legion of Honor, presented by Napoleon III."

In his own country, Mr. Goodyear was scarcely less unfortunate. His patents were infringed and violated by others, even after the decision of the courts seemed to place his rights beyond question. He was too thoroughly the inventor and too little the man of business to protect himself from the robberies of the wretches who plundered him of the profits of his invention. It is said that his inability to manage sharp transactions made him the victim of many who held nominally fair business relations with him. The United States Commissioner of Patents, in 1858, thus spoke of his losses:

"No inventor, probably, has ever been so harassed, so trampled upon, so plundered by that sordid and licentious class of infringers known in the parlance of the world, with no exaggeration of phrase, as 'pirates.' The spoliation of their incessant guerrilla warfare upon his defenseless rights have, unquestionably, amounted to millions."

Failing to accomplish any thing in Europe, Mr. Goodyear returned to this country, and continued his labors. His health, never strong, gave way under the continued strain, and he died in New York in July, 1860, in the sixtieth year of his age, completely worn out. Notwithstanding his great invention—an invention which has made millions for those engaged in its manufacture—he died insolvent, and left his family heavily in debt. A few years after his death an effort was made to procure from Congress a further seven years' extension of his patent for vulcanization, for the benefit of his family and his creditors. The men who had trampled his rights under foot while living were resolved, however, that he should not have justice done him in death; and, through their influence, that august body, in strange contrast with its usual lavish generosity in the matter of land grants and the like, coldly declined to do any thing for the family of the man to whom civilization owes so much, and the effort proved abortive.

But, though unfortunate in a pecuniary sense, though he died without freeing himself from the embarrassments which haunted him through life, there can be no question that Charles Goodyear richly merits the place which we have given him in this gallery of "Our Self-made Men;" not only on account of the great merit and usefulness of his discovery or invention, but because that invention has been the source of many a "great fortune" to others, as it might, indeed, have been to him, had his rights been respected, or properly protected when infringed. It is sad to reflect that he died poor who has given wealth to so many, and accomplished results so beneficent to mankind. Yet he did not fail entirely of his reward in life; he lived to see his invention give rise to large factories in the United States, and in England, France, and Germany, which employ sixty thousand operatives, and produce over five hundred different kinds of articles, to the amount of eight millions of dollars annually. He lived to see boots and shoes, clothing, caps, hats, articles of commerce and of pleasure, mechanical, scientific, and surgical instruments, toys, belting for machinery, packing for the steam-engine, and many other articles now in common use, made of the material, the discovery and perfection of which cost him long and sorrowful years of toil. He lived to hear his name mentioned by millions as one of their greatest benefactors; to know that he had conferred upon the world benefits of which those who had robbed him could not deprive his fellow-men; and to feel that he had at length accomplished his mission—a mission which has been productive of good alone.

"THE MADHOUSE IS THE PROPER PLACE FOR HIM."

CHAPTER XV.

ELI WHITNEY.

AT the close of the Revolution the States of South Carolina and Georgia presented large tracts of land to the gallant General Nathaniel Greene, to whose genius they were indebted for their relief from British tyranny. Soon after this grant was made, General Greene removed his family to Mulberry Grove, a fine plantation on the Georgia side of the Savannah River. Here he died in 1786, from sunstroke, but his family continued to reside on the place. The mansion of Mrs. Greene was noted for its hospitality, and was frequently filled with guests who came to pay their respects to the widow of the most brilliant and best trusted subordinate of the immortal Washington.

To this mansion there came one day, in the year 1792, ELI WHITNEY, then a young man recently from New England. He was a native of Westborough, Massachusetts, where he was born on the 8th of December, 1765. Of his youth but little is known, save that he was gifted with unusual mechanical genius, the employment of which enabled him to overcome some of the difficulties incident to his poverty, and to acquire the means of obtaining a good common school education. Adding to this the labors of a teacher, he earned a sum sufficient to carry him through Yale College, where he was graduated in the summer of 1792, a few months before his arrival in Georgia. He had come South to accept the offer of a situation as teacher, but the place had been filled before his arrival, and, being without friends in that section, he sought employment from Mrs. Greene. Though pleased with his modesty and intelligence, that lady could not avail herself of his services as a tutor, but invited him to make her house his home as long as he should desire to remain in Georgia. He was sick in body and disheartened by his first failure, and gladly accepted her invitation. While her guest he made her a tambour frame of an improved pattern, and a number of ingenious toys for her children, which so delighted the good lady that she enthusiastically declared him capable of doing any thing.

Not long after Mr. Whitney's arrival at the plantation, Mrs. Greene was entertaining a number of visitors from the surrounding country, several planters of considerable wealth being among the number, when one of the guests turned the conversation upon the subject of cotton-raising, by declaring that he had met with such poor success that he was ready to abandon the undertaking. His trouble was not, he said, that cotton would not grow in his land, for it yielded an abundant return, but that the labor of clearing it from the seed was so enormous that he could not do more than pay expenses after selling it.

His case was simply one among a thousand. The far Southern States were admitted by every one to be admirably adapted to the cultivation of cotton, but, after it was grown and picked, the expense of cleaning it destroyed nearly all the profits of the transaction. The cleaning process was performed by hand, and it was as much as an able-bodied negro could do to clean one pound per day in this manner. Disheartened by this difficulty, which no one had yet been able to remove, the planters of the

South were seriously contemplating the entire abandonment of this portion of their industry, since it only involved them in debt. Their lands were heavily mortgaged, and general ruin seemed to threaten them. All felt that the invention of a machine for cleaning or ginning the cotton would not only remove their difficulties, but enable them to plant the green cotton-seed, from the use of which they were then almost entirely debarred, because, although more productive and of a better quality than the black, and adapted by nature to a much greater variety of climate, it was much more difficult to clean, and therefore less profitable to cultivate.

These facts were discussed in the conversation at Mrs. Greene's table, and it was suggested by one of the company that perhaps the very urgency of the case would induce some ingenious man to invent a machine which should solve the problem, and remove all the difficulties in the way.

"Is it a machine you want?" said Mrs. Greene, eagerly. "Then, gentlemen, you should apply to my young friend, Mr. Whitney; *he* can make any thing."

She at once sent for Whitney, and introduced him to her guests, who repeated to him the substance of their conversation, and urged him to undertake the invention of what was so much needed. The young man protested that he had never seen either a pod of cotton or a cotton-seed in his life, and was utterly incompetent for the task they proposed. In spite of this, however, his new acquaintances urged him to attempt it, and assured him that if successful his invention would make his fortune. Whitney would promise nothing more than to think of the matter, and the planters departed in the belief that nothing would come of their entreaties, and that the culture of cotton would languish until it should finally die out.

Whitney *did* think of the matter, and the result was that he decided to attempt the production of a machine which should clean cotton both expeditiously and cheaply. It was late in the season, and unginned cotton, or cotton from which the seeds had not been removed, was hard to procure. With considerable difficulty he succeeded in finding a few pounds on the wharf at Savannah, and at once securing his prize, he carried it home in his hands.

Mrs. Greene being confidentially informed of his plans, provided him with a room in the cellar of her house, where he could carry on his work in secret. All that winter he worked

WHITNEY WATCHING THE FIRST COTTON-GIN.

at it, with a patience and energy which could not fail of success. Many difficulties confronted him. To carry on his work successfully, he needed tools of a certain description, which were not to be had in Savannah, or even in Charleston, upon any terms. But when was the genius of a Yankee ever baffled by difficulties? Whitney's mechanical skill came to his aid, and he conquered this obstacle by manufacturing all the implements he needed. He wanted wire, but none was to be found, and he was compelled to make all that he used. A score or more of drawbacks presented themselves, and were overcome in this way, and all through the winter the young inventor applied himself with diligence to his task. The children and servants regarded him with the greatest curiosity. They heard him hammering and sawing in his room, the doors of which were always kept locked, and into which they were never allowed to enter. Mrs. Greene was kept fully informed of his progress. When sure of success, Whitney revealed the secret to a Mr. Miller, a gentleman of means, who consented to enter into a copartnership with him for the manufacture of the machines, after the completion of the model should have enabled Whitney to secure a patent for his invention.

Whitney had hoped to keep his work secret from all others, but this proved to be impossible. It became rumored about the country that the young man from New England, who was living at Mrs. Greene's, was engaged in inventing a machine which would clean cotton with the rapidity of thought, and the most intense eagerness was manifested to see the wonderful production, which every one felt would entirely revolutionize cotton culture in the South. Whitney endeavored to guard his invention from the public curiosity, but without success. Before he had completed his model, some scoundrels broke into the place containing it, and carried it off by night. He succeeded in recovering it, but the principle upon which it depended was made public, and before the model was completed and a patent secured, a number of machines based on his invention had been surreptitiously made, and were in operation.

In spite of this discouraging circumstance, Whitney brought his invention to perfection, and in the spring of 1793 set up his first cotton gin, under a shed on Mrs. Greene's plantation, and invited a number of the neighboring planters to witness its operation.

His machine was very simple, but none the less ingenious on that account. The cotton was placed in a trough, the bottom of which consisted of parallel rows of wire, placed like the bars in a grating, but so close together that the seed could not pass through them. Underneath this trough revolved an iron roller, armed with teeth formed of strong wires projecting from the roller, which passed between the wire bars, and, seizing the cotton, drew it through the bars and passed it behind the roller, where it was brushed off the wire teeth by means of a cylindrical brush. The seed, unable to pass through the bars, were left behind, and, completely stripped of the fiber, ran out in a stream through a spout at one end of the trough. It was found that the cotton thus ginned was cleaned thoroughly,* and far better than it could be done by hand, and that a single man, by this process, could clean as much as three hundred pounds in a day.

The spectators were delighted with Whitney's machine, and urged him to lose no time in putting it in the market. They predicted an unlimited success for it, and assured the inventor that it would not only make his own fortune, but also render cotton culture the source of wealth to the South. They did not exaggerate. As soon as it was made known to the public, Whitney's machine came into general use. Planters had no longer any thing to fear from the labor and expense of prepar-

* The cotton for which Whitney's machine accomplished so much, was the short staple, which is the principal product of the South. The Sea Island cotton could not be cleaued by it, on account of the length and delicacy of its fiber; and this species, for the want of some cheap and expeditious method of preparing it, has seldom been grown to a greater quantity than fifty thousand bags of three hundred pounds each. Consequently, it has always commanded a high price.

ing their great staple for market. Whitney's genius had swept away all their difficulties, and they reaped a golden harvest from it. They were enabled to send their cotton promptly and cheaply to market, where it brought good prices. With the money thus obtained they paid their debts, and increased their capacity for cultivation. Every year the area devoted to cotton-growing became more extended, and the prosperity of the South became greater and more durable. In 1793, the total export of cotton from the United States was ten thousand bales; in 1860, it was over four millions of bales. Hundreds of millions of dollars were brought into the South by this invention—so that it is no exaggeration to say that the remarkable prosperity enjoyed by the South at the commencement of our late civil war was due entirely to the genius of Eli Whitney. This opinion is fortified by the following remarks of Judge Johnson, uttered in a charge to the jury in a suit brought by Whitney, in Savannah, in 1807, to sustain the validity of his patent:

"With regard to the utility of this discovery . . . the whole interior of the Southern States was languishing, and its inhabitants emigrating for want of some object to engage their attention and employ their industry, when the invention of this machine at once opened views to them which set the whole country in active motion. From childhood to age it has presented to us a lucrative employment. Individuals who were depressed with poverty, and sunk in idleness, have suddenly risen to wealth and respectability. Our debts have been paid off, our capitals have increased, and our lands have trebled themselves in value. We can not express the weight of the obligation which the country owes to this invention. The extent of it can not now be seen."

Surely, the reader will exclaim, if such was the profit of this invention to the country at large, what a vast fortune must it have been to its inventor! Let us see. In May, 1793, Whitney and Miller went to Connecticut and established a factory for the construction of cotton gins. They were in possession of a patent which was supposed to pledge to them the protection of the United States. The demand for the machine was increasing every day, and it seemed that they would reap a golden harvest from it. They were disappointed. The machine was so simple that any competent mechanic could easily manufacture one after examining the model, and this temptation to dishonesty proved too strong for the morality of the cotton-growing community. In a short time there were hundreds of fraudulent machines at work in the South, made and sold in direct and open violation of Whitney's rights. In vain the inventor brought suit against those who infringed his patent. It was rare that a jury in a cotton State gave a verdict in his favor. In Georgia it was boldly asserted that Whitney was not the inventor of the cotton gin, but that some persons in Switzerland had invented something similar to it, and the substitution of teeth, cut in an iron plate, instead of wire, was claimed as superseding his invention. The Legislature of South Carolina granted him the beggarly sum of $50,000 for the use of his invention by the planters of that State; but it was only by going to law, and after several tedious and vexatious suits, that he was able to secure this sum. Tennessee agreed to allow him a percentage for the use of each saw for a certain period, but afterward repudiated her contract. The action of North Carolina forms the only bright page in this history of fraud and wrong. That State allowed him a percentage for the use of each saw for the term of five years, and promptly collected the money and paid it over to the patentee. For fourteen years Whitney continued to manufacture his machines, reaping absolutely no profit from his investments, and earning merely a bare support. During all this time his rights were systematically violated, suits were wrongfully decided against him by various Southern courts, and he was harassed and plundered on every side. America never presented a more shameful spectacle than was exhibited when the courts of the cotton-growing regions united with the piratical infringers of Whitney's rights in robbing their greatest benefactor. In 1807, Whitney's partner died, and his factory was destroyed by fire. In the same year his patent expired, and he sought its renewal from Congress. Here again he was met with the ingratitude of the cotton States. The Southern members, then all powerful in the Government, united in opposing the extension of his patent, and his petition was rejected. At the same time a report was industriously circulated that his machine injured the fiber of the cotton; but it is a significant fact that, although the planters insisted vehemently upon this assertion while Whitney was seeking an extension of his patent, not one of them discontinued the use of his machine, or sought to remedy the alleged defect.

Whitney, thoroughly disheartened, now abandoned the manufacture of cotton gins in disgust, wound up his affairs, and found himself a poor man. In spite of the far-reaching benefits of his invention, he had not realized one dollar above his expenses. He had given millions upon millions of dollars to the cotton-growing States, he had opened the way for the establishment of the vast cotton-spinning interests of his own country and Europe, and yet, after fourteen years of hard labor, he was a poor man, the victim of a wealthy, powerful, and, in his case, a dishonest class, who had robbed him of his rights and of the fortune he had so fairly earned. Truly, "wisdom is better than strength, but the poor man's wisdom is despised."

Whitney, however, was not the man to waste his time in repining. He abandoned his efforts to protect his cotton gin because of his conviction that there was not honesty enough in the country to sustain him in his rights, but he did not abandon with it the idea of winning fortune. He promptly turned his genius in another direction, and this time with success.

The fire-arms then in use were heavy, clumsy weapons, and effective only at very short range. He examined the system closely, and quickly designed several important improvements in them, especially in the old-fashioned musket. Although his improved arms were not to be compared with the terribly effective weapons of to-day, they were admitted to be the best then in use. By examining the Springfield musket, which is due almost entirely to his genius, the reader can form an accurate estimate of the service he rendered in this respect. He has the honor of being the inaugurator of the system of progressive improvement in fire-arms, which has gone on steadily and without flagging for now fully sixty years past.

Some time before abandoning the manufacture of the cotton gin, Mr. Whitney established an arms factory in New Haven, and obtained a contract from the Government for ten thousand stand of arms, to be delivered in two years. At this time he not only had to manufacture the machinery needed by him for this purpose, but had to invent the greater part of it. This delayed the execution of his contract for eight years, but at the expiration of that time he had so far perfected his establishment, which had been removed to Whitneyville, Conn., that he at once entered into contracts for thirty thousand more arms, which he delivered promptly at the appointed time. His factory was the most complete in the country, and was fitted up in a great measure with the machinery which he had invented, and without which the improved weapons could not be fabricated. He introduced a new system into the manufacture of fire-arms, and one which greatly increased the rapidity of construction. "He was the first manufacturer of fire-arms who carried the division of labor to the extent of making it the duty of each workman to perform by machinery but one or two operations on a single portion of the gun, and thus rendered all the parts adapted to any one of the thousands of arms in process of manufacture at the same time."

His success was now marked and rapid. His factory was taxed to its fullest capacity to supply the demand for arms. His genius was rewarded at last, and he acquired a fortune which enabled him not only to pass the evening of his days in comfort, but also to leave a handsome estate to his family. He married a daughter of Judge Pierpont Edwards, a lady of fine accomplishments and high character. He died at New Haven on the 8th of January, 1825, in his sixtieth year.

CHAPTER XVI.

CHAUNCEY JEROME.

MANY readers of these pages doubtless remember the huge old-fashioned clocks, tower-like in shape, that in the days of their childhood ornamented the remote corner of the hall, or stood solemnly near the chimney in the sitting-room of the old homestead,—such a clock as that which greeted little Paul Dombey, when he commenced to be a man, with its "How, is, my, lit, tle, friend?—how, is, my, lit, tle, friend?" Very different from the bright, pretty timepieces of to-day, which go ticking away, as if running a race with time, was the clock of the olden days, as it stood, solemn and dark, in its accustomed corner, from which the strength of two men was necessary to move it, sending the sound of its slow, steady strokes into all parts of the house. And in the night, when all within was still, how its deep beats throbbed in the dark hall louder and sterner even than in the day. There was something eminently respectable about an old clock of this kind, and it would have been audacity unheard of for any member of the family to doubt its reliability. Set once a year, it was expected to retain its steady-going habits for the rest of the twelvemonth. You dared not charge it with being slow; and as for being too fast, why, the very idea was absurd. There was sure to be some white-capped, silver-haired old lady, whose long years had been counted by the venerable pendulum with unerring precision, ready to defend the cause of the clock, to vouch for its accuracy, and to plead its cause so well and so skillfully, that you were ready to hide your face in shame at the thought of having even suspected the veracity of so venerable and so honored an institution.

Truth to say, however, these old clocks, to the masses of the people of this country, were objects of admiration, and nothing more; for their exceeding high price placed them beyond the reach of all save the wealthier classes. A good clock cost from seventy-five to one hundred and fifty dollars, and the most indifferent article in the market could not be obtained for less than twenty-five dollars. At the opening of the present century, the demand for them was so small that but three hundred and fifty clocks were made in the State of Connecticut, which was then, as at present, the one most largely engaged in this branch of American industry. To-day the annual manufacture of Connecticut is about six hundred thousand clocks of all kinds, which command a wholesale price of from fifty cents upward, the greater number bringing the maker less than five dollars. Thus the reader will see that, while the business of the clock-maker has prospered so extraordinarily, valuable timepieces have been brought within the reach of even the poorest.

The man to whom the country is indebted for this wonderful and beneficial increase is CHAUNCEY JEROME, who was born at Canaan, Connecticut, in 1793. His father was a blacksmith and nail-maker, to which trade he added the cultivation of the little farm on which he lived; and being poor, it was necessary for him to labor hard in all his callings in order to provide his family with a plain subsistence. Young Chauncey had little or no time given him for acquiring an education.

He learned to read and write, but went no further; for, when he was but a little more than seven years old, and barely able to do the lightest kind of labor, he was put to work on the farm to help his father, who kept him at this until he was nine, when he took him into his shop. All the nails then in use were made by hand, for there were no huge iron works in the country to send them out by the ton; and such articles were scarce and high. The boy was set to work to make nails, and for two years pursued his vocation steadily. He was a manly little fellow, and worked at his hammer and anvil with a will, resolved that he would become thorough master of his trade; but when he had reached the age of eleven, the sudden death of his father made an entire change in his career, and threw him upon the world a helpless and penniless orphan.

In order to earn his bread, he hired himself to a farmer, receiving for his labor nothing but his "victuals and clothes," the latter being of the plainest and scantiest kind. He worked very hard; but his employer was cold and indifferent to him at all times, and occasionally used him very badly. The boy was naturally of a cheerful disposition, and it did him good service now in helping to sustain him in his hard lot. Four years were passed in this way, and when he was fifteen years old his guardian informed him that he had now reached an age when he must begin his apprenticeship to some regular trade.

The boy was very anxious to learn clock-making, and begged his guardian to apprentice him to that trade; but the wise individual who controlled his affairs replied, sagely, that clock-making was a business in which he would starve, as it was already overdone in Connecticut. There was one man, he said, engaged in that trade who had been silly enough to make two hundred clocks in one year, and he added that it would take the foolish man a life-time to sell them, or if they went off quickly, the market would be so glutted that no dealer would have need to increase his stock for years to come. Clock-making, he informed the boy, had already reached the limit of its expansion in Connecticut, and offered no opportunities at all. The carpenter's trade, on the other hand, was never crowded with good workmen, and always offered the prospect of success to any enterprising and competent man. It was the custom then to regard boys as little animals, possessed of a capacity for hard work, but without any reasoning powers of their own. To the adage that "children should be seen and not heard," the good people of that day added another clause, in effect, "and should never pretend to think for themselves." It was this profound conviction that induced parents and guardians, in so many instances, to disregard the wishes of the children committed to their care, and to condemn so many to lives for which they were utterly unfitted. So it was with the guardian of Chauncey Jerome. He listened to the boy's expression of a preference, it is true, but paid no attention to it, and ended by apprenticing his ward to a carpenter.

The life of an apprentice is always hard, and in those days it was especially so. No negro slave ever worked harder, and but few fared worse, so far as their bodily comfort was concerned, than the New England apprentices of the olden time. Masters seemed almost to regard the lads indentured to them as their property, and in return for the support they gave them exacted from them the maximum amount of work they were capable of performing. They granted them no privileges, allowed them no holidays, except those required by the law, and never permitted the slightest approach to laziness. Chauncey Jerome's master proved no exception to the rule, and when the boy exhibited an unusual proficiency and quickness in his trade, the only notice his employer took of it was to require more work of him. When only a little over sixteen years old, this boy was able to do the work of a full-grown man, and a man's work was rigorously exacted of him. When sent to work at a distance from his employer's home, he invariably had to make the entire journey on foot, with his tools on his back, sometimes being required to go as far as thirty miles in one day in this way. His mother was living at some distance from the place where his master resided, and whenever he visited her, he had to walk all night in order to avoid using his master's time, not one hour of which was allowed him.

In 1811, he informed his master that he was willing to undertake to clothe himself if he could have the five months of the cold season to himself. As this part of the year was always a dull period, and apprentices were little more than an expense to their masters, young Jerome's employer promptly consented to the proposed arrangement. Jerome, now eighteen years old, had never relinquished his old desire to become a clock-maker. He had watched the market closely, and questioned the persons engaged in the business, and he found that, so far from the market being over-stocked, there was a ready sale for every clock made. Greatly encouraged by this, he resolved to devote the five months of his freedom to learning the business, and to apply himself entirely to it at the expiration of his apprenticeship. As soon as he had concluded his bargain with his master, he set out for Waterbury on foot, and upon arriving there, sought and obtained work from a man who made clock-dials for the manufacturers of clocks.

He worked with his new employer awhile, and then formed an arrangement with two journeymen clock-makers. Having perfected their plans, the three set out for New Jersey in a lumber wagon, carrying their provisions with them. The two clock-makers were to make and set up the works, and Jerome was to make the cases whenever they should succeed in selling a clock on their journey. Clock-making was then considered almost perfect. It had been reduced to a regular system, and the cost of construction had been very greatly lessened. A good clock, with a case seven feet high, could now be made for forty dollars, at which price it yielded a fair profit to the maker. The three young men were tolerably successful in their venture. Jerome worked fifteen hours a day at case-making, and by living economically, managed to carry some money with him when he went back to his master's shop in the spring. For the remaining three years of his apprenticeship he employed his winters in learning the various branches of clock-making, and not only earned enough money to clothe himself, but laid by a modest sum besides.

In 1814, being twenty-one years of age and his own master, he set up a carpenter shop of his own, being not yet sufficiently master of clock-making to undertake that on his own account. In 1815, he married. Times were hard. The war with England had just ended, and labor was poorly compensated. He is said at this time to have "finished the whole interior of a three-story house, including twenty-seven doors and an oak floor, nothing being found for him but the timber," for the beggarly sum of eighty-seven dollars—a task which no builder would undertake to-day for less than a thousand dollars. Still, he declared that, in spite of this poor rate of compensation, he was enabled to save enough to make a partial payment on a small dwelling for himself. It required a constant struggle, however, to live at this rate, and in the winter of 1816, being out of work, and having a payment on his house to meet in the spring, he determined to go to Baltimore to seek work during the winter. He was on the eve of starting, when he learned that Mr. Eli Terry, the inventor of the wooden clocks which were so popular fifty years ago, was about to open a large factory for them in an adjoining town. He walked to the town, and made his application to Mr. Terry, who at once engaged him at liberal wages. Mr. Terry's factory was then the largest in the country, and, as he used wooden instead of metal works, he was able to manufacture his best clocks at fifteen dollars, and other grades in proportion. This reduction in price largely increased the sale of his clocks, and in a comparatively short time after opening his factory, Mr. Terry made and sold about six thousand clocks a year.

Jerome was determined that he would spare no pains to make himself master of every detail of clock-making, and applied himself to the business with so much intelligence and energy, that by the spring of 1817 he felt himself competent to undertake their manufacture on his own account. He began his operations very cautiously, at first buying the works already made, putting them together, and making the cases himself. When he had finished two or three, he would carry them about for sale, and as his work was well done, he rarely had any difficulty in disposing of them. Gradually he increased his business, and in a year or two was able to sell every clock he could make, which kept him constantly busy. A Southern dealer having seen one of his clocks, was so well pleased with it that he gave the maker an order for twelve exactly like it, which the latter agreed to furnish at twelve dollars each. It was an enormous order to Jerome, and seemed to him almost too good to be real. He completed the clocks at the stipulated time, and conveyed them in a farmer's wagon to the place where the purchaser had agreed to receive them. The money was paid to him in silver, and as the broad pieces were counted into his hand, he was almost ready to weep for joy. One hundred and forty-four dollars was the largest sum he had ever possessed at one time, and it seemed almost a fortune to him. His clocks were taken to Charleston, South Carolina, and sold. They gave entire satisfaction; and when, some years later, he commenced to ship regular consignments to the Southern cities, he found no difficulty in disposing of his wares.

Mr. Jerome's success was now more decided. He was enabled to pay for his house in a short time, and having, soon afterward, an opportunity to dispose of it at a fair profit, he did so, and took clock-works in payment. He bought land and timber, and paid for them in clocks, and his affairs prospered so well that, before long, he began to employ workmen to assist him, and to dispose of his clocks to peddlers and merchants, instead of carrying them around for sale himself. As his business increased, he invented and patented labor-saving machinery for the manufacture of the various parts of the clock, and thus greatly decreased the cost of construction. He designed new and ornamental cases, and exerted himself to render the exterior of his clocks as tasteful and attractive as possible. His business now increased rapidly, and he was soon compelled to take in a partner. He began to ship his clocks to the Southern States, sending them by sea. They met with a ready sale, but all his ventures of this kind were subject to serious risks. The works, being of wood, would frequently become damp and swollen on the voyage, thus rendering them unfit for use. Mr. Jerome endeavored in various ways to remedy this defect, but was finally compelled to admit that, until he could change the nature of the wood, he could not prevent it from being influenced by moisture.

He passed many sleepless nights while engaged in seeking this remedy, for he plainly foresaw that unless the defect could be removed, the days of the wooden clock business were numbered.

In the midst of his depression, the idea occurred to him, one night while lying awake, that the works of a clock could be manufactured as cheaply of brass as of wood. The thought came to him with the force of a revelation. He sprang out of bed, lit his candle, and passed the rest of the night in making calculations which proved to him that he could not only make brass works as cheaply as wooden ones, but, by the employment of certain labor-saving machinery, at a cost decidedly less. There was one important obstacle in his way, however. The machinery requisite for cutting brass works cheaply was not in existence. Before making known his plans, Mr. Jerome set to work to invent the clock-making machinery which has made him famous among American inventors. When he had completed it, he commenced to make brass clocks, which he sold at such a low price that wooden clocks were speedily driven out of the market. Little by little, he brought his machinery to perfection, applying it to the manufacture of all parts of the clock; and to-day, thanks to his patience and genius, clock-making in the United States has become a very simple affair. By the aid of Jerome's machinery, one man and one boy can saw veneers enough for three hundred clock cases in a single day. By the aid of this same machinery, six men can manufacture the works of one thousand clocks in a day; and a factory employing twenty-five workmen can turn out two thousand clocks per week. By the aid of this same machinery, the total cost of producing a good clock of small size has been brought down to forty cents.

As the reader will suppose, Jerome made a large fortune—a princely fortune—for himself, and entirely revolutionized the clock-making trade of the Union. Thanks to him, scores of fortunes have been made by other manufacturers also, and American clocks have become famous all over the world for their excellence and cheapness. "Go where you will, in Europe, Asia, Africa, or America, you will be sure to come upon Yankee clocks. To England they go by the shipload. Germany, France, Russia, Spain, Italy, all take large quantities. Many have been sent to China and to the East Indies. At Jerusalem, Connecticut clocks tick on many a shelf, and travelers have found them far up the Nile, in Guinea, at the Cape of Good Hope, and in all the accessible places of South America."

After conducting his business for some years, Mr. Jerome organized the Jerome Clock-Making Company, of New Haven. It began its operations with a large capital, and conducted them upon an extensive scale. In a few years Mr. Jerome retired from the active management of its affairs, but continued nominally at its head as its president. He built for himself an elegant mansion in New Haven, where he gathered about him his family and the friends which his sterling qualities and upright character had drawn to him, and here he hoped to pass the remainder of his days.

He was doomed to a bitter disappointment. Although nominally at the head of the Clock Company, he left its control entirely to his partners, who, by injudicious management, brought it at length to the verge of bankruptcy. They made energetic efforts to ward off the final catastrophe, but without success, and in 1860, almost before Mr. Jerome was aware of the full extent of the trouble, the Company was ruined. Its liabilities were heavy, and every dollar's worth of Jerome's property was taken to meet them. Honest to the core, he gave up every thing. His elegant mansion was sold, and he was forced to remove to an humble cottage, a poorer man than when he had first set up for himself as a carpenter.

He was not the man to repine, however, and he at once began to look about him for employment. He was sixty-seven years old, and it was hard to go out into the world to earn his bread again, but he bore his misfortunes bravely, and soon succeeded in obtaining the employment he desired. The great Clock Company of Chicago engaged him at a liberal salary to superintend their manufactory in that city, which position he still holds. The Company manufacture his own clocks, and are fortunate in having the benefit of his genius and experience. Were he a younger man, there can be no doubt that he would win a second fortune equal to that which was swept from him so cruelly, through no fault of his own. As it is, we can only venture to hope that his sturdy independence and indomitable energy will provide him with the means of passing the closing years of his life in comfort. Few men have done the world better service, or been more worthy of its rewards.

ELIAS HOWE, JR.

CHAPTER XVII.

ELIAS HOWE, Jr.

ONE of the busiest parts of the busy thoroughfare of Broadway, in the city of New York, is the point of its intersection with Fourth Street. Thousands and tens of thousands of people pass and repass there daily, but few ever pause to look at the curious machine which stands in the window of the shop at the north-west corner of these two streets. This machine, clumsy and odd-looking as it is, nevertheless has a history which makes it one of the most interesting of all the sights of the great city. It is the first sewing-machine that was ever made.

Elias Howe, its maker, was born in the town of Spencer, Massachusetts, in 1819. He was one of eight children, and it was no small undertaking on the part of his father to provide a maintenance for such a household. Mr. Howe, Sen., was a farmer and miller, and, as was the custom at that time in the country towns of New England, carried on in his family some of those minor branches of industry suited to the capacity of children, with which New England abounds. When Elias was six years old, he was set, with his brothers and sisters, to sticking wire teeth through the leather straps used for making cotton cards. When he became old enough he assisted his father in his saw-mill and grist-mill, and during the winter months picked up a meager education at the district school. He has said that it was the rude and imperfect mills of his father that first turned his attention to machinery. He was not fitted for hard work, however, as he was frail in constitution and incapable of bearing much fatigue. Moreover, he inherited a species of lameness which proved a great obstacle to any undertaking on his part, and gave him no little trouble all through life. At the age of eleven he went to live out on the farm of a neighbor, but the labor proving too severe for him, he returned home and resumed his place in his father's mills, where he remained until he was sixteen years old.

When at this age, he conceived an ardent desire to go to Lowell to seek his fortune. One of his friends had just returned from that place, and had given him such a wonderful description of the city and its huge mills, that he was eager to go there and see the marvel for himself. Obtaining his father's consent, he went to Lowell, and found employment as a learner in one of the large cotton-mills of the city. He remained there two years, when the great financial disaster of 1837 threw him out of employment and compelled him to look for work elsewhere. He obtained a place at Cambridge, in a machine-shop, and was put to work upon the new hemp-carding machinery of Professor Treadwell. His cousin, Nathaniel P. Banks, afterward governor of Massachusetts, member of Congress, and major-general, worked in the same shop with him, and boarded at the same house. Howe remained in Cambridge only a few months, however, and was then given a place in the machine-shop of Ari Davis, of Boston.

At the age of twenty-one he married. This was a rash step for him, as his health was very delicate, and his earnings were but nine dollars per week. Three children were born to him in quick succession, and he found it no easy task to provide food, shelter, and clothing for his little family. The light-heartedness for which he had formerly been noted entirely deserted him, and he became sad and melancholy. His health did not improve, and it was with difficulty that he could perform his daily task. His strength was so slight that he would frequently return home from his day's work too much exhausted to eat. He could only go to bed, and in his agony he wished "to lie in bed forever and ever." Still he worked faithfully and conscientiously, for his wife and children were very dear to him; but he did so with a hopelessness which only those who have tasted the depths of poverty can understand.

About this time he heard it said that the great necessity of the age was a machine for doing sewing. The immense amount of fatigue incurred and the delay in hand-sewing were obvious, and it was conceded by all who thought of the matter at all that the man who could invent a machine which would remove these difficulties would make a fortune. Howe's poverty inclined him to listen to these remarks with great interest. No man needed money more than he, and he was confident that his mechanical skill was of an order which made him as competent as any one else to achieve the task proposed. He set to work to accomplish it, and, as he knew well the dangers which surround an inventor, kept his own counsel. At his daily labor, in all his waking hours, and even in his dreams, he brooded over this invention. He spent many a wakeful night in these meditations, and his health was far from being benefited by this severe mental application. Success is not easily won in any great undertaking, and Elias Howe found that he had entered upon a task which required the greatest patience, perseverance, energy, and hopefulness. He watched his wife as she sewed, and his first effort was to devise a machine which should do what she was doing. He made a needle pointed at both ends, with the eye in the middle, that should work up and down through the cloth, and carry the thread through at each thrust; but his elaboration of this conception would not work satisfactorily. It was not until 1844, fully a year after he began the attempt to invent the machine, that he came to the conclusion

HOWE'S FIRST IDEA OF THE SEWING-MACHINE.

that the movement of a machine need not of necessity be an imitation of the performance of the hand. It was plain to him that there must be another stitch, and that if he could discover it his difficulties would all be ended. A little later he conceived the idea of using two threads, and forming a stitch by the aid of a shuttle and a curved needle with the eye near the point. This was the triumph of his skill. He had now invented a perfect sewing-machine, and had discovered the essential principles of every subsequent modification of his conception. Satisfied that he had at length solved the problem, he constructed a rough model of his machine of wood and wire, in October,

1844, and operated it to his perfect satisfaction. His invention is thus described:

"He used a needle and a shuttle of novel construction, and combined them with holding surfaces, feed mechanism and other devices, as they had never before been brought together in one machine. . . . . One of the principal features of Mr. Howe's invention is the combination of a grooved needle, having an eye near its point, and vibrating in the direction of its length, with a side-pointed shuttle for effecting a locked stitch, and forming, with the threads, one on each side of the cloth, a firm and lasting seam not easily ripped. The main action of the machine consists in the interlocking of the loop, made by the thread carried in the point of the needle through the cloth, with another thread passed through this loop by means of a shuttle entering and leaving it at every stitch. The thread attached to this shuttle remains in the loop and secures the stitch as the needle is withdrawn to be ready to make the next one. At the same time the cloth, held by little projecting pins to the baster plate, is carried along with this by what is called the 'feed motion' just the length of a stitch, the distance being readily adjusted for finer or coarser work. . . . . The cloth is held in a vertical position in the machine, and the part to be sewed is pressed against the side of the shuttle-race by a presser plate hinged on its upper edge, and capable of exerting any required pressure on the cloth, according as the adjusting screw that regulates it is turned. A slot, or perforation through the plate, also extended through the side of the shuttle-race near the bottom, admits the passage of the needle; and when this is pushed in the shuttle can still pass freely over it. The shuttle is pushed one way and then the other through its race or trough by picker staves. The thread for the needle is supplied by a bobbin, the movement of which is checked by a friction band, this securing the proper tension, and the slack of the thread is duly taken up by a suitable contrivance for the purpose. Thus, all the essential features of the most approved sewing-machine were first found in that of Mr. Howe; and the machines of later date are, in fact, but modifications of it."

At this time, he had abandoned his work as a journeyman mechanic, and had removed to his father's house. Mr. Howe, Sen., had established in Cambridge a machine-shop for the cutting of strips of palm-leaf used in the manufacture of hats. Elias and his family lived under his father's roof, and in the garret of the house the half-sick inventor put up a lathe, where he did a little work on his own account, and labored on his sewing-machine. He was miserably poor, and could scarcely earn enough to provide food for his family; and, to make matters worse, his father, who was disposed to help him, lost his shop and its contents by fire. Poor Elias was in a most deplorable condition. He had his model in his head, and was fully satisfied of its excellence, but he had not the money to buy the materials needed in making a perfect machine, which would have to be constructed of steel and iron, and without which he could not hope to convince others of its value. His great invention was useless to him without the five hundred dollars which he needed in the construction of a working model.

In this dilemma, he applied to a friend, Mr. George Fisher, a coal and wood merchant of Cambridge, who was a man of some means. He explained his invention to him, and succeeded in forming a partnership with him. Fisher agreed to take Howe and his family to board with him while the latter was making the machine, to allow his garret to be used as a workshop, and to advance the five hundred dollars necessary for the purchase of tools and the construction of a model. In return for this he was to receive one-half of the patent, if Howe succeeded in patenting his machine. About the first of December, 1844, Howe and his family accordingly moved into Fisher's house, and the little workshop was set up in the garret. All that winter he worked on his model. There was little to delay him in its construction, as the conception was perfectly clear in his mind. He worked all day, and sometimes nearly all night, and in April, 1845, had his machine so far advanced that he sewed a seam with it. By the middle of May the machine was completed, and in July he sewed with it the seams of two woolen suits, one for himself and the other for Mr. Fisher. The sewing was so well done that it outlasted the cloth.

It has been stated by Professor Renwick and other scientific men that Elias Howe "carried the invention of the sewing-machine further on toward its complete and final utility than any other inventor has ever brought a first-rate invention at the first trial." Those who doubt this assertion should examine the curious machine at the corner of Broadway and Fourth Street, and their doubts will be dispelled; for they will find in it all the essentials of the best sewing-machine of to-day.

Having patented his machine, Howe endeavored to bring it into use. He was full of hope, and had no doubt that it would be adopted at once by those who were so much interested in the saving of labor. He first offered it to the tailors of Boston; but they, while admitting its usefulness, told him it would never be adopted by their trade, as it would ruin them. Considering the number of machines now used by the tailoring interest throughout the world, this assertion seems ridiculous. Other efforts were equally unsuccessful. Every one admitted and praised the ingenuity of the machine, but no one would invest a dollar in it. Fisher became disgusted, and withdrew from his partnership, and Howe and his family moved back to his father's house. Thoroughly disheartened, he abandoned his machine. He then obtained a place as engineer on a railroad, and drove a locomotive until his health entirely broke down.

With the loss of his health his hopes revived, and he determined to seek in England the victory which he had failed to win here. Unable to go himself, he sent his machine by his brother Amasa, in October, 1846. Upon reaching London, Amasa sought out Mr. William Thomas, of Cheapside, and explained to him his brother's invention. He found Mr. Thomas willing to use the machine in his business, but upon terms more favorable to himself than to the inventor. He offered the sum of twelve hundred and fifty dollars for the machine which Amasa Howe had brought with him, and agreed to pay Elias fifteen dollars per week if he would enter his service, and adapt the machine to his business of umbrella and corset making. As this was his only hope of earning a livelihood, Elias accepted the offer, and, upon his brother's return to the United States, sailed for England. He remained in Mr. Thomas's employ for about eight months, and at the end of that time left him, having found him hard, exacting, and unreasonable.

Meanwhile his sick wife and three children had joined him in London, and he had found it hard to provide for them on the wages given him by Mr. Thomas; but after being thrown out of employment his condition was desperate indeed. He was in a strange country, without friends or money, and often he and his little family went whole days without food. Their sufferings were very great, but at length Howe was able (probably by assistance from home) to send his family back to his father's house. He himself remained in London, still hoping to bring his machine into use. It was in vain, however, and so, collecting what few household goods he had acquired in England, he shipped them to America, and followed them thither himself in another vessel, pawning his model and patent papers to pay his passage. When he landed in New York he had half a crown in his pocket, and there came to him on the same day a letter telling him that his wife was dying with consumption in Cambridge. He could not go to her at once, as he had no money, and was too feeble to undertake the distance on foot. He was compelled to wait several days until he could obtain the money for his fare to Cambridge, but at length succeeded in reaching that place just in time to see his wife die. In the midst of his grief he received the announcement that the vessel containing the few household goods which he had shipped from England had been lost at sea. It seemed to him that Fate was bent upon destroying him, so rapid and stunning were the blows she dealt him.

But a great success was now in store for him, and he was to rise out of his troubles to the realization of his brightest hopes. Soon after his return home he obtained profitable employment, and, better still, discovered that his machine had become famous during his absence. Fac-similes of it had been constructed by unscrupulous mechanics, who paid no attention to the patents of the inventor, and these copies had been exhibited in many places as "wonders," and had even been adopted in many important branches of manufacture. Howe at once set to work to defend his rights. He found friends to aid him, and in August, 1850, began those famous suits which continued for four years, and were at length decided in his favor. His adversaries made a bold resistance, but the decision of Judge Sprague, in 1854, settled the matter, and triumphantly established the rights of the inventor.

In 1850, Howe removed to New York, and began in a small way to manufacture machines to order. He was in partnership with a Mr. Bliss, but for several years the business was so unimportant that upon the death of his partner, in 1855, he was enabled to buy out that gentleman's interest, and thus become the sole proprietor of his patent. Soon after this his business began to increase, and continued until his own proper profits and the royalty which the courts compelled other manufacturers to pay him for the use of his invention grew from $300 to $200,000 per annum. In 1867, when the extension of his patent expired, it is stated that he had earned a total of two millions of dollars by it. It cost him large sums to defend his rights, however, and he was very far from being as wealthy as was commonly supposed, although a very rich man.

In the Paris Exposition of 1867, he exhibited his machines, and received the gold medal of the Exposition, and the Cross of the Legion of Honor, in addition, as a compliment to him as a manufacturer and inventor.

He contributed money liberally to the aid of the Union in the late war, and enlisted as a private soldier in the Seventeenth Regiment of Connecticut Volunteers, with which command he went to the field, performing all the duties of his position until failing health compelled him to leave the service. Upon one occasion the Government was so much embarrassed that it could not pay the regiment of which he was a member. Mr. Howe promptly advanced the money, and his comrades were saved from the annoyances which would have attended the delay in paying them. He died at Brooklyn, Long Island, on the 3d of October, 1867.

Mr. Howe will always rank among the most distinguished of American inventors; not only because of the unusual degree of completeness shown in his first conception of the sewing-machine, but because of the great benefits which have sprung from it. It has revolutionized the industry of the world, opened new sources of wealth to enterprise, and lightened the labor of hundreds of thousands of working people. Many a pale-faced, hollow-eyed woman, who formerly sat sewing her life away for a mere pittance, blesses the name of Elias Howe, and there is scarcely a community in the civilized world but contains the evidence of his genius, and honors him as the benefactor of the human race.

CHAPTER XVIII.

RICHARD M. HOE.

TO write the complete history of the printing press would require years of patient labor and research, and a much larger space than the limits of the present work will permit. There are few subjects more attractive or more worthy of consideration than the history of this wonderful invention, which seems more like a romance than a narration of facts. The historian who should essay the task would be required to carry his reader back to the darkest ages of the world, and, beginning with the stamps used for affixing hieroglyphical characters to the now crumbling ruins of Egypt and Nineveh, trace the gradual development of the beneficent conception from the signets of the Israelites, and the stamps used by the Romans for marking certain kinds of merchandise, through the rude process of the Chinese, Japanese, and Tartars, to the invention of Johannes Guttenberg, and, finally, to the wonderful lightning steam-presses of to-day.

In these pages it is not proposed to offer to the reader any such narrative. On the contrary, the story of the printing press will be taken up just as it was on the point of reaching its greatest perfection, since our subject concerns only the man who brought it to that state.

This man, RICHARD MARCH HOE by name, was born in the city of New York, on the 12th of September, 1812. His father, Robert Hoe, was a native of the village of Hose, Leicester, England, and the son of a wealthy farmer. Disliking his father's pursuit, he apprenticed himself to a carpenter. When only sixteen years old, the elder Hoe purchased his indentures from his master and sailed for the United States. He was almost penniless when he reached New York, and in this condition entered the store of Mr. Grant Thorburn one day in search of employment. Mr. Thorburn manifested a sudden and strong liking to the youth, took him to his own house, and when he was prostrated with the yellow fever, during the epidemic of 1804, nursed him tenderly throughout. Setting to work immediately upon his arrival in New York, he made friends rapidly, and prospered in his trade so well that when but twenty years old he was able to marry. His bride was a daughter of Matthew Smith, of Westchester, and a sister of Peter Smith, the inventor of the hand printing press, which bears his name. With this gentleman and Matthew Smith, jr., his brother, Robert Hoe entered into partnership. Their business was that of carpentering and printers' joinery; but after Peter Smith had completed the invention of his hand press, it gradually grew into the manufacture of presses and printers' materials. Both of the brothers died in 1823, and Robert Hoe succeeded to the entire business.

The manufactory of "Robert Hoe & Co." was originally located in the centre of the old block between Pearl and William Streets, and Pine Street and Maiden Lane. Soon after their establishment there, the city authorities ran Cedar Street right through their building, and they removed to Gold Street, near John. They have been twice burned out here, but still occupy these premises with their counting-room and lower shop.

Printing by steam had long attracted the attention of persons engaged in the art, and many essays had been made in this direction by different inventors, both in this country and in Europe. The most successful results were the Adams press, the invention of Mr. Isaac Adams, of Boston, Mass., and the Napier press, that of a British artisan. It was the latter which was the means of identifying Mr. Hoe with the steam press.

The Napier press was introduced into this country in 1830, by the proprietors of the *National Intelligencer*, but when it arrived, these gentlemen were not able to release it from the Custom-house. Major Noah, himself the proprietor of a newspaper, was at that time Collector of the port of New York, and he, being anxious to see the press in operation, requested Mr. Hoe to put it together. Mr. Hoe performed this task successfully, although the press was a novelty to him, and was permitted to take models of its various parts before it was reshipped to England. It was found to be a better press than any that had ever been seen in this country, and the *Commercial Advertiser*, of New York, and the *Chronicle*, of Philadelphia, at once ordered duplicates of it from England.

Mr. Hoe was very much pleased with this press, but believed that he could construct a much better one. "To this end he despatched his new partner, Mr. Sereno Newton, to England to examine all the improvements in machinery there, and bring home samples of such as he thought might be advantageously adopted in this country. Mr. Newton, besides being an ingenious mechanic, was well-read in books, and was considered one of the first mathematicians in New York. Returning from his mission, he constructed a new two-cylinder press, which soon superseded all others then in use." Mr. Hoe's health failed, compelling him, in 1832, to retire from the business.

Young Richard M. Hoe had been brought up in his father's business, after receiving a fair education. He inherited his father's inventive genius, combined with a rare business capacity, and from the first was regarded as the future hope of the establishment. Upon the withdrawal of his father, a partnership was established between himself, his brother Robert, Mr. Newton, and his cousin Matthew Smith, but the style of the firm remained unchanged.

Richard Hoe's first invention was conceived in 1837, and consisted of a valuable improvement in the manufacture of grinding saws. Having obtained a patent for it in the United States, he visited England in that year for the same purpose. By his process circular saws may be ground with accuracy to any desired thickness. He readily obtained a patent in England, as the excellence of his invention commended it to every one. While there he gave especial attention to the improvements which had been made in the printing press, in the manufacture of which his firm was still largely engaged. Returning to New York, he devoted himself entirely to this branch of his business, and soon produced the machine known as "Hoe's Double-Cylinder Press," which was capable of making about six thousand impressions per hour. The first press of this kind ever made was ordered by the New York *Sun*, and was the admiration of all the printers of the city. This style of press is now used extensively for printing country newspapers.

As long as the newspaper interest of the country stood still, "Hoe's Double-Cylinder Press" was amply sufficient for its wants, but as the circulation of the journals of the large cities began to increase, the "double-cylinder" was often taxed far beyond its powers, A printing press capable of striking off papers with much greater rapidity was felt to be an imperative and still-increasing need. It was often necessary to hold the forms back until nearly daylight for the purpose of issuing the latest news, and in the hurry which ensued to get out the morning edition, the press very frequently met with accidents.

Mr. Hoe was fully alive to the importance of improving his press, and, in 1842, he began to experiment with it for the purpose of obtaining greater speed. It was a serious undertaking, however, and at every step fresh difficulties arose. He spent four years in experimenting, and at the end of that time was almost ready to confess that the obstacles were too great to be overcome. One night, in 1846, while in this mood, he resumed his experiments. The more he pondered over the subject the more difficult it seemed. In despair, he was about to relinquish the effort for the night, when suddenly there flashed across his mind a plan for securing the type on a horizontal cylinder. This had been his great difficulty, and he now felt that he had mastered it. He sat up all night, working out his design, and making a note of every idea that occurred to him, in order that nothing should escape him. By morning the problem which had baffled him so long had been solved, and the magnificent "Lightning Press" already had a being in the inventor's fertile brain.

He carried his model rapidly to perfection, and, proceeding with it to Washington, obtained a patent. On his return home he met Mr. Swain, the proprietor of the Baltimore *Sun* and Philadelphia *Ledger*, and explained his invention to him. Mr. Swain was so much pleased with it that he at once ordered a four-cylinder press, which was completed and ready for use on the 31st of December, 1848. This press was capable of making ten thousand impressions per hour, and did its work with entire satisfaction in every respect.

This was a success absolutely unprecedented—so marked, in

fact, that some persons were inclined to doubt it. The news flew rapidly from city to city, and across the ocean to foreign lands, and soon wherever a newspaper was printed men were talking of Hoe's wonderful invention. Orders came pouring in upon the inventor with such rapidity that he soon had as many on hand as he could fill in several years. In a comparatively brief period the *Herald, Tribune,* and *Sun,* of New York, were boasting of their "Lightning Presses," and soon the *Traveller* and *Daily Journal,* in Boston, followed their example. Mr. Hoe was now not only a famous man, but possessed of an assured business for the future, which was certain to result in a large fortune. By the year 1860, besides supplying the principal cities of the Union (fifteen lightning presses being used in the city of New York alone), he had shipped eighteen presses to Great Britain, four to France, and one to Australia. Two of the presses sent to England were ordered for the London *Times.*

Mr. Hoe continued to improve his invention, adding additional cylinders as increased speed was desired, and at length brought it to the degree of perfection exhibited in the splendid ten-cylinder press now in use in the offices of our leading journals, which strikes off twenty-five thousand sheets per hour. Whether more will be accomplished with this wonderful machine the future alone can determine, but the inventor is said to be still laboring to improve it.

In 1858, Mr. Hoe purchased the patent rights and manufactory of Isaac Adams, in Boston, and since then has carried on the manufacture of the Adams press from that place. He has also established a manufactory in England, where he conducts a profitable business in both the Adams and the Hoe press. Over a million and a half of dollars are invested in these establishments in New York, Boston, and London, in land, buildings, and stock. The firm manufacture presses of all kinds, and all materials used by printers except type and ink. They also manufacture circular saws, made according to Mr. Hoe's process.

Mr. Hoe, now fifty-eight years of age, is still as vigorous and active as many a younger man. Besides being one of the most prominent and distinguished inventors and manufacturers in the country, he is justly esteemed for his many virtues and his commanding business talents. He is still the active head of the house which he has carried to such a brilliant success, and is the possessor of an ample fortune, which his genius and industry have secured to him. He is courteous and obliging to all, and very liberal to those whose needs commend them to his benevolence.

The ten-cylinder press costs fifty thousand dollars, and is regarded as cheap at that immense sum. It is one of the most interesting inventions ever made. Those who have seen it working in the subterranean press-rooms of the journals of the great metropolis will not soon forget the wonderful sight. The ear is deafened with the incessant clashing of the machinery; the printed sheets issue from the sides of the huge engine in an unceasing stream; the eye is bewildered with the mass of lines and bands; and it seems hard to realize that one single mind could ever have adjusted all the various parts to work harmoniously.

The following is a description of the ten-cylinder steam printing-press now used in the office of the New York *World*. It is one of the best specimens of its kind to be seen in the great city:

The dimensions of the press are as follows: Entire length, 40 feet; width, 15 feet; height, 16 feet. The large horizontal cylinder in the center is about 4½ feet in diameter, and on it are placed the "forms" of type for the four pages of one side of the paper. Each of these constitutes a segment of a circle, and the whole four occupy a segment of only about one-fourth of the surface of the cylinder, the other three-fourths being used as an ink-distributing surface. Around this main cylinder, and parallel with it, are ten smaller impression cylinders, according to the number of which a press is termed a four, six, or ten-cylinder press. The large cylinder being set in revolution, the form of types is carried successively to all the impression cylinders, at each of which a sheet is introduced and receives the impression of the types as the form passes. Thus as many sheets are printed at each revolution of the main cylinder as there are impression cylinders around it. One person is required at each impression cylinder to supply the sheets of paper, which are taken at the proper moment by fingers or grippers, and after being printed are conveyed out by tapes and laid in heaps by means of self-acting flyers, thereby dispensing with the hands required in ordinary machines to receive and pile the sheets. The grippers hold the sheet securely, so that the thinnest newspaper can be printed without waste.

The ink is contained in a fountain placed beneath the main cylinder, and is conveyed by means of distributing rollers to the distributing surface on the main cylinder. This surface being lower or less in diameter than the form of types, passes by the impression cylinders without touching them. For each impression there are two inking rollers, which receive their supply of ink from the distributing surface of the main cylinder, and raise and ink the form as it passes under them, after which they again fall to the distributing surface.

Each page of the paper is locked up on a detached segment of the large cylinder, called by the compositors a "turtle," and this constitutes its bed and chase. The column-rules run parallel with the shaft of the cylinder, and are consequently straight, while the head, advertising, and dash-rules are in the form of segments of a circle. The column-rules are in the form of a wedge, with the thin part directed toward the axis of the cylinder, so as to bind the type securely, and at the same time to keep the ink from collecting between the types and the rules. They are held down to the bed by tongues projecting at intervals along their length, which slide into rebated grooves, cut crosswise in the face of the bed. The spaces in the grooves between the column-rules are accurately fitted with sliding blocks of metal even with the surface of the bed, the ends of the blocks being cut away underneath to receive a projection on the sides of the tongues of the column-rules. The form of type is locked up in the bed by means of screws at the foot and sides, by which the type is held as securely as in the ordinary manner upon a flat bed, if not even more so. The speed of the machine is limited only by the ability of the feeders to supply the sheets. Twenty-five hundred is about as many as a man can supply in an hour, and multiplying this by ten—one man being at each cylinder—we have 25,000 sheets an hour as the capacity of the press.

CHAPTER XIX.

SAMUEL COLT.

SAMUEL COLT was born at Hartford, Connecticut, on the 19th of July, 1814. He was descended from one of the original settlers of that city, and his father, who possessed some means, was a man of great energy, intelligence, and enterprise. The senior Colt began life as a merchant, and afterward became a manufacturer of woolen, cotton, and silk goods. The mother of our hero was the daughter of Major John Caldwell, a prominent banker of Hartford, and is said to have been a woman of superior character and fine mental attainments.

It was within the power of the parents of Samuel Colt to give him a thorough education, and this they were anxious to do; but he was always so full of restless energy that he greatly preferred working in the factory to going to school. He loved to be where he could hear the busy looms at work, and see the play of the intricate machinery in the great building. In order to gratify him, his father placed him in his factory at the age of ten years, and there he remained for about three years, leaving it only at rare intervals and for short periods of time, which he passed in attendance upon school and working on a farm. When he was thirteen his father declared that he would not permit him to grow up without an education, and sent him to a boarding-school at Amherst, Massachusetts. He did not remain there long, for the spirit of adventure came over him with such force that he could not resist it. He ran away from school and shipped as a boy before the mast on a vessel bound for the East Indies. The ship was called the Coroo, and was commanded by Captain Spaulding.

The voyage was long, and the lad was subjected to great hardships, which soon convinced him that running away to sea was not as romantic in real life as in the books he had read,

THE BOY COLT INVENTING THE REVOLVER.

but his experience, though uncomfortable enough, failed to conquer his restless spirit. While at sea in the Coroo he had an abundance of leisure time for reflection, but instead of devoting it to meditating upon the folly of his course, he spent it in inventing a revolving pistol, a rough model of which he cut in wood with his jack-knife. This was the germ of the invention which afterward gave him such fame, and it is not a little singular that the conception of such a weapon should have come to a boy of fourteen.

Returning home, he became an apprentice in his father's factory at Ware, Massachusetts. He was put into the dyeing and bleaching department, and was thoroughly trained in it by Mr. William T. Smith, a scientific man, and one of the best practical chemists in New England. Young Holt manifested a remarkable aptitude for chemistry, and when but a mere boy was known as one of the most successful and dexterous manipulators in New England.

When he had reached his eighteenth year, the old spirit of restlessness came over him again, and he embarked in an unusually bold undertaking for one so young, in which, however, he was much favored by the circumstance that he was very much older in appearance than in reality, commonly passing for a full-grown man. Assuming the name of Dr. Coult, he traveled throughout the Union and British America, visiting nearly every town of two thousand inhabitants and over, lecturing upon chemistry, and illustrating his lectures with a series of skillful and highly popular experiments. His tour was entirely successful, and he realized in the two years over which it extended quite a handsome sum. The use which he made of the money thus acquired was characteristic of the man.

He had never abandoned the design of a revolving pistol which he had conceived on board the Coroo, and he now set to work to perfect it, using the proceeds of his lectures to enable him to take out patents in this country and in Europe. He spent two years in working on his model, making improvements in it at every step, and by 1835 had brought it to such a state of excellence that he was enabled to apply for a patent in the United States. His application was successful. Before it was decided, however, he visited England and France, and patented his invention in those countries. Though now only twenty-one years old, he had given seven years of study and labor to his "revolver," and had brought it to a state of perfection which was far in advance of his early hopes.

"At this time, and, indeed, for several years after, he was not aware that any person before himself had ever conceived the idea of a fire-arm with a rotating chambered breech. On a subsequent visit to Europe, while exploring the collection of fire-arms in the Tower of London and other repositories of weapons of war in England and on the continent, he found several guns having the chambered breech, but all were so constructed as to be of little practical value, being far more liable to explode prematurely and destroy the man who should use them than the objects at which they might be aimed. Unwilling, however, to seem to claim that which had been previously invented, he read before the Institution of Civil Engineers in England (of which he was the only American associate), in 1851, an elaborate paper on the subject, in which he described and illustrated, with appropriate drawings, the various early inventions of revolving fire-arms, and demonstrated the principles on which his were constructed."

Having secured patents in the United States and in the principal countries of Europe, Mr. Colt exerted himself to organize a company for the manufacture of his revolver. He met with considerable opposition, for it was commonly asserted that his pistol would never be of any practical value. The wise ones said it was too complicated for general use, and that its adoption would be attended by the killing or maiming of the majority of those who used it. The inventor disregarded these birds of ill omen, however, and, persevering in his efforts, finally succeeded in securing the aid of some capitalists in New York. A company was formed in 1835, called the "Patent Arms Company," with a capital of $300,000, and an armory was established at Paterson, New Jersey. Mr. Colt then endeavored to induce the Government of the United States to adopt the arm in the military and naval service. Strange as it now seems, however, the officers of the army and navy were not disposed to regard the revolver with favor. They declared that the percussion cap was entirely unreliable, and that no weapon requiring it could be depended on with certainty; that there was great danger that two or more of the charges would explode at the same time; and that the arm was liable to get out of order very easily. They further protested that it was much more difficult to repair than the arms then in use, and that this alone rendered it unfit for adoption by the Government. Notwithstanding these objections were fully met by Mr. Colt, who explained carefully the principles of his weapon, it was two years before the Government consented to give the revolver a trial.

In 1837, the Florida war raged with great violence, and the Seminoles, secure in their fastnesses in the Everglades, were enabled to bid defiance to all the efforts of the army of the United States. Their superior skill in the use of the rifle gave them an advantage which the bravery and determination of our troops could not overcome. In this emergency, the Government consented to make a trial of Colt's revolver. A regiment under Lieutenant-Colonel Harvey was armed with this weapon, and its success was so marked from the first that the Government promptly gave an order for more, and ended by making it the principal arm of the troops in Florida. The savages were astounded and disheartened at seeing the troops fire six or eight times without reloading; and when the war was brought to a close, as it soon was, it was plain to all that the revolver had played a decisive part in the struggle. It was a great triumph for Colonel Colt, but in the end proved a source of misfortune. The speedy termination of the war put an end to the demand for his weapon, and his business fell off so greatly that in 1842 the Patent Arms Company was compelled to close its establishment and wind up its affairs.

For five years none of the revolvers were manufactured, and, meanwhile, the stock which had been put in the market was entirely exhausted by the demand which had set in from Texas and the Indian frontier. In 1847 the war with Mexico began, and General Taylor, who had witnessed the performance of the revolver in Florida, was anxious to arm the Texan Rangers with that weapon. He sent Captain Walker, the commander of the Rangers, to Colonel Colt to purchase a supply. Walker was unsuccessful. Colt had parted with the last one that he possessed, and had not even a model to serve as a guide in making others. The Government now gave him an order for one thousand, which he agreed to make for $28,000; but there was still the difficulty caused by having no model to work by. In this dilemma, he advertised extensively for one of his old pistols, to serve as a model, but failing to procure one, was compelled to make a new model. This was really a fortunate circumstance, as he made several improvements in the weapon, which officers who had used it suggested to him, so that his weapons were very much better than the old ones. Having no factory of his own, Colonel Colt hired an armory at Whitneyville, near New Haven, where he produced the first thousand pistols ordered by the Government. These gave entire satisfaction, and further orders from the War Department came in rapidly. Colonel Colt now hired and fitted up larger and more complete workshops in Hartford, and began business on his own account, supplying promptly every order that was given him. The weapon proved most effective during the Mexican War, and the orders of the Government were sufficiently large to allow the inventor to reap a handsome profit from them, and lay the foundations of his subsequent business success.

At the close of the war, Colonel Colt was apprehensive that the demand for his weapon would again drop off, as it had done after the Florida campaign; but he was agreeably disappointed. The success of the revolver in Mexico had made it generally and favorably known throughout the country, and there was now a steady and even a growing demand for it. The discovery of gold in California, which so quickly followed the cessation of hostilities, greatly stimulated this demand, for the most essential part of the gold seeker's outfit was a revolver; and the extraordinary emigration to Australia, which set in somewhat later, still further extended the market for his weapon. Convinced by this time that there would be no considerable falling off in his orders, Colonel Colt began to take steps to assure the permanency of his business.

The experience of the American officers during the Mexican War enabled them to point out many improvements to the inventor, who promptly adopted them. This made his pistol almost a new weapon, and the most formidable small arm then in use. He obtained a new patent for it, as thus improved, and it was adopted by the Government as the regular arm of the army and navy, different sizes being made for each service. The Crimean and Indian wars, which followed soon after, brought the inventor large orders from the British Government, and during the next few years his weapon was formally introduced into the armies of the leading States of Europe.

His success was so rapid that, as early as 1851, it became necessary to provide still more ample accommodations for his manufactory. The next year he began the execution of a plan, the magnitude of which caused many of his friends to tremble for his future prosperity. He resolved to build the largest and most perfect armory in the world, one which should enable him to manufacture his weapons with greater rapidity and nicety than had ever yet been possible.

Just to the south of the Little or Mill River there was a piece of meadow land, about two hundred and fifty acres in extent, generally regarded as useless, in consequence of its being submerged every spring by the freshets in the river. Colonel Colt bought this meadow for a nominal sum, and, to the astonishment of the good people of Hartford, proceeded to surround it with a strong dike, or embankment. This embankment was two miles in length, one hundred and fifty feet wide at the base, from thirty to sixty feet wide at the top, and from ten to twenty-five feet high. Its strength was further increased by planting willows along the sides; and it was thoroughly tested just after its completion by a freshet of unusual severity. Having drained the meadow, Colonel Colt began the erection of his armory upon the land inclosed by the embankment. It was constructed of Portland stone, and consisted of three buildings—two long edifices, with a third connecting them in the center, the whole being in the form of the letter H. The front parallel was five hundred by sixty feet, the rear parallel five hundred by forty feet, and the central building two hundred and fifty by fifty feet—the front parallel and central building being three stories in height. Connected with these buildings were other smaller edifices for offices, warerooms, watchmen's houses, etc.

In 1861, the demand for the arms had become so enormous that the armory was doubled in size, the new buildings being similar in style to the old. "In this establishment there is ample accommodation for the manufacture of one thousand fire-arms per day," which is more than the arsenals at Harper's Ferry and Springfield combined could turn out in the same time previous to the war. In 1861, Colt's armory turned out about one hundred and twenty thousand stand of arms, and in 1860, the two armories before mentioned made about thirty-five thousand between them. A portion of the armory at Hartford is devoted to the fabrication of the machinery invented by Colonel Colt for the manufacture of his pistols. This machinery is usually sold to all parties purchasing the right to manufacture the revolver. Colonel Colt supplied in this way a large part of the machinery used in the Government manufactory at Enfield, in England, and all of that used in the Imperial armory at Tulin, in Russia. Near the armory, and in the area inclosed by the dike, Colonel Colt erected a number of tasteful cottages for his workmen, and warehouses for other kinds of business. His entire expenditure upon his land and buildings here amounted to more than two million five hundred thousand dollars.

"Among his other cares, the intellectual and social welfare of his numerous employés were not forgotten. Few mechanics are favored with as convenient residences as those he has erected for them; and a public hall, a library, courses of lectures, concerts, the organization of a fine band of music, formed entirely from his own workmen, to whom he presented a superb set of musical instruments, and of a military company of his operatives, provided by him with a tasteful uniform, and otherwise treated by him with great liberality, were among the methods by which he demonstrated his sympathy with the sons of toil."

The Hartford armory is the largest and most complete in the world, in extent and perfection of machinery. All the articles needed with the revolver, such as the powder flask, balls, lubricator, bullet molds, cartridges, etc., are made here on a large scale. The establishment is a noble monument to the inventive genius and business capacity of its founder.

In addition to his inventions of fire-arms, Colonel Colt invented a submarine battery, which was thoroughly tested by the officers of the United States Navy, and is said to be one of the most formidable engines for harbor defense ever known. He also invented a submarine telegraph cable, which he laid and operated with perfect success, in 1843, from Coney Island and Fire Island to the city of New York, and from the Merchants Exchange to the mouth of the harbor. His insulating material consisted of a combination of cotton yarn with asphaltum and beeswax; the whole was inclosed in a lead pipe. This was one of the most successful experiments of the early days of submarine telegraphy, and entitles Colonel Colt to a conspicuous place in the list of those who brought that science to perfection.

After the permanent establishment of his business, in 1847 and 1848, Colonel Colt's success was rapid. He acquired a large fortune, and built an elegant and tasteful mansion in Hartford, where he resided, surrounded with all the luxuries of wealth and taste. In 1855, he married Miss Elizabeth Jarvis, daughter of the Rev. Dr. Jarvis, of Portland, Connecticut, a lady of great beauty and superior character and accomplishments. She still survives him.

He repeatedly visited Europe after his settlement at Hartford, and as the excellence of his weapons had made his name famous the world over, he was the recipient of many attentions from the most distinguished soldiers of Europe, and even from some of the monarchs of the Old World. In 1856, being on a visit to Russia, with his family, he was invited with them to be present at the coronation of the Emperor Alexander II. He was decorated by nearly all the Governments of Europe, and by some of the Asiatic sovereigns, with orders of merit, diplomas, medals, and rings, in acknowledgment of the great services he had rendered to the world by his invention.

He died, at his residence in Hartford, on the 10th of January, 1862, in the forty-eighth year of his age. The community of which he was a member lost in him one of its most enterprising and public-spirited citizens, and the country one of the best representatives of the American character it has ever produced.

CHAPTER XX.

SAMUEL F. B. MORSE.

SAMUEL FINLEY BREESE MORSE is the eldest son of the late Jedediah Morse, one of the most distinguished Presbyterian clergymen of New England. He was born at Charlestown, Massachusetts, on the 27th of April, 1791, was carefully educated in the common schools of his native town, and at an early age entered Yale College, where he graduated in 1810. He exhibited an early fondness for art as well as studies of a scientific character, and while a student at Yale displayed an especial aptness for chemistry and natural philosophy. Upon leaving college he decided to adopt the profession of an artist, and was sent abroad to study under the tuition of West and Copley and Allston.

"When Allston was painting his 'Dead Man Restored to Life,' in London," says Mr. Tuckerman, in his *Book of the Artists*, "he first modeled his figure in clay, and explained to Morse, who was then his pupil, the advantages resulting from a plan so frequently adopted by the old masters. His young countryman was at this time meditating his first composition—a dying Hercules—and proceeded at once to act upon this suggestion. Having prepared a model that exhibited the upper part of the body—which alone would be visible in the picture—

SAMUEL F. B. MORSE.

he submitted it to Allston, who recognized so much truth in the anatomy and expression that he urgently advised its completion. After six weeks of careful labor, the statue was finished and sent to West for inspection. That venerable artist, upon entering the room, put on his spectacles, and as he walked around the model, carefully examining its details and general effect, a look of genuine satisfaction beamed from his face. He rang for an attendant and bade him call his son. 'Look here, Raphael,' he exclaimed, as the latter appeared; 'did I not always tell you that every painter could be a sculptor?' We may imagine the delight of the student at such commendation. The same day one of his fellow pupils called his attention to a notice issued by the Adelphi Society of Arts, offering a prize for the best single figure, to be modeled and sent to the rooms of the association within a certain period. The time fixed would expire in three days. Morse profited by the occasion, and placed his 'Dying Hercules' with the thirteen other specimens already entered. He was consequently invited to the meeting of the society on the evening when the decision was to be announced, and received from the hands of the Duke of Norfolk, the presiding officer, and in the presence of the foreign ambassadors, the gold medal. Perhaps no American ever started in the career of an artist under more flattering auspices; and we can not wonder that a beginning so successful encouraged the young painter to devote himself assiduously to study, with a view of returning to his own country fully prepared to illustrate the historical department of the art."

Morse spent four years in Europe in close study, and was then obliged to return to America by lack of means to carry on his education in the Old World. He had not indeed reached the high degree of proficiency which he had hoped to obtain before returning home, but he was possessed of natural talents and acquired skill which fairly entitled him to recognition as one of our leading artists. This recognition never came to him, however, and his artist life in this country was a series of sorrowful disappointments. He found no opportunity of devoting himself to the higher branches of his art, and was obliged to confine himself entirely to portrait painting as a means of livelihood. His artist career is thus referred to by Mr. Tuckerman:

"Morse went abroad under the care of Allston, and was the pupil of West and Copley. Hence he is naturally regarded by a later generation as the connecting bond that unites the present and the past in the brief annals of our artist history. But his claim to such recognition does not lie altogether in the fact that he was a pioneer; it has been worthily evidenced by his constant devotion to the great cause itself. Younger artists speak of him with affection and respect, because he has ever been zealous in the promotion of a taste for, and a study of, the fine arts. Having entered the field at too early a period to realize the promise of his youth, and driven by circumstances from the high aims he cherished, misanthropy was never suffered to grow out of personal disappointment. He gazed reverently upon the goal it was not permitted him to reach, and ardently encouraged the spirit which he felt was only to be developed when wealth and leisure had given his countrymen opportunities to cultivate those tastes upon the prevalence of which the advancement of his favorite pursuit depends. When, after the failure of one of his elaborate projects, he resolved to establish himself in New York, he was grieved to find that many petty dissensions kept the artists from each other. He made it his business to heal these wounds and reconcile the animosities that thus retarded the progress of their common object. He sought out and won the confidence of his isolated brothers, and one evening invited them all to his room ostensibly to eat strawberries and cream, but really to beguile them into something like agreeable intercourse. He had experienced the good effect of a drawing club at Charleston, where many of the members were amateurs; and on the occasion referred to covered his table with prints, and scattered inviting casts around the apartment. A very pleasant evening was the result, a mutual understanding was established, and weekly meetings unanimously agreed upon. This auspicious gathering was the germ of the National Academy of Design, of which Morse became the first president, and before which he delivered the first course of lectures on the fine arts ever given in this country."

In 1829 Mr. Morse went abroad for the purpose of completing his art studies. He remained in Europe for more than three years, residing in the principal cities of the Continent. During his absence he was elected "Professor of the Literature of the Fine Arts" in the University of the City of New York. He set out on his return home to accept this professorship in the autumn of 1832, sailing from Havre on board the packet-ship "Sully."

As has been stated, he had manifested a decided fondness for Chemistry and Natural Philosophy while at Yale College, where he was a pupil of Professor Silliman in the former science, and of Professor Day in the latter, and after his departure from college he had devoted all his leisure time to the pursuit of these studies. So great was his fondness for them that some of his friends declared their belief that he ought to abandon art and devote himself to science. In 1826–27 he had delivered, at the Athenæum in New York, the course of fine-art lectures to which reference has been made, and on alternate nights of the same season Professor J. Freeman Dana had lectured upon electro-magnetism, illustrating his remarks with the first electro-magnet (on Sturgeon's principle) ever seen in this country. Morse and Dana had been intimate friends, and had often held long conversations upon the subject of magnetism, and the magnet referred to had at length been given to the former by Professor Torrey. The interest which he had thus conceived in this instrument had never diminished, and his investigations and studies had never ceased, so that at the time of his departure from France in the "Sully," in 1832, he was one of the best informed men upon the subject to be found in any country.

Among his fellow-passengers were a number of persons of intelligence and cultivation, one of whom had but recently witnessed in Paris some highly interesting experiments with the electro-magnet, the object of which was to prove how readily the electric spark could be obtained from the magnet, and the rapidity with which it could be disseminated. To most of the passengers this relation was deeply interesting, but to all save one it was merely the recital of a curious experiment. That one exception was Mr. Morse. To him the development of this newly-discovered property of electricity was more than interesting. It showed him his true mission in life, the way to his true destiny. Art was not his proper field now, for however great his abilities as an artist, he was possessed of genius of a higher, more useful type, and it was henceforth his duty to employ it. He thought long and earnestly upon the subject which the words of his fellow-passenger had so freshly called up, pacing the deck under the silent stars, and rocked in his wakeful berth by the ocean whose terrors his genius was to tame, and whose vast depths his great invention was to set at naught. He had long been convinced that electricity was to furnish the means of rapid communication between distant points, of which the world was so much in need; and the experiments which his new acquaintance had witnessed in Paris removed from his mind the last doubt of the feasibility of the scheme. Being of an eminently practical character, he at once set to work to discover how this could be done, and succeeded so well that before the "Sully" reached New York he had conceived "not merely the idea of an electric telegraph, but of an electro-magnetic and chemical recording telegraph, substantially and essentially as it now exists," and had invented an alphabet of signs, the same in all important respects as that now in use. "The testimony to the paternity of the idea in Morse's mind, and to his acts and drawings on board the ship, is ample. His own testimony is corroborated by all the passengers (with a single exception), who testified with him before the courts, and was considered conclusive by the judges; and the date of 1832 is therefore fixed by this evidence as the date of Morse's conception, and realization also—so far as the drawings could embody the conception—of the telegraph system which now bears his name."

But though invented in 1832, it was not until 1835 (during which time he was engaged in the discharge of the duties of his professorship in the University of the City of New York) that he was enabled to complete his first recording instrument. This was but a poor, rude instrument, at the best, and was very far from being equal to his perfected invention. It embodied his idea, however, and was a good basis for subsequent improvements. By its aid he was able to send signals from a given point to the end of a wire half a mile in length, but as yet there was no means of receiving them back again from the other extremity. He continued to experiment on his invention, and made several improvements in it. It was plain from the first that he needed a duplicate of his instrument at the other end of his wire, but he was unable for a long time to have one made. At length he acquired the necessary funds, and in July, 1837, had a duplicate instrument constructed, and thus perfected his plan. His telegraph now worked to his entire satisfaction, and he could easily send his signals to the remote end of his line and receive replies in return, and answer signals sent from that terminus. Having brought it to a successful completion, he exhibited it to large audiences at the University of New York, in September, 1837. In October, 1837, Professor Morse filed a caveat to secure his invention, but his patent was not obtained until 1840.

He now entered upon that period of the inventor's life which has proved so disastrous to many, and so wearying and disheartening to all—the effort to bring his invention into general use. It was commonly believed that, although the invention was successful when used for such short distances as had been tried in the City of New York, it would fail when tested by longer lines. Morse was confident, however, that this was not the case, and in December, 1837, he went to Washington to solicit from the Government an appropriation for the construction of an experimental line from Washington City to Baltimore—a distance of forty miles. This line he declared would thoroughly test the practicability and utility of the telegraph. His petition was laid before Congress, and a committee appointed to consider it. He stated his plan to this body, and proved its practicability by actual experiments with his instruments. Considerable interest in the subject was thus aroused in Congress and throughout the country, but he derived no benefit from it. If men spoke of his telegraph, it was only to ridicule it, or to express their doubts of its success. This was especially the case in Congress, and it was very uncertain whether that body would sustain the report from the committee in favor of the invention. The session wore away in this manner, and at length ended without any action being taken in the matter.

Having failed to secure the assistance of Congress, Professor Morse went to Europe in the spring of 1838, for the purpose of enlisting the aid of the governments there in bringing his invention into use. He was unsuccessful. In England a patent was refused him, and in France he merely obtained a worthless *brevet d'invention.* He tried several other countries, but was equally unsuccessful in all, and he returned home almost disheartened, but not entirely cast down. For four years he had to struggle hard for a living. He was very poor, and, as one of his friends has since declared, had literally "to coin his mind for bread." His sturdy independence of character would not allow him to accept assistance from any one, although there were friends ready and even anxious to help him in his troubles. Alone and manfully he fought his way through these dark days, still hopeful of success for his invention, and patiently seeking to improve it wherever opportunity presented itself. At length, in 1840, he received his long-delayed patent from the General Government, and, encouraged by this, determined to make another effort to bring his telegraph into use.

He was not able to do so until the session of Congress of 1842–43, when he presented a second petition to that body, asking its aid in the construction of an experimental line between Baltimore and Washington. He had to encounter a great degree of skepticism and ridicule, with many other obstacles, not the least of which was the difficulty of meeting the expense of remaining in Washington and urging his invention upon the Government. Still he persevered, although it seemed to be hoping against hope, as the session drew near its close, and his scanty stock of money grew daily smaller. On the evening of the 3d of March, 1843, he returned from the Capitol to his lodgings utterly disheartened. It was the last night of the session, and nothing had been done in the matter of his petition. He sat up late into the night arranging his affairs so as to take his departure for home on the following day. It was useless to remain in Washington any longer. Congress would adjourn the next day, and his last hope of success had been shattered.

On the morning of the 4th of March he came down to the breakfast-table gloomy and despondent. Taking up the morning journal, he ran over it listlessly. Suddenly his eye rested upon a paragraph which caused him to spring to his feet in complete amazement. It was an announcement that, at the very last hour of the session of the previous night, a bill had been passed by Congress appropriating the sum of thirty thousand dollars for the purpose of enabling Professor Morse to construct an experimental line of telegraph between Baltimore and Washington. He could scarcely believe it real, and, as soon as possible, hastened to the Capitol to seek authentic information. The statement was confirmed by the proper authorities, and Morse's dearest wish was realized. The hour of his triumph was at hand, and his long and patient waiting was rewarded at last.

Work on the telegraph line was immediately begun, and carried on actively. At first, an insulated wire was buried under ground in a lead pipe, but this failing to give satisfaction, the wire was elevated upon poles. On the 27th of May, 1844, the line was completed, and the first trial of it made in the presence of the Government officials and many other distinguished men. Professor Morse was confident of success; but this occasion was a period of the most intense anxiety to him, for he knew that his entire future was staked upon the result of this hour. Among the company present to witness the trial was the Secretary of the Treasury, John C. Spencer. Although very much interested in the undertaking, he was entirely ignorant of the principles involved in it, and, therefore, very apprehensive of its failure. It was upon this occasion that he asked one of Professor Morse's assistants how large a bundle could be sent over the wires, and if the United States mail could not be sent in the same way.

When all was in readiness, Professor Morse seated himself at the instrument, and sent his first message to Baltimore. An answer was promptly returned, and messages were sent and replies received with a rapidity and accuracy which placed the triumph of the invention beyond the possibility of doubt. Congratulations were showered upon the inventor, who received them as calmly as he had previously borne the scoffs of many of these same men. Yet his heart throbbed all the while with a brilliant triumph. Fame and fortune both rose proudly before him. He had won a great victory, and conferred a lasting benefit upon his race.

The success of the experimental line brought Professor Morse numerous offers for the use of his invention. Telegraph companies were organized all over the country, and the stock issued by them was taken up as fast as offered. At the present day, not only the United States, but the whole world, is covered with telegraph lines. In July, 1862, just eighteen years after the completion of Morse's experimental line, it was estimated that the lines then in operation throughout the world amounted to an aggregate length of 150,000 miles. The Morse system is adopted on the principal lines of the United States, on all the lines of the Eastern continent, and exclusively on all the continental lines of Europe, "from the extreme Russian north to the Italian and Spanish south, eastward through the

Turkish empire, south into Egypt and northern Africa, and through India, Australia, and parts of China."

The rapid growth of the telegraph interest of the United States placed Professor Morse in the possession of a large fortune, which was greatly increased by the adoption of his invention in Europe. The countries which had refused him patents at first now did honor to his genius. Nor was he the only gainer by this. In France, especially, the benefits of his invention were great. The old system of semaphore telegraphs had been an annual expense to the government of that country of 1,100,000 francs, but Morse's telegraph yielded to the French Government, in the first three years after its introduction, a total revenue of 6,000,000 francs.

Fortune was not Morse's only reward. Honors were showered upon him from all parts of the world. In 1848, his *alma mater*, Yale College, conferred on him the complimentary degree of LL.D., and since then he has been made a member of nearly all the American scientific and art academies. From European Governments and scientific and art associations he has received more honors than have ever fallen to the share of any other American. In 1848, he received from the Sultan of Turkey the decoration of the *Nishaun Iftichar* in diamonds, and subsequently gold medals of scientific merit were awarded him by the King of Prussia, the King of Würtemburg, and the Emperor of Austria. The gift of the King of Prussia was set in a massive gold snuff-box. In 1856, the Emperor Napoleon III gave him the Cross of Chevalier of the Legion of Honor; in 1857, he received from the King of Denmark the Cross of Knight of the Danebrog; and in 1858, the Queen of Spain sent him the Cross of Knight Commander of the order of Isabella the Catholic. In 1859, a convention of the representatives of the various European powers met in Paris, at the instance of the Emperor Napoleon III, for the purpose of determining upon the best means of giving Professor Morse a collective testimonial. France, Russia, Sweden, Belgium, Holland, Austria, Sardinia, Tuscany, Turkey, and the Holy See were represented, and their deliberations resulted in the presentation to Professor Morse, in the name of their united governments, of the sum of 400,000 francs, as an honorary and personal reward for his labors. In 1856, the telegraph companies of Great Britain gave him a banquet in London, at which Mr. William Fothergill Corke, himself the distinguished inventor of a system of telegraphy, presided.

Professor Morse is also the inventor of submarine telegraphy. In 1842, he laid the first submarine telegraph line ever put down, across the harbor of New York, and for this achievement received the gold medal of the American Institute. On the 10th of August, 1843, he addressed a communication to the Secretary of the Treasury, in which he avowed his belief that a telegraphic cable could and would be laid across the Atlantic ocean, for the purpose of connecting Europe and America. His words upon this occasion clearly prove that the idea of the Atlantic telegraph originated with him. They were as follows: "The practical inference from this law is, that a telegraphic communication on the electro-magnetic plan may with certainty be established across the Atlantic ocean. Startling as this may now seem, I am confident the time will come when this project will be realized."

In February, 1854, Mr. Cyrus W. Field, of New York, ignorant of Professor Morse's views upon this subject, wrote to him to ask if he considered the working of a cable across the Atlantic practicable. The Professor at once sought an interview with Mr. Field, and assured him of his entire confidence in the undertaking. He entered heartily into Mr. Field's scheme, and rendered great aid in the noble enterprise which has been described elsewhere in these pages. He was present at each attempt to lay the cable, and participated in the final triumph by which his prediction, made twenty-three years previous, was verified.

Professor Morse is now in his eightieth year. He resides during the winter in the city of New York, and passes his summers at his beautiful country seat, near Poughkeepsie, on the Hudson. He bears his great honors with the same modesty which marked his early struggles, and is the center of a host of friends whom he has attached to himself by the tenderest ties. "Courage and patience have been his watchwords, and although the snows of time have bleached his hair, the same intelligence and enterprising spirit, the same urbane disposition that endeared him to the friends of his youth, still cause all who know him to rejoice in the honorable independence which his great invention has secured to his age."

IV.

PUBLISHERS.

CHAPTER XXI.

JAMES HARPER.

SOME years ago a gentleman having business with the great house of Harper & Brothers asked one of the employés of that establishment, "Which one is Harper, and which are the brothers?" He was answered, "Either one is Harper, and all the rest are the brothers." This reply fully sets forth the difficulty which must be experienced by any one attempting to write the story of the life of either member of this house. In such an undertaking it is very difficult to select "Harper," and impossible to pass by the "Brothers." The interests of each were so thoroughly in harmony with those of all the others, and there was such perfect unanimity of sentiment existing between them with regard to their private as well as their public affairs, that it is hardly possible to separate them. Since, however, it is not consistent with the design of this work to relate the history of the "house," it is the purpose of the writer to select the eldest of the brothers as the representative of the group, and to offer him to the reader as a type of the American publisher.

The grandfather of JAMES HARPER came to this country

from England about the year 1740, and was one of the first of the American Methodists. His son Joseph was born in 1766. He married Elizabeth Kollyer, and settled at Newtown, on Long Island, as a farmer. It was here that James, their eldest child, was born, on the 13th of April, 1795. He grew up with a vigorous constitution, and the pure influences of his home, together with the sound religious training which he received from his parents, laid the foundation of those simple and steady habits for which he was noted through life. In the winter he attended the district school, and in the summer he worked on his father's farm. Thus his life passed away quietly and healthfully until he had completed his fifteenth year.

It now became necessary for him to make some choice of a profession in life, and when the matter was presented to him he promptly decided to become a printer. His father cheerfully seconded his wishes, and he was accordingly apprenticed to a printer in New York. On the morning of his departure from home, when the family assembled for "prayers," his mother, who was a woman of superior character, took the father's place and led the worship. With trembling tones she commended her boy to the love and protection of the Saviour, and when the moment of leave-taking came she sent him forth into the world with the tender warning never to forget his home or his religious duties, or "that he had good blood in him."

The change from his happy home to the place of "devil" in the printing office was one which tried the lad's fortitude to the utmost. His position was but little better than that of a menial, and not only was all the drudgery and disagreeable work put upon him, but he was made the sport of the workmen, some of whom used him even roughly. He bore it all good-naturedly, however, devoting himself to his trade with the determination to master it.

The printing office in which he was employed was located near Franklin Square, then occupied by the best people of the city. Often, as young Harper passed across the square to and from his work, his rough "country clothes" drew upon him the ridicule of the children of these "goodly citizens." They teazed and insulted him, and sometimes carried their cruelty to the extremity of offering him bodily violence. He bore it patiently for a time, but at length determined to put a stop to it. He was physically the superior of any of his tormentors, and had put up with their conduct merely from his sincere desire to avoid a "street fight." In accordance with his new resolution, however, when one of them approached him one day and asked for his card, he set down a bucket which he was carrying, and, seizing the fellow, kicked him across the square, saying to him: "That's my card, take good care of it. When I am out of my time, and set up for myself, and you need employment, as you will, come to me, bring the card, and I will give you work." "Forty-one years after," says the writer upon whose authority this incident is related, "when Mr. Harper's establishment was known throughout all the land, after he had borne the highest municipal honors of the city, and had become one of our wealthiest men, the person who had received the card came to Mr. James Harper's establishment and asked employment, claiming it on the ground that he had kept the card given him forty-one years before."

In a little while James was joined by his brother John, who was apprenticed to another printer in the city, and the two lads spent with each other much of their leisure time. Both worked hard. James soon became noted as the best pressman in the city, his great personal strength enabling him to work the old-fashioned hand-press with ease. It is said that if he disliked a fellow pressman and wished to be rid of him, he merely put forth his immense strength and outworked him. The man being unable to keep up with him, was obliged to retire.

"The habits of his rural home followed him to the city. In an age when every body drank ardent spirits freely, he was strictly temperate, and the cold water disciple justified his faith by his works. With the cheerful constancy of the fathers of his church he quietly resisted the temptations of the city. He opened a prayer-meeting in the house of an old colored woman in Ann Street, and joined the John Street Methodist Church. Meanwhile, to their simple and thrifty method of life, James and his brother added work out of hours, so that when their apprenticeship was ended they had a little money saved."

James' excellent habits and great skill as a workman had given entire satisfaction to his master during the whole period of his apprenticeship, and he informed the young man at the expiration of his indentures that he was willing to employ him again at fair wages. The young workman surprised him by telling him that he intended to set up for himself, and that all he wanted from him now was a certificate that he was fit to be trusted with a book. This was given, and James and his brother John took their little capital, which was increased by a loan of a few hundred dollars from their father, and renting a small room in Dover Street, set up an office on their own account, and began business under the firm name of J. & J. Harper. Their capital was small—less than the annual wages of some of their workmen to-day—but they were sustained by industry, determination, and high moral principle. When they began business, it was with a tacit agreement that each would endeavor to deserve the confidence of the other, and of their fellow-men. There was to be no evasion of principle, no sharp practice, in their house. They were resolved to make money, but to make it honestly. They would engage in no transaction which should cause a doubt of their integrity in the breast of the good mother who had sent them forth with her blessing.

More than fifty years have passed away since then, and the Harpers have prospered steadily, and so greatly, too, that for many years their house has stood at the head of the publishing interest of America. Their career is an instructive one, giving an emphatic denial to the assertion we hear so often repeated, that an "over-honest" man can not make money in New York. Shut your ears to the calumny, young man, just staring out in life. "Honesty *is* the best policy;" and it is only by scrupulous honesty that enduring success can be obtained. Trickery and sharp practice may earn wealth rapidly, but depend upon it they have their reward; for it is a curious fact in the history of man that wealth acquired by knavery rarely stays with its possessors for more than a generation, if so long.

In starting out, the young Harpers printed books to order, attempting nothing at their own risk. They did a part of the composition and press-work with their own hands, and were, perhaps, the hardest workers in their establishment. Their first job was two thousand copies of Seneca's Morals, and was intrusted to them by Evert Duyckinck, a famous publisher of that day. The books were delivered in August, 1817, and gave entire satisfaction.

Immediately after this, they undertook to stereotype an edition of the "Book of Common Prayer" for the Protestant Episcopal Church of New York, supposing that they would be able to make a fair profit at the rate at which they had agreed to do the work. It was their original intention to do the composition themselves, and have the stereotyping done at one of the large establishments of the city; but upon a closer investigation they found that this would cost them more than they had agreed to do the work for. In this dilemma, they resolved to learn the art of stereotyping themselves, and perform that portion of their contract on their own premises. It was a tedious undertaking; but they went through with it determinedly, and at the proper time delivered the books to the officials of the Episcopal Church. Their profit was not very large, but they had become stereotypers as well as printers, and had added a valuable department to their business. Further than this, their Prayer Book was pronounced the best piece of stereotyping that had ever been seen in the city, and won the young men congratulations on all sides. They next undertook twenty-five hundred copies of Mair's "Introduction to Latin," which they delivered in December, 1817.

In April, 1818, they put forth their first venture on their own account. This consisted of five hundred copies of Locke's "Essay upon the Human Understanding." These were readily disposed of, and their success encouraged them to further efforts. They proceeded very cautiously, and it was for a long time their custom, when contemplating the publication of a book, and especially in the case of a reprint, to send to the leading booksellers in the large cities of the Union, and ascertain how many copies each one would take. Thus they pushed their way forward, seizing upon every favorable opportunity for the publication of original and foreign works. They rarely made an unsuccessful venture, and as each worked hard, and had constantly in view, above all other subjects, the success of the house, they gradually extended their business until they secured the foremost place among the publishers of the United States.

Beginning with works of a dry, philosophic nature, the Harpers have extended their operations into every department of literature. Their catalogue of publications, issued in 1869, lies on the writer's table. It is a duodecimo volume of two hundred and ninety-six closely-printed pages, and embraces a list of several thousand volumes. In this list are histories, biographies, travels, adventures, novels, poems, educational works, works on science, art, philosophy, metaphysics—in short, books on every topic familiar to man. In the department of fiction, the success of this house has been remarkable. They have published between four and five hundred novels, in cloth and paper bindings, and the demand for their early publications of this kind is still sufficiently active to compel them to keep a stock always on hand. When they began to issue their Library of Select Novels, they did so with a distinct purpose in view. Novel-reading has always been a passion with Americans, but at the period referred to the best novels were published at such high prices that but few could afford to buy them. The masses were compelled to put up with the cheap, flashy stories which were so well known some years ago as "yellow covers." This style of fiction, now confined to the lowest class of readers, at that time found its way into almost every house, and the popular taste was at a very low ebb. The Harpers felt sure that by issuing the best, and only the best, English novels at a low price, they would not only meet a real want on the part of the public, but in great measure supersede the "yellow covers," with all their pernicious influences. The sequel proved the correctness of these views, and resulted in large profits to them.

Soon after commencing business, James and John Harper received their younger brothers, Joseph Wesley and Fletcher, into their establishment as apprentices. These young men were taught the business thoroughly, and when they had completed their apprenticeship were admitted into the firm as partners, the former entering the firm in 1823, and the latter in 1826. In 1825 the style of the firm was changed to Harper &

Brothers, and the business was removed to 81 and 82 Cliff Street, on a portion of the site of the present establishment. It was then the largest printing-house in New York, employing fifty workmen and ten hand presses.

In 1850, the Harpers decided to commence the publication of a monthly periodical, and, accordingly, in the summer of that year they issued the first number of "Harper's New Monthly Magazine," which, in point of popularity, stands to-day, after a career of twenty years, at the head of American magazines, and boasts of a circulation of 180,000 copies. The recognition of another want of the public led, in 1857, to the establishment of an illustrated newspaper, "Harper's Weekly," which has at present a circulation of 100,000 copies. In 1869 they began the publication of a new weekly fashion paper, called "the Bazaar," which has reached a circulation of 75,000 copies.

From the first, the Harpers made their house a popular establishment. They sought public favor by legitimate means, and generally managed to retain it in the same way. From an early period in their history, their imprint on a book has been sufficient to secure its sale; and they have managed to identify themselves so thoroughly with American progress that the whole country feels an interest in their success. By studying the popular taste closely, they were enabled to publish in rapid succession works suited to it; and by fair and liberal dealings with authors they soon drew around them a corps of the best writers in the Union.

Their success was rapid, and by the year 1853 their establishment had increased in size so much that it occupied "nine large contiguous buildings, full of costly machinery of every kind, with stores of plates and books." On the 10th of December of that year, a workman in one of the upper rooms carelessly threw a piece of lighted paper into what he supposed to be a pail of water, but which proved to be camphene. In a few minutes the building was in flames; all efforts to save it were in vain. The fire spread rapidly, and in a few hours the entire establishment was in ruins. The loss was one million of dollars, of which sum only about one-fourth was covered by insurance.

It was a terrible blow, but James Harper and his brothers wasted no time in repining. Before the embers had ceased smoking they were taking active measures to reëstablish their business. From the wreck of their establishment they saved a part of the stereotype plates, which had been stored in the vaults, out of the way of the fire. They immediately rented Sheffield's paper warehouse, at the corner of Beekman and Gold Streets, and went to work with greater energy than ever. "Presses were employed in New York, Philadelphia, and Boston. Nothing was forgotten. The next monthly issue of the *Magazine* had been made ready, and it was reproduced at the earliest moment. One regular contributor, then in Chicago, received the first news of the fire by a brief telegram: 'Copy destroyed. Send fresh copy immediately.' Before the ruins were cleared away the plans of the new buildings were ready, and the buildings themselves were rapidly finished."

The new establishment of Harper & Brothers is one of the wonders of the great city in which it is located. The buildings are of iron and brick, and cover half an acre of ground. The establishment really consists of two buildings. The front building faces Franklin Square, and is a magnificent iron structure, painted white. Behind this is the second building, which fronts on Cliff Street. A court-yard intervenes between them, spanned by several bridges, connecting them. Each building is seven stories in height, and completely fire-proof.

There are no openings in the floors for communication, but the various floors are connected by circular stairways of iron, placed outside the building. The front building, or that which faces Franklin Square, is used for storerooms, salesrooms, and the editorial and business offices of the establishment. In the rear building the various branches of the book manufacture are carried on. The author's manuscript is received here and sent back to him a complete book. Every portion of the work is done under the same roof, and it is well done. The building is filled with the most costly and complete machinery for saving time and labor. Besides the machinery used in other departments, it contains in its press-room forty-three Adams presses for book work, and five cylinder presses for printing the "Weekly" and the "Bazaar." About 600 persons, 250 of whom are females, are employed in the establishment; and it is to the credit of both employers and employés that but few changes occur in this force. Many of the employés have been with the firm since its first entrance into business. The old man in charge of the vaults—a curiosity in his way—has been in the service of the house for fifty years, and to leave it now would, doubtless, break his heart; for none of the Harpers are as proud of their reputation as he is. The most perfect system reigns throughout every department, and every thing goes on promptly and in its proper place.

"Of course," says a writer who many years has witnessed the operations of the house, "the development and organization of such a business were due not to one brother alone, but to the coöperation of all. . . . The business was to James, as to the others, the great central interest, but prosperity could not relax his steady character. He did not forget his early faith, nor the counsels and the habits of his Long Island home. He remained strictly a 'temperance man,' and his marvelous physical vigor was claimed by the temperance advocates as that of a cold-water man. He was long an official member of John-Street Church, and when he left his house in Rose Street, and went to live in the upper part of the city, he joined the congregation of St. Paul's Church, in the Fourth Avenue. But with all his fidelity to his ancestral faith, he cherished the largest charity, and by much experience of the world had learned to agree with his favorite apostle, James, that pure religion and undefiled, is to visit the fatherless and widows, and keep himself unspotted from the world. Thus, with all his conviction and devotion, there was nothing hard or fanatical in his feeling or conduct, and he held pleasant personal relations with men of every faith. Few men indulged in so little harsh criticism of others, and he expressed censure or disapprobation by humorous indirection rather than by open accusation. 'We must not be too hard,' he was fond of saying, 'it is so difficult to know all the circumstances. If you should insist, for instance, that the use of tobacco is a sin, dear me! dear me!'

"Mr. Harper was a Whig during the days of that party, and a natural conservative. But in politics he showed the same moderation and toleration. 'Don't try to drive men too roughly, my dear sir; it is much easier to draw than to push.' He took no conspicuous or active part in politics, except in 1844, when he was elected Mayor of the city. He was constantly asked to serve in Congress and in other public stations, but he steadily declined, saying, with a sly smile, that he preferred to stick to the business that he understood.

"To that business his heart and life were given. Of late years its active cares had naturally fallen into the hands of his younger associates; but he never relaxed his interest and devotion. 'While I was dressing,' said a much younger neighbor, 'I used to see Mayor Harper coming out of his house to go down town, and felt ashamed of myself. Early at the office, he opened and looked over the mail, and during the hours of the morning he passed from one room to another, his shrewd eye seeing every thing, and measuring men and work, chatting and jesting as he went. But out of those shrewd eyes looked a kind and gentle heart. He knew by name the men and women and children employed in the various parts of the great buildings, interested himself in their family stories, and often won a confidence that was never betrayed. His charities, which were ample, were thus intelligent and effective, and poor men as well as women bent to kiss his calm, unchanged face as he lay in his coffin."

To the very last, James Harper retained his physical and mental vigor, and was looked up to by all the members of the house as its brightest ornament. To the last, he was one of the best known and most honored citizens of the great metropolis. His great wealth had not ruffled the serenity of his spirit, or caused the slightest variation in his conduct. To the last he was the Christian merchant, citizen, and father, offering to his children in himself a noble model by which to shape their lives.

It had been his custom at family prayers to ask of God protection from sudden death, but for some time before his death he ceased to do so. His family noticed this, and one of them asked his reason for the omission. He answered quietly, "The Lord knows best."

On the 25th of March, 1869, he was at his usual post in his office, and after business hours, as was his habit, set out with his daughter for a drive in the Central Park. As he neared the Park the pole of his carriage broke suddenly, and the horses, becoming frightened, dashed off furiously, dragging the carriage after them. Mr. Harper and his daughter were both thrown violently upon the pavement. The latter was but slightly injured, but Mr. Harper was taken up insensible, and conveyed to St. Luke's Hospital, which was close at hand. He never regained consciousness, but lingered until fifteen minutes after seven on the evening of the 27th, when he expired, surrounded by all his family, excepting his wife, who had long been an invalid. His death was regarded as a calamity to the city, and all classes of the community united to do honor to his memory.

CHAPTER XXII.

JAMES T. FIELDS.

THE old "corner book-store" at the intersection of Washington and School Streets, in the city of Boston, is one of the most notable places in the New England metropolis. The memory of the oldest inhabitant can not recall a time when this corner was not devoted to its present uses; and around it, in the long years that have passed since the first book merchant first displayed his wares here, there have gathered a host of the most interesting, as well as the most brilliant, souvenirs of our literary history. Here were sold, in "the days that tried men's souls," those stirring pamphlets that sounded the death-knell of British tyranny in the New World; and it was from this old corner that the tender songs of Longfellow, the weird conceptions of Hawthorne, the philosophic utterances of Emerson, first found their way to the hearts of the people.

In 1834, the corner book-store was kept by Carter & Bendee, and was then the leading book-house in Boston. One morning in that year there entered the office of the proprietors a young lad from New Hampshire, who stated that he came to seek employment in their service. His bright, intelligent appearance was in his favor, scarcely less than the testimonials which he brought, vouching for his integrity and industry. His application was successful, and he entered the service of Messrs. Carter & Bendee, being given the lowest clerkship in the establishment and a salary barely sufficient to support him.

This lad was JAMES T. FIELDS. He was born in Portsmouth, New Hampshire, on the 30th of December, 1820. His father was a captain in the merchant service, and died when the boy was only four years old, leaving him to the care and guidance of one of the best of mothers. He was educated at the common schools of the city, and was thence transferred to the high school. He exhibited a remarkable fondness for study, and at the early age of thirteen graduated at the high school, taking the first honors of his class. He was regarded as one of the best classical scholars in the institution, and during his course took several prizes in Latin and Greek composition. Unusual abilities as a poet were also manifested very early, and when but twelve years old he wrote a poem in blank verse, which attracted the attention of the late Chief Justice Woodbury, then Governor of New Hampshire, who was so much surprised and gratified to find such talent in so young a boy, that he earnestly advised him to endeavor to complete his studies at Harvard University. This, indeed, was the chief desire of the boy, but a collegiate education required means which he could not command, and he was forced to go out into the world to seek his fortune. Having secured a good elementary education, however, he was resolved that he would not abandon his efforts to acquire knowledge. All his leisure time, after going to Boston to live, was devoted to reading and study. While neglecting no duty in his business, he gave the hours which most boys devote to amusement to severe mental labor. Young as he was, he was ambitious.

He knew that knowledge was power, especially in the community in which he lived, and he was resolved that this power should be his. The result is plainly seen in his subsequent career. Although deprived of the advantages of a collegiate course, Mr. Fields has more than made up that deficiency by his faithful labors, and there are few men in New England to-day possessed of more varied and extensive mental accomplishments than he. Upon going to Boston he promptly identified himself with the Mercantile Library Association of that place, availing himself of its advantages, and exerting all the influence of which he was possessed to insure its success. When but eighteen years old, he was chosen to deliver an anniversary poem before the association. The value of the compliment will be better appreciated by the reader when it is stated that the oration upon that occasion was pronounced by Edward Everett.

His industry in his business duties was great. He entered the house of Carter & Bendee with the determination to rise in it. He worked faithfully, and was the first at his post in the morning, and the last to leave it at night. When the style of the firm was changed to Allen & Ticknor, he was promoted to a more important place. He proved himself from the first one of the most valuable and trustworthy assistants in the house, and his merits were promptly recognized. From the lowest place in the house, he worked his way up steadily until he became the manager of the establishment. Each promotion brought with it an increase of salary. Knowing well that "a penny saved at present is a pound gained in future" to a young man striving to rise in the world, he practiced the most conscientious economy. He made himself thoroughly acquainted with every detail of the publishing trade; and although, of late years, he has had the supervision more especially of the literary department of his large business, there are few publishers in this country more intimate with the business and mechanical branches of their trade.

In 1846, just twelve years after his entrance into the house, his clerkship came to an end, and he became a partner in the establishment, the style of the firm being Ticknor & Fields. He took an active share in the business; and while full credit must be given to Mr. Ticknor for the extraordinary success which the firm enjoyed, it can not be denied that Mr. Fields' share in this work was very great, and fully equal to that of his partner. His acknowledged literary abilities won him friends among the most gifted writers of the country, and these naturally sought his assistance in presenting their works to the world. Their friendship induced an intelligent confidence in his literary taste and mercantile integrity, and it was a decided gain for them to secure one so generally esteemed and trusted as their publisher. Young writers, still struggling for fame, felt that in submitting their works to his inspection they would receive the patient examination of not only a conscientious reader, but of one whose own literary abilities rendered him unusually competent for the task. The public generally learned to share this confidence in his literary judgment. And so it came to pass that the imprint of Ticknor & Fields was universally accepted as a sufficient guarantee of the excellence of any book, and rarely failed to insure its success. Naturally, the house was proud of this confidence, and it is pleasant to record that they have never abused it. There is, perhaps, no other publishing firm in the Union whose catalogue is so free from objectionable or worthless publications as that issued by this house.

Gradually Messrs. Ticknor & Fields became the recognized publishers of a large number of the leading writers of this country and of Great Britain. In their catalogue we find the names of Longfellow, Bryant, Whittier, Holmes, Aldrich, Agassiz, Beecher, Alice Cary, Cummins, Dana, Emerson, Hawthorne, Gail Hamilton, Lowell, Parton, Saxe, Sprague, Stowe, Bayard Taylor, Thoreau, and Tuckerman, in American literature; and in English literature, the names of Browning, Dickens, George Eliot, Mrs. Jameson, Kingsley, Owen Meredith, Charles Reade, and Tennyson. With their English authors they maintain the pleasantest relations, recognizing their moral right to their works, and paying them a fair royalty upon the sales of their books. Of their relations with their American authors, a popular periodical says:

"There are no business men more honorable or generous than the publishers of the United States, and especially honorable and considerate toward authors. The relation usually existing between author and publisher in the United States is that of a warm and lasting friendship, such as now animates and dignifies the intercourse between the literary men of New England and Messrs. Ticknor & Fields. . . . . The relation, too, is one of a singular mutual trustfulness. The author receives his semi-annual account from the publisher with as ablute a faith in its correctness as though he had himself counted the volumes sold."

In 1865, the firm removed from the old corner stand to a new and elegant establishment on Tremont Street, near the Common, and in the same year Mr. Howard Ticknor, who had succeeded his father in the business, withdrew from it. New partners were admitted, and the style of the firm became Fields, Osgood & Co., Mr. Fields still remaining at the head of the house.

The new book store is one of the handsomest and most attractive in the country. The store proper is eighty feet deep by fifty feet wide, and is fitted up handsomely in hard wood.

There is no paint about it, every piece of wood in use presenting its natural appearance. On the right in entering are the book shelves and counters, and on the opposite side the desks devoted to the magazine department. At the rear are the counting rooms and the private office of Mr. J. R. Osgood, the active business man of the concern. The second story is elegantly and tastefully fitted up. It contains the luxurious private office of Mr. Fields, in which are to be seen excellent likenesses of his two dearest friends, Longfellow and Dickens; and the parlor of the establishment, which is known as the Author's Room. This is a spacious and handsomely-appointed room, whose windows, overlooking the Common, command one of the prettiest views in New England. It is supplied with the leading periodicals of the day, and choice volumes of current literature. Here one may always find one or more of the "gifted few," whose names are familiar to the reader; and frequent reunions of the book-making fraternity are designed to be held here, under the genial auspices of the literary partner of the house.

It is not often that men win success in both literature and mercantile life. Good authors have usually made very poor business managers, and *vice versa;* but the subject of this memoir, besides winning a great success as a merchant, and that in one of the most hazardous branches of mercantile life, has also won an enviable reputation as a man of letters. His poems have made him well known, both in this country and in England. Besides the poems recited before various literary associations, he has published two volumes of fugitive pieces. The first appeared in 1843, while he was still a clerk, and the second in 1858. His poems abound in humor, pathos, and a delicate, beautiful fancy. One of his friends has said of him:

"Little of the sad travail of the historic poet has Mr. Fields known. Of the emaciated face, the seedy garment, the collapsed purse, the dog-eared and often rejected manuscript, he has never known, save from well-authenticated tradition. His muse was born in sunshine, and has only been sprinkled with the tears of affection. Every effort has been cheered to the echo, and it is impossible for so genial a fellow to fail of an ample and approving audience for whatever may fall from his lip or pen."

The following lines, from his second volume, will serve as a specimen of the "homely beauty" of Mr. Fields' muse, though it hardly sets forth all his powers:

She came among the gathering crowd
  A maiden fair, without pretense,
And when they asked her humble name,
  She whispered mildly, "Common Sense."

Her modest garb drew every eye,
  Her ample cloak, her shoes of leather;
And when they sneered, she simply said,
  "I dress according to the weather."

They argued long and reasoned loud,
  In dubious Hindoo phrase mysterious;
While she, poor child, could not divine
  Why girls so young should be so serious.

They knew the length of Plato's beard,
  And how the scholars wrote in Laturn;
She studied authors not so deep,
  And took the Bible for her pattern.

And so she said, "Excuse me, friends,
  I feel all have their proper places,
And *Common Sense* should stay at home
  With cheerful hearts and smiling faces."

Mr. Fields has been a frequent contributor to his own periodicals, his latest effort being a paper devoted to personal recollections of Charles Dickens, which was published in the "Atlantic Monthly" soon after the death of the great master.

He has made several extended tours throughout Europe, where he has enjoyed social advantages rarely opened to travelers. One of his friends says that, in his first visit to the Old World, "he passed several months in England, Scotland, France, and Germany, visiting the principal places of interest, and forming most delightful and profitable intimacies with the most distinguished *litcrateurs* of the day. He was a frequent guest at the well-known breakfasts of the great banker-poet of 'The Pleasures of Memory' and of 'Italy,' and listened or added his own contributions to the exuberant riches of the hour, when such visitors as Talfourd, Dickens, Moore, and Landor were the talkers." He also formed a warm friendship with Wordsworth, and, during his stay in Edinburgh, with Professor Wilson and De Quincey. The writings of the last-named author were published by Ticknor and Fields, in eighteen volumes, and were edited by Mr. Fields, at the author's own request.

Mr. Fields is now in his fiftieth year, but shows no sign of age, save the whitening of his heavy, curling beard. He is still young and active in mind and body. He is of medium height, and well proportioned, with an erect carriage. Polished and courteous in manner, he is easily accessible to all. To young writers he is especially kind, and it is a matter of the truest pleasure to him to seek out and bring to notice genuine literary merit. He has a host of friends, and is widely popular with all classes.

V.

EDITORS.

CHAPTER XXIII.

JAMES GORDON BENNETT.

JAMES GORDON BENNETT was born at New Mill, Keith, in Banffshire, on the north-eastern coast of Scotland, about the year 1800. His relatives were Roman Catholics, and he was brought up in a Catholic family of French origin. In his fourteenth year, having passed through the primary schools of his native place, he entered the Roman Catholic Seminary at Aberdeen, for the purpose of studying for the priesthood of that Church. During the two or three years which he passed here he was a close student, and acquired the basis of an excellent education.

In 1817 he came into possession of a copy of Benjamin Franklin's autobiography, which had been recently published in Scotland. The perusal of this little book changed the course of his whole life. It induced him to abandon all thoughts of the priesthood, and to try his fortune in the New World, in which the great philosopher had succeeded so well before him. A little more than a year later he left Glasgow, and in May, 1819, being now about twenty years old, landed at Halifax,

Nova Scotia. He had less than twenty-five dollars in his purse, knew no vocation save that of a book-keeper, and had not a friend on this side of the ocean.

He secured a few pupils in Halifax, and gave lessons in book-keeping, but his profits were so small that he determined to reach the United States as soon as possible. Accordingly he made his way along the coast to Portland, Maine, where he took passage for Boston in a small schooner. He found great difficulty in procuring employment, for Boston then, as now, offered but few inducements to new-comers. He parted with his last penny, and was reduced to the most pressing want. For two whole days he went without food, and a third day would doubtless have been added to his fast had he not been fortunate enough to find a shilling on the Common, with which he procured the means of relieving his hunger. He now obtained a salesman's place in the bookstore of Messrs. Wells & Lilly, who, upon discovering his fitness for the place, transferred him to their printing-office as proof-reader; but his employers failed about two years after his connection with them began, and he was again thrown out of employment.

From Boston he went, in 1822, to New York, where he obtained a situation on a newspaper. Soon after his arrival in the metropolis he was offered, by Mr. Wellington, the proprietor of the "Charleston (S. C.) Courier," the position of translator from the Spanish, and general assistant. He accepted the offer, and at once repaired to Charleston. He remained there only a few months, however, and then returned to New York.

He now proposed to open a "Permanent Commercial School," at 148 Fulton Street, and advertised to teach the usual branches "in the inductive method." His advertisement set forth that his pupils would be taught "reading, elocution, penmanship, and arithmetic; algebra, astronomy, history, and geography;

moral philosophy, commercial law, and political economy; English grammar and composition, and, also, if required, the French and Spanish languages by natives of those countries." This elaborate scheme was never put into execution, as Mr. Bennett did not receive a sufficient number of applications to warrant him in opening the school. He next attempted a course of lectures on political economy at the old Dutch Church in Ann Street, but this enterprise was also a pecuniary failure. In 1825 he purchased the "New York Courier," a Sunday paper, but did not succeed with it. He continued to write for the press, principally for one or two papers, selling his articles where he could, and in 1826 formed a regular connection with the "National Advocate," a Democratic journal. To his duties in this position he applied himself with an energy and industry never surpassed, and rarely equaled, in his profession. He took an active part in politics, and wrote regularly and constantly for his paper, acquiring considerable reputation by his articles against the tariff and on banks and banking. He now embarked in journalism as the business of his life, and with the determination to succeed. In order to win success, he knew he must first learn to master himself. He neither smoked, drank, nor gambled. He indulged in no species of dissipation, but was temperate and prudent in all things. A few years later he said of himself, "I eat and drink to live, not live to eat and drink. Social glasses of wine are my aversion; public dinners are my abomination; all species of gormandizing my utter scorn and contempt. When I am hungry, I eat; when thirsty, drink. Wine or viands taken for society, or to stimulate conversation, tend only to dissipation, indolence, poverty, contempt, and death."

In 1827 the "National Advocate" changed hands, and, under its new proprietors, supported John Quincy Adams for President. Mr. Bennett, being a supporter of Martin Van Buren, then a United States Senator, resigned his position on the paper, and soon after, in connection with the late M. M. Noah, established "The Enquirer," which warmly espoused the cause of Andrew Jackson in the Presidential canvass of 1828. About this time he became a recognized member of the Tammany Society.

In the spring of 1828 he went to Washington, where he resided for some time as the correspondent of "The Enquirer." In looking through the library of Congress one day, he found an edition of Horace Walpole's letters, which he read with a keen relish. These suggested the idea of a series of similar letters to his own paper, and he at once put his plan into execution. His letters were written and published. They were "spicy," pleasant in style, full of gossip about the distinguished personages who thronged the capital every winter, and, withal, free from any offensive personality. They were read with eagerness, and widely copied by the press throughout the country. Yet he was poorly paid for them, and at a time when he had made a "real hit" was forced to labor hard for a bare subsistence. He did all kinds of literary work. He wrote editorials, letters, sketches, poetry, stories, police reports, in short, every thing that a newspaper had use for, and yet his earnings were barely more than sufficient to afford him a decent support.

In 1829, the "Courier and Enquirer" were united under one management, and Mr. Bennett was made assistant editor, with James Watson Webb as his chief. In the autumn of that year he became associate editor. Says Mr. James Parton (by no means an ardent admirer of Mr. Bennett):

"During the great days of the 'Courier and Enquirer,' from 1829 to 1832, when it was incomparably the best newspaper on the continent, James Gordon Bennett was its most efficient hand. It lost him in 1832, when the paper abandoned General Jackson and took up Nicholas Biddle, and in losing him lost its chance of retaining the supremacy among American newspapers to this day. We can truly say that at that time journalism, as a thing by itself and for itself, had no existence in the United States. Newspapers were mere appendages of party, and the darling object of each journal was to be recognized as the organ of the party it supported. As to the public, the great public, hungry for interesting news, no one thought of it. Forty years ago, in the city of New York, a copy of a newspaper could not be bought for money. If any one wished to see a newspaper, he had either to go to the office and subscribe, or repair to a bar-room and buy a glass of something to drink, or bribe a carrier to rob one of his customers. The circulation of the 'Courier and Enquirer' was considered something marvelous when it printed thirty-five hundred copies a day, and its business was thought immense when its daily advertising averaged fifty-five dollars. It is not very unusual for a newspaper now to receive for advertising, in one day, six hundred times that sum. Bennett, in the course of time, had a chance been given to him, would have made the 'Courier and Enquirer' powerful enough to cast off all party ties, and this he would have done merely by improving it as a vehicle of news. But he was kept down upon one of those ridiculous, tantalizing, corrupting salaries, which are a little more than a single man needs, but not enough for him to marry upon. This salary was increased by the proprietors giving him a small share in the small profits of the printing-office; so that, after fourteen years of hard labor and Scotch economy, he found himself, on leaving the great paper, a capitalist to the extent of a few hundred dollars. The chief editor of the paper which he now abandoned sometimes lost as much in a single evening at the card-table. It probably never occurred to him that this poor, ill-favored Scotchman was destined to destroy his paper and all the class of papers to which it belonged. Any one who examines a file of the 'Courier and Enquirer' of that time, and knows its interior circumstances, will see plainly enough that the possession of this man was the vital element in its prosperity. He alone knew the rudiments of his trade. He alone had the physical stamina, the indefatigable industry, the sleepless vigilance, the dexterity, tact, and audacity needful for keeping up a daily newspaper in the face of keen competition."

Mr. Bennett left the "Courier and Enquirer" in 1832, the cause of his action being the desertion of General Jackson by that journal. He at once started a cheap partisan paper, called "The Globe," devoted to the interests of Jackson and Van Buren. It failed to receive the support of the Democratic party, however, and went down after a precarious existence of thirty days.

Undismayed by this failure, Mr. Bennett removed to Philadelphia, and invested the remainder of his capital in a daily Democratic journal, called "The Pennsylvanian," of which he was the principal editor, laboring hard to win for it the assistance and support of the party. He had rendered good and admitted service to the Democracy, but was to experience the ingratitude for which political organizations are proverbial. He applied to Martin Van Buren and other prominent leaders of the party to aid him in securing a loan of twenty-five hundred dollars for two years, which sum would have enabled him to establish his paper on a paying basis, but the politicians turned deaf ears to his appeals, and his paper failed, after a brief and desperate struggle.

He came back to New York about the beginning of 1835, a

little sore from his unsuccessful battle with fate, but far from being dismayed or cast down. His failures to establish party organs had convinced him that success in journalism does not depend upon political favor, and he determined to make one more effort to build up a paper of his own, and this time one which should aim to please no party but the public. That there was need of an independent journal of this kind he felt sure, and he knew the people of the country well enough to be confident that if such a journal could be properly placed before them, it would succeed. The problem with him was how to get it properly before them. He had little or no money, and it required considerable capital to carry through the most insignificant effort of the kind. He made several efforts to inspire other persons with his confidence before he succeeded. One of these efforts Mr. Parton thus describes, in his *Life of Horace Greeley*: "An incident connected with the job-office of Greeley & Co. is perhaps worth mentioning here. One James Gordon Bennett, a person then well known as a smart writer for the press, came to Horace Greeley, and, exhibiting a fifty-dollar bill and some other notes of smaller denominations as his cash capital, wanted him to join in setting up a new daily paper, 'The New York Herald.' Our hero declined the offer, but recommended James Gordon to apply to another printer, naming one, who he thought would like to share in such an enterprise. To him the editor of 'The Herald' did apply, and with success."

The parties to whom Mr. Greeley referred Mr. Bennett were two young printers, whom he persuaded, after much painstaking, to print his paper and share with him its success or failure. He had about enough cash in hand to sustain the paper for ten days, after which it must make its own way. He proposed to make it cheap—to sell it at one penny per copy, and to make it meet the current wants of the day. The "Sun," a penny paper, was already in existence, and was paying well, and this encouraged Mr. Bennett to hope for success in his own enterprise.

He rented a cellar in Wall Street, in which he established his office, and on the 6th of May, 1835, issued the first number of "The Morning Herald." His cellar was bare and poverty-stricken in appearance. It contained nothing but a desk made of boards laid upon flour barrels. On one end of this desk lay a pile of "Heralds" ready for purchasers, and at the other sat the proprietor writing his articles for his journal and managing his business. Says Mr. William Gowans, the famous Nassau-Street bookseller: "I remember to have entered the subterranean office of its editor early in its career, and purchased a single copy of the paper, for which I paid the sum of one cent United States currency. On this occasion the proprietor, editor, and vendor was seated at his desk, busily engaged in writing, and appeared to pay little or no attention to me as I entered. On making known my object in coming in, he requested me to put my money down on the counter and help myself to a paper, all this time he continuing his writing operations. The office was a single oblong underground room; its furniture consisted of a counter, which also served as a desk, constructed from two flour barrels, perhaps empty, standing apart from each other about four feet, with a single plank covering both; a chair, placed in the center, upon which sat the editor busy at his vocation, with an inkstand by his right hand; on the end nearest the door were placed the papers for sale."

Standing on Broadway now, and looking at the marble palace from which the greatest and wealthiest newspaper in the Union sends forth its huge editions, one finds it hard to real-

HOW THE "NEW YORK HERALD" BEGAN.

ize that just thirty-four years ago this great journal was born in a cellar, an obscure little penny sheet, with a poor man for its proprietor. Yet such was the beginning of "The New York Herald."

The prospect was not a pleasant one to contemplate, but Mr. Bennett did not shrink from it. He knew that it was in him to succeed, and he meant to do it, no matter through what trials or vicissitudes his path to fortune lay. Those who heard his expressions of confidence shook their heads sagely, and said the young man's air-castles would soon fade away before the blighting breath of experience. Indeed, it did seem a hopeless struggle, the effort of this one poor man to raise his little penny sheet from its cellar to the position of "a power in the land." He was almost unknown. He could bring no support or patronage to his journal by the influence of his name, or by his large acquaintance. The old newspaper system, with its clogs and dead-weights, was still in force, and as for newsboys to hawk the new journal over the great city, they were a race not then in existence. He had to fight his battle with poverty alone and without friends, and he did fight it bravely. He was his own clerk, reporter, editor, and errand boy. He wrote all the articles that appeared in "The Herald," and many of the advertisements, and did all the work that was to be performed about his humble office.

"The Herald" was a small sheet of four pages of four columns each. Nearly every line of it was fresh news. Quotations from other papers were scarce. Originality was then, as now, the motto of the establishment. Small as it was, the paper was attractive. The story that its first numbers were scurrilous and indecent is not true, as a reference to the old files of the journal will prove. They were of a character similar to that of "The Herald" of to-day, and were marked by the same industry, tact, and freshness, which make the paper to-day the most salable in the land.

Says Mr. Parton: "The first numbers were filled with nonsense and gossip about the city of New York, to which his poverty confined him. He had no boat with which to board arriving ships, no share in the pony express from Washington, and no correspondents in other cities. All he could do was to catch the floating gossip, scandal, and folly of the town, and present as much of them every day as one man could get upon paper by sixteen hours' labor. He laughed at every thing and every body,—not excepting himself and his squint eye,—and though his jokes were not always good, they were generally good enough. People laughed, and were willing to expend a cent the next day to see what new folly the man would commit or relate. We all like to read about our own neighborhood; this paper gratified the propensity.

"The man, we repeat, had really a vein of poetry in him, and the first numbers of 'The Herald' show it. He had occasion one day to mention that Broadway was about to be paved with wooden blocks. This was not a very promising subject for a poetical comment, but he added: 'When this is done, every vehicle will have to wear sleigh-bells, as in sleighing times, and Broadway will be so quiet that you can pay a compliment to a lady, in passing, and she will hear you.' This was nothing in itself; but here was a man wrestling with fate in a cellar, who could turn you out two hundred such paragraphs a week, the year round. Men can growl in a cellar; this man could laugh, and keep laughing, and make the floating population of a city laugh with him. It must be owned, too, that he had a little real insight into the nature of things around him—a little Scotch sense, as well as an inexhaustible fund of French vivacity. Alluding, once, to the 'hard money' cry by which the lying politicians of the day carried elections, he exploded that nonsense in two lines: 'If a man gets the wearable or the eatable he wants, what cares he if he has gold or paper money?' He devoted two sentences to the Old School and New School Presbyterian controversy: 'Great trouble among the Presbyterians just now. The question is whether or not a man can do any thing toward saving his own soul.' He had also an article upon the Methodists, in which he said that the two religions nearest akin were the Methodist and the Roman Catholic. We should add to these trifling specimens the fact that he uniformly maintained, from 1835 to the crash of 1837, that the prosperity of the country was unreal, and would end in disaster."

These things served the end for which they were intended. They brought "The Herald" conspicuously before the public. While engaged in them, the proprietor was anxiously planning the means of making his paper a great *newspaper*. He worked sixteen or seventeen hours each day. He rose before five o'clock in the morning, and gave three hours to writing his editorials and the witty paragraphs to which allusion has been made. At eight o'clock he went to his cellar, or "office," and was at his post there during the morning, selling his papers, receiving advertisements, and often writing them for those who were not able to prepare them, doing such other work as was necessary, and finishing his editorial labors. At one o'clock he went into Wall Street, gathering up financial news and interesting items of the street. He returned to his office at four o'clock, and remained there until six, when the business of the day was over. In the evening he went to the theater, a ball, concert, or some public gathering, to pick up fresh items for his paper.

All this while, however, he was losing money. He had a heavy load to carry, and though he bore it unflinchingly and determinedly, the enterprise seemed doomed to failure for lack of funds. At this juncture, he resolved to make the financial news of the day a special feature of "The Herald." The monetary affairs of the country were in great confusion—a confusion which was but the prelude to the crash of 1837; and Wall Street was the vortex of the financial whirlpool whose eddies were troubling the whole land. Every body was anxious to get the first news from the street, and to get it as full and reliable as possible. At this time, too, our relations with France were exceedingly critical—a circumstance which served to increase the trouble in financial matters. Appreciating the anxiety which was generally felt on this subject, Mr. Bennett resolved to create a demand for "The Herald" among the business men of the country. On the 13th of June, 1835, just five weeks after the establishment of the paper, he printed his first money article—the first that ever appeared in an American newspaper. It was as follows:

COMMERCIAL.

Stocks yesterday maintained their prices during the session of the Board, several going up. Utica went up 2 per cent.; the others stationary. Large quantities were sold. After the Board adjourned and the news from France was talked over, the fancy stocks generally went down 1 to 1½ per cent.; the other stocks quite firm. A rally was made by the bulls in the evening under the trees, but it did not succeed. There will be a great fight in the Board to-day. The good people up town are anxious to know what the brokers think of Mr. Livingston. We shall find out, and let them know.

The cotton and flour markets rallied a little. The rise of cotton in Liverpool drove it up here a cent or so. The last shippers will make 2½ per cent. Many are endeavoring to produce the impression that there will be a war. If the impression prevails, naval stores will go up a good deal. Every eye is outstretched for the "Constitution." Hudson, of the Merchants News Room, says he will hoist out the first flag. Gilpin, of the Exchange News Room, says he will have her name down in his room one hour before his competitor. The latter claims having beat Hudson yesterday by an hour and ten minutes in chronicling the "England."

The money article was a success, and appeared regularly in "The Herald" after this. It created a demand for the paper among the merchants, and increased its circulation so decidedly that at the end of the third month the daily receipts and expenditures balanced each other. Mr. Bennett now ventured to engage a cheap police reporter, which gave him more time to attend to other duties.

The paper now seemed on the point of becoming a success, when it received a severe and unlooked-for blow. The printing-office was burned down, and the gentlemen who had printed "The Herald" were so much discouraged that they refused to renew their connection with it. Mr. Bennett knew that he was too near to success to abandon the enterprise, and courageously put his wits to work to devise means to carry on the paper. By the greatest and most indomitable exertions he managed to secure the means of going on with it, and bravely resumed its publication alone.

A few months after this the "great fire" swept over New York, and laid nearly the whole business portion of the city in ashes. This was Mr. Bennett's opportunity. The other journals of the city devoted a brief portion of their space to general and ponderous descriptions of the catastrophe, but Mr. Bennett went among the ruins, note-book and pencil in hand, and gathered up the most minute particulars of the fire. He spent one-half of each day in this way, and the other half in writing out reports of what he thus learned. These reports he published in "The Herald." They were free, graphic, offhand sketches of the fire and its consequences, and were so full and complete that they left little or nothing connected with the incidents they described to be added. Mr. Bennett also went to the expense of publishing a picture of the burning of the Merchants Exchange, and a map of the burnt district—a heavy expense for his little journal. The result proved the sagacity of his views. "The Herald" reports of the fire created a heavy demand for the paper, and its circulation increased rapidly. Yet its success was not assured.

When his first year closed, Mr. Bennett found his paper still struggling for existence, but with a fair prospect of success, if it could follow up the "hit" it had made with its reports of the fire. About this time he received an offer from Dr. Benjamin Brandreth to advertise his pills in "The Herald," and a contract was at once concluded between them. The money thus paid to the paper was a considerable sum, and proved of the greatest assistance to it. All the money received was conscientiously expended in the purchase of news. The circulation grew larger as its news facilities increased, and for some years its proprietor expended all his profits in making the paper more attractive.

At the close of the fifteenth month of its career Mr. Bennett increased the size of "The Herald," and raised the price of it to two cents per copy. His success was now assured, and continued to increase, as, under his able and far-seeing management, his paper expanded and enlarged its facilities for securing and making public the promptest and most reliable news of the day. Since that time his success has been unvarying. He has made "The Herald" the leading newspaper of the world, for no other journal upon the globe can compare with it in liberality and energy in the collection of news or in promptness and completeness of detail in laying it before the public. Its growth has been slow, but sure. Every step has been won by hard and conscientious labor, as well as by the force of real genius. Other journals have been compelled to follow the example of "The Herald," but none have surpassed it. It still stands at the head of the newspaper press of the world, and we are justified in believing that it will continue to stand there as long as its founder's hand controls it.

Instead of the little penny sheet of thirty-four years ago, "The New York Herald" of to-day is an immense journal, generally of twelve, and often of sixteen pages of six columns each, making a total of from seventy-two to ninety-six closely printed columns of matter. From four to nine pages are filled with advertisements, classified with the utmost exactness. No reader has to search the paper over for the article or advertisement he wishes to see; each subject has its separate place, which can be discovered at a glance. Its advertisements have reference to every trade, profession, or calling known to civilized man, and are a faithful mirror of the busy age in which we live. Its news reports are the freshest, most complete, and most graphic of any American journal, and are collected at an expenditure of more time, care, and money than any other journal sees fit to lay out. It has its correspondents in all parts of the world, and when news is worth sending, these are instructed to spare no pains or expense in transmitting it at once. During the late war it had a small army of attachés in the field, and its reports were the most eagerly sought of all by the public. During the Abyssinian war its reporters and correspondents furnished the London press with reliable news *in advance of their own correspondents.* Any price is paid for news, for it is the chief wish of Mr. Bennett that "The Herald" shall be the first to chronicle the events of the day.

"The Herald" office is now located at the corner of Broadway and Ann Street. The building, of white marble, is five stories in height, and is one of the handsomest in the country. It is the most complete newspaper establishment in existence. It has two cellars, in which are placed the two steam-engines that drive the huge presses which strike off the various editions of "The Herald." Every thing is in perfect order, and the machinery shines like polished gold and silver. The proprietor's eye is upon the whole establishment, and he is quick to notice and reprimand a fault. The street floor contains the business office of the journal, a magnificent room, gorgeous with marble, plate-glass, black walnut, and frescoes. The editorial rooms are above, and near them are the reporters' rooms. The top floor constitutes the finest composing room in the world, from which speaking-tubes and vertical railways communicate with all the other parts of the building. Every department of the paper has a responsible head, and the most rigid discipline prevails throughout the office. There are twelve editors, thirty-five reporters, and four hundred and fifty-three other employés, making a total force of five hundred men engaged upon "The Herald." The circulation of the various editions of the paper amounts to tens of thousands. It is to be found in every town of importance in the land, and its daily receipts from advertisements alone are counted by tens of thousands of dollars.

Mr. Bennett rarely writes for the paper now. He assembles his editors in his council at noon every day, hears their suggestions, decides what topics shall be treated in the next day's issue, and assigns to each man the subject upon which he is to write. In his absence his place at the council-board is filled by his son, or by the managing editor. Mr. Bennett in this way exercises a close supervision over all the articles that appear in "The Herald," and imparts to them a considerable share of his personality.

Mr. Bennett is married, and has two children, a son, James Gordon Bennett, jr., who will succeed his father in the ownership of "The Herald," and a daughter. He lives on Fifth Avenue at present, his favorite residence, at Washington Heights, having been recently destroyed by fire. He is said to be a courtly and agreeable host, and one who rarely fails to send away his visitors with a pleasant impression of himself.

In person he is tall and firmly built, and walks with a dignified carriage. His head is large, and his features are prominent and irregular. He has a thoroughly Scotch face, and is cross-eyed. His forehead is broad and high, betokening great capacity and force of character. His expression is firm and somewhat cold—that of a man who has had a hard fight with fortune, and has conquered it. He is reserved in his manner to strangers, but always courteous and approachable. To his friends he is genial and unreserved. He is finely educated, and is said to be a man of excellent taste. His favorite studies are history and biography, and he still pursues them with a keen relish. His home is one of the most elegant in the city. He is proud of his success, as he may well be, and very proud of the fact that he owes it to himself alone. While he was building the new "Herald" office, he was waited on by the president of one of the national banks of the city, who said to him:

"Mr. Bennett, we know that you are at great expense in erecting this building, besides carrying on your immense business. If you want any accommodation, you can have it at our bank."

"Mr. ——," replied Mr. Bennett, "before I purchased the land, or began to build, I had on deposit two hundred and fifty thousand dollars in the Chemical Bank. There is not a dollar due on 'The Herald' building that I can not pay. I would pay off the mortgage to-morrow, if the owner would allow me to do so. When the building is opened, I shall not owe one dollar to any man, if I am allowed to pay. I owe nothing that I can not discharge in an hour. I have not touched one dollar of the money on deposit in the bank, and while that remains I need no accommodation."

CHAPTER XXIV.

ROBERT BONNER.

ROBERT BONNER was born in the north of Ireland, near the town of Londonderry, about the year 1824. He came to this country when a mere child, and was brought up in the State of Connecticut, where he received a good common-school education.

Manifesting a decided liking for the printer's trade, he was placed at an early age in the office of the "Hartford Courant," where he took his first lessons in the art of setting type. He entered upon the business with the determination to learn it thoroughly, and when he had mastered his trade soon acquired the reputation of being the best workman in Hartford. As a compositor, he was not only neat and thorough, but was remarkably rapid as well. On one occasion, when the "Courant" was endeavoring to publish the "President's Message" in advance of all its competitors, Mr. Bonner is said to have worked at the rate of seventeen hundred ems an hour—a feat absolutely unparalleled.

In 1844, he removed to New York and engaged in the office of a new journal, called the "American Republican," then lately established as the organ of the American party in that city, upon which he worked steadily during its brief career. His wages were small, and it was only by practicing the most rigid economy that he could live upon them.

When the "Republican" suspended publication, Mr. Bonner was employed in the office of the "Evening Mirror," published by Morris, Willis & Fuller. Here he made himself so useful, that the business of getting up or displaying advertisements attractively was soon left entirely to him. His taste in this department was almost faultless, and the advertisements of the "Mirror" soon became noted for their neat and handsome appearance.

At this time there was published in New York a small, struggling paper, exclusively mercantile in its character, called the "Merchants' Ledger." This paper was almost entirely dependent upon its advertising patronage, and the attention of its proprietor was called to Mr. Bonner's skill, as exhibited in the "Mirror," in displaying advertisements to the greatest advantage. The result was that Mr. Bonner received an offer, which he accepted, to take charge of this paper. This was the origin of his connection with the journal which he has since rendered famous.

Being fond of composition, he made frequent contributions to the editorial columns of the paper, which were well received by the general public, but which seem to have aroused the petty jealousy of the proprietor of the "Ledger."

Soon after forming his connection with the "Ledger," Mr. Bonner purchased it. From his boyhood up, it had been his ambition to become the proprietor of a journal which should be carried out upon his own ideas, and he believed that the "Ledger" offered him the best means of doing this. It was generally doubted at that time that a literary paper could flourish in New York—Boston and Philadelphia having apparently monopolized such enterprises. Mr. Bonner, however, had a clearer view of the matter, and was convinced from the first that the great center of American industry was the very best place for such an undertaking. He proceeded very cautiously at first, however, changing the character of his paper very gradually, from a commercial to a literary journal.

At this time Fanny Fern was the great literary sensation of the day. She had just published her "Ruth Hall," which had attracted universal attention, and had given rise to a sharp discussion in the public press as to whether she was the sister of N. P. Willis or not. Mr. Bonner resolved to profit by her sudden notoriety, and requested her to write a story for the "Ledger," for which he offered to pay her twenty-five dollars per column. She declined the proposition. He then offered her fifty dollars a column, and, upon a second refusal, increased his offer to seventy-five dollars a column. She was pleased with the energy exhibited by Mr. Bonner, and flattered by his eagerness to secure her services, but declared that she would write no more for the newspapers. A little later Mr. Bonner was offered a story from her, about ten columns long. He at once accepted her proposition, and upon the receipt of the manuscript sent her a check for one thousand dollars.

With this story began that wonderful career of the "Ledger" which seems more like a dream than hard reality. The story was double-leaded, and made to fill twenty columns of the paper. The "Ledger" itself was changed from its old style to its present form, and made a purely literary journal. The price paid for the story was unparalleled in the history of American journalism, and Mr. Bonner spread the announcement far and wide that he was publishing a serial for which he had given one hundred dollars a column. His advertisements were to be seen in almost every newspaper of respectable circulation throughout the Union. In form they were different from any that had preceded them. "Fanny Fern writes for the 'Ledger.'" "Buy the 'New York Ledger,'" etc., appeared, dozens of times repeated, until men were absolutely tired of seeing the announcement. Nothing had ever been brought to the public notice so prominently before. For awhile people were astonished at the audacious boldness of "the 'Ledger' man." Then they began to buy the paper. Since then the demand for it has steadily increased.

The venture was successful. Fanny Fern's reputation and Mr. Bonner's energy and boldness made a demand for the "Ledger," at once, and out of the profits of the story for which he had paid such an unheard-of price Mr. Bonner purchased a handsome residence in New York City.

There was as much originality as boldness in the peculiar style in which Mr. Bonner advertised his paper. As before stated, nothing of the kind had ever been seen before, and the novelty of the announcements at once attracted attention. It was seen that they were expensive also, and people naturally felt some curiosity to see for themselves the paper for which a man was willing to assume such risk and expense. These announcements sometimes covered a whole page of a daily paper; sometimes the page would be almost entirely blank, with only a few lines in each column containing the announcement. Again the advertisement would be the opening chapters of a story, which would be sure to excite the curiosity of the reader, and induce him to purchase the remaining chapters in the "Ledger" itself. It is to the credit of the "Ledger" that it rarely loses a subscriber. It has become a family paper.

A recent writer thus refers to Mr. Bonner's early experience in advertising:—

"His mode of advertising was new, and it excited both astonishment and ridicule. His ruin was predicted over and over again. But as he paid as he went along, he alone would be the sufferer. He was assailed in various ways. Men sneered at his writers, as well as at the method in which he made them known. He had no competition. Just then it was announced that the Harpers were to put a first-class weekly into the field. The announcement was hailed with delight by many classes. Men who had been predicting Bonner's ruin from the start were anxious to see it accomplished. He had agents in all the leading cities in the land. These held a monopoly of the 'Ledger.' The book men and newspaper men, who were left out, were quite willing to have the 'Ledger' go under. The respectability and wealth of the house, its enterprise, with the class of writers it could secure, made the new paper a dangerous rival. Mr. Bonner concluded to make the first issue serviceable to himself. His paragraph advertising was considered sensational, and smacking of the charlatan. He resolved to make it respectable. He wrote half a column in sensational style: 'Buy Harper's Weekly!'—'Buy Harper's Weekly!'—'Buy Harper's Weekly!'—'Buy Harper's Weekly!'—and so on through the half column. Through his advertising agent he sent this advertisement to the 'Herald,' 'Tribune,' and 'Times,' and paid for its insertion. Among the astonished readers of this 'Ledger' style of advertising were the quiet gentlemen who do business on Franklin Square. The community were astonished. 'The Harpers are waking up!' 'This is the Bonner style!' 'This is the way the Ledger man does it!' were heard on all sides. The young Harpers were congratulated by the book men every-where on the enterprise with which they were pushing the new publication. They said nothing, and took the joke in good part. But it settled the respectability of the 'Ledger' style of advertising. It is now imitated by the leading publishers, insurance men, and most eminent dry goods men in the country. The sums spent by Mr. Bonner in advertising are perfectly marvelous. He never advertises unless he has something new to present to the public. He pays from five to twenty-five thousand dollars a week when he advertises."

Mr. Bonner well knew that all his advertising would be worth nothing in the end unless he made the "Ledger" worthy of the public patronage, and he exerted himself from the first to secure the services of a corps of able and popular writers. In his arrangements with his contributors, he inaugurated a system of liberality and *justness* which might well put his rivals to shame.

When Mr. Everett was engaged in his noble effort to assist the ladies of the Mount Vernon Association in purchasing the home and tomb of Washington, Mr. Bonner proposed to him to write a series of papers for the "Ledger," for which he offered him ten thousand dollars, the money to be appropriated to the purchase of Mount Vernon. Mr. Everett accepted the offer, and the celebrated Mount Vernon Papers were the result. This was a far-sighted move on the part of Robert Bonner. Under ordinary circumstances Mr. Everett would probably have declined to "write for the 'Ledger;'" but in a cause so worthy he could not refuse. The association of his name with the journal was of incalculable service to it, and the Mount Vernon Papers were to its proprietor his very best advertisement. (We are viewing the matter commercially.) The sale of the paper was wonderfully increased, and a golden harvest was reaped.

This connection of Mr. Everett with the "Ledger" led to a warm personal friendship between himself and its proprietor, which was broken only by the statesman's death—a circumstance which speaks volumes for the private worth of the younger man. Mr. Everett continued to write for the paper after his Mount Vernon articles were finished, and is said to have earned over fifty thousand dollars by his able contributions to it.

Soon after the completion of the Mount Vernon Papers, Mr. Bonner secured the services of George Bancroft, the historian, who contributed a series of admirable articles. Mr. Everett's connection with the "Ledger" had settled the question that it was not beneath the dignity of the most eminent literateur in the land to write for it. Fanny Fern's husband, Mr. James Parton, Alice and Phœbe Carey, Mrs. Southworth, and a host of others have helped, and still help, to fill its columns.

But perhaps its most profitable contributor, next to Mr. Everett, is Henry Ward Beecher. That wonderful gift of the great preacher which enables him to touch so constantly upon subjects nearest to the hearts of most men, would make him invaluable to any paper. Mr. Bonner was struck with this after hearing him preach several times, and resolved to secure his services for the "Ledger." He proposed, to the parson's utter astonishment, that Mr. Beecher should write a story for the paper, and coupled it with the offer of a sum which many persons would consider a fortune. The field was utterly new to Mr. Beecher. Novel-writing was something he had never even thought of; but after some hesitation he accepted the offer. Soon after this, the publication of "Norwood" was begun in the columns of the "Ledger." The story was longer than was at first agreed upon, and Mr. Bonner paid its author a handsome sum in addition to the amount originally offered. The reward was princely, but not out of proportion to the service rendered by Mr. Beecher, who has won thousands of readers for the paper. Mr. Beecher still writes for the "Ledger," and there is no present prospect of his genial and useful contributions coming to a close.

Mr. Bonner has made his paper useful to young people as well as those of maturer years. Each number contains articles, briefly and pointedly written, upon some popular and useful topic, so that thousands find not only amusement, but valuable hints and profitable instruction in the "Ledger."

It was for a long time the custom of the newspaper press to indulge in sneers at the "Ledger," and, at the least, to treat it with a species of mild contempt. In order to stop this, its proprietor secured and published a series of articles from James Gordon Bennett of "The Herald," Henry J. Raymond of "The Times," and Horace Greeley of "The Tribune." By thus identifying the leading journalists of the country with his enterprise, he effectually silenced the scoffers, and with them the "lesser lights" of the press.

It was said by some over-careful persons that the "Ledger" was not a proper paper for young persons to read. Mr. Bonner at once secured the services of the Presidents of the twelve principal colleges of the Union, and articles from each of these gentlemen appeared in his paper. After this it was not to be presumed that a journal which had among its contributors twelve such distinguished guides of youth could be unfit for any one to read.

In order to make still less room for doubt on this subject, a series of articles by twelve distinguished clergymen soon after appeared in the "Ledger."

Indeed, the greatest care is exercised to exclude from the columns of the paper any thing savoring in the least of impurity. It is the proprietor's aim to make it a help as well as an amusement to its readers, and his object is to elevate, not to degrade them.

The "Ledger" now circulates over three hundred thousand copies per week, and is growing in the public favor. From the profits of his business Mr. Bonner has built a splendid marble publishing-house at the corner of William and Spruce Streets, in New York, from which the "Ledger" is now issued. It is one of the most complete establishments in the world, and is fitted up with every convenience necessary to the performance of the work upon the paper in the most perfect and expeditious manner. Mr. Bonner has created all this by his own energy and business talent, and richly deserves the success he enjoys. He resides in an elegant mansion in New York, and has also a handsome country seat at Morrisania, in Westchester County. He is married, and has a family.

Mr. Bonner's great wealth has enabled him to achieve a distinction of another kind. He is famous as the owner of the finest horses in America. His stables are located in Twenty-seventh Street, and are the most perfect of their kind in this country. They contain every thing needed for the comfort and care of the horses, and the men employed in them are thoroughly skilled in their business. The horses are seven in number. First on the list is "Dexter," who has made his mile in the unprecedented time of 2:17¼ in harness, and 2:18 under the saddle. He is the fastest horse in the world. "Lantern," a splendid bay, fifteen and a half hands high, has made his mile in 2:20. "Pocahontas," the most perfectly formed horse in existence, has made her mile in 2:23; while "Peerless," a fine gray mare, has followed close on to her in 2:23½. "Lady Palmer" has made two miles with a three hundred and fifty pound wagon and driver in 4:59, while her companion, "Flatbush Mare," has made a two-mile heat to a road wagon in 5:01¼. The "Auburn Horse," a large sorrel, sixteen and a half hands high, with four white feet and a white face, was declared by Hiram Woodruff to be the fastest horse he ever drove. These horses cost their owner over two hundred thousand dollars, and he would not part with them for double that sum. He does not race them for money, but drives them for his own use, and holds the reins himself.

VI.

LAWYERS.

CHAPTER XXV.

JOHN MARSHALL.

TO the writer's mind the most perfect specimen of the American lawyer known to our history was JOHN MARSHALL, of Virginia, Chief Justice of the United States. Profoundly learned in the law, irresistible in argument, and possessed of an eloquence which drew men in throngs to listen to him, he was also the soul of honor. Neither in his private nor professional life could the most malicious find an action open to reproach. Simple and earnest as a child, he was yet a tower of strength to the cause of justice. Occupying the highest place in our judiciary system, he was never unduly elated by his honors, and while gaining and awarding fortunes in the discharge of his professional duties, he was himself so true a man that the most brazen suitor would not have dared to offer him a bribe. He was in all things the simple, honest gentleman, the fearless advocate, the just judge, and the meek and earnest follower of his Saviour. Although belonging to a past generation, his story is presented here because I wish to offer to those who seek to follow him in his noble calling the purest and highest model our history affords.

John Marshall was born in Fauquier County, Virginia, on the 24th of September, 1755. He was the oldest of a family of fifteen children, and was the son of Colonel Thomas Marshall, a planter of moderate fortune. During the Revolution, Colonel Marshall commanded a regiment of Virginia troops, and won considerable distinction at the battles of the Great Bridge, Germantown, Brandywine, and Monmouth. At the Brandywine the regiment bore the brunt of the attack of the British army, led by Cornwallis in person.

John Marshall was born in a region so thinly settled as to be almost cut off from civilization. The people were plain and even rough in their habits, and the mode of life which prevailed in his native county doubtless did much to lay the foundation of those habits of simplicity for which he was noted in after life. Schools were almost unknown in this region, and such as were in operation were so rude in character that Colonel Marshall, who was a man of education and culture, decided not to attempt to train his children in them. Being unable to raise the means of sending them to better schools in other parts of the Colony, he determined to become their teacher himself, and applied himself to his task with a devotion which was signally rewarded by the brilliant career of his eldest son. He laid especial weight upon their acquiring a thorough knowledge of the English language and of history, and sought to cultivate in them a love for the poetry of their native tongue. Referring in after life to his father's devoted labors, Judge Marshall once said, with great feeling, "To him I owe the solid foundation of all my success in life." John Marshall did ample justice to his father's labors, and when only fourteen years old was thoroughly familiar with the writings of Shakespeare, Dryden,

Milton, and Pope, and could repeat by heart nearly the whole of the "Essay on Man." These poets were always his favorites, and in mature life he would quote them with readiness and the keenest relish.

He showed such marked talent that his father determined to make an effort to secure him a better education than his private labors could impart to him, and accordingly sent him for a year to the school of the Rev. Mr. Campbell, in Westmoreland County, where he received a good drilling in English and Latin. At this school began his acquaintance with James Monroe, who was then one of Mr. Campbell's pupils. Returning home at the end of the year, he continued his studies under the Rev. Mr. Thompson.

He studied hard and was an industrious reader. Poetry and romance were his favorites, but he read history with the deepest interest. He was quiet and thoughtful in manner, and full of a dreamy, poetic enthusiasm. He loved to wander in the thick woods, and would pass many of his leisure hours in gazing at the beauties of nature. His constitution was a sound and vigorous one, and he was not only fond of manly and athletic sports, but excelled in them. He had no inclination toward dissipation, and the simple, healthful life of his home was calculated to develop his physical powers to the utmost. Colonel Marshall did not neglect the moral training of his children, but always impressed upon them the importance of Christianity as the basis of their characters, rearing them in that simple code of true gentility which was so dear to our fathers, but of which we of to-day are fast losing sight.

Being destined for the bar, young Marshall began his legal studies at the age of eighteen, but in two years they were interrupted by the troubles with Great Britain, which terminated in open hostilities. A volunteer company was raised in the neighborhood, and John Marshall promptly attached himself to it. He took a prominent part in the questions of the day, and expressed himself boldly in favor of resistance. In 1775 Patrick Henry made his memorable appeal for volunteers to drive the Loyalist Governor, Lord Dunmore, out of Virginia. Three companies were immediately organized in Marshall's neighborhood. Among these were the famous "Culpepper Minute Men." Marshall's father was elected major of the regiment, and he himself was chosen a lieutenant in the Minute Men. The force at once hastened to the lower counties, and bore a conspicuous part in the battle of Great Bridge. In July, 1776, Marshall's company was assigned to the Eleventh Virginia Regiment of the Continental Army, and sent North. In May, 1777, he was made captain of his company. He participated in the fight at Iron Hill, and in the battles of Germantown, Brandywine, and Monmouth, and shared the sufferings of the army at the memorable encampment of Valley Forge. Until the close of 1779 he was constantly in active service. He was always patient, cheerful, and hopeful. In the severest hardships to which the army was exposed his spirits never sank. One of his comrades said that he did more than any other man to keep alive the hopes of the army during the terrible winter at Valley Forge, and another has declared that "the officers of the Virginia line appeared to idolize him." His conduct attracted the attention of Washington, who conceived a warm friendship for him, and Marshall, on his part, returned the friendship of his chief with a feeling almost of worship. Washington frequently appointed him deputy judge advocate during the winter.

At the close of 1779 he went to Virginia to take command of a new corps which the Legislature was about to raise. The project remaining under discussion for some months, he passed the time in attendance upon a course of lectures on law, delivered by George Wythe, and a course of lectures on natural philosophy, delivered by the Rev. Dr. Madison, afterward Bishop of Virginia, at William and Mary College, in Williamsburg. The next summer he received his license to practice law. Meanwhile, the project for raising troops had taken the shape of a definite failure, and he now set out to rejoin the army. Too poor to pay his passage to the North, he walked the entire distance from Williamsburg, Virginia, to Philadelphia, upon reaching which city he was so travel-worn and shabby in appearance, that the landlord of the hotel at which he wished to stop refused him admittance. He joined the army in due time, and remained with it until the spring of 1781, when he resigned his commission, a few months before the close of the war.

With the return of peace the courts were again thrown open, and Marshall began that brilliant legal career which has made him one of the most famous men in our history. His success was marked from the first, as his professional talents were such as to make themselves felt anywhere, and his personal popularity aided him greatly in overcoming the difficulties which lie in the path of a young aspirant to legal honors. In 1782, the people of Fauquier elected him to the House of Delegates in the General Assembly of the Commonwealth, and in the fall of that year he was appointed one of the Council of State. In January, 1783, he was married to Miss Mary Willis Ambler, with whom he lived in the most perfect happiness for over fifty years. His bride was a woman of great personal beauty, and in every respect a fitting helpmate for such a man—than which no higher tribute could be paid her. About this time, Mr. Marshall decided not to return to Fauquier, but to locate himself permanently in Richmond, where he could enjoy many more professional advantages. In spite of this, however, his old friends in Fauquier re-elected him to the Legislature, and in 1787 he sat in that body as representative from the county of Henrico.

He was very plain and even careless in his personal attire, and this often led to amusing occurrences. Soon after he began the practice of his profession in Richmond, he was strolling through the streets one morning, dressed in a plain linen suit and a straw hat. The hat was held under his arm, and was filled with cherries, of which he ate as he walked. In passing the Eagle Hotel, he stopped to exchange salutations with the landlord, and then continued his walk. Sitting near the landlord, on the hotel porch, was a Mr. P——, an elderly gentleman from the country, who had come to the city to engage counsel in an important case which was to be tried in a day or two. The landlord referred him to Marshall as the best lawyer in the city; but the old gentleman was so much prejudiced against the young advocate, by his careless appearance, that he refused to engage him. On entering court, Mr. P—— was a second time referred to Marshall by the clerk of the court, and a second time he refused to employ him. At this moment entered Mr. V——, a venerable-looking legal gentleman, in a powdered wig and black coat, whose dignified appearance produced such an impression on Mr. P—— that he engaged him at once. In the first case which came on, Marshall and Mr. V—— each addressed the court. "The vast inferiority of his advocate was so apparent that at the close of the case Mr. P—— introduced himself to young Marshall, frankly stated the prejudice which had caused him, in opposition to advice, to employ Mr. V——; that he extremely regretted the error, but knew not how to remedy it. He had come to the city with one hundred dollars as his lawyer's fee, which he had paid, and had but five left, which, if Marshall chose, he would cheerfully give him for assisting in the case. Marshall, pleased with the incident, accepted the offer, not, however, without passing a sly joke at the *omnipotence* of a powdered wig and black coat."

In 1788, Mr. Marshall was elected to the Virginia Convention which met in June of that year for the purpose of considering the question of the adoption or rejection of the Federal Constitution. The debates in this body were among the most brilliant in history. Marshall took a decided stand in favor of the Constitution, and is believed to have done more than any other man, save Mr. Madison, to secure its adoption. He added greatly to his reputation by his labors in this body, and the close of the session found his practice very much enlarged. He was anxious to devote himself entirely to his professional duties; but he was urged so vehemently to accept a seat in the Legislature from the city of Richmond, that he was forced to consent. He sat in that body from 1789 to 1791, and in those sessions which were marked by the brilliant contests between the Federalists and Republicans took a decided stand with the former, and sustained his position by an array of arguments against which his opponents were powerless. The struggle was one of great bitterness, but Marshall, although victorious in it, made no enemies among his antagonists.

For the next three years he devoted himself industriously to his profession, appearing in public only to defend with masterly eloquence the course of President Washington with reference to the insolent conduct of Citizen Genet, the French Agent. In 1795, he was again elected to the Legislature, "not only without his approbation, but against his known wishes;" but yielding to the desires of his friends he took his seat in that body. The great question of the day was the adoption of "Jay's Treaty" with Great Britain. In Virginia, a bitter opposition assailed the treaty, and the entire State rang with denunciations of it. Even the influence of Washington was powerless to stay the tide of popular passion excited against the treaty and those who upheld it. Meetings were held in Richmond, and the treaty was fiercely denounced. Marshall now came to the rescue, and before a meeting of the citizens of that place made such an unanswerable argument in favor of the treaty, that the men who had been foremost in assailing it now united in the adoption of resolutions indorsing the policy of the Administration. In the Legislature his efforts were equally successful, and the opponents of the Administration were forced to abandon their constitutional objections to the treaty, and to content themselves with a simple denial of the expediency of the measure at that time. President Washington attached so much importance to these services that he offered to his old friend and comrade the position of Attorney-General of the United States, but Marshall declined the offer, as he wished to devote himself to his practice, which had now become very lucrative. He continued to sit in the Legislature, which did not interfere with his private business, and remained the constant and vigilant friend of Washington's Administration. In 1796, he was offered the post of Minister to France, as Mr. Monroe's successor, but he declined it for the same reason which had made him refuse the Attorney-Generalship. In 1797, when the offer was repeated, this time by President Adams, Marshall yielded to the entreaties of Washington, and went to France with Pinckney and Gerry, as Envoy Extraordinary. The object of the mission was to remove the obstructions placed by France in the way of American commerce. The Envoys were unsuccessful, but a correspondence took place between Marshall and Talleyrand, which was a source of great satisfaction to American publicists, and raised Marshall still higher in their esteem and confidence. Upon his return home in 1798, he was given a public reception in New York by the citizens, and a public dinner by the two Houses of Congress, "as an evidence of affection for his person, and of their grateful approbation of the patriotic firmness with which he had sustained the dignity of his country during his important mission." He subsequently took a prominent part in support of the measures of retaliation directed against France by the Administration, which were sharply assailed by the opposition. He resumed his practice in Richmond, but was again drawn from it by a message from Washington, who requested him to visit him at Mt. Vernon. He did so, and the result was that he yielded to the solicitations of his old chieftain, and consented to accept a seat in Congress. He was elected to the Lower House of that body in 1799. During the canvass, President Adams offered him a seat in the Supreme Court of the United States, but he declined it.

His career in Congress was brief, but brilliant. The Federalist party was hard pressed by the Republicans, and he promptly arrayed himself on the side of the former, as the champion of the Administration of John Adams. The excitement over the "Alien and Sedition Laws" was intense, but he boldly and triumphantly defended the course of the Administration. Mr. Binney says of him that, in the debates on the great constitutional questions, "he was confessedly the first man in the House. When he discussed them, he exhausted them; nothing more remained to be said; and the impression of his argument effaced that of every one else."

His great triumph was his speech in the Jonathan Robbins affair. Robbins had committed a murder on board an English ship-of-war, and had sought refuge from punishment in the United States. In accordance with one of the provisions of

Jay's Treaty, his surrender had been demanded by the British Minister, on the ground that he was a British subject, and he had been surrendered by President Adams. The opposition in Congress made this act a pretext for a famous assault upon the Administration, and a resolution was introduced into the House of Representatives by Mr. Livingston, censuring the President for his course in the matter. This resolution produced an extended debate in the House, in the course of which Marshall defended the President in a speech of great force and eloquence. Judge Story has said of this speech, that "it was *rèponse sans rèplique*—an answer so irresistible that it admitted of no reply. It silenced opposition, and settled then and forever the points of national law upon which the controversy hinged."

In May, 1800, Mr. Adams offered Marshall a seat in his Cabinet as Secretary of War, but before he could enter upon the duties of that office he was made Secretary of State, in which capacity he acted for a short while, conducting several important negotiations during that time, and leaving behind him several of the most magnificent state papers to be found in our archives. During his occupancy of this position, it became necessary to appoint a Chief Justice of the United States, and Marshall took advantage of the occasion to urge upon the President the propriety of tendering the place to a distinguished gentleman who had been a faithful friend to the Administration; but Mr. Adams quietly informed him that he had made up his mind to confer the honor upon the man best suited to it, and that he had sent to the Senate the name of John Marshall, of Virginia. This appointment, which came to him entirely unsolicited, was made on the 31st of January, 1801, and was unanimously confirmed by the Senate.

He held the position of Chief Justice for more than thirty-four years, and this period is justly regarded as the most brilliant portion of the history of our highest court, a court of which a famous judge has said:

"The decisions of the Supreme Court of the United States have raised the renown of the country not less than they have confirmed the Constitution. In all parts of the world its judgments are spoken of with respect. Its adjudications of prize law are a code for all future time. Upon commercial law it has brought us nearly to one system, befitting the probity of a great commercial nation. Over its whole path, learning and intelligence and integrity have shed their combined luster."

Although holding so high a post in the General Government, he continued to take a warm interest in the affairs of his native State, and in 1828 was a delegate to the Charlottesville Convention, which met for the purpose of recommending to the Legislature a system of internal improvements best suited to the needs of the State. In 1829, he was a member of the Convention which met in Richmond for the purpose of revising the Constitution of the State. Though now quite old and feeble, he took an active part in the debates of the Convention, and was mainly instrumental in effecting the settlement of the disputes between the eastern and western sections of the State.

In 1805, Judge Marshall published, in five volumes, his "Life of Washington." The first volume was devoted to the history of the Colonies, from their settlement to the commencement of the Revolution. This work has always held the first position in our Revolutionary annals, and won for its author a place in the front rank of American writers. It is, all in all, the best biography of Washington in existence.

Sterling honesty was exemplified in Judge Marshall's whole career. His word was indeed as good as his bond. He would never argue in behalf of a cause which he had reason to think unjust, and he scorned to take a legal advantage at the expense of moral honesty. He once indorsed a bond to the amount of several thousand dollars. The drawer failed, and Marshall paid it, although he knew he could avoid it, as the holder had forfeited his claim in law by requiring more than legal interest.

He was generous to a fault. Once, as he passed through Culpepper County, he met with Captain S——, one of his old comrades in the Revolution. In the course of the conversation which ensued, S—— told him that his estate was burdened with a mortgage for $3,000, which was about to fall due, and that, as he was unable to pay it, he saw nothing but ruin in store for him. At his departure, Marshall handed a note to the servant who brought his horse to the door, and told him to give it to his master. This was done as Marshall was riding away, and upon opening the note Mr. S—— found that it contained a check for the amount of the mortgage. Mounting his horse, he soon overtook Marshall, and, though he thanked him warmly for his generosity, refused to accept it. Marshall strenuously urged its acceptance, but the other persistently refused. Finally, the former suggested a compromise. Marshall took up the mortgage, and thus satisfied the first claim, but as his friend was never prosperous, he never asked for the payment of the debt.

William Wirt has left us the following description of his personal appearance: "He is tall, meager, emaciated; his muscles relaxed, and his joints so loosely connected as not only to disqualify him apparently for any vigorous exertion of body, but to destroy every thing like harmony in his air or movements. Indeed, in his whole appearance and demeanor,—dress, attitudes, gesture, sitting, standing, or walking,—he is as far removed from the idolized graces of Lord Chesterfield as any other gentleman on earth."

"In spite, however, of this ungainly person," says a writer, "no one was a greater social favorite than the Chief Justice. The people of Richmond regarded his eccentric figure with strong personal affection as well as respect. The black eyes, under their bushy gray brows, beamed with good nature, and the lips were habitually smiling. The courtesy of the Judge was one of his most beautiful traits. It was the spontaneous exhibition of the simple and kindly emotions of his heart. Pure benevolence and philanthropy displayed itself in every word which he uttered. He gave his hand to the plain yeoman clad in homespun as courteously and sincerely as to the greatest personage in the country. He had the same simple smile and good-humored jest for both, and seemed to recognize no difference between them. It was instructive to estimate in the good Chief Justice the basis and character of true politeness. John Randolph, one of the most fastidious and aristocratic of men, left his opinion that Marshall's manner was perfect good breeding. In dress and bearing, it would be difficult to imagine any one more simple than Judge Marshall. He presented the appearance of a plain countryman, rather than a Chief Justice of the United States. He had a farm in Fauquier County, and another near Richmond, and he would often return from the latter to take his seat on the bench with burrs sticking to his clothes. His great passion was the game of quoits, and he was a member of the club which met, as it still meets, at Buchanan's Spring, near the city, to play at this game. Here the Governor of Virginia, the Chief Justice, and the most eminent lawyers of the Court of Appeals, were found by a French gentleman, Baron Quinet, with their coats off, gayly pitching quoits, with the ardor of a party of urchins. In these simple amusements passed the hours of leisure which Judge Marshall could steal from his exhausting judicial toil.

At such times he seemed to become a boy again, and to forget the ermine. His fondness for other social enjoyments was great. He was the center of a brilliant circle of men, many of whom were famous, and the tradition of their dinner parties, and the jests which they circulated, is still preserved."

It was his custom always to provide for his table himself when at home, and he might be seen every morning at the Shockoe Hill Market, with his basket on his arm, engaged in making his purchases. Upon one of these occasions he noticed a fashionably-dressed young man, swearing violently because he could not find any one willing to carry home for him a turkey which he had just purchased, and which his foolish pride would not permit him to carry himself. Approaching him quietly, the Judge asked where he lived, and upon being told, said, "I am going that way, and will carry it for you." Taking the turkey, he set out and soon reached the young man's door. Upon receiving his turkey, the young man thanked him for his trouble, and asked, "How much shall I pay you?" "Oh, nothing," replied the Judge, smiling, "you are welcome. It was on my way, and no trouble." So saying, the Judge departed, and the young man, with a faint suspicion of the truth, turned to a bystander, and asked, in some confusion, "Who is that polite old gentleman who brought home my turkey for me?" "That is John Marshall, the Chief Justice of the United States," was the reply. "Why, then, did *he* bring home my turkey?" stammered the fop. "To give you a deserved rebuke," said the gentleman, "and to teach you to conquer your silly pride."

Reference has been made to his carelessness in regard to his personal appearance. A wager was once laid among his friends in Richmond that he could not dress himself without leaving about his clothing some mark of his carelessness. The Judge good-humoredly accepted the wager. A supper was to be given to him upon these conditions. If his dress was found faultless upon that occasion, the other parties were to pay for the entertainment; but if any carelessness could be detected about his dress or in his appearance, the expense was to fall upon him. Upon the appointed evening the gentlemen and the Judge met at the place agreed upon, and to the surprise of all, the Judge's dress seemed faultless. He appeared the very perfection of neatness and taste. The supper followed, the Judge being in high glee over his victory. Near the close of the repast, however, one of the guests, who sat next to Judge Marshall, chanced to drop his napkin, and stooping down to pick it up, discovered that the Judge had put on one of his stockings with the wrong side out. Of course the condition of affairs was immediately reversed, and, amid roars of laughter, the Chief Justice acknowledged his defeat.

The means of locomotion in the Southern States being limited in the days of Judge Marshall, it was his custom to travel about the country, when holding his circuit courts, in an old-fashioned and very much dilapidated gig. His plain and even rusty appearance often led him into ludicrous adventures, which he related to his friends with keen enjoyment. At other times people to whom he was personally unknown were astonished to find that this shabbily-dressed old man was the famous Chief-Justice Marshall. One of his adventures is thus related by an eye-witness:

"It is not long since a gentleman was traveling in one of the counties of Virginia, and about the close of the day stopped at a public-house to obtain refreshment and spend the night. He had been there but a short time when an old man alighted from his gig, with the apparent intention of becoming his fellow-guest at the same house. As the old man drove up, he observed that both the shafts of his gig were broken, and that they were held together by withes formed from the bark of a hickory sapling. Our traveler observed, further, that he was plainly clad, that his knee-buckles were loosened, and that something like negligence pervaded his dress. Conceiving him to be one of the honest yeomanry of our land, the courtesies of strangers passed between them, and they entered the tavern. It was about the same time that an addition of three or four young gentlemen was made to their number—most of them, if not all, of the legal profession. As soon as they became conveniently accommodated, the conversation was turned by the latter upon an eloquent harangue which had that day been delivered at the bar. The other replied that he had witnessed the same day a degree of eloquence no doubt equal, but that it was from the pulpit. Something like a sarcastic rejoinder was made to the eloquence of the pulpit, and a warm and able altercation ensued, in which the merits of the Christian religion became the subject of discussion. From six o'clock until eleven the young champions wielded the sword of argument, adducing with ingenuity and ability every thing that could be said pro and con. During this protracted period, the old gentleman listened with all the meekness and modesty of a child, as if he was adding new information to the stores of his own mind; or perhaps he was observing, with philosophic eye, the faculties of the youthful mind, and how new energies are evolved by repeated action; or, perhaps, with patriotic emotion, he was reflecting upon the future destinies of his country, and on the rising generation upon whom these future destinies must devolve; or, most probably, with a sentiment of moral and religious feeling, he was collecting an argument which—characteristic of himself—no art would be 'able to elude and no force resist.' Our traveler remained a spectator, and took no part in what was said.

MARSHALL'S DEFENCE OF CHRISTIANITY.

"At last one of the young men, remarking that it was impossible to combat with long-established prejudices, wheeled around, and, with some familiarity, exclaimed, 'Well, my old gentleman, what think you of these things?' If, said the traveler, a streak of vivid lightning had at that moment crossed the room, their amazement could not have been greater than it was with what followed. The most eloquent and unanswerable appeal was made, for nearly an hour, by the old gentleman, that he ever heard or read. So perfect was his recollection, that every argument used against the Christian religion was met in the order in which it was advanced. Hume's sophistry on the subject of miracles was, if possible, more perfectly answered than it had already been done by Campbell. And in the whole lecture there was so much simplicity and energy, pathos and sublimity, that not another word was uttered. An attempt to describe it, said the traveler, would be an attempt to paint the sunbeams. It was now a matter of curiosity and inquiry who the old gentleman was. The traveler concluded it was the preacher from whom the pulpit eloquence was heard; but no—it was the Chief Justice of the United States."

Judge Marshall was a simple and earnest Christian, and held in the deepest abhorrence the fashionable skepticism of his day. His conduct was consistent with his profession, and to the last this good and great man repeated night and morning the simple prayer he had learned at his mother's knee.

For many years he suffered from an affection of the bladder, and was at length compelled to resort to a surgical operation for relief. This had the desired effect, but he was soon after taken with an attack of "liver complaint." He repaired to Philadelphia for medical treatment, but failed to derive any benefit from it, and died in that city on the 6th of July, 1835.

His body was conveyed to Richmond for interment, and he

now sleeps by the side of his wife in the Shockoe Hill Cemetery in that city. The spot is marked by a plain slab of marble, over which the weeds and the rank grass are growing, and on which may be read the following inscription, dictated (saving the last date) by himself:

"John Marshall, son of Thomas and Mary Marshall, was born 24th of September, 1755; intermarried with Mary Willis Ambler, the 3d of January, 1783; departed this life the 6th day of July, 1835."

JAMES T. BRADY.

CHAPTER XXVI.

JAMES T. BRADY.

THE father of James T. Brady was born in Ireland, and came to this country during the second war with England, and just after his marriage. Mr. Brady opened a school for boys, in New York, soon after his arrival, and it was in that city, on the 9th of April, 1815, that his eldest son, JAMES TOPHAM BRADY, was born. Other children followed, there being seven in all, two boys (James T., and Judge John R. Brady) and five girls. Mr. Brady, senior, was a man of rare abilities, and his wife was a woman of great personal beauty and high character, "one of those mothers," says a distinguished gentleman, who knew her, "whose quiet virtues shed their blessed influence over families, and are felt so long in their durable effect upon children."

James T. Brady grew up with a sound, vigorous constitution, and at an early age was put at his studies in his father's school. He was only seven years old when he began, and though so young, he worked hard, storing his "big head"—which seemed too big for the little feet below it—with knowledge. He endeared himself very greatly to his school-fellows, and formed with several of them friendships which continued through life. "He was so noted," says one of his former school-fellows, "for his loving kindliness as a boy, that it almost obliterates every other recollection." His amiable traits developed with his years. He always delighted in acts of kindness, and could never bear to give pain, even to the most insignificant animal or insect. He detested hunting and fishing, which he regarded as a needless sacrifice of life. Yet while so tender and gentle in his disposition, he was brave and fearless, unusually independent, and, above all, as mirthful and fond of a jest at fifty as at sixteen.

Before he had completed his education, his father abandoned the profession of teaching for that of a lawyer, and young Brady entered his office as office-boy and student, it being his desire to become an advocate. He was bright, quick-witted, and remarkably apt in his studies. His buoyant spirits and ready repartee often led him into encounters with his elders, who were generally forced to confess that his tongue was too much for them. His father encouraged him to form his own opinions, and to hold them tenaciously until convinced of his error. He made rapid progress in his legal studies, and soon acquired such proficiency in the management of the details of the office business that every thing which did not absolutely need his father's personal attention was left to him.

Although fond of social enjoyment, and full of the fire and joyfulness of youth, he knew how to seclude himself from the pleasures he relished so much. He was a hard and faithful student, allowing nothing to draw him from his books when he meant to devote himself to them. He read not only law, but history, poetry, biography, romance, in short, every thing that could store his mind with useful knowledge or add to its natural graces. He slept at the office, and often sat up the entire night engaged in study. Abbott speaks as follows of the early studies of Napoleon II., and it requires no straining of language or ideas to apply his remarks to this portion of the life of James T. Brady: "So great was his ardor for intellectual improvement that he considered every day as lost in which he had not made perceptible progress in knowledge. By this rigid mental discipline he acquired that wonderful power of concentration by which he was ever enabled to simplify subjects the most difficult and complicated." Mr. Brady, senior, was very proud of the energy and talent displayed by his son, and when the latter was nineteen years old the father said to a friend who had been speaking to him of the promise of the boy: "Yes, sir; he is a boy of great promise, a boy of splendid intellect and noble character. Young as he is, I regard him as a walking encyclopœdia; his mind seems to gild every subject it touches."

In the year 1835, when but twenty years old, Mr. Brady was admitted to the bar. "There were giants in those days" at the New York bar, and the young man was now entering an arena in which his powers were to be tested to the utmost. His native eloquence was well known to his friends, and naturally he was not ignorant of it; but he did not, like so many young men in his calling, trust entirely to his powers of pleading. He had long since recognized the truth of Lord Erskine's declaration that "no man can be a great advocate who is no lawyer," and had stored his mind with a knowledge of the theories of his profession which few men in coming to the bar have ever equaled.

In his first important case he was opposed to Charles O'Conor, and was unsuccessful. He was engaged in a suit to recover a certain sum of money from an insurance company, which his client claimed was due him for certain goods which had been destroyed by fire. As Brady himself saw, he had a very weak case, and Mr. O'Conor had no trouble in demolishing it; yet the young counsel conducted it with a skill and an eloquence which made him from that hour a marked man in his profession. Yet he had to contend against that obstacle which meets most public men at the outset of their careers—the feeling which actors call "stage fright." He said that on this occasion every thing around him grew suddenly black, and he could not even see the jury. By steadying himself against his table, and keeping his eyes in the direction of the jury, he continued to speak until he had recovered his self-control.

The case which brought him most prominently before the public, and which may be said to have established his fame as a lawyer, was a peculiar one. Some newsboys had been arrested for selling the "Sunday Morning News" on the morning of the Sabbath day. It was claimed that the selling of the paper on the streets on Sunday was contrary to law, and that the boys disturbed the congregations in the churches by their cries. One of these boys had been arrested at the instance of Mr. Gerard, and this brought on a suit to determine the rights of the lads, in which Mr. Brady appeared for the newsboys. Considerable feeling was manifested on the subject, and when the trial came on the court-room was crowded. The verdict of the jury was against him, but Mr. Brady won a remarkable triumph by his management of the case, and the whole city rang with his eloquence. So great was the effect of his speech upon the audience, that many of them who were total strangers to him crowded around him as he left the court-house to congratulate him. Though defeated in the verdict of the jury, this case was a great triumph for Mr. Brady. It established his fame as an advocate, and advanced him at once to a foremost place at the bar. Business flowed in upon him more rapidly than he could attend to it, and from this time to the close of his labors he was always in the possession of a large and lucrative practice.

Mr. McKeon has said of him: "We may refer to the period of his introduction to the bar of this city as an epoch in its history. In looking back at the past, we see rising before us George Wood, treading with no uncertain step through the labyrinth of the law of real property; Daniel Lord, following, with his legal eye, commerce over the long and dreary waste of waters; David Graham, the younger, and Ogden Hoffman, standing in full panoply of intellectual power before our criminal tribunals. Into the lists where stood these proud knights young Brady sprang, ready to contend with the mightiest of them. How well he contended many of you well remember, and the honors paid to his memory are justified by the triumphs he has won."

He grew rapidly in popularity, and in the esteem and confidence of his fellow-citizens, and was intrusted with numerous cases of a class which had rarely until then been seen in the hands of a young lawyer. His practice soon extended into the Supreme Court of the State, which at that time met quarterly, at New York, Albany, Utica, and Rochester. The practice of this court was entirely in the hands of men of high standing in their profession,—the great lawyers of the State,—and it was no slight honor to our young lawyer to hold a place, and a proud place, too, among them.

He won additional honors in the famous India-rubber suits, which have been mentioned elsewhere in this volume, acting as one of the counsel of Charles Goodyear, and being associated with Daniel Webster. Brady applied himself with intense energy to master the case, and when the trial came off at Trenton, in the United States Circuit Court, before Justices Grier and Dickerson, he opened the case in a speech which lasted two days, and which Daniel Webster said in the beginning of his remarks had so exhausted it as to leave him nothing to say.

Turning to Mr. Brady, Mr. Webster said, "You have cut a highway through this case, and if it is won, it will be because of the manner in which you have brought it before the court." The suit was won by Goodyear.

"In connection with the India-rubber cases is a fact which testifies to his character. A salary of twenty-five thousand dollars a year for life was offered to be settled on him by the rubber company, if he would advise a certain course; but not deeming it right, he rejected the offer. When in France, in 1851, the rubber cases coming in controversy there, Mr. Brady substantially gave in French, to Etienne Blanc, the French advocate, the materials for his brief."

Mr. Brady practiced law for thirty-four years, and during the major part of that time there was scarcely a case of great importance, in either the civil or criminal courts, in which he did not figure. He was compelled to refuse case after case from lack of time to give to it; and yet he frequently found time to respond to the appeals of the courts to defend men indicted for capital offenses who were unable to procure counsel. In some of these cases he had scarcely any chance of preparation, but he always managed to secure the acquittal of his client, in spite of this drawback. The spirit of kindliness which had so endeared him to his boyhood's friends pervaded every action of his maturer life, and he never displayed more energy, more unceasing vigilance, more irresistible eloquence, than when pleading the cause of some poor wretch who could only reward him with his thanks.

His readiness in mastering a case was remarkable, and was greatly assisted by his profound knowledge of the law. As a rule, in the ordinary run of cases, it was merely necessary for him to comprehend the particular case under consideration, since he was already familiar with the law bearing upon it.

This readiness is admirably illustrated in the following reminiscence related of him by the Hon. Luther R. Marsh. Mr. Marsh was engaged in a case of great importance, in which he desired Mr. Brady's assistance in the trial. Marsh had thoroughly and patiently studied the case, but Brady was totally ignorant of it. Nevertheless, he told Mr. Marsh he would do his best, and that he (Marsh) must open the case as fully and exhaustively as he could, without reference to him. Mr. Marsh did so, and says that when he sat down he thought he had *exhausted* the case, and was wondering what Brady could find to say in addition to it. To his astonishment and delight, Brady rose, and in his argument presented seven new and telling points.

In the examination of a witness, he could be severe and decisive when he had occasion to suspect that the person was trying to evade the truth; but in general his manner was kind and considerate, and he succeeded in eliciting evidence by his forbearance which others could not have extorted by bullying. Upon one occasion, he was convinced that a witness was about to relate a "made-up" story, and he at once fixed upon the man a look so piercing that the fellow was overwhelmed with confusion and could not go on with his evidence. Brady promptly changed his tactics, sent for a glass of water for the witness, and soothed him so effectually that the heart of the man was won, and, abandoning his false tale, he made a simple statement of the truth.

The independence of character exhibited by Mr. Brady has already been adverted to. Having once traced out the line of duty, nothing could make him swerve from it, and he was as bold in the defense of the rights of his clients as of his own. Mr. Edwards Clarke, from whose excellent memoir is gleaned much of the information upon which this sketch is based, relates the following incidents in illustration of this quality of the man:

"The trial of Baker for the murder of Poole furnished a notable instance of Mr. Brady's intrepidity in behalf of a client. It was at the height of the 'Know-Nothing' excitement, and Poole, after receiving the fatal bullet, having exclaimed, 'I die an American,' succeeded in causing himself to be regarded as a martyr to the cause. Lingering for days with—as the *post-mortem* proved—a bullet deeply imbedded in his heart, the interest and excitement became intense; and on the day of his funeral twenty thousand men walked in solemn procession behind the coffin of the martyred 'rough.' In such a state of public feeling, Baker was put on trial for his life. At the opening of the charge by the judge, aroused by its tenor, Mr. Brady seized a pen and commenced writing rapidly, indignation showing itself in his set lips and frowning brow. The moment the judge ceased he was on his feet, and began: 'You have charged the jury thus and thus. I protest against your so stating it.' The judge said he would listen to the objections after the jury had retired. 'No!' exclaimed the indignant orator, 'I choose that the jury should hear those objections;' and, defying interference, he poured forth impetuously forty-five separate and formal objections, couching them all emphatically in words of personal protest to the judge. The force of the judge's charge on that jury was pretty effectually broken. The indignation of the advocate at this time was real, not simulated; and he, at least, of the New York bar dared to defy and to denounce injustice, even when clad in ermine.

"Another instance of his intrepidity before a judge was in the Busteed case. The judge had threatened to convict him for contempt. Busteed had apologized, and Brady also, with his matchless grace and courtesy, had tendered Busteed's apology; but the judge still said that he should send him to prison. 'You will, will you?' said Brady; 'I say you will not.' And, citing authority after authority against his power to do so, he dared him to thus stretch his prerogative. The judge thought best to excuse Mr. Busteed."

Perhaps one of the best instances of his moral courage to be found was his conduct with reference to the late Edwin M. Stanton. He was associated with Mr. Stanton in the Sickles trial, and conceived a warm personal attachment to him. Mr. Brady remained a Democrat to the last, and was an active member of Tammany Hall. Upon one occasion, during a meeting of the Tammany Committee, when the name of Stanton was received with hisses and yells of objurgation, Brady rose, and facing the crowd told them "that he knew they hated Edwin M. Stanton, but he, a Democrat, knew him, and held him in his heart of hearts." It was a bold declaration, considering the time and place, even for one so highly esteemed as James T. Brady.

As before remarked, Mr. Brady never relied upon his eloquence alone for success at the bar. He had a profound respect for his profession, and scorned its trickeries. He worked faithfully over the cases intrusted to him, studied them carefully, and never brought them to trial till he was thorough master of the law bearing upon them. This enabled him frequently to present issues which a less learned man would not have dreamed of. When he was retained as counsel for Huntington the forger, he conceived the idea that the man was morally unaccountable for his deed, and his theory of moral insanity, as developed by him in this case, is one of the most powerful arguments upon the subject to be found in any language. He read every thing he could find on the subject of insanity, and when he went into court there was not a physician in the land better informed with respect to it than he. The cases in which he was frequently engaged required an unusual acquaintance with medical jurisprudence, and he was regarded as one of the best authorities on the subject in the country.

His power over a jury was remarkable. He never lost sight of the "twelve peers," and by his dexterous management soon had them so thoroughly under the influence of his magnetic mind that they hung upon his words, followed his every act, laughed or cried as he willed, and seemed capable of thinking only as he permitted them. He defended fifty-one men for their lives in the course of his practice, and brought them all off in safety.

Mr. Clarke, from whose memoir I have already quoted, relates the following incidents in his career:

"The case of a young man charged with murder, in what was claimed to be an accidental fracas, attracted a good deal of interest. He was a Mason, and that society applied to Mr. Brady to defend him, tendering twenty-five hundred dollars as a fee; but for some cause he declined the case. Not long after, one afternoon, a neatly-dressed, modest young girl came to the office and asked for Mr. Brady. Told to walk into his private office, she timidly approached his desk, and saying, 'Mr. Brady, they are going to hang my brother, and you can save him. I've brought you this money; please don't let my brother die,' she burst into tears. It was a roll of two hundred and fifty dollars, which the poor girl had begged in sums of five and ten dollars. The kind-hearted man heard her story. 'They shall not hang your brother, my child,' said he, and putting the roll of bills in an envelope, told her to take it to her mother, and he would ask for it when he wanted it. The boy was cleared. In Mr. Brady's parlor hangs an exquisite picture, by Durand,

"THEY ARE GOING TO HANG MY BROTHER, AND YOU CAN SAVE HIM!"

with a letter on the back asking him to accept it as a mark of appreciation for his generous kindness in defending this poor boy. Mr. Brady prized *that* picture. . . . .

"Once when, in the height of his appeal to the jury, a dog began barking vigorously, he whirled around, shook his finger at the dog and said, gravely, with the quickness of thought, 'I am Sir Oracle, and when I ope my lips let no dog bark!'

"An Irishman once came to his office: 'And are yez Misther Brady?' 'I am; come in, Patrick. What is it you wish?' 'I ax yer pardon; I ought n't to intrude upon yez.' 'But what is it, Patrick?' 'Well, yer honor, it is n't for the likes o' me to be comin' troublin' yer honor.' 'But tell me what you want, Pat.' 'Well, yer honor, I came to see ye about a friend of mine as met wid an accident.' 'An accident?' said Mr. Brady; 'then why do n't you go for a doctor?' 'Arrah, sure, you 're the docther for my friend; he had an accident which wants yer honor.' 'Well, what *was* it?' 'Well, yer honor, he was arristed for a thrifle of a burglary, shure.' Quick as Mr. Brady was, with the readiness of his race, for repartee, he sometimes met his match among his own countrymen. He was once examining an unwilling witness who persistently called him Mr. O'Brady. At length, even his proverbial good nature being a little ruffled, he said to the witness: 'You need not call me Mr. O'Brady. I 've mended my name since I came here and dropped the O.' 'Have ye, now? 'Pon my sowl it 's a pity ye did n't mend yer manners at the same time.'"

In politics Mr. Brady was a Democrat of the States-Rights school, yet he always maintained that it was the duty of the citizen to render the promptest obedience to the General Government. At the outset of the late war he gave his support to the Government in its war measures, though he did not separate himself from the Democratic party. He was frequently solicited by his friends to accept political honors, but he steadily refused, saying that he wanted no honors outside of his profession.

In person Mr. Brady was slender and delicate in appearance. What attracted the gazer at once was his massive head—a head which measured in its circumference twenty-four and three-eighths inches. Age seemed to have no effect upon his face. Severe mental labor in the course of years took away some of the rosy hues of youth, but otherwise it continued as fresh and as winning as when a boy.

Mr. Brady never married, but no one was more widely removed from the typical old bachelor than he. If he had no family of his own, he was the head of a family of devoted relatives, who gave him ample scope for the exercise of the domestic affections which were so strong in him. Very soon after entering upon the practice of his profession his parents died, leaving his brother and five sisters, all much younger than himself, helpless. The young lawyer at once declared that the care of these dear ones should be his first thought, and he devoted himself to his practice with redoubled energy, in order to provide for them. He brought his personal expenses down to a low figure, and resolutely kept them there, yet all the while he was lavish in his generosity to those whom he loved. He once said to a friend who asked him why he had never married: "When my father died he left five daughters, who looked to me for support. All the affection which I could have had for a wife went out to those sisters, and I have never desired to recall it." He transferred a share of this affection to the children of those sisters and of his brother, and was never so happy as when in their company. In his will he mentions one of his nieces as his "dearly beloved Toot."

He was very fond of literature, especially of poetry, and

devoted a considerable portion of his time to literary efforts of his own. His great fame as a lawyer so overshadowed the success he won in literature that few besides himself knew how much pleasure the popularity of his writings gave him.

In the exercise of his profession Mr. Brady won a large fortune. His income was princely during the greater part of his life, but he saved comparatively little. He delighted in giving to others. His relatives were the constant recipients of substantial evidences of his affection for them, and his charities to the poor were in keeping with his generous nature. He could not look upon suffering unmoved, and "never turned his face from any poor man."

His last appearance in public was at the Gerard dinner, where he was as brilliant and genial as ever. He seemed to have a foreboding of his approaching end, however, for the next day he said to one of his family: "I feel that it is the last time I shall ever appear on a like public occasion." His fears were prophetic. He was seized with an attack of paralysis on the morning of the 9th of February, 1869, and breathed his last at five o'clock in the afternoon of the same day. He died in the communion of the Catholic Church, and was buried from St. Patrick's Cathedral, in the city of New York. His death drew forth expressions of sympathy and respect from all parts of the Union and from men of all shades of opinion. All felt that a good and useful man, a great advocate, and an incorruptible citizen had been taken away.

His was a happy fate. He died in the fullness of his fame, before age had weakened his faculties or chilled his heart, and dying thus, it may be said of him, as he once said of another, that he was "a man who had no guile in his nature, and who died leaving no living creature to rejoice at his death."

VII.

ARTISTS.

CHAPTER XXVII.

BENJAMIN WEST.

AT a time when America was regarded in Europe as a savage region, and when Americans were looked upon as little better than barbarians by the people of the mother country, it was no slight achievement for an American artist to rise by the force of his genius to the proud position of President of the Royal Academy of Great Britain.

The man who won this triumph was BENJAMIN WEST. He was born in Springfield, Pennsylvania, on the 10th of October, 1738. His parents were Quakers, plain, simple people, who feared God, lived a just life, and desired above all other things that their children should become pious and useful men and women. The old mansion-house where the future artist was born was situated in Chester County, and is still standing. It is not far from Philadelphia, and the place is now called Westdale. His father's family emigrated from England to America with William Penn, at his second visit, in 1699. John West married the daughter of Thomas Pearson, by whom he had ten children. Of these, Benjamin was the youngest son. His mother was a woman of great piety, and, being once in attendance upon a memorable religious revival, at which she was terribly agitated by the preaching of one Edward Peckover, an itinerant Quaker minister, was taken with premature labor, of which Benjamin West was born.

It was predicted that a child who had been brought into the world under such circumstances would be a man of more than ordinary fame, and the good mother treasured these prophecies in her heart, and watched the career of her boy with the keenest interest.

When he was but seven years old, he was left one day to watch beside the cradle of the infant child of his eldest sister, who, though married, was still living at home. Being unusually silent for a long time, his mother concluded that she would go and see what he was doing. Upon entering the room where he had been left with his charge, she saw him kneeling by a chair which he had placed close up to the cradle, gazing at the infant, and making what she supposed to be marks on a paper which lay on the chair. Stealing up behind him softly, she saw to her astonishment that this boy, only seven years old, had executed, with black and red ink and a pen, an accurate though rude likeness of the sleeping babe. This was the first evidence he had ever given of his predilection for art, and was indeed a most surprising performance for so young a child.

The next summer a party of Indians came to Springfield to pay their annual visit, and to please them little Benjamin showed them some sketches of birds and flowers which he had executed with pen and ink. The savages were delighted with them, and presented him with the red and yellow pigments with which they colored their ornaments. In addition to this gift, they taught him how to prepare these colors, to which he added another, namely, indigo, which his mother gave him

THE TRUANT'S SECRET DISCOVERED.

from her laundry. His colors were rude enough, but his pencils were ruder. They were made of the hairs which he had pulled from a cat's back and fastened in the end of a goose-quill. Soon after this, a relative from Philadelphia, chancing to visit the old homestead, was struck with the talent of the little fellow, and upon his return to the city sent him a box of colors, with pencils and canvas and a few prints. He was only nine years old, but he was a born artist. He had never seen any painting of merit, and the few prints which his relative gave him were the most finished productions he had ever seen. The box of colors was his most precious possession, and it opened to him new fields of enjoyment. The day of its arrival he gave himself up entirely to the pleasure of examining it. "Even after going to sleep," says his biographer, "he awoke more than once during the night, and anxiously put out his hand to the box, which he had placed by his bedside, half afraid that he might find his riches only a dream. Next morning he rose at break of day, and, carrying his colors and canvas to the garret, proceeded to work. Every thing else was now unheeded; even his attendance at school was given up. As soon as he got out of the sight of his father and mother, he stole to his garret, and there passed the hours in a world of his own. At last, after he had been absent from school some days, the master called at his father's house to inquire what had become of him. This led to the discovery of his secret occupation. His mother, proceeding to the garret, found the truant; but so much was she astonished and delighted by the creation of his pencil, which also met her view when she entered the apartment, that, instead of rebuking him, she could only take him in her arms and kiss him with transports of affection. He made a new composition of his own out of two of the engravings, which he had colored from his own feeling of the proper tints; and so perfect did the appearance already appear to his mother, that, although half the canvas yet remained uncovered, she would not suffer him to add another touch to what he had done. Mr. Galt, West's biographer, saw the picture in the state in which it had thus been left sixty-seven years afterward; and the artist himself used to acknowledge that in none of his subsequent efforts had he been able to excel some of the touches of invention in this his first essay."

His next effort was a landscape, which comprehended a view of a river, with vessels in the stream and cattle browsing on the banks. He could not have been much over ten years of age at this time, and the picture, though insignificant in itself, is remarkable as the work of a child. He subsequently presented it to his friend, Mr. William Henry, of Lancaster, whose family still retain possession of it. He visited Philadelphia soon after, and received a few simple instructions in the practical portion of his art, after which he went about through the towns of the vicinity of his home, painting portraits of his friends. At length he was sent for by Mrs. Ross, of Lancaster, a lady famed for her great beauty, to paint the portraits of herself and her family—a great honor for a lad of twelve.

It was in Lancaster, in the year 1750, that he made the acquaintance of Mr. William Henry. That gentleman became deeply interested in the precocious boy, and frequently came to watch him at his portrait-painting. One day he said to Benjamin, that if he (Henry) could paint equally well he would not waste his time upon portraits, but would devote himself to historical subjects. In the course of the conversation to which this remark gave rise, Mr. Henry proposed to him to make an attempt in this direction, and suggested to him "The Death of Socrates" as his first subject. The little artist frankly avowed that he had never heard of the great philosopher, and Mr. Henry at once went to his library and brought out a volume of Plutarch, from which he read to the boy the beautiful story of the wise man's death. West listened with the deepest interest, and expressed his perfect readiness to undertake the task, but feared he would have difficulty in painting the figure of the slave who presented the poison, and which he thought ought to be naked, since he had hitherto painted only men with their clothes on. Mr. Henry had in his employ a young man of fine appearance, and upon hearing West's objection at once sent for him. As the workman entered the room Henry pointed to him, and said to West, "There's your model." West took the hint, painted the picture, which was purchased by Mr. Henry, and thenceforth determined that in his art he would look only into nature for his models.

At the age of sixteen he returned to Springfield. He was anxious to continue his career as an artist, and as his parents were satisfied that he was now old enough to enter upon some permanent occupation, they agreed that his wishes should be submitted to a public meeting of the Society of Friends. The meeting was called, and the matter was laid before them, the boy himself being present. His relatives and friends were all very proud of his talents, but as the profession of an artist was so entirely at variance with all Quaker habits and ideas, they felt that the subject was one which ought not to be rashly decided. Silence prevailed for a long time after the opening of the meeting, but at length John Williamson, moved by the Spirit, rose and addressed the assemblage, declaring his belief that as the youth had not derived his fondness for art from any of his associations or surroundings, and since it was so manifestly a special gift from the Creator, it was their plain duty to bid him go forward in the path that had been marked out for him, and to wish him God-speed in his efforts. At the close of his remarks silence again fell upon the assembly. Then the women rose, and approaching the lad, one by one, kissed him on the cheek, and the men, laying their hands on his head, prayed that the Lord might verify in his life the value of the gift which had induced them, in spite of their religious tenets on the subject, to allow him to enter upon the permanent exercises of the profession so dear to his heart.

Thus was he dedicated to his art, and at the same time separated to a certain degree from his Quaker brethren. Not long after this he violated every principle of the Quaker dispensation by volunteering under Major Sir Peter Halket to go in search of the remains of Braddock's army.

In 1756, at the age of eighteen, he established himself in Philadelphia as a portrait painter, and soon after removed to New York, where he painted portraits at five guineas a head, occasionally attempting an historical piece. When he was twenty years old he made a visit to Europe—a visit which decided his destiny. A famine in the south of Europe induced a Philadelphia merchant to dispatch a vessel laden with flour to Leghorn, and his son, who was to take passage in the ship, proposed to West to accompany him, and thus secure an opportunity of seeing the art-treasures of the Old World. West promptly accepted the invitation, and some of his friends in New York provided him with an outfit for the voyage. Upon arriving at Gibraltar, the vessel was boarded by a British officer, who proved to be a kinsman of the son of the owner of the ship, and he not only passed them without molestation, but enabled them to secure unusual facilities in the voyage up the Mediterranean. West arrived in Rome in July, 1759, and was kindly received by the English Lord Grantham, to whom he bore letters of introduction.

"Among the distinguished persons whom Mr. West found in Rome, was the celebrated Cardinal Albani. At an evening party, the Cardinal became curious to witness the effect which the works of art in the Belvidere and Vatican would produce on the young artist. The whole company, which consisted of the principal Roman nobility and strangers of distinction then in Rome, were interested in the event, and it was arranged, in the course of the evening, that, on the following morning, they should accompany West to the palaces. At the hour appointed, the company assembled, and a procession consisting of upwards of thirty of the most magnificent equipages in the capital of Christendom, and filled with some of the most erudite characters in Europe, conducted the young Quaker to view the masterpieces of art. It was agreed that the 'Apollo' should be first submitted to his view, because it was the most perfect work among all the ornaments of Rome, and, consequently, the best calculated to produce that effect which the company were anxious to witness. The statue then stood in a case, inclosed with doors, which could be so opened as to disclose it at once to full view. West was placed in the situation where it was seen to the most advantage, and the spectators arranged themselves on each side. When the keeper threw open the doors, the artist felt himself surprised with a sudden recollection altogether different from the gratification which he had expected, and without being aware of the force of what he said, exclaimed, 'My God! how like it is to a young Mohawk warrior.' The Italians, observing his surprise and hearing the exclamation, were excessively mortified to find that the god of their idolatry was compared to a savage. They mentioned their chagrin, and asked West to give some more distinct explanation, by informing them what sort of people the Mohawk Indians were. He described to them their education, their dexterity with the bow and arrow, the admirable elasticity of their limbs, and how much their active life expands the chest, while the quick breathing of their speed in the chase dilates the nostrils with that apparent consciousness of vigor which is so nobly depicted in the 'Apollo.' 'I have seen them often,' added he, 'standing in that very attitude, and pursuing with an intense eye the arrow which they had just discharged from the bow.' The Italians were delighted with this descriptive explanation, and allowed that a better criticism had never been pronounced on the merits of the statue."

Soon after his arrival in Rome, West painted a portrait of Lord Grantham, which won him considerable reputation. It was at first attributed to Raphael Meugs, but when the true artist was announced, and the circumstances of his history became known, West found himself suddenly famous, with orders enough to place him at once in comfortable circumstances. Cardinal Albani and Lord Grantham were very kind to him during his stay in Rome, and Raphael Meugs advised him to make a careful tour of study through the Italian art capitals. While in Rome he painted two pictures, "Cimon and Iphigenia," and "Angelica and Medora," which were well received, and during this period he was elected a member by the Academies of Florence, Bologna, and Parma. He made the tour advised by Meugs, remaining in Italy several years. Thence he proceeded to France, where he passed a short time in studying the French masters, after which he went to England, intending to sail from that country for America, where he had left his heart behind him in the keeping of a young Quakeress of Philadelphia.

He reached London in 1763, and while continuing his studies here, whither his reputation had preceded him from Italy, undertook some commissions for Archbishop Drummond and several other church dignitaries. These attracted general admiration, and his countrymen residing in London were prompt to recognize and proclaim his genius. He had relatives living in England, so that he was not an entire stranger there. His success was marked from the first, and his friends urged him to profit by so favorable a beginning, give up his idea of returning to America, and make his permanent home in England. This he at length decided to do, and devoted himself with increased ardor to his labors. In two years he considered himself sufficiently well established to send to Philadelphia for his betrothed. This lady, Miss Elizabeth Shewell, came out to England under the care of his father, and in the same year, 1765, West was married to her in London. She was a lady of great amiability of character, and by the English was often spoken of as the Philadelphia beauty.

Soon after his arrival in England he produced a large painting on a subject from Tacitus, "Agrippina Landing with the Ashes of Germanicus." It was a decided success. George the Third was deeply impressed with it, and congratulated West warmly upon its merits. At the same time the king gave him a commission for a painting,—the subject to be "The Death of Regulus,"—and thus began the friendship between the monarch and the artist, which lasted for nearly forty years. He was a hard worker, and during his long life his pictures followed each other in rapid succession. They are estimated by a writer in Blackwood's Magazine at three thousand in number. Mr. Dunlap says that they would cover a wall ten feet high and a quarter of a mile long if arranged side by side on a flat surface. The most famous are his "Death of Wolfe;" "Regulus, a Prisoner to the Carthaginians;" "The Battle of La Hogue;" "The Death of Bayard;" "Hamilcar Swearing the Infant Hannibal at the Altar;" "The Departure of Regulus;"

"Agrippina Landing with the Ashes of Germanicus;" "Christ Healing the Sick;" "Death on the Pale Horse;" "The Descent of the Holy Ghost on the Saviour in the Jordan;" "The Crucifixion;" and "Christ Rejected."

The picture which brought him most prominently before the public, and which placed his popularity beyond dispute, was "The Death of Wolfe at Quebec." It was fashionable at this time to treat nothing but subjects from ancient history, and when West announced his intention of painting a picture of contemporary history his friends warned him that he was incurring a serious risk. Nevertheless he finished his "Death of Wolfe," and it was exhibited in the National Gallery. The public "acknowledged its excellence at once, but the lovers of old art—called classical—complained of the barbarism of boots, buttons, and blunderbusses, and cried out for naked warriors, with bows, bucklers, and battering rams." Lord Grosvenor was much pleased with the picture, and finally purchased it, though he did so with hesitation, daunted to some extent by the fierce storm of opposition with which the critics received it. Sir Joshua Reynolds, then the President of the Royal Academy, and the Archbishop of York, called on West and protested against his barbarous innovation, but he declared to them that "the event to be commemorated happened in the year 1759, in a region of the world unknown to Greeks and Romans, and at a period of the world when no warrior who wore classic costume existed. The same rule which gives law to the historian should rule the painter." When the king saw the picture he was delighted both with it and West's originality, and declared that he was sorry Lord Grosvenor had been before him in purchasing it. This was the inauguration of a new era in British art, and Sir Joshua Reynolds was obliged to declare, "West has conquered. I foresee that this picture will not only become one of the most popular, but will occasion a revolution in art." This frank avowal was as honorable to Sir Joshua as to West.

West painted for George the Third a number of subjects taken from the early history of England, and received from the same monarch a commission for a series of paintings illustrating the progress of revealed religion, with which the king designed to ornament the chapel at Windsor Castle. Of these twenty-eight were finished when the Prince of Wales, afterward George the Fourth, came into power as Prince Regent, and the commission was withdrawn. The artist then began a series of grand religious subjects, upon which he was still engaged when death called him to rest from all his labors. Of those which were completed, "Death on the Pale Horse" and "Christ Healing the Sick" are the best known in this country.

In 1792, upon the death of Sir Joshua Reynolds, West was made President of the Royal Academy. The king wished to confer upon him the honor of knighthood, but he declined it, alleging that he was not wealthy enough to support the dignity of the position. In consequence of dissensions in the Academy, West resigned his presidency in 1802. The post was filled for a year by James Wyatt, the architect, and at the close of that time West was re-elected by every ballot but one—that of Fuseli, who voted for Mrs. Lloyd, a member of the Academy, declaring that he considered "one old woman as good as another." West continued in this office until his death.

The close of his life was blessed with ample means, and, as he was in the full possession of all his faculties and covered with art's supremest honors, it may be regarded as the happiest portion of his career. His house was always open to Americans visiting England, and few things pleased him more than to listen to news from his native village. He was a kind and judicious friend to young artists, especially to those of his own country studying in England, and took a lively pleasure in their success. Leigh Hunt, whose mother was a relative of West, has left us the following description of him:

"The appearance of West was so gentlemanly that the moment he changed his gown for a coat he seemed to be full dressed. The simplicity and self-possession of the young Quaker, not having time enough to grow stiff—for he went early to Rome—took up, I suppose, with more ease than most would have done, the urbanities of his new position. Yet this man, so well bred, and so indisputably clever in his art, whatever might be the amount of his genius, had received a homely or careless education, and pronounced some of his words with a puritanical barbarism; he would talk of his art all day. There were strong suspicions of his leaning to his native side in politics, and he could not restrain his enthusiasm for Bonaparte. How he managed these matters with the higher powers in England I can not say."

Possessed originally of a sound and vigorous constitution, which he had not weakened by any species of dissipation, West lived to a good old age, and died in London on the 11th of March, 1820, in his eighty-second year. He was buried in St. Paul's Cathedral, by the side of Sir Joshua Reynolds, and under the same great dome which covers the tombs of Nelson and Wellington.

CHAPTER XXVIII.

JOHN ROGERS.

THERE is scarcely a family of means and taste in the country but is the possessor of one or more of Rogers's groups in plaster. You see them in every art or book-store window, and they are constantly finding new admirers, and rendering the name of the talented sculptor more and more a household word.

JOHN ROGERS, to whom the world is indebted for this new branch of art, was born at Salem, Massachusetts, on the 30th of October, 1829. His ancestors were among the original settlers of the colony, and have resided in Salem for generations. His father, a merchant of moderate means and good reputation, was anxious to train his son to some regular and profitable business. As the basis of this, he gave the boy a good education in the common schools of the town, and in 1845, when he was sixteen years old, placed him in a dry-goods store in Boston to learn the business. He remained there for two years.

He gave early evidence of his artistic genius, and when a mere child had shown a taste and talent for drawing which increased with his years, and made him eager to become an artist. His parents, however, were desirous of seeing him rich rather than famous, and did all in their power to discourage him from making choice of a vocation which they considered but little better than vagabondage. They magnified the difficulties and trials of an artist's career, and so far succeeded in their efforts that he entirely abandoned his wish to make art a means of livelihood. He was not willing to forsake it altogether, however—he was too true an artist at heart for that—but contented himself for the time with continuing his efforts, merely as a means of personal enjoyment.

In 1847, feeling satisfied that he was not suited to a mercantile life, Mr. Rogers gave up his clerkship in Boston, and obtained a place in the corps of engineers engaged in the construction of the Cochituate Water Works. Here he had a fine opportunity for cultivating his talent for drawing, but the constant labor which he underwent so injured his eyes that he was compelled to give up his position. His physician advised him to make an ocean voyage for the purpose of re-establishing his health. Acting upon this advice, he made a short visit to Spain, and returned home very much improved by the voyage and the rest his eyes had enjoyed.

In 1848, soon after his return to this country, he entered a machine shop in Manchester, New Hampshire, to learn the trade of a machinist. He worked at this trade for a period of seven years, applying himself to it with great diligence and determination, and acquiring much mechanical skill and a thorough knowledge of the trade. He rose steadily through the various grades of his new calling—from the bench of the apprentice to the post of draughtsman in the designing department.

During this period he devoted himself enthusiastically to his art. Soon after his return from Spain, he had observed a young man modeling a figure in clay, and by closely observing him had learned the process, which until then was unknown to him. The labor of the youth pleased him very much, and the more because he saw in it a new means of artistic expression. He at once procured some clay, and, taking it to his room, commenced to practice upon the lesson which he had just received. From this time forward he continued his art labors, giving to them all the leisure time he could spare from his duties in the shop, where he was compelled to work from five A. M. until seven P. M. He would go to his room after supper, and by the light of a tallow candle work late into the night, modeling figures in clay, and bringing new fancies into shape. He says that frequently, although exhausted by his severe labor at the shop, he would be unable to sleep until he had molded into clay the idea which possessed his mind. These night studies, superadded to his daily duties, proved very trying to him. Yet he persevered, encouraged by his success with his figures. He endeavored to persuade some of his relatives to aid him in securing a better education as an artist, such as would have enabled him to abandon the machine shop; but they turned a deaf ear to him, and he was thus compelled to continue his daily task, which, under these circumstances, naturally grew more and more irksome.

In 1856, he was enabled to better his condition for a short time. He was offered the place of manager of a railroad machine-shop at Hannibal, Missouri, and promptly accepted it. In six months, however, he was out of employment, the panic of 1857 having caused the machine-shop to suspend operations. Having a little money in hand, which he had saved from his wages, he resolved to visit Europe, and study the works of the great masters in his art, and, if he could, to take lessons in sculpture from some competent teacher in the Old World. He went to Paris and Rome, remaining in those cities for a period of eight months, and endeavoring to share the enthusiasm for the great works around him which the artist world manifested. At the end of that time he came home convinced that classic art had no attractions for him, and was almost ready to declare that he had none of the true inspiration of an artist.

He did not stop long in the East upon his return. Going West at once, he obtained a situation in the office of the Surveyor of the city of Chicago. In this position he worked hard and faithfully, and his employers soon found that in him they had obtained a prize.

Meantime, although so much disheartened by his failure to accomplish any thing in Europe, he did not abandon his art studies, but continued to model figures in clay, and shortly after his arrival in Chicago, gave one of his groups to some ladies of that city, to be sold at a fair in behalf of some benevolent purpose. This was the "Checker Players," and was the first of his efforts ever submitted to the public. Its success was immediate. It proved one of the most attractive features of the fair, and the newspapers pronounced it one of the most satisfactory evidences of native genius ever seen in Chicago. Mr. Rogers was much pleased with its success, and soon followed it with "The Town Pump," one of his most popular compositions.

The popularity which these efforts attained, opened John Rogers's eyes to a correct perception of his true mission in life. He was not capable of accomplishing any thing in classic art, but here was a field in which a renown, unique and brilliant, might be won, and in which he might endear himself to thousands of hearts in the great world in which he lived. Both fame and wealth seemed opening up before him. He did not hesitate long, but resolved to follow the leadings of his genius. Having heard that a new process of flexible molds had been invented, by which the most intricate designs could be cast with ease, he came to New York in 1859, bringing with him his "Checker Players" and "Town Pump," and the model of a new group on which he was then engaged. Seeking an Italian familiar with the new process, he engaged him to cast his figures in plaster by means of it, and from him he learned how to practice the new method himself.

He now put forth his "Slave Auction," which he had modeled in Chicago and brought to New York with him. The antislavery excitement was then at its height, and this effort aroused the sympathy and won Mr. Rogers the support of the greater part of the people of the Northern States. There was a large demand for the group, and Mr. Rogers soon found himself obliged to employ assistance to fill the orders which kept crowding in upon him. By selecting a subject which was of the deepest interest to the people of the country, he had thus attracted attention to his merits, and he felt sure that by keeping the people supplied with works illustrative of the topics of the day, he would win the success to which he aspired.

He now ventured to establish himself permanently in New York, and, renting the garret of a Broadway building, set up his studio in it, and issued this modest card: "John Rogers, Artist, Designs and Executes Groups of Figures in Composition at his Studio, 599 Broadway." The success of his works had been so marked as to induce him to believe that he would have no difficulty in establishing a permanent business, and he set to work with enthusiasm. In quick succession he produced his "Fairy's Whisper" and "Air Castles," the latter of which is the only commission he has ever executed. The war began soon after, and supplied him with an abundance of popular subjects. These war subjects attracted universal attention, and sold as rapidly as he could supply them. A New York journal thus describes the "sensation" which they created in that city:

"All day, and every day, week in and week out, there is an ever-changing crowd of men, women, and children standing stationary amid the ever-surging tides of Broadway, before the windows of Williams & Stevens, gazing with eager interest upon the statuettes and groups of John Rogers, the sculptor. These works appeal to a deep popular sentiment. They are not pretentious displays of gods, goddesses, ideal characters, or stupendous, world-compelling heroes. They are illustrations of American domestic and especially of American military life—not of our great generals or our bold admirals, or the men whose praises fill all the newspapers, but of the common soldier of the Union; not of the common soldier, either, in what might be called his high heroic moods and moments, when, with waving sword and flaming eye, he dashes upon the enemy's works, but of the soldier in the ordinary moments and usual occupations of every-day camp life. For the last year or more Mr. Rogers has been at work mainly on groups of this latter class and character. Thus he has given us 'The Returned Volunteer, or How the Fort was Taken,' being a group of three gathered in a blacksmith's shop, the characters consisting of the blacksmith himself, standing with his right foot on the anvil block, and his big hammer in his hands, listening eagerly, with his little girl, to a soldier who sits close by on his haunches, narrating 'how the fort was taken.' We have also another group of three, 'The Picket Guard,' spiritedly sketched, as in eager, close, and nervous search for the enemy; the 'Sharpshooters,' another group of three, or rather of two men and a scarecrow, illustrating a curious practice in our army of deceiving the enemy; the 'Town Pump,' a scene in which a soldier, uniformed and accoutered, is slaking his thirst and holding blessed converse beside the pump with a pretty girl who has come for a pail of water; the 'Union Refugees,' a pathetic and noble group, consisting of a stalwart and sad-faced East Tennesseean or Virginian, who, accompanied by his wife, who leans her head upon his bosom, and by his little boy, who looks up eagerly into his face, has started off from home with only his gun upon his shoulder and his powder-horn by his side, to escape the tyranny of the rebels; 'The Camp Fire, or Making Friends with the Cook,' in which a hungry soldier, seated upon an inverted basket, is reading a newspaper to an 'intelligent contraband,' who is stirring the contents of a huge and ebullient pot hung over the fire; 'Wounded to the Rear, or One More Shot,' in which a soldier is represented as dressing his wounded leg, while his companion, with his left arm in a sling, is trying to load his gun to take another shot at the enemy, at whom he looks defiantly; 'Mail Day,' which tells its own story of a speculative soldier, seated on a stone and racking his poor brains to find some ideas to transcribe upon the paper which he holds upon his knee, to be sent perchance to her he loves; 'The Country Postmaster, or News from the Army,' which, though a scene from civil life, tells of the anxiety of the soldier's wife or sweetheart to get tidings from the brave volunteer who is periling his life on the battle-field; 'The Wounded Scout, or a Friend in the Swamp,' representing a soldier, torn, and bleeding, and far gone, rescued and raised up by a faithful and kind-hearted negro—which we think is one of the best, if not the very best, of Mr. Rogers's works; and lastly, a group called 'The Home Guard, or Midnight on the Border,' in which a heroic woman, accompanied by a little girl, is represented as stepping out, pistol in hand, to confront the assailants of her humble home."

In 1862 Mr. Rogers removed his studio to the corner of Fifth Avenue and Twenty-sixth Street, where he still remains. He has followed up the earlier productions named above with

"The Bushwhacker," a scene representing a Tennessee loyalist dogging the footsteps of the Southern army; "Taking the Oath and Drawing Rations," the best and certainly the most popular of his works,—a group of four, representing a Southern lady with her little boy, compelled to take the oath of allegiance in order to obtain rations for her family. A negro boy, bearing a basket for his mistress, leans on the barrel watching the proceeding with the most intense interest. The woman's face is wonderful, and it expresses eloquently the struggle in her breast between her devotion to the South and her love for the boy before her, and the officer tendering the oath almost speaks the sympathy which her suffering has awakened in him. The other works of our artist are "Uncle Ned's School," "The Charity Patient," "The School Examination," "The Council of War," "The Courtship in Sleepy Hollow," "The Fugitive's Story," "Challenging the Union Vote," and "Rip Van Winkle."

The process by which these exquisite groups are produced is exceedingly simple, but is one requiring considerable skill and delicacy of manipulation, and although the casting could readily be done by competent assistants, Mr. Rogers conscientiously gives his personal attention to every detail of the process. The artist takes a mass of wet clay of the desired consistency and size, and fashions it roughly with his hands to something like the proper shape. "It is sometimes necessary to make a little frame of wire upon which to lay the clay, to hold it in its proper place, the wire being easily made to take any form. The rough figure is then finished with the molding stick, which is simply a stick of pine with a little spoon of box-wood attached to each end, one spoon being more delicate than the other. With this instrument the artist works upon the clay with surprising ease. The way in which the works are reproduced is as follows: When the clay model is complete, a single plaster cast is taken for a pattern, and is finished with the most scrupulous care by Mr. Rogers himself. This cast is used as a pattern for making whatever number of molds may be needed to supply the demand for any particular group or statue. The molds are made of glue softened with water, so as to be about as limber as India-rubber. This is poured over the pattern while in a warm and liquid condition; it is, therefore, necessary to surround the pattern with a stiff case to hold the glue in place. This case is made of plaster, and is built up by hand around the pattern. When the glue has become sufficiently hard, it is cut by a thin sharp knife and pulled off the pattern. The parts are put together and bound by cord, making a perfect glue mold. The plaster of Paris is then poured into the mold inverted. A number of crooked pieces of wire are also placed in the mold to strengthen the figure. In about twenty minutes the plaster sets so as to allow the case to be opened, and the glue mold to be pulled off. To his proficiency in the mechanical part of his art Mr. Rogers attributes a considerable measure of his success, as it enables him to execute with facility every suggestion of his imagination, and to secure the perfect reproduction of his works by those to whom he intrusts that labor."

By placing his works at popular prices, ranging from $10 to $25 each, Mr. Rogers has insured the largest sale and greatest popularity for them, and has thus become a national benefactor. It is now within the power of every person of moderate means to possess one or more of his exquisite groups, and in this way the artist has not only secured to himself a sure means of wealth, but has done much to encourage and foster a popular love for, and appreciation of, the art of which he is so bright an ornament.

It was a bold venture to depart so entirely from all the precedents of art, but the result has vindicated both the artist's genius and his quick appreciation of the intelligence of his countrymen. "We can not enter into the feelings of ancient Greece," says a popular journal, in summing up his efforts, "and our artists who spend their time in attempting to reproduce that ancient art are only imitators. Their works interest only a small class of connoisseurs, and that interest is an antiquarian interest. It is not a vital, living interest, such as a Greek felt in his own work. It is not the natural, healthful, artistic feeling, the feeling for the beauty of realities, except in so far as it represents the feeling for the eternal attributes of beautiful form. It is an effort on the part of our artists to impose the forms and features of another age upon this one,—a task as impossible in art as in society, religion, and national politics."

Mr. Rogers is now in his forty-first year, and of all our American artists is, perhaps, the one best known to the masses, and the most popular. He is of medium height, carries himself erectly, and is quick and energetic in his movements. His face is frank, manly, and open, and the expression, though firm and resolute,—as that of a man who has fought so hard for success must be,—is winning and genial. He is a gentleman of great cultivation of mind, and is said by his friends to be one of the most entertaining of companions. In 1865 he married a daughter of Mr. C. S. Francis, of New York, and his fondness for domestic life leads him to pass his leisure hours chiefly by his own fireside.

HIRAM POWERS.

CHAPTER XXIX.

HIRAM POWERS.

HIRAM POWERS was born in Woodstock, Vermont, on the 29th of July, 1805. He was the eighth in a family of nine children, and was the son of a farmer who found it hard to provide his little household with the necessaries of life. He grew up as most New England boys do, sound and vigorous in health, passing the winters in attendance upon the district schools, and the summers in working on the farm. "The only distinctive trait exhibited by the child was mechanical ingenuity; he excelled in caricature, was an adept in constructiveness, having made countless wagons, windmills, and weapons for his comrades, attaining the height of juvenile reputation as the inventor of what he called a 'patent fuse.'"

The Powers family lived just over the river, opposite the village, and all joined heartily in the effort to keep the wolf from the doors. Mr. Powers, Sen., was induced to become security for one of his friends, and, as frequently happens, lost all he had in consequence. Following close upon this disaster came a dreadful famine in the State, caused by an almost total failure of the crops. "I recollect," says Mr. Powers, "we cut down the trees, and fed our few cows on the browse. We lived so long wholly on milk and potatoes, that we got almost to loathe them. There were seven of us children, five at home, and it was hard work to feed us."

One of the sons had managed to secure an education at Dartmouth College, and had removed to Cincinnati, where he was at this time editing a newspaper. Thither his father, discouraged by the famine, determined to follow him. Accordingly, placing his household goods and his family in three wagons, and being joined by another family, he set out on the long journey to the West. This was in 1819, when young Hiram was fourteen years old. It cost him a sharp struggle to leave his old home, and as they climbed the hills beyond Woodstock he lingered behind with his mother to take a last view of the place. They crossed the State, and passing through western New York came to the vicinity of Niagara Falls. They were near enough to the great cataract to hear its solemn roar sounding high above the silent woods. The boy was eager to visit it, but the distance was too great to the falls, and he was forced to relinquish this pleasure. Continuing their journey westward, they reached the Ohio River, down which stream they floated on a flatboat until they came to Cincinnati, then a city of fourteen thousand inhabitants.

Through the assistance of his eldest son, the editor, Mr. Powers was enabled to secure a farm not far from Cincinnati, and removing his family to it, began the task of clearing and cultivating it. Unfortunately for the new-comers, the farm was located on the edge of a pestilential marsh, the poisonous exhalations of which soon brought the whole family down with the ague. Mr. Powers the elder died from this disease, and Hiram was ill and disabled from it for a whole year. The family was broken up and scattered, and our hero, incapable of performing hard work so soon after his sickness, obtained a place in a produce store in Cincinnati, his duty being to watch the principal road by which the farmers' wagons, laden with grain and corn whisky, came into the city, and to inform the men in charge of them that they could obtain better prices for their produce from his employers than from any other merchants in the city. It was also a part of his duty to help to roll the barrels from the wagons to the store. He made a very good "drummer," and gave satisfaction to his employers, but as the concern soon broke up, he was again without employment.

His brother, the editor, now came to his assistance, and made a bargain with the landlord of a hotel in the city to establish a reading-room at his hotel. The landlord was to provide the room and obtain a few paying subscribers; the editor was to stock it with his exchange newspapers, and Hiram was to be put in charge of it and receive what could be made by it. The reading-room was established, but as the landlord failed to comply with his agreement, Powers was forced to abandon the undertaking.

"About that time," said he, in relating his early life to the Rev. Dr. Bellows, some years ago, "looking around anxiously for the means of living, I fell in with a worthy man, a clock-maker and organ-builder, who was willing to employ me to collect bad debts in the country. He put me on an old horse which had one very bad fault. He was afflicted with what the Western people called the 'swaleys,' and could not go down-hill. I frequently had to dismount and back him down, as the only way of getting along. The road often lay through forests and clearings, in mire, and among the roots of the beeches, with which my poor beast was constantly struggling. I would sometimes emerge from a dark wood, five miles through, perhaps, and find myself near a clearing where the farmer's house I was seeking lay, half a mile off the road.

Picking up a stout club to defend myself against the inevitable dog, which, in the absence of men-folks, guarded every log-house, I plodded across the plowed field, soon to be met by the ferocious beast, who, not seeing a stranger more than once a month, was always furious and dangerous. Out would come, at length, the poor woman, too curious to see who it was that broke up her monotonous solitude, to call off the dog, who generally grew fiercer as he felt his backer near him, and it was commonly with a feeling as of a bare escape of my life that I finally got into the house. It was sad enough, too, often to find sickness and death in those fever-stricken abodes—a wan mother nursing one dying child, with perhaps another dead in the house. My business, too, was not the most welcome. I came to dun a delinquent debtor, who had perhaps been inveigled by some peddler of our goods into an imprudent purchase, for a payment which it was inconvenient or impossible to make. There, in the corner, hung the wooden clock, the payment for which I was after, ticking off the last minutes of the sick child—the only ornament of the poor cabin. It was very painful to urge my business under such circumstances. However, I succeeded, by kindness, in getting more money than I expected from our debtors, who would always pay when they could. I recollect, one night, almost bewailing my success. I had reached the entrance of a forest, at least nine miles through, and finding a little tavern there, concluded it was prudent to put up and wait till morning. There were two rough-looking fellows around, hunters, with rifles in their hands, whose appearance did not please me, and I fancied they looked at each other significantly when the landlord took off my saddle-bags and weighted them, feeling the hundred dollars of silver I had collected. I was put into the attic, reached by a ladder, and, barricading the trap-door as well as I could, went to sleep with

POWERS' DISTRUST OF THE HUNTERS.

one eye open. Nothing, however, occurred, and in the morning I found my wild-looking men up as early as I, and was not a little disturbed when they proposed to keep me company across the forest. Afraid to show any suspicion, I consented, and then went and looked at the little flint-pistol I carried, formidable only to sparrows, but which was my only defense.

"About two miles into the wood, my fierce-looking friends, after some exchange of understanding as to their respective ways and meeting-point, started off on different sides of the road in search of game, as they said, but, as I feared, with the purpose of robbing and perhaps murdering me at some darker spot in the forest. I had gone perhaps two miles farther, when I heard the breaking of a twig, and, looking on one side, saw a hand signaling me to stop. Presently an eye came out behind the tree, and then an arm, and I verily thought my hour had come. But, keeping straight on, I perceived, almost instantly, to my great relief, two fine deer, who appeared not at all disturbed by a man on horseback, though ready enough to fly from a gun, and began to suspect that the robber I was dreading was, after all, only a hunter in the honest pursuit of his living. The crack of the rifle soon proved that the deer, and not my saddle-bags, were the game aimed at, and I found my imagination had for twelve hours been converting very harmless huntsmen into highwaymen of a most malicious aspect."

His employer was so well pleased with the success of his young collector that he offered to give him a place in the factory, saying there would always be plenty of rough work at which an inexperienced hand could employ himself. "I could refuse no proposition that promised me bread and clothes," said he, "for I was often walking the streets hungry, with my arms pressed close to my sides to conceal the holes in my coat sleeves." His first task was to thin down with a file some brass plates which were to be used as parts of the stops of an organ. Powers was expected to do merely the rough work, after which the plates were to pass into the hands of the regular finisher. His employer, knowing that the task was one which would require time, told him he would look in in a few days, and see how he had succeeded. The young man's mechanical talent, on which he had prided himself when a boy in Vermont, now did him good service, and he applied himself to his task with skill and determination. When his employer asked for the plates, he was astonished to find that Powers had not only done the rough work, but had finished them much better than the regular finisher had ever done, and this merely by his greater nicety of eye and his undaunted energy. He had blistered his hands terribly, but had done his work well. His employer was delighted, and, finding him so valuable an assistant, soon gave him the superintendence of all his machinery, and took him to live in his own family.

As has been stated, his employer's business was the manufacture of organs and clocks. Powers displayed great skill in the management of the mechanical department of the business, and this, added to the favor shown him by the "boss," drew upon him the jealousy of the other workmen. There hung in the shop at this time an old silver bull's-eye watch, a good time-piece, but very clumsy and ungainly in appearance. Powers was anxious to become its owner. Being too poor to buy it, he hit upon the following expedient for obtaining it. He had carefully studied the machine used in the shop for cutting out wooden clock wheels, and had suggested to his employer several improvements in it. The workmen, however, had ridiculed his suggestions, and had denounced as the most barefaced presumption his belief that he could improve a machine which had come all the way from Connecticut, where, they said, people were supposed to know something about clocks. Nevertheless, he maintained his opinions, and told his employer that if he would give him the silver watch, he would invent a much better machine. His offer was accepted, and in ten days he produced a machine, not only much simpler than the old one, but capable of performing twice as much and better work. The workmen promptly acknowledged his success, and his employer gave him the watch. "The old watch," said he, a few years ago, "has ticked all my children into existence, and three of them out of this world. It still hangs at the head of my bed."

About this time, in a chance visit to the Museum in Cincinnati, he saw a plaster cast of Houdon's "Washington." It was the first bust he had ever seen, and he says it moved him strangely. He had an intense desire to know how it was done, and a vague consciousness that he could do work of the same kind if he could find an instructor. The instructor he soon found in a German living in the city, who made plaster casts and busts, and from him he learned the secret of the art. He proved an apt pupil, and surprised his teacher by his proficiency. His first effort at modeling from life was the bust of a little daughter of Mr. John P. Foote. She sat to him during the hours he could spare from his regular work. His model was made of beeswax, as he was afraid that clay would freeze or stiffen. His success encouraged him very greatly. "I found I had a correct eye," said he, "and a hand which steadily improved in its obedience to my eye. I saw the likeness, and knew it depended on the features, and that, if I could copy the features exactly, the likeness would follow just as surely as the blood follows the knife. I found early that all the talk about catching the expression was mere twaddle; the expression would take care of itself if I copied the features exactly."

The true principles of his art seemed to come to him naturally, and having the genius to comprehend them so readily, he had the courage to hold on to them often in the face of adverse criticism. While conscious of having a perfectly correct eye, however, he did not scorn the humbler method of obtaining exactness by mathematical measurement. The following incident, which he related to Dr. Bellows, illustrates this:

"One of the first busts I ever made was of an artist, a Frenchman, who came over with Mrs. Trollope. He proposed to paint my picture, while I was to make his bust. He was older, and considered himself much my superior, and, indeed, undertook to be my instructor. I was to begin. His first *canon* was that I was to use no measurements, and he quoted Michael Angelo's saying—'A sculptor should carry his compasses in his eyes, not in his fingers.' I humbly submitted to his authority, and finished the bust without a single measurement. He was very triumphant at what he called the success of his method. I begged permission of him, now that the bust was completed, to verify my work by the dividers. He graciously consented, and I was pleased to find how nearly I had hit the mark. A few imperfections, however, appeared, and these, in spite of his objections, I corrected without his knowledge, for I was determined to have the bust as near right as I could make it. It had taken me, however, at least five times as long to measure the distances with my eyes as it would have done to measure them with the calipers, and I saw no advantage in the longer and more painful effort. The measurements are mere preparations for the artist's true work, and are, like the surveyor's lines, preparatory to the architect's labor. When my subject, in his turn, undertook my portrait, he was true to his own principles, and finished it without measurements. I then, though with some horror at my temerity, asked permission to verify his work with the dividers, and found at the first stroke a difference of at least half an inch in the distance between the eyes. He looked very much mortified, but said that it was done to 'give the effect.' I have had no misgivings since about the economy and wisdom of using the calipers freely. To be useful, they must be applied with the greatest precision—so small are the differences upon which all the infinite variety in human countenances depends. With the aid of my careful measurements, I do in one day what it would cost me a week or two's work to accomplish without, and I am then able to give my exclusive attention to the modeling."

He did not regularly devote himself to his art, however, but remained in the employment of the organ and clock maker for some time longer, giving his leisure hours to constant practice. When he was about twenty-three years old, a Frenchman named Herview opened in Cincinnati a museum of natural history and wax figures. The latter had been very much broken and disfigured in transportation, and their owner, in despair, begged Powers to undertake the task of restoring them. The figures were representations of distinguished men and women, and as Powers readily saw that it would be impossible to repair them without having proper likenesses as his guides, he proposed to the Frenchman to make an entirely new composition of the old materials, and one which should attract attention by its oddity. This was agreed to, and the result was a hideous and ungainly figure, which Powers proposed should be called the "King of the Cannibal Islands," but to his amazement the Frenchman advertised it as the embalmed body of a South Sea man-eater, "secured at immense expense." Powers declared to his employer that the audience would discover the cheat and tear down the museum; but the "man-eater" drew immense crowds, and was regarded as the most wonderful natural curiosity ever seen in the West. The Frenchman was so well pleased with it that he employed the artist permanently as "inventor, wax-figure maker, and general mechanical contriver in the museum.

Powers remained in the Frenchman's employ for seven years, hoping all the while to earn money enough to devote himself entirely to art, which had now become his great ambition. His experience was not a pleasant one. Some of it was so singular, not to say ludicrous, that he shall relate one portion of it in his own language:

"One of the first things I undertook, in company with Herview, was a representation of the infernal regions after Dante's description. Behind a grating I made certain dark grottoes, full of stalactites and stalagmites, with shadowy ghosts and pitchforked figures, all calculated to work on the easily-excited imaginations of a Western audience, as the West then was. I found it very popular and attractive, but occasionally some countryman would suggest to his fellow-spectator that a little motion in the figures would add much to the reality of the show. After much reflection I concluded to go in among the figures dressed like the Evil One, in a dark robe, with a death's-head and cross-bones wrought upon it, and with a lobster's claw for a nose. I had bought and fixed up an old electrical machine, and connected it with a wire, so that, from a wand in my hand, I could discharge quite a serious shock upon any body venturing too near the grating. The plan worked admirably, and excited great interest; but I found acting the part of wax-figure two hours every evening in the cold no sinecure, and was put to my wits to devise a figure that could be moved by strings, and which would fill my place. I succeeded so well that it ended in my inventing a whole series of automata, for which the old wax-figures furnished the materials, in part, and which became so popular and so rewarding, that I was kept seven years at the business, my employer promising me, from time to time, an interest in the business, which he quite forgot to fulfill. When, at last, I found out the vanity of my expectations, I left him. He knew I kept no accounts, but he did not know that I reported all the money he gave me to my wife, who did keep our accounts. He tried to cheat me, but I was able to baffle him through her prudence and method. For I had married in this interval, and had a wife and children to support."

Powers was now thirty years old, and had acquired considerable reputation in Cincinnati as an artist. His abilities coming to the notice of Mr. Nicholas Longworth, of that city, that good genius of young men of talent called on him and offered to buy out the museum and establish him in the business. The offer was declined with thanks. Mr. Longworth then proposed to send him to Italy to study his profession, but this, too, being declined, Mr. Longworth urged him to go to Washington and try his fortune with the public men of the country. To this Powers consented, and, aided by his generous friend, he repaired to the national capital in 1835, and spent two years there. During this period he modeled busts of Andrew Jackson, J. Q. Adams, Calhoun, Chief Justice Marshall, Woodbury, Van Buren, and others. Being unable to secure a model of Webster in Washington, the statesman invited him to go with him to Marshfield for that purpose. Powers accepted the invitation, and declares that he looks back upon his sojourn there as one of the most delightful portions of his life.

General Jackson was very kind to him, and won his lasting

esteem and gratitude. Upon being asked if he would sit for his bust, the old hero hesitated, and, looking at the artist nervously, asked: "Do you daub any thing over the face? Because," he added, "I recollect poor Mr. Jefferson got nearly smothered when they tried to take his bust. The plaster hardened before they got ready to release him, and they pounded it with mallets till they nearly stunned him, and then almost tore off a piece of his ear in their haste to pull off a sticking fragment of the mold. I should not like that." Powers assured him that such a terrible process would not be necessary, but that he only wished to look at him for an hour a day, sitting in his chair. The General brightened up at once, and cordially told him it would give him pleasure to sit for him. He at once installed the artist in a room in the White House, and gave him a sitting of an hour every morning until the model was done.

Mr. Powers regards the bust of Jackson as one of his best efforts, and the President himself was very much pleased with it. After he had completed his model, Mr. Edward Everett brought Baron Krudener, the Prussian Minister to Washington, to see it. The Baron was a famous art critic, and poor Powers was terribly nervous as he showed him the bust. The Baron examined it closely, and then said to the artist, "You have got the General completely: his head, his face, his courage, his firmness, his identical self; and yet it will not do! You have also got all his wrinkles, all his age and decay. You forget that he is President of the United States and the idol of the people. You should have given him a dignity and elegance he does not possess. You should have employed your *art*, sir, and not merely your *nature*." The artist listened in silence, and Mr. Everett stood by without saying a word, "conscious," as he afterward confessed, "of a very poor right to speak on such a subject," after listening to so famous a critic. "*I* did not dare," says Powers, "in my humility and reverence for these two great men, to say what I wanted to in reply; to tell the Baron that my 'art' consisted in concealing art, and that my 'nature' was the highest art I knew or could conceive of. I was content that the 'truth' of my work had been so fully acknowledged, and the Baron only confirmed my resolution to make truth my only model and guide in all my future undertakings."

One of his sitters in Washington was Senator Preston, of South Carolina, who conceived such an interest in him that he wrote to his brother, General Preston, of Columbia, South Carolina, a gentleman of great wealth, urging him to come to the artist's assistance, and send him to Italy. General Preston at once responded to this appeal, of which Powers was ignorant, and wrote to the artist to draw on him for a thousand dollars, and go to Italy at once, and to draw on him annually for a similar sum for several years. Powers was profoundly touched by this noble offer, and accepted it as frankly as it had been made. He sent his models to Italy, and took his departure for the Old World in 1837. Speaking of Mr. Preston's generosity, he said, two years ago: "I have endeavored to requite his kindness by sending him works of mine, equal in money value to his gifts; but I can never extinguish my great obligations. I fear he do n't like me since the war,—for I could not suppress my strong national feelings for any man's friendship,—but I like and honor him; I would do any thing in my power to show him my inextinguishable gratitude."

He reached Florence in advance of his models, and while waiting for them made two busts, one of a professor in Harvard College, and the other of an American lady. A severe domestic affliction, however, which came upon him soon after his arrival in Italy, affected him so greatly that he was not able to return to his work for a long time. Then he applied himself to his busts, which were warmly praised by the artists in Florence and by his countrymen traveling abroad. Thorwaldsen visited him in his studio, and pronounced his bust of Webster the best work of its kind in modern times, and praises from other distinguished artists were equally as warm. Orders came in rapidly from English and Italians, and from Americans in Europe, and the sculptor soon had as much business as he could attend to. He gave his leisure time to work on an ideal figure, which, when completed, was purchased by an English gentleman of wealth. This was "The Greek Slave," the most popular of all his works. Duplicates of it were exhibited in America and at the Crystal Palace in England, and won him praise from all quarters. This single work established his fame as an artist, and brought him orders from all parts of the civilized world. His statue of "Eve," which had preceded "The Greek Slave" by a year, had been pronounced by Thorwaldsen fit to be any man's master-piece, but it had not created such a furore as "The Greek Slave." Subsequently he made an exquisite bust of the Grand Duchess of Tuscany, with which the Grand Duke was so pleased that he called on Powers, and asked him as a favor to himself to apply to him whenever he could do him a service. Powers asked permission to take a cast of the Venus, and this much-coveted boon, which had been denied to other artists for years, was at once granted to him.

Since then his works have been numerous. Among these are "The Fisher Boy," of which three duplicates in marble have been made; "Il Penseroso;" "Proserpine," a bust; "California;" "America," modeled for the Crystal Palace at Sydenham, England; "Washington" and "Calhoun," portrait statues, the former for the State of Louisiana, and the latter for the State of South Carolina; and "Benjamin Franklin" and

"Thomas Jefferson," in the Capitol at Washington. His works are all marked by beauty and vigor of conception as well as by exquisite finish. Beautiful as his ideal figures are, he yet excels in his busts and statues of the great men of his native land. His "Jefferson" and "Franklin" are wonderful works, and his "Calhoun" is said to be almost life-like. This last was wrecked on the coast of Long Island on its voyage to America, and remained in the sea for some time, but being well packed was found, when raised, to be only slightly damaged by the water.

Mr. Powers has now resided in Italy for thirty-three years. Motives of economy have controlled his action, for he would gladly return to his own land did he feel justified in doing so. He has thus stated the reasons which have influenced his long residence abroad:

Sculpture is universal. The human form is of no country, and may be studied with equal advantage at home and abroad. The opportunities of studying it abroad are so immeasurably greater than at home, that I do not see how it is possible, without great loss, to neglect them.

1. It is impossible to model successfully without living models; and in America, in my time, it was almost at the peril of reputation, both for model and sculptor, that an artist employed the living model, even if he could procure it. Now, I understand, a few models may be obtained in New York; but they are so rare and so expensive, that it is almost ruinous to employ them. It costs two or three dollars there to secure a model which here may be had for half a day for forty cents. There is no want of models here; but their history is a sad one, and makes one often seriously lament the necessity for employing them. Young women, especially, are driven to this employment by the want of bread. I have numerous offers of their services made by parents who are in great distress. I make it a point to discourage all who come to me from entering the business, and am only conquered when I feel sure that, if I decline, they will be driven to other studios. I prefer only professional models, already thoroughly committed to the calling, as I shrink from the responsibility of leading any into so perilous a vocation. They are

usually accompanied by their mothers, and I strive to treat them in a way to save their self-respect and delicacy—a very hard task, which too often breaks down in less scrupulous hands.

2. The opportunities of anatomical studies are here nearly perfect, and free from all expense. The medical schools not only illustrate anatomy by surgery on the cadaver, but standing by the side of the dead body is a living one, in which the action of the muscles dissected before the student may be studied in life. These colleges are open to all artists, and furnish the best possible schooling in anatomy, a thorough acquaintance with which is indispensable to the sculptor, and can only be obtained in America at great cost.

3. Marble is no cheaper here than in New York, the long sea-carriage costing no more to America than the short land-carriage does from the quarries to Florence or Rome. But good workmen, who can not be dispensed with, are so abundant and so cheap here, so rare and so dear at home, that that alone is a decisive reason for coming abroad. Even here it is a heavy expense to procure sufficient and competent workmen; at home it is almost at ruinous cost and with nearly insuperable difficulty. I have two workmen—as good, certainly, as the best in America—to the finest of whom I pay only four dollars a day. He could make twice that cutting weeping-willows on American tomb-stones. What could he not justly demand in wages from a New York sculptor? I employ a dozen workmen in my studios; the poorest, at work on pedestals and rough work, earn about half a dollar a day; the moderately skilled, a little over a dollar. The whole cost me about fifteen dollars per day, which is wonderfully low. Then, my rent—which could not, for my extensive accommodations, be less than two thousand five hundred dollars a year in any eligible position which the public would visit—reaches only about four hundred and fifty dollars annually.

But, 4. The general expenses of maintaining a family are so much less here than at home, that a man without capital, possesssing a profession so slow in reaching its pecuniary returns as an artist's, finds an immense inducement to live abroad. It is true that, music and accomplishment in languages apart, the opportunities of a substantial education for one's children are not as good here as at home. There are, however, less temptations to vice, and less exposures to the American habit of hard drinking among young men; but, no doubt, the general influences here, in the way of developing a manly, energetic, and self-relying character, are less favorable than at home. There is a softness, a disposition to take life easy, and a want of moral earnestness in Italy, which are not favorable to youthful ambition and independence. On the other hand, the money-getting propensities and social rivalries of America tend to harden human character, and to bring out a severe selfishness which is offensive. On the whole, the balance is on our side, and, other things apart, American youth are better brought up in America. But the artist must make this sacrifice to his art.

Mr. Powers is sixty-five years old, but is in full possession of his mental and physical strength. He is a genuine American, notwithstanding his long residence abroad, and has always a warm welcome for his countrymen visiting his studio. He is a favorite with the younger artists, who find in him a kind and judicious friend. Scorning servile imitation, he still exhibits in his works the freshness of his youth and the genuine originality which was the basis of his fame.

CHAPTER XXX.

EMMANUEL LEUTZE.

EMMANUEL LEUTZE, by adoption an American, was born in the village of Emingen, near the city of Reutlingen, in Wurtemberg, on the 24th of May, 1816. His father emigrated to America during the infancy of his son, and the future artist spent his youth in the city of Philadelphia and the town of Fredericksburg, Virginia. He received a good common school education, and passed his time in comparative seclusion from society, reading and studying, but showing no especial fondness for art. At length, during his father's last illness, in which he nursed him with great devotion, he took up drawing to beguile the weary hours of the sick-room, and succeeded so well in his attempts that after his father's death he continued his efforts under the instruction of a competent drawing master. He improved rapidly, and was so well satisfied with his success that he determined to adopt the profession of an artist as the one best suited to his talents and inclination.

Having acquired considerable skill in drawing, he attempted rude portraits of men and beasts, and at length undertook to copy from memory a colored print after Westall. He completed it, and resolved to show it to some of his friends. In his impatience for the colors to dry, he placed the painting before

FILIAL DEVOTION SHAPES A GREAT CAREER.

the fire and went to summon his friends, but found, to his dismay, upon returning with them, that the heat had blistered the canvas so that the picture was hardly recognizable. Yet, in spite of this, his critics saw such evidences of genius in the painting that they urged the young artist to continue his labors, and predicted a great success for him.

Leutze, however, was not willing to venture upon another composition, either partly or wholly original, but applied himself with zeal to learn the rudiments of his art, and with such success that when his portraits appeared at the Artist's Fund Exhibition, a year or two later, they received high praise, both from critics and the public. An enterprising publisher, attracted by these portraits, engaged him to go to Washington and paint the portraits of the leading statesmen of the country, to be engraved for a "national work." Leutze at once proceeded to the capital, full of hope and enthusiasm, but soon found that the schemes of the politicians whose faces he was to transmit to canvas engrossed them so much that they would not give him the sittings he desired. After waiting impatiently for a considerable time he threw up the engagement in disgust, and went into the woods of Virginia to console himself by communing with nature. For some time he wandered about, making desultory sketches, and abandoning himself to a melancholy which was closely akin to despair. When this feeling was at its height, a friend, before unknown, came to his aid.

"A gentleman, whose rich domain he chanced to approach in his wayward rovings, perceived his abilities, understood his unhappiness, and aroused him from inaction by a call upon his professional skill. The artist obeyed, but he could not subdue the mood which possessed him. No brilliant scene arose to his fancy, no humorous incident took form and color from his pencil, and the fair landscape around appeared to mock rather than cheer his destiny. He could not bring himself into relation with subjects thus breathing of hope and gayety, but found inspiration only in the records of human sorrow. As the royal mourner bade her companions sit upon the ground and 'tell sad stories of the death of kings,' the pensive artist found something analogous to his own fate in the story of Hagar and Ishmael. He painted them as having followed up a spent water-course, in hopes of finding wherewith to quench their thirst, and sinking under the disappointment. He neither saw nor painted the angel of God who showed the fountain in the wilderness, and yet the angel was there, for now the sufferer acknowledges that early vicissitudes nerved him for high endeavor, rendered his vision piercing, his patience strong, and his confidence firm, and that this incidental effort to triumph over difficulties was the first of a series which inspired his subsequent career."

In 1840 he produced a painting which he called "An Indian Contemplating the Setting Sun." It was exhibited in Philadelphia, and won general praise for the artist. Better than this, it secured him the friendship of the late Edward L. Carey, of that city, who, recognizing his genius, determined to help him on in his labors. Mr. Carey was successful in inducing his friends to give Leutze a number of commissions, and these enabled him to carry out his wish to visit Europe and complete his studies. Instead of going to Italy, as was then the almost universal practice, he determined to study in Germany, and accordingly sailed for that country. He went by way of Holland, and after a long and trying voyage reached Amsterdam in January, 1841. Pausing here for awhile to familiarize himself with the master-pieces of the Dutch school, he repaired to Dusseldorf, where he became a pupil of the celebrated painter Lessing, under whom he made marked progress. His reception by the artists of Dusseldorf was at once hearty and encouraging, and won for that school and its members his enthusiastic devotion. He became Lessing's pupil at the personal request of the master, and these two gifted men were soon bound to each other by the ties of an undying friendship.

Leutze devoted himself to historical subjects from the first, and soon after his arrival in Dusseldorf began his picture of "Columbus Before the Council of Salamanca." When it was finished, it was visited by Director V. Schadow, who praised it warmly, and requested the artist to offer it to the Art Union of Dusseldorf, which at once purchased it. This high compliment to a beginner and a stranger proved an additional stimulus to Leutze, and he soon after produced a companion picture to his first, "Columbus in Chains," which procured him the gold medal of the Brussels Art Exhibition, and was subsequently purchased by the Art Union of New York.

Remaining two years in Dusseldorf, Leutze went to Munich to study the works of Cornelius and Kaulbach, and while there painted another scene in the life of the Great Discoverer, "Columbus before the Queen." Upon completing this picture he went to Venice, Rome, and the other Italian cities, making careful studies of the masters of that school. He gave two years to his travels, visiting the Tyrol, and reveling in the magnificent scenery through which he journeyed. He went into Switzerland, sketching the glorious beauties of its Alps, and reached the Rhine at Strasbourg. Then, sailing down that beautiful river, he set foot once more in Dusseldorf, glad, as he declared, to end his wanderings in the midst of his friends. Here he determined to locate himself permanently, and soon after his return he married.

He lived in Dusseldorf for fourteen years, devoting himself assiduously to his art. His labors were incessant. Historic subjects make up the vast bulk of his productions during this period, and in his treatment of them he adhered closely to the style of the Dusseldorf school. The best known of his works during this portion of his career are "The Landing of the Norsemen in America;" "Cromwell and his Daughter;" "The Court of Queen Elizabeth;" "Henry VIII. and Anne Boleyn;" "The Iconoclast," and his famous and brilliant series of pictures illustrative of the events of the American War of Independence. The most prominent of these were, "Washington Crossing the Delaware;" "Washington at Monmouth;" "Washington at the Battle of Monongahela;" "News from Lexington;" "Sergeant Jasper," and "Washington at Princeton." These are fine paintings, possessing striking characteristics, and are all more or less popular. "Washington Crossing the Delaware" is perhaps the best known, since it has been engraved, and sold in all parts of the country in that form.

During his absence in Germany, Leutze did not forget the country of his choice, as his devotion to American subjects amply testifies. When he had won a proud name in his art by his labors in Dusseldorf, and had laid by money enough to justify him in returning to a land where art was in its infancy, and not over-remunerative, he came back to the United States, after an absence of eighteen years, and opened a studio in New York. He found a vast improvement in the public taste and in the demand for works of art since his departure for the Old World, and, better still, found that his peculiar field, the historic, was the one most suited to the tastes of the American public.

It was his intention, in coming back to this country, to devote the time during which he supposed he would be compelled to wait for orders, to looking around him and familiarizing himself with the changes that had taken place in the Union during his absence; but he was never able to carry out this design, as he had no leisure time. His European reputation had preceded him hither, and he had scarcely opened his doors in New York before he was obliged to refuse orders, for lack of time to execute them. His hands were full from the first, and he at once took rank as the most thoroughly popular and accomplished artist in the country.

Early in 1860 he received from the Government of the United States a commission to decorate one of the marble stairways in the Capitol at Washington with a mural painting. The painting was to be executed in fresco, and he chose as his subject, "Westward the Star of Empire Takes its Way." He entered upon the undertaking with the keenest delight, and in order to make himself thoroughly acquainted with the true character of frontier scenery and life, performed what was then the long and difficult journey to the Rocky Mountains, where he made numerous sketches. Returning to the States, he sailed for Europe, and went to Munich to learn from Kaulbach the new stereochromatic process which has now superseded the fresco-painting of the middle ages. Returning to Washington, he applied himself to his task, and in a couple of years completed it.

The picture is the largest and finest mural painting in America, and adorns the magnificent stairway at the north end of the west corridor of the House of Representatives. It is lighted from a sky-light in the roof, and is seen to the best advantage from the upper corridor. The coloring is softer and more life-like than is often seen in such paintings. The surface of the wall is rough, but the work has been done by such a master hand that one seems to be gazing upon real life. It is a wonderful picture—one that will repay weeks of study.

The scene represents a train of emigrants crossing the Rocky Mountains. They have reached the summit of the range, from which a glorious view stretches out before them to the westward. The adventurers consist of the usual class of emigrants, men, women, and children. There are several wagons and a number of horses in the train. The faces of the emigrants express the various emotions which fill their hearts as they gaze upon the glorious scene before them. Some are full of life and vigor, and hope beams in every feature, while others are struggling with sickness and despair. The advance of the train has been momentarily checked by a huge tree which has fallen across the trail, and two stout men, under the direction of the leader of the party, who is sitting on his horse, are engaged in hewing it away with axes. Two others have climbed to the summit of the neighboring rocky crag, on which they have planted the banner of the Republic, which is seen flapping proudly from its lofty perch. In the foreground stands a manly youth, clasping his father's long rifle firmly, and gazing toward the promised land with a countenance glowing with hope and energy. His sister, as hopeful as himself, is seated by her mother's side, on a buffalo-robe which has been thrown over a rock. The mother's face is sad, but patient. She knows well the privations, toils, and hardships which await them in the new home-land, but she tries to share the enthusiasm and hope of her children. She clasps her nursing infant to her breast, and listens to her husband, who stands by and points her to the new country where they will have a home of their own. Her face is inexpressibly beautiful. The rich, warm light of the rising sun streams brightly over the whole scene, and gives to it a magical glow. The legend, "Westward the Star of Empire Takes its Way," is inscribed over the painting, in letters of gold.

An elaborate illuminated border, illustrative of the advance of civilization in the West, surrounds the painting, and is in itself one of the most perfect works of art in the Capitol.

Leutze received the sum of $20,000 for this painting. After completing it, some matters connected with his family required him to make a visit to Dusseldorf, and upon reaching that place he was warmly welcomed by the artists, on the 10th of June, 1863, at their club. "About one hundred and fifty lords of art," says a letter from Dusseldorf, "assembled at the 'Mahlkasten,' just outside of the Hof-Garten. This is the club-house of the painters, and, with its gardens, is their property. Leutze was received with music, and when he came within reach of the assembled company, there was a general rush to shake his hands, kiss his cheeks, and hug him. The old fellows were much affected at the scene, and were heartily glad to see their old companion once more. The guest made a short and feeling address, whereupon all went in to supper. Here two of the artists had arrayed themselves, one as a negro, the other as an Indian; and these brought in the first dishes and handed them to Leutze. Andreas Achenbach sat at Leutze's right, and his old friend Tryst at his left. After dinner, the calumet cf peace was passed around; there was speaking and drinking of healths, with songs afterward in the illuminated garden. The occasion appears to have been a very pleasant and right merry one, and is said to have been the happiest festival ever given by the Society of Artists."

Returning to the United States a few months later, Leutze repaired to Washington, where he had permanently settled. He was given several commissions by the Government, and at once began to design his subjects. They were only in the cartoon, however, at the time of his death. One of these, "Civilization," was to have been placed in the Senate Chamber, and was partly finished. It is said to have given promise of being his finest production. He also left a sketch of an immense picture, "The Emancipation." He was always a hard worker, and this doubtless contributed to bring about his death, which took place on the 18th of July, 1868. The immediate cause was apoplexy, superinduced by the intense heat.

"Mr. Leutze," says a writer in the Annual Cyclopedia, "was altogether the best educated artist in America, possessed of vast technical learning, of great genius, and fine powers of conception. His weakest point was in his coloring, but even here he was superior to most others."

"Leutze," says Mr. Tuckerman, "delights in representing adventure. He ardently sympathizes with chivalric action and spirit-stirring events; not the abstractly beautiful or the simply true, but the heroic, the progressive, the individual, and earnest phases of life, warm his fancy and attract his pencil. His forte is the dramatic. . . . If Leutze were not a painter, he would certainly join some expedition to the Rocky Mountains, thrust himself into a fiery political controversy, or seek to wrest a new truth from the arcana of science. . . . We remember hearing a brother artist describe him in his studio at Rome, engaged for hours upon a picture, deftly shifting palette, cigar, and maul-stick from hand to hand, as occasion required; absorbed, rapid, intent, and then suddenly breaking from his quiet task to vent his constrained spirits in a jovial song, or a romp with his great dog, whose vociferous barking he thoroughly enjoyed; and often abandoning his quiet studies for some wild, elaborate frolic, as if a row was essential to his happiness. His very jokes partook of this bold heartiness of disposition. He scorned all ultra refinement, and found his impulse to art not so much in delicate perception as in vivid sensation. There was ever a reaction from the meditative. His temperament is Teutonic—hardy, cordial, and brave. Such men hold the conventional in little reverence, and their natures gush like mountain streams, with wild freedom and unchastened enthusiasm."

VIII.

DIVINES.

CHAPTER XXXI.

HENRY WARD BEECHER.

HENRY WARD BEECHER was born in Litchfield, Connecticut, on the 24th of June, 1813, and was the eighth child of Dr. Lyman Beecher, the famous Presbyterian divine of New England. Dr. Beecher was regarded as one of the most powerful champions of orthodox Christianity in the land of the pilgrims, and had the good fortune to be the father of a family whose members have become celebrated for their intellectual gifts.

The most of these gave early promise of their future distinction, but the subject of this memoir was regarded as the dunce of the family. He grew up as the children of most New England clergymen of that day climbed the road to manhood. His father's family was large, and the salary paid by the congregation never exceeded eight hundred dollars, and was not always promptly paid at that. The good people of the land of steady habits well knew how to drive hard bargains with the Lord's messengers, and were adepts in the art of securing the "best talent" at the lowest price. The stern, hard struggle for a livelihood in which the father was engaged prevented him from giving much personal attention to his children, and the mother of young Henry dying when he was but three years old, the boy was left very much to himself. Like most ministers' children, he was obliged to "set an example to the village," and this boy was dosed with Catechism and his father's stern and gloomy theological tenets until he was sick of them.

"In those days," says Mrs. Stowe, "none of the attentions were paid to children that are now usual. The community did not recognize them. There was no child's literature; there were no children's books. The Sunday-school was yet an experiment in a fluctuating, uncertain state of trial. There were no children's days of presents and *fetes*, no Christmas or New Year's festivals. The annual thanksgiving was only associated with one day's unlimited range of pies of every sort—too much for one day—and too soon things of the past. The childhood of Henry Ward was unmarked by the possession of a single child's toy as a gift from any older person, or a single *fete*. Very early, too, strict duties devolved upon him. A daily portion of the work of the establishment, the care of the domestic animals, the cutting and piling of wood, or tasks in the garden, strengthened his muscles and gave vigor and tone to his nerves. From his father and mother he inherited a perfectly solid, healthy organization of brain, muscle, and nerves, and the uncaressing, let-alone system under which he was brought up gave him early habits of vigor and self-reliance."

When but three or four years old he was sent to the Widow Kilbourn's school, where he said his letters twice a day, and passed the rest of his time in hemming a brown towel or a checked apron. It was not expected that he would learn very much from Marm Kilbourn, but the school kept him out of the way of the "home folks" for the greater part of the day.

He was a winning, sweet-faced child, with long golden curls, of which he was very proud. Some of his female playfellows at school, thinking it a shame that a boy should look so much like a girl, cut off one or two of his curls with a pair of shears made of scraps of tin, and when the little fellow complained of his loss at home it was decided that the best way to protect him from such attacks in future was to cut his hair close to his head, which was done at once. Little Henry was commonly thought a dull child. His memory was lamentably deficient, and his utterance was thick and indistinct, so much so that he could scarcely be understood in reading or speaking. This was caused partly by an enlargement of the tonsils of his throat, and partly by timidity. The policy of repression worked badly in his case, and had there not been so much real good at the basis of his character it might have led this gentle, yearning boy far from the useful channel along which his life has flown.

His stepmother was a lady of fine mental culture, of elegant breeding and high character, but she was an invalid, and withal thoroughly imbued with the gloomy sternness of her husband's faith. One day little Henry, who was barely able to manage the steady-going old family horse, was driving her in the chaise. They passed a church on their way, and the bell was tolling for a death. "Henry," said Mrs. Beecher, solemnly, "what do you think of when you hear a bell tolling like that?" The boy colored and hung his head in silence, and the good lady went on. "*I* think, was that soul prepared? It has gone into *eternity*." The little fellow shuddered, in spite of himself, and thought, no doubt, what a dreadful thing it was to be a Christian.

So it was with the religion that was crammed into him. There was no effort made to draw him to religion by its beauty and tenderness. He rarely heard of the Saviour as the loving one who took little children in His arms and blessed them, but was taught to regard Him as a stern and merciless judge, as one who, instead of being "touched with the feeling of our infirmities," makes those infirmities the means of wringing fresh sufferings from us. Sunday was a day of terror to him, for on that day the Catechism was administered to him until he was more than sick of it. "I think," said he to his congregation, not long since, referring to this part of his life, "that to force childhood to associate religion with such dry morsels is to violate the spirit, not only of the New Testament, but of common sense as well. I know one thing, that if I am 'lax and latitudinarian,' the Sunday Catechism is to blame for a part of it. The dinners that I have lost because I could not go through 'sanctification,' and 'justification,' and 'adoption,' and all such questions, lie heavily on my memory! I do not know that they have brought forth any blossoms. I have a kind of grudge against many of those truths that I was taught in my childhood, and I am not conscious that they have waked up a particle of faith in me. My good old aunt in heaven—I wonder what she is doing. I take it that she now sits beauteous, clothed in white, that round about her sit chanting cherub children, and that she is opening to them from her larger range sweet stories, every one fraught with thought, and taste, and feeling, and lifting them up to a higher plane. One Sunday afternoon with my aunt Esther did me more good than forty Sundays in church with my father. He thundered over my head, and she sweetly instructed me down in my heart. The promise that she would read Joseph's history to me on Sunday was enough to draw a silver thread of obedience through the entire week; and if I was tempted to break my promise, I said, 'No; Aunt Esther is going to read on Sunday;' and I would do, or I would not do, all through the week, for the sake of getting that sweet instruction on Sunday.

"And to parents I say, Truth is graded. Some parts of God's truth are for childhood, some parts are for the nascent intellectual period, and some parts are for later spiritual developments. Do not take the last things first. Do not take the latest processes of philosophy and bring them prematurely to the understanding. In teaching truth to your children, you are to avoid tiring them."

"The greatest trial of those days," says Mrs. Stowe, "was the Catechism. Sunday lessons were considered by the mother-in-law as inflexible duty, and the Catechism as the *sine qua non.* The other children memorized readily, and were brilliant reciters, but Henry, blushing, stammering, confused, and hopelessly miserable, stuck fast on some sand-bank of what is required or forbidden by this or that commandment, his mouth choking up with the long words which he hopelessly miscalled, was sure to be accused of idleness or inattention, and to be solemnly talked to, which made him look more stolid and miserable than ever, but appeared to have no effect in quickening his dormant faculties."

At the age of ten he was a well-grown, stout, stocky boy, strong and hearty, trained to hard work, and to patient obedience of his elders. He was tolerably well drilled in Calvinism, and had his head pretty well filled with snatches of doctrine which he caught from his father's constant discussions; but he was very backward in his education. He was placed at the school of the Rev. Mr. Langdon, at Bethlehem, Connecticut, and it was hoped that the labors of this excellent tutor would result in making something of him. He spent a winter at this school, and boarded at a neighboring farm-house, whose kind-hearted mistress soon became so much attached to him that she indulged him to an extent which he had never known at home. With his gun on his shoulder, he passed the greater part of his hours out of school in tramping over the pretty Connecticut hills in search of game, or, lying down on the soft grass, would pass hours in gazing on the beautiful landscape, listening to the dull whirr of the partridges in the stubble-field or the dropping of the ripe apples in the orchard. The love of nature was strong in the boy, and his wonderful mistress taught him many of the profoundest lessons of his life. He made poor progress at the school, however, and his father was almost in despair. The whole family shook their heads in solemn forebodings over the failure of this child of ten to become a mental prodigy.

Miss Catharine Beecher, his eldest sister, was then teaching a young ladies' school in Hartford, and she proposed to take the boy and see what could be done with him. There were thirty or forty girls in the school, and but this one boy, and the reader may imagine the amount of studying he did. The girls were full of spirits, and in their society the fun-loving feature of his disposition burst out and grew with amazing rapidity. He was always in mischief of some kind, to the great delight of the girls, with whom he was extremely popular, and to the despair of his sister, who began to fear that he was hopelessly stupid.

The school was divided into two divisions in grammar recitations, each of which had its leader. The leaders chose their "sides" with great care, as these contests in grammar were esteemed the most important part of the daily exercises. Henry's name was generally called last, for no one chose him except as a matter of necessity. He was sure to be a dead weight to his leader.

"The fair leader of one of these divisions took the boy aside to a private apartment, to put into him with female tact and insinuation those definitions and distinctions on which the honor of the class depended.

"'Now, Henry, A is the indefinite article, you see, and must be used only with the singular noun. You can say *a man*, but you can't say *a men*, can you?' 'Yes, I can say *Amen*, too,' was the ready rejoinder. 'Father says it always at the end of his prayers.'

"'Come, Henry, now don't be joking. Now, decline He.' 'Nominative he, possessive his, objective him.' 'You see, his is possessive. Now, you can say his book, but you can't say him book.' 'Yes, I do say hymn book, too,' said the impracticable scholar, with a quizzical twinkle. Each one of these sallies made his young teacher laugh, which was the victory he wanted.

"'But now, Henry, seriously, just attend to the active and passive voice. Now, *I strike*, is active, you see, because if you strike you do something. But, *I am struck*, is passive, because if you are struck you don't do any thing, do you?'

"'Yes, I do; I strike back again.'

"Sometimes his views of philosophical subjects were offered gratuitously. Being held rather of a frisky nature, his sister appointed his seat at her elbow when she heard her classes. A class in natural philosophy, not very well prepared, was stumbling through the theory of the tides. 'I can explain that,' said Henry. 'Well, you see, the sun, he catches hold of the moon and pulls her, and she catches hold of the sea and pulls that, and this makes the spring tides.'

"'But what makes the neap tides?'

"'Oh, that's when the sun stops to spit on his hands.'"

It will hardly surprise the reader to be told that Master

Henry remained with his sister only six months, and was returned at the end of that time to his father as an indifferent scholar and a most inveterate joker.

A change now occurred in his life. When he was twelve years old his father removed to Boston to assume the charge of the Hanover-Street Church. Here the boy had a chance to see something more than nature, and to employ his powers of observation in receiving impressions from the daily life and aspect of a large and crowded city. His father entered him at the Boston Latin School, and appealed to him not to disgrace his name any longer by his stupidity. The appeal roused the little fellow's pride, and he set to work to show to his family that he was not the dunce they had thought him. He went at his studies manfully, mastering the tedious puzzle of the Latin verbs and nouns, and acquiring a respectable acquaintance with the grammar of that language. It was a terrible task to him, for he had no liking for the language, and did his work merely to please his father and escape disgrace. His success cost him a share of his health, and his vigorous constitution began to show the effects of such intense application. His father noticed this, and as a diversion to his mind advised him to enter upon a course of biographical reading. He read the lives of Captain Cook, Nelson, and the great naval commanders of the world, and at once became possessed of the desire to go to sea. This feeling made him restless and discontented, and he resolved to leave home and ship on board some vessel sailing from the harbor. He hovered about the wharves, conversing with the sailors and captains, and sometimes carrying his little bundle with him. But the thoughts of home were too strong for him, and he could never quite summon up resolution enough to run away. In a fit of desperation he wrote a letter to his brother, telling him of his wish to go to sea, and informing him that he should first ask his father's permission, and if that were not granted he should go without it. This letter he dropped where his father would be sure to find it. The old gentleman soon discovered it, and, reading it, put it into his pocket without comment. The next day he asked the boy if he had ever thought of any definite avocation for his future life.

"Yes," said Henry, "I want to go to sea. I want to enter the navy, be a midshipman, and rise to be a commander."

"Oh, I see," said the Doctor, cheerfully; "but in order to prepare for that you must study mathematics and navigation."

"I am ready, sir."

"Very well. I'll send you up to Amherst next week, to Mount Pleasant, and then you 'll begin your preparatory studies at once. As soon as you are well prepared, I presume I can make interest to get you an appointment."

The boy was delighted, and the next week started for Amherst. The Doctor felt sure that the sailor scheme would never come to any thing, and exclaimed, exultantly, as he bade his son good-by, "I shall have that boy in the ministry yet."

At the Mount Pleasant Institute he roomed with his teacher in mathematics, a young man named Fitzgerald, and a warm friendship sprung up between them. Fitzgerald saw that his pupil had no natural talent or taste for mathematics; but instead of despairing in consequence of this discovery, he redoubled his efforts. Appealing to his pupil's pride and ambition, he kept him well to his task, and succeeded in implanting in him a fair knowledge of the science. Young Beecher also took lessons in elocution from Professor John E. Lovell. Under the instructions of this able teacher, he learned to manage his voice, and to overcome the thickness and indistinctness of utterance which previous to this had troubled him so much. He continued at this school for three years, devoting himself to study with determination and success, and taking rank as one of the most promising pupils of the school.

During his first year at Mount Pleasant, he became deeply impressed with a sense of his religious responsibility at a famous revival which was held in the place, and from that time resolved to devote himself entirely to preparing for his entrance into the ministry when he should attain the proper age. Henceforth he applied himself with characteristic energy to his studies and to his religious duties, and rose steadily in the esteem of his teachers and friends. He entered Amherst College upon the completion of his preparatory course, and graduated from that institution in 1834.

In 1832, Dr. Beecher removed from Boston to Cincinnati, to enter upon the Presidency of Lane Seminary, to which he had been elected. Henry followed him to the West after his graduation at Amherst, and completed his theological studies at the seminary, under the tuition of his father and Professor Stowe, the latter of whom married Henry's sister Harriet, in 1836. Having finished his course, he was ordained.

"As the time drew near in which Mr. Beecher was to assume the work of the ministry," says Mrs. Stowe, "he was oppressed by a deep melancholy. He had the most exalted ideas of what ought to be done by a Christian minister. He had transferred to that profession all those ideals of courage, enterprise, zeal, and knightly daring which were the dreams of his boyhood, and which he first hoped to realize in the naval profession. He felt that the holy calling stood high above all others; that to enter it from any unholy motive, or to enter and not do a worthy work in it, was a treason to all honor.

"His view of the great object of the ministry was sincerely and heartily the same with that of his father, to secure the regeneration of the individual heart by the Divine Spirit, and thereby to effect the regeneration of human society. The problem that oppressed him was, how to do this. His father had used certain moral and intellectual weapons, and used them strongly and effectively, because employing them with undoubting faith. So many other considerations had come into his mind to qualify and limit that faith, so many new modes of thought and inquiry, that were partially inconsistent with the received statements of his party, that he felt he could never grasp and wield them with the force which could make them efficient. It was no comfort to him that he could wield the weapons of his theological party so as to dazzle and confound objectors, while all the time conscious in his own soul of objections more profound and perplexities more bewildering. Like the shepherd boy of old, he saw the giant of sin stalking through the world, defying the armies of the living God, and longed to attack him, but the armor in which he had been equipped for the battle was no help, but only an incumbrance!

"His brother, who studied with him, had already become an unbeliever and thrown up the design of preaching, and he could not bear to think of adding to his father's trials by deserting the standard. Yet his distress and perplexity were so great that at times he seriously contemplated going into some other profession. . . . .

"In his last theological term he took a Bible class in the city of Cincinnati, and began studying and teaching the Evangelists. With the course of this study and teaching came a period of spiritual clairvoyance. His mental perplexities were relieved, and the great question of "what to preach' was solved. The shepherd boy laid aside his cumbrous armor, and found in a clear brook a simple stone that smote down the giant; and so, from the clear waters of the Gospel narrative Mr. Beecher drew forth that 'white stone with a new name,' which was to be the talisman of his ministry. To present Jesus Christ personally as the Friend and Helper of humanity, Christ as God impersonate, eternally and by a necessity of His nature helpful, and remedial, and restorative; the Friend of each individual soul, and thus the Friend of all society,—this was the one thing which his soul rested on as a worthy object in entering the ministry. He afterward said, in speaking of his feelings at this time, 'I was like the man in the story to whom a fairy gave a purse with a single piece of money in it, which he found always came again as soon as he had spent it. I thought I knew at least one thing to preach. I found it included every thing.'"

Upon being ordained, Mr. Beecher married, and accepted a call to Lawrenceburg, Indiana, a little town on the Ohio River, about twenty miles below Cincinnati. His salary was small and the work was hard. He was not only pastor, but sexton as well, and in this capacity he swept out the church, made the fires, filled and trimmed the lamps, and rang the bell. Says he, "I did all but come to hear myself preach—that they had to do."

He did not remain here long, however, but soon accepted a call to Indianapolis, the capital of the State, where he lived for eight years. He occupied a tasteful cottage on the outskirts of the town, and gathered about him his household treasures, which consisted of his family, his library, his horse, cow, pigs, and chickens. He was an enthusiast in matters of agriculture and horticulture, and besides importing from the East the best varieties of fruit-trees, roses, etc., he edited a horticultural paper, which had a fair circulation.

The eight years of his ministry in Indianapolis make up a period of hard and useful work. He held two services on Sunday, and five meetings during the week in various parts of the city, and with the consent of his people gave three months of each year to missionary work in other parts of the State. While engaged in this latter duty he traveled about the State on horseback and preached daily.

His experience in the ministry, as well as his study of the lives of the apostles, convinced him that success in his profession—by which I mean the successful winning of souls to God—was not to be won by preaching controversial or dry doctrinal sermons. He must seize upon some vital truth, admitted by all parties, and bring that home to men's minds. He must preach to them of their daily, hourly trials and temptations, joys and comforts, and he resolved that this should be the character of his preaching. Then came the question, how shall one man know that which is uppermost in the thoughts of the many? He went into the places of public resort, where men were accustomed to lounge and to gather to hear the news, and made it his practice to listen to their conversations. In this way he began to know the people to whom he preached as few pastors know their flocks, and he was enabled by this knowledge to apply his teachings to their daily lives, and to send them forth to their duties warned by his reproofs or cheered by his intelligent counsel and sympathy. This practice, modified at times as circumstances have required, he has steadfastly continued, and in it lies the secret of his success as a preacher. Said a gentleman, not long since, himself a member of a different denomination, "Beecher's sermons do me more good than any I hear elsewhere. They never fail to touch upon some topic of importance that has engaged my thoughts during the week. Dropping all doctrinal technicalities, and steering clear of the vexed questions of theology, he talks to me in such a way that I am able to carry Christ into the most trifling of my daily affairs, and to carry Him there as my Sympathizer and Helper, as well as my Judge." He soon became the most popular preacher in the city, and, thanks to the genuineness of his gifts and the earnestness of his zeal, he was enabled to add many to the kingdom of Christ who had been drawn to hear him merely by their curiosity. Among these was his brother Charles, whose skepticism has been spoken of elsewhere in this chapter. Becoming deeply impressed at a revival in Indianapolis, Charles Beecher, by his brother's advice, took a Bible class, and began to teach the story of Christ. The plan worked most happily. Charles solved all the questions which had perplexed his mind, reëntered upon his religious life with increased fervor, and soon afterward entered the ministry.

In August, 1847, Mr. Beecher received a call to Plymouth Church, Brooklyn, which had just been founded. He promptly accepted it. Breaking up his home in Indiana, he removed to Brooklyn, and was publicly installed pastor of Plymouth Church on the 11th of November, 1847. He at once "announced in Plymouth pulpit the same principles that he had in Indianapolis, namely, his determination to preach Christ among them not as an absolute system of doctrines, not as a bygone historical personage, but as the living Lord and God, and to bring all the ways and usages of society to the test of His standards. He announced to all whom it might concern, that he considered temperance and antislavery as a part of the Gospel of Christ, and should preach them to the people accordingly."

It is no part of my purpose to consider Mr. Beecher as a politician. I deal with him here not as the partisan of a political organization, but as a minister of the Gospel. In politics he has always been a Republican of the Radical type, but has generally inclined to a conservative construction of that creed. Many of his warmest friends take issue with him in his political views, and he has not always been able to lead his congregation with him in this respect.

Soon after assuming the charge of Plymouth Church Mr. Beecher became a regular contributor to "The Independent," a paper which he had helped to establish. His articles were marked with an asterisk, and were widely read. They dealt with every topic of interest, principally with slavery, and were vigorous and full of thought. A number of them were afterward collected and published in book form as the "Star Papers." Since then he has acted as editor of "The Independent," and is at present the editor of "The Christian Union." He has written a novel of New England life, called "Norwood," for "The New York Ledger," and still writes a weekly paper for that journal. He is at present engaged upon a "Life of Christ," which is to be the crowning labor of his life. Besides these labors, he has been until recently almost constantly in the lecture field, and has spoken frequently before popular assemblies on the political questions of the day.

These labors have filled up the leisure time left him after discharging his duties as pastor of his church, which have never been neglected upon any occasion. In this field his work has been faithful and constant. He has labored in it for nearly twenty-three years, and his work has not been without its reward. Such sermons as his could not fail of doing good even if spoken to half a dozen people. How great, then, must be their effect when addressed to the vast audiences to which he speaks! His congregation averages over twenty-five hundred at every service, being the largest regular congregation in existence. His sermons are reported by a stenographer, and are printed each week in pamphlet form, and in this manner find their way into thousands of hands. The "Plymouth Pulpit," in which they are published, has a regular weekly circulation of six thousand copies, and it is estimated that each copy is read by at least five persons, which gives the preacher, in addition to his own congregation, an audience of more than thirty thousand persons per week.

When Plymouth Church was organized, the wise heads predicted a failure for it; but it has grown and prospered, until it is now the most compact and the best organized congregation in America. It is dependent upon no synod or other religious body, but manages its affairs entirely as it pleases. The control is vested in a board of trustees, of which Mr. Beecher is *ex-officio* a member. He has no superiority in this board unless called by its members to preside over its meetings. His influence is of course all-powerful; but as the trustees are shrewd business men, they sometimes carry out their own views in preference to his. The church is supported by the sale of its pews. This yields it an annual income of between forty and fifty thousand dollars. The pastor receives a handsome salary—said to be the largest in the United States—and the rest goes into the treasury of the church. As the period of the annual sale of pews approaches, Mr. Beecher makes it his practice to preach a sermon in which he reviews the questions of the day, and as far as possible marks out his course with regard to them during the ensuing year. This he does in order that every one purchasing a seat in Plymouth Church may know just what is in store for him from the pulpit. The surplus revenue, after the pastor's salary and the current expenses are paid, has until recently been devoted to extinguishing the debt upon the church. That burden now being off the shoulders of the congregation, the money is applied to missionary work in Brooklyn. "Two missions have been largely supported by the funds derived from Plymouth Church, and the time and personal labor of its members. A mechanics' reading-room is connected with one of these. No church in the country furnishes a larger body of lay teachers, exhorters, and missionaries in every department of human and Christian labor."

Plymouth Church is located in Orange Street, between Hicks and Henry Streets, in Brooklyn, and not far from the Fulton Ferry. Many strangers, whose expectations are based upon the fame of the pastor, are disappointed in the plain and simple exterior of red brick, as they come prepared to see a magnificent Gothic temple. The interior, however, rarely fails to please all comers. It is plain and simple, but elegant and comfortable. It is a vast hall, around the four sides of which sweeps an immense gallery. The interior is painted white, with a tinge of pink, and the carpets and cushions of the seats are of a rich, warm red. The rows of seats in the body of the church are semicircular, and those in the gallery rise as in an amphitheater, from the front to the wall. At the far end of the church is a raised platform containing merely a chair and a table. The table is a pretty ornament, and is the "Plymouth Pulpit." It is made of wood brought from the Garden of Gethsemane. In the gallery behind the pulpit is the great organ—one of the largest and finest in the Union. The church will seat over twenty-five hundred people, but in order to do this, chairs are placed in the aisles. These chairs are sold as well as the pews.

Every Sunday morning the streets are filled with persons on their way to attend the services at Plymouth Church. They come not only from Brooklyn, but from New York, and even from Jersey City and Hoboken. The yard and street in front of the church are quickly filled with the throng, but the doors are guarded by policemen, and none but pew-holders are permitted to enter the church until ten minutes before the hour for service. Without this precaution the regular congregation would be crowded out of their seats every Sunday by strangers.

At ten minutes before the hour for service the doors are thrown open, and very soon there is not even standing room in the vast interior, and generally the vestibules are full.

Near the pulpit is placed a basket of exquisite flowers, and sometimes the entire platform is decorated in the same way. Most commonly some little child perches itself up among the flowers, and this pretty sight never fails to bring a smile of pleasure to the pastor's face as he enters the church. He comes in through a little door under the gallery, behind the pulpit. He is dressed in a plain suit of black, with a Byron collar and a black stock. His movements are quiet and graceful, although quick and energetic. His manner in opening the services is quiet and earnest, and at once impresses his hearers with the solemnity of the occasion. He reads the Bible in an easy, unconstrained manner, as if he enjoyed the task, and in his prayers, which are extempore, he carries the hearts of all his hearers with him to the Throne of Grace. He joins heartily in the singing, which is congregational. It was feared that the organ would prove a great temptation to do away with this style of singing, but this has not been the case. The magnificent instrument is used only to accompany the congregation, and there swells up such a volume of harmony from this vast throng as is never listened to outside of Plymouth Church. The singing is wonderful.

The gem of the whole service, however, is the sermon; and these sermons are characteristic of the man. They come warm and fresh from his heart, and they go home to the hearer, giving him food for thought for days afterward. To attempt to describe his manner would be to paint the sunbeam. Eloquence can be felt, but it can not be described. He enchains the attention of his auditors from the first, and they hang upon his utterances with rapt eagerness until the close of the sermon.

He knows human nature thoroughly, and he talks to his people of what they have been thinking of during the week, of trials that have perplexed them, and of joys which have blessed them. He takes the clerk and the merchant to task for their conduct in the walks of business, and warns them of the snares and pitfalls which lie along their paths. He strips the thin guise of honesty from the questionable transactions of Wall Street, and holds them up to public scorn. He startles many a one by his sudden penetration and denunciation of what that one supposes to be the secrets of his heart. His dramatic power is extraordinary. He can hardly be responsible for it, since it breaks forth almost without his will. It is simply unavoidable with him. He moves his audience to tears, or brings a mirthful smile to their lips, with a power that is irresistible. His illustrations and figures are drawn chiefly from nature, and are fresh and striking. They please the subtlest philosopher who hears him, and illuminate the mind of the average listener with a flood of light. He can startle his people with the terrors of the law, but he prefers to preach the Gospel of Love. "God's love for those who are scattered and lost," he says, "is intenser and deeper than the love even of a mother. . . . God longs to bring you home more than you long to get there. He has been calling, calling, calling, and listening for your answer. And when you are found, and you lay your head on the bosom of Jesus, and you are at rest, you will not be so glad as He will be who declared that, like a shepherd, he had joy over one sinner that repented more than over ninety and nine just persons that needed no repentance."

Religion is to him an abiding joy; it is perfect love, and casteth out fear. It has no gloom, no terror in it, and he says to his people: "If God gave you gayety and cheer of spirits, lift up the careworn by it. Wherever you go, shine and sing.

In every household there is drudgery; in every household there is sorrow; in every household there is low-thoughted evil. If you come as a prince, with a cheerful, buoyant nature, in the name of God, do not lay aside those royal robes of yours. Let humor bedew duty; let it flash across care. Let gayety take charge of dullness. So employ these qualities that they shall be to life what carbonic acid is to wine, making it foam and sparkle."

The sum and substance, the burden of all his preaching is Christ: "'Behold the Lamb of God, that taketh away the sin of the world!' I present Jesus to you as the atoning Saviour; as God's sacrifice for sin; as that new and living way by which alone a sinful creature can ascend and meet a pure and just God. I bring this question home to you as a sinner. O man! full of transgressions, habitual in iniquities, tainted and tarnished, utterly undone before God, what will you do with this Jesus that comes as God's appointed sacrifice for sin, your only hope and your only Saviour? Will you accept him? Will you, by personal and living faith, accept him as your Saviour from sin? I ask not that you should go with me into a discourse upon the relations of Christ's life, of his sufferings, of his death; to the law of God, or to the government of God. Whatever may be the philosophy of those relations, the matter in hand is one of faith rather than of philosophy; and the question is, Will you take Christ to be your soul's Saviour?"

Having selected his theme, and formed a general plan of treatment, Mr. Beecher trusts a great deal to the inspiration of the moment for his language and illustrations. Some time ago, in reply to a friend who asked how he prepared his sermons, he said he generally has an idea during the week as to what he will preach about on Sunday, but does not attempt any thing like systematic preparation until an hour or two before going into the pulpit. Sometimes it is easy to block out a sermon; but again it is hard work, and he does not fairly get into it until the first bell rings. He writes out the headings of his subject, and marks the proper places for illustration. He does not confine himself to this written outline, however, but, once in the pulpit, changes it according to the impulse of the moment. He never preaches the same sermon twice, though he may use the same text several times, treating it in a different way each time. He endeavors to preach his best sermons on stormy days, in order that the desire to hear his best efforts may keep his congregation from degenerating into "fair-weather Christians." "Once," he said, laughing, "it snowed or rained every Sabbath in a certain winter, and the effort I had to make to remain faithful to this rule came near killing me." When asked if he studied his prayers, he answered promptly: "Never. I carry a feeling with me such as a mother would have for her children were they lost in a great forest. I feel that on every side my people are in danger, and that many of them are like babes, weak and helpless. My heart goes out in sorrow and in anxiety toward them, and at times I seem to carry all their burdens. I find that when one's heart is wrapped and twined around the hearts of others, it is not difficult to pray."

The church is provided with a large lecture-room, a study for the pastor, and an elegant parlor. Mr. Beecher does not pay pastoral visits to his people, unless he is sent for to visit the sick and dying, or persons seeking help in their religious struggles. His parishioners are scattered over so wide a territory that a systematic course of visiting would consume all his time In place of these visits, he meets his congregation at stated times in social gatherings in the church parlor, and these evenings are looked forward to with eagerness by both pastor and people.

The most characteristic meeting of this congregation, however, even more so than the Sunday services, is the Friday evening meeting, which is held in the lecture-room. This room is plain and simple. It is provided with comfortable seats and a grand piano. There is no pulpit in it, but a small table and a chair are placed for the pastor on a low platform covered with green baize. The object is to banish every thing like formalism, and to make the meeting as free and unconstrained as a social gathering. As at the Sunday services, the house is full, but now the persons present are almost entirely members of the church. Strangers rarely come to these meetings, and in staying away from them miss the chance of seeing the true inner life of Plymouth Church. A gentleman who was present at one of them, a few years ago, wrote the following account of it for the "Atlantic Monthly:"

Mr. Beecher took his seat on the platform, and, after a short pause, began the exercises by saying, in a low tone, these words: "Six twenty-two."

A rustling of the leaves of hymn-books interpreted the meaning of this mystical utterance, which otherwise might have been taken as announcing a discourse upon the prophetic numbers. The piano confirmed the interpretation; and then the company burst into one of those joyous and unanimous singings which are so enchanting a feature of the services of this church. Loud rose the beautiful harmony of voices, constraining every one to join in the song, even those most unused to sing. When it was ended, the pastor, in the same low tone, pronounced a name, upon which one of the brethren rose to his feet, and the rest slightly inclined their heads. . . . The prayers were all brief, perfectly quiet and simple, and free from the routine or regulation expressions. There were but two or three of them, alternating with singing; and when that part of the exercises was concluded, Mr. Beecher had scarcely spoken. The meeting ran alone, in the most spontaneous and pleasant manner. . . . There was a pause after the last hymn died away, and then Mr. Beecher, still seated, began, in the tone of conversation, to speak somewhat after this manner:

"When," said he, "I first began to walk as a Christian, in my youthful zeal I made many resolutions that were well meant, but indiscreet. Among others, I remember I resolved to pray, at least once, in some way, every hour that I was awake. I tried faithfully to keep this resolution, but never having succeeded a single day, I suffered the pangs of self-reproach, until reflection satisfied me that the only wisdom possible, with regard to such a resolve, was to break it. I remember, too, that I made a resolution to speak upon religion to every person with whom I conversed,—on steamboats, in the streets, anywhere. In this, also, I failed, as I ought; and I soon learned that, in the sowing of such seed, as in other sowings, times, and seasons, and methods must be considered and selected, or a man may defeat his own object, and make religion loathsome."

In language like this he introduced the topic of the evening's conversation, which was, How far, and on what occasions, and in what manner, one person may invade, so to speak, the personality of another, and speak to him upon his moral condition. The pastor expressed his own opinion, always in the conversational tone, in a talk of ten minutes' duration, in the course of which he applauded, not censured, the delicacy which causes most people to shrink from doing it. He said that a man's personality was not a macadamized road for every vehicle to drive upon at will, but rather a sacred inclosure, to be entered, if at all, with the consent of the owner, and with deference to his feelings and tastes. He maintained, however, that there *were* times and modes in which this might properly be done, and that every one *had* a duty to perform of this nature. When he had finished his observations, he said the subject was open to the remarks of others; whereupon a brother instantly rose and made a very honest confession.

He said that he had never attempted to perform the duty in question without having a palpitation of the heart, and a complete turning over of his inner man. He had often reflected upon this curious fact, but was not able to account for it. He had not allowed this repugnance to prevent his doing the duty; but he always had to rush at it and perform it by a sort of *coup de main*, for if he allowed himself to think about the matter, he could not do it at all. He concluded by saying that he should be very much obliged to any one if he could explain this mystery.

The pastor said: "May it not be the natural delicacy we feel, and ought to feel, in approaching the interior consciousness of another person?"

Another brother rose. There was no hanging back at this meeting; there were no awkward pauses; every one seemed full of matter. The new speaker was not inclined to admit the explanation suggested by the pastor. "Suppose," said he, "we were to see a man in imminent danger of immediate destruction, and there was one way of escape, and but one, which *we* saw, and he did not, should we feel any delicacy in running up to him and urging him to fly for his life? Is it not a want of faith on our part that causes the reluctance and hesitation we all feel in urging others to avoid a peril so much more momentous?"

Mr. Beecher said the cases were not parallel. Irreligious persons, he remarked, were not in imminent danger of immediate death; they might die to-morrow; but in all probability they would not, and an ill-timed or injudicious admonition might forever repel them. We must accept the doctrine of probabilities, and act in accordance with it in this particular, as in all others.

Another brother had a puzzle to present for solution. He said that he too had experienced the repugnance to which allusion had been made; but what surprised him most was, that the more he loved a person, and the nearer he was related to him, the more difficult he found it to converse with him upon his spiritual state. Why is this? "I should like to have this question answered," said he, "if there *is* an answer to it."

Mr. Beecher observed that this was the universal experience, and he was conscious himself of a peculiar reluctance and embarrassment in approaching one of his own household on the subject in question. He thought it was due to the fact that we respect more the personal rights of those near to us than we do those of others, and it was more difficult to break in upon the routine of our ordinary familiarity with them. We are accustomed to a certain tone which it is highly embarrassing to jar upon.

Captain Duncan related two amusing anecdotes to illustrate the right way and the wrong way of introducing religious conversation. In his office there was sitting one day a sort of lay preacher, who was noted for lugging in his favorite topic in the most forbidding and abrupt manner. A sea captain came in, who was introduced to this individual.

"Captain Porter," said he, with awful solemnity, "are you a captain in Israel?"

The honest sailor was so abashed and confounded at this novel salutation, that he could only stammer out an incoherent reply; and he was evidently disposed to give the tactless zealot a piece of his mind, expressed in the language of the quarter-deck. When the solemn man took his leave, the disgusted captain said, "If ever I should be coming to your office again, and that man should be here, I wish you would send me word, and I'll stay away."

A few days after another clergyman chanced to be in the office, no other than Mr. Beecher himself, and another captain came in, a roistering, swearing, good-hearted fellow. The conversation fell upon sea-sickness, a malady to which Mr. Beecher is peculiarly liable. The captain also was one of the few sailors who are always sea-sick in going to sea, and gave a moving account of his sufferings from that cause. Mr. Beecher, after listening attentively to his tale, said, "Captain Duncan, if I was a preacher to such sailors as your friend here, I should represent hell as an eternal voyage, with every man on board in the agonies of sea-sickness, the crisis always imminent, but never coming."

This ludicrous and most unprofessional picture amused the old salt exceedingly, and won his entire good will toward the author of it; so that after Mr. Beecher left, he said, "That's a good fellow, Captain Duncan. I like *him*, and I'd like to hear him talk more."

Captain Duncan contended that this free and easy way of address was just the thing for such characters. Mr. Beecher had shown him, to his great surprise, that a man could be a decent and comfortable human being although he was a minister, and had so gained his confidence and good will that he could say *any thing* to him at their next interview. Captain Duncan finished his remarks by a decided expression of his disapproval of the canting regulation phrases so frequently employed by religious people, which are perfectly nauseous to men of the world.

This interesting conversation lasted about three-quarters of an hour, and ended, not because the theme seemed exhausted, but because the time was up. We have only given enough of it to convey some little idea of its spirit. The company again broke into one of their cheerful hymns, and the meeting was dismissed in the usual manner.

During the late war, Mr. Beecher took an active and energetic part in support of the cause of the Union. His labors were so severe that his health was considerably impaired, and his voice began to fail him. His physicians ordered him to seek rest and recreation in a tour through Europe, and he reluctantly obeyed them. He was much benefited by his visit to the Continent, but on his return to England, on his way home, being solicited to speak in that country in behalf of the Union, he delivered a series of powerful appeals, which exhausted the greater part of the strength he had gained on the Continent, and caused him to return home almost as ill as when he went abroad.

Soon after his return the war closed, and he went to Charleston to deliver the address at Fort Sumter upon the occasion of the rehoisting of the flag of the United States over that work. The news of the assassination of Mr. Lincoln met him upon his return to Brooklyn, and drew from him one of his most memorable sermons. At the close of hostilities, he preached a sermon to his congregation, urging forgiveness and conciliation toward the South as the policy of the hour, saying truly that that crisis was a rare opportunity which would never come again, if spurned. The sermon was unpopular, and caused him some trouble even in his own congregation.

Mr. Beecher is now fifty-seven years old, but is still in the flush of his intellectual vigor. His eye is as bright, his step as firm and elastic, and his voice as clear and ringing as when he preached his first sermon. His powers have grown with his work, and every year he seems to rise higher in his intellectual supremacy. As a pulpit orator, he has no superior, and certainly there is no man in all this round earth whose eloquence has been productive of greater good to the cause he serves. He is a stout, stocky man in appearance, with a large square face and heavy features. It is the face of a great orator and a genial, warm-hearted man. He is careful and temperate in all his habits—except that he will work too hard—and enjoys robust health. He lives plainly and dresses simply. He impresses one at once with his immense energy, and you would recognize him immediately as a man of unusual power in his community. Said a friend not long since, "I was standing by Beecher in a book-store to-day. He was perfectly still, as he was waiting for a parcel to be done up, but he reminded me of a big locomotive full of steam and fire, and ready to display its immense force at any moment."

Mr. Beecher is not only a preacher, but a capital farmer. He has a model farm at Peekskill, on the Hudson, and is brimful of agricultural and horticultural theories, which he carries into practice successfully. His love for flowers is a perfect passion, and dates from his boyhood. He is an excellent mechanic, and makes the repairs on his own premises, as far as he can, with a keen relish, which he has doubtless inherited from his father. He is thoroughly read in history, and as an art critic has no superior. His house is filled with art gems, which are his pride. He has not lost the love of reverie which marked his boyhood, but he is eminently a practical man, and prefers the practical questions of theology to those merely theoretical. He is as little like the typical parson as one can imagine, and yet he is one whose place will be hard to fill when he is gone, and whose works will live in the grateful memory of those whom his counsel has saved from sin, and his sympathy encouraged to continue in the path of duty.

CHAPTER XXXII.

PETER CARTWRIGHT.

ONE of the most remarkable men in the American ministry is PETER CARTWRIGHT, the "Backwoods Preacher." Sixty-seven years of ministerial labors have passed over his head, and yet he still continues in the field in which he has done such good service, and retains all the popularity and much of the fire of his younger days.

He was born in Amherst County, Virginia, on the 1st of September, 1785. His father had been a soldier in the Revolutionary War, and his mother was an orphan. Shortly after the close of the war, the Cartwrights removed from Virginia to Kentucky, which was then an almost unbroken wilderness. The journey was accompanied with considerable danger, as the Indians were not yet driven west of the Ohio, but the family reached their destination in safety. For two years they lived on a rented farm in Lincoln County, Kentucky, and at the end of that time removed to what was called the Green River Country, and settled in Logan County, nine miles south of Russellville, the county seat, and within one mile of the State line of Tennessee.

The portion of Logan County in which young Cartwright's childhood and youth were passed was the very last place one would have cared to bring up a candidate for the ministry. It was called "Rogue's Harbor," and was thickly settled with fugitives from justice from all parts of the Union. They actually constituted a majority of the inhabitants of the district, and when the respectable citizens sought to bring them to justice they readily "swore each other clear," and thus set the law at defiance. They carried on such a course of outrage and violence that the respectable citizens were at length compelled to combine for defence against them by means of an organization known as the Regulators. Several fierce encounters took place between the desperadoes and the Regulators, in which many lives were lost, before the supremacy of the law was established.

"When my father settled in Logan County," says Mr. Cartwright, "there was not a newspaper printed South of Green River, no mill short of forty miles, and no schools worth the name. Sunday was a day set apart for hunting, fishing, horse-racing, card-playing, balls, dances, and all kinds of jollity and mirth. We killed our meat out in the woods, wild, and beat our meal and hominy with a pestle and mortar. We stretched a deer-skin over a hoop, burned holes in it with the prongs of a fork, sifted our meal, baked our bread, eat it, and it was first-rate eating, too. We raised, or gathered out of the woods, our own tea. We had sage, bohea, cross-vine, spice, and sassafras teas in abundance. As for coffee, I am not sure that I ever smelled it for ten years. We made our sugar out of the water of the maple-tree, and our molasses, too. These were great luxuries in those days. We raised our own cotton and flax. We water-rotted our flax, broke it by hand, scutched it, picked the seed out of the cotton with our fingers; our mothers and sisters carded, spun, and wove it into cloth, and they cut and made our garments and bed-clothes, etc. And when we got on a new suit thus manufactured, and sallied out into company, we thought ourselves *as big as any body.*"

Young Peter grew up in this rough country with a constitution of iron, and a fair share of Western courage, independence, and energy. He was sent by his father to a neighboring school, but the teacher was an indifferent one, and he learned merely to read and write and cipher imperfectly.

He was a "wild, wicked boy," he tells us, and grew up to delight in horse-racing, card-playing, and dancing. His father seems to have enjoyed having so dashing a son, but his mother, who was a pious woman, took his course seriously to heart, and wept and prayed over her boy as only a Christian mother can. She often talked to him, and moved him so deeply that he frequently vowed to lead a better life; but his pleasures were too tempting, and he fell back again into his old habits. His father presented him with a race-horse and a pack of cards, and he became known among his youthful companions as one of the most fearless riders and the luckiest fellow at cards in the county. The good mother wept and prayed all the more, and the boy hid his cards from her to keep her from burning them.

In 1801, when he was sixteen years old, a change came over him. He had been out with his father and brother to attend a wedding in the neighborhood. The affair was conducted with all the uproarious merriment incident to those days, and when Peter returned home and began to think over it, he felt condemned at having passed his time in such a manner. "My mother was in bed," says he. "It seemed to me, all of a sudden, my blood rushed to my head, my heart palpitated, in a few minutes I turned blind, an awful impression rested on my mind that death had come to me and I was unprepared to die. I fell on my knees and began to ask God to have mercy on me. My mother sprang from her bed, and was soon on her knees by my side, praying for me, and exhorting me to look to Christ for mercy, and then and there I promised the Lord if he would spare me I would seek and serve Him, and I never fully broke that promise. My mother prayed for me a long time. At length we lay down, but there was little sleep for me. Next morning I rose, feeling wretched beyond expression. I tried to read in the Testament, and retired many times to secret prayer through the day, but found no relief. I gave up my race-horse to my father and requested him to sell him. I went and brought my pack of cards and gave them to mother, who threw them into the fire, and they were consumed. I fasted, watched, and prayed, and engaged in regular reading of the Testament. I was so distressed and miserable that I was incapable of any regular business."

Several months passed away, during which time Peter had seasons of comfort and hopes of forgiveness, but during the greater portion he was wretched and miserable, filled with such a fear of the devil that he was almost convinced that Satan was really present with him to keep him from God. A camp-meeting, held in the vicinity of his father's house, in the spring of 1801, completed his conversion and gave him peace.

"To this meeting," says he, "I repaired a guilty, wretched sinner. On the Saturday evening of said meeting I went, with weeping multitudes, and bowed before the stand, and earnestly prayed for mercy. In the midst of a solemn struggle of soul, an impression was made on my mind as though a voice said to me: 'Thy sins are all forgiven thee.' Divine light flashed all around me, unspeakable joy sprang up in my soul. I rose to my feet, opened my eyes, and it really seemed to me as if I was in heaven; the trees, the leaves on them, and every thing seemed, and I really thought were, praising God. My mother raised the shout, my Christian friends crowded around me and joined me in praising God. . . I have never doubted that the Lord did, then and there, forgive my sins and give me religion." He went on his way rejoicing, and in June, 1801, was formally received into the Methodist Episcopal Church. In May, 1802, he was appointed an exhorter. He shrank from accepting the position, as he distrusted his own abilities, but finally yielded to his presiding elder's wishes and entered upon his work. In the fall of that year his parents removed to Lewiston County, toward the mouth of the Cumberland River.

Although he was but eighteen years old, his presiding elder had detected in him signs of unusual promise, and had resolved to bring him into active labor for the Church at once, and accordingly, upon his departure for his new home, Peter was given authority to lay out and organize a new circuit, the plan of which he was to submit to the presiding elder for approval. The boy hesitated, frightened by the magnitude of the task, but being encouraged by his superiors, accepted the trust, and thus began his labors as a preacher of the Word. Upon reaching his new home, he attended a tolerably good school in the vicinity, hoping to acquire a better education, but the pupils and teacher persecuted him so sorely that he was obliged to withdraw. Determining to lose no time in waiting for an education, he at once began the work of preaching. Being possessed of strong natural sense, a ready wit, and being thoroughly imbued with the spirit of frontier life, he was just the man to carry the Gospel home to the hearts of the rude pioneers of the great West. His manner was that of a backwoodsman, and he had no city airs and graces to offend the plain, rough people to whom he preached. He was emphatically one of them. He offered them the plain Gospel, and gave theological theories a wide berth.

His plan of operations was adapted to the rudest intellect. It was to thunder the terrors of the law into the ears of his converts, or, in his own words, to "shake them over hell until they smelt brimstone right strong," and make them see the fearful condition in which they lay by reason of their sin. Man was to him a wretched, degraded creature, and the only way to bring him to God was to drive him there by the terrors of the law. Our preacher had very little faith in the quieter, more persuasive means of grace. His first effort was to give the souls of his hearers a good shaking up, bring them face to face with hell and its torments, and then, having forced them to flee from the wrath to come, to trust to their future Christian experience for the means of acquiring a knowledge of the tender mercies of the Saviour. It must be confessed that this was the only plan open to him in the field in which he labored. The people to whom he preached were a rude, rough set, mainly ignorant and superstitious, and many of them sunk in the depths of drunkenness and viciousness. The Western country was almost a wilderness. Vast forests and boundless prairies lay on every hand, with but here and there a clearing with a solitary log cabin in it, or but two or three at the most. The people lived in the most perfect solitude, rarely seeing any but the members of their own households. Solitude and danger made them superstitious, and the absence of schools kept them in ignorance. They drank to keep off the blues, and when they came together for amusement they made the most of their opportunities, and plunged into the most violent sports, which were not always kept within the bounds of propriety. Churches were as scarce as schools, and until the Methodist circuit riders made their appearance in the West, the people were little better than heathen. The law had scarcely any hold upon these frontiersmen. They were wild and untamed, and personal freedom was kept in restraint mainly by the law of personal accountability. They were generous and improvident, frank, fearless, easy-going, and filled with an intense scorn for every thing that smacked of Eastern refinement or city life. They were proud of their buckskin and linsey-woolsey clothes, their squirrel caps, and their horny hands and rough faces. They would have been miserable in a city mansion, but they were lords and kings in their log-cabins. To have sent a preacher bred in the learned schools of New England to such a people would have been folly. The smooth cadences, the polished gestures, and, above all, the manuscript sermon of a Boston divine, would have disgusted the men and women of the frontier. What cared they for predestination or free-will, or for any of the dogmas of the schools? They wanted to hear the simple, fundamental truths of the Gospel, and they wanted to hear them from a man of their own stamp. They wanted a "fire and brimstone" preacher, one whose fiery eloquence could stir the very depths of their souls, and set their simple imaginations all ablaze; one who could shout and sing with true Western abandon; who could preach in his shirt-sleeves, sleep with them on the bare ground, brave all the dangers of a frontier life, and, if necessary, thrash any one who dared to insult him. Such was the man for these sturdy, simple Western folk, and such a man they found in Peter Cartwright.

Peter went at the task before him with a will. The country being sparsely settled, people had to travel a long way to get to church, and it became a matter of expediency for the clergy to hold religious gatherings at stated points, and to continue them for several days, so that those who desired to attend might be able to avoid the necessity of going home every evening and coming back next day. Church edifices being scarce, these meetings were held in the woods, and a large encampment was formed by the people in attendance. This was the origin of the camp-meeting system, which for many years was the only effective way of spreading the Gospel in the West. It was at a camp-meeting that Peter obtained religion, and he has ever since been a zealous advocate of, and a hard worker at, them. From the first he was successful. The fame of the "boy preacher" went abroad into all the land, and people came in to the camp from a hundred miles around to hear him. He had little education, but he knew his Bible thoroughly, and was a ready speaker, and, above all, he knew how to deal with the people to whom he preached. He made many converts, and from the first took rank as the most popular preacher in the West.

Peter not only believed in the overruling power of God, but he was firmly convinced of the active and personal agency of the devil in human affairs. Many of the follies and faults of the people around him took place, he averred, because they were possessed of devils. Each camp-meeting was to him a campaign against Satan, and in his opinion Satan never failed to make a good fight for his kingdom. Certainly some very singular things did occur at the meetings at which he was present, and, naturally, perhaps, some persons began to believe that Peter Cartwright possessed supernatural powers. The following incident, related by him, not only explains some of the phenomena to which I allude, but also the manner in which he was regarded by some of the unconverted:

"A new exercise broke out among us, called the 'jerks,' which was overwhelming in its effects upon the bodies and minds of the people. No matter whether they were saints or sinners, they would be taken under a warm song or sermon, and seized with a convulsive jerking all over, which they could not by any possibility avoid, and the more they resisted, the more they jerked. If they would not strive against it, and pray in good earnest, the jerking would usually abate. I have seen more than five hundred persons jerking at one time in my large congregations. Most usually persons taken with the jerks, to obtain relief, as they said, would rise up and dance. Some would run, but could not get away. Some would resist; on such the jerks were very severe.

"To see those proud young gentlemen and young ladies, dressed in their silks, jewelry, and prunella, from top to toe, take the jerks, would often excite my risibilities. The first jerk or so you would see their fine bonnets, caps, and combs fly, and so sudden would be the jerking of the head that their long, loose hair would crack almost as loud as a wagoner's whip.

"At one of my appointments, in 1804, there was a very large congregation turned out to hear the 'Kentucky boy,' as they called me. Among the rest there were two very finely dressed, fashionable young ladies, attended by two brothers with loaded horsewhips. Although the house was large, it was crowded. The two young ladies, coming in late, took their seats near where I stood, and their two brothers stood in the door. I was a little unwell, and I had a phial of peppermint in my pocket. Before I commenced preaching I took out my phial and swallowed a little of the peppermint. While I was preaching the congregation was melted into tears. The two young gentlemen moved off to the yard fence, and both the young ladies took the jerks, and they were greatly mortified about it. . . .

"As I dismissed the assembly, a man stepped up to me and warned me to be on my guard, for he had heard the two brothers swear they would horsewhip me when meeting was out for giving their sisters the jerks. 'Well,' said I, 'I'll see to that.'

"I went out and said to the young men that I understood they intended to horsewhip me for giving their sisters the jerks. One replied that he did. I undertook to expostulate with him on the absurdity of the charge against me, but he swore I need not deny it, for he had seen me take out a phial in which I carried some truck that gave his sisters the jerks. As quick as thought came into my mind how I would get clear of my whipping, and, jerking out the peppermint phial, said I, 'Yes; if I gave your sisters the jerks I'll give them to you.' In a moment I saw he was scared. I moved toward him, he backed, I advanced, and he wheeled and ran, warning me not to come near him or he would kill me. It raised the laugh on him, and I escaped my whipping. . . .

"I always looked upon the jerks as a judgment sent from God, first, to bring sinners to repentance, and, secondly, that God could work with or without means, and that he could work over and above means and do whatsoever seemeth him good to the glory of his grace and the salvation of the world. There is no doubt in my mind that, with weak-minded, ignorant, and superstitious persons, there was a great deal of sympathetic feeling with many that claimed to be under the influence of this jerking exercise, and yet with many it was perfectly involuntary. It was on all occasions my practice to recommend fervent prayer as a remedy, and it almost universally proved an effectual antidote."

The excitement of the religious revivals plunged many of the people into excesses. They prophesied, dreamed dreams, and saw visions, and troubled the young preacher exceedingly, but he set his face sternly against all such disorders, and pronounced their visions and messages to be from the devil. One of these dreamers came to him one day and told him he had a message from heaven for him.

"Well," said Cartwright, "what is it?"

"It has been revealed to me," said the fellow, "that you are never to die, but are to live forever."

"Who revealed that to you?"

"An angel."

"Did you see him?" asked Cartwright, dryly.

"O, yes; he was a beautiful, white, shining being."

"Did you smell him?" asked Peter, bluntly.

The man looked at him in amazement, and the preacher continued, sternly, "Well, did the angel you saw smell of brimstone? He must have smelled of brimstone, for he was from a region that burns with fire and brimstone, and consequently from hell, for he revealed a great lie to you if he told you I was to live forever."

The dreamer turned off abruptly, and disappeared amidst the jeers of the crowd that had listened to the conversation.

On the 16th of September, 1806, Mr. Cartwright was ordained a deacon in the Methodist Episcopal Church by Bishop Asbury, and on the 4th of October, 1808, Bishop McKendree ordained him an elder. Upon receiving deacon's orders he was assigned to the Marietta Circuit. His appointment dismayed him. Says he: "It was a poor, hard circuit at that time. Marietta and the country round were settled at an early day by a colony of Yankees. At the time of my appointment I had never seen a Yankee, and I had heard dismal stories about them. It was said they lived almost entirely on pumpkins, molasses, fat meat, and bohea tea; moreover, that they could not bear loud and zealous sermons, and they had brought on their learned preachers with them, and they read their sermons and were always criticising us poor backwoods preachers. When my appointment was read out it distressed me greatly. I went to Bishop Asbury and begged him to supply my place and let me go home. The old father took me in his arms and said: 'O, no, my son; go in the name of the Lord. It will make a man of you.'

"Ah, thought I, if this is the way to make men, I do not want to be a man. I cried over it bitterly, and prayed, too. But on I started, cheered by my presiding elder, Brother J. Sale. If I ever saw hard times, surely it was this year; yet many of the people were kind and treated me friendly. I had hard work to keep soul and body together. The first Methodist house I came to the brother was a Universalist. I crossed over the Muskingum River to Marietta. The first Methodist family I stopped with there, the lady was a member of the Methodist Episcopal Church, but a thorough Universalist. She was a thin-faced, Roman-nosed, loquacious Yankee, glib on the tongue, and you may depend upon it I had a hard race to keep up with her, though I found it a good school, for it set me to reading my Bible. And here permit me to say, of all the isms I ever heard of, they were here. These descendants of the Puritans were generally educated, but their ancestors were rigid predestinarians, and as they were sometimes favored with a little light on their moral powers, and could just 'see men as trees walking,' they jumped into Deism, Universalism, Unitarianism, etc., etc. I verily believe it was the best school I ever entered. They waked me up on all sides; Methodism was feeble, and I had to battle or run, and I resolved on the former."

Just before he was made an elder, Mr. Cartwright left his circuit, and went home on a visit to recruit. He had made a good fight with poverty during his labors, and at the time of his departure for home he was in a condition sufficiently hard to test any man's fortitude. "I had been from my father's house for three years," says he; "was five hundred miles from home, my horse had gone blind, my saddle was worn out, my bridle reins had been eaten up and replaced (after a sort) at least a dozen times, and my clothes had been patched till it was difficult to detect the original. I had concluded to make my way home and get another outfit. I was in Marietta, and had just seventy-five cents in my pocket. How I would get home and pay my way I could not tell."

He did reach home, however, after many characteristic adventures, and obtained another outfit, and while there he took an important step—he married. "After a mature deliberation and prayer," he says, "I thought it was my duty to marry, and was joined in marriage to Frances Gaines, on the 18th of August, 1808, which was her nineteenth birthday." Peter and his bride knew that a hard life was in store for them, but they felt strong in the love they bore each other. They were simple backwoods folk, and their wants were few. "When I started as a traveling preacher," he said fifty-three years afterward, "a single preacher was allowed to receive eighty dollars per annum if his circuit would give it to him; but single preachers in those days seldom received over thirty or forty dollars, and often much less; and had it not been for a few presents made us by the benevolent friends of the church, and a few dollars we made as marriage fees, we must have suffered much more than we did. But the Lord provided, and, strange as it may appear to the present generation, we got along without starving or going naked." There is something awe-inspiring in the simple trust in God which this good man displayed in every stage of his life. Once satisfied that he was in the path of duty, he never allowed the future to trouble him. He provided for it as far as he could, and left the rest to the Master whose work he was doing. Poverty and hardship had no terrors for this brave young couple, and it was very far from their thoughts to wait until a better day to marry. They would go out hand in hand into the world and meet their trials together. Children would come, they knew, and those little mouths would have to be fed, but they would be industrious, saving, and patient, and "God would provide."

Peter Cartwright's mission was to plant the Methodist Episcopal Church in the West as well as to preach the Gospel. For that end he worked and prayed. The Methodist Episcopal Church was his haven of safety. Without, all was storm and darkness; within its fold all was peace and light. He believed his church to be the best door to heaven, if indeed it was not in his estimation the only one. He was a fanatic, pure and simple, as regarded his own denomination, but a fanatic full of high and noble purposes, and one whose zeal was productive only of good. This fanaticism was necessary to the success of his labors. It was his perfect belief that his was the only church in which sinners could find perfect peace that carried him through the difficulties which encompassed him. Men were dying all around him, and they must come into his church. They had other denominations close at hand, but they, in his estimation, would not do. The Methodist Episcopal Church was a necessity for sinners, therefore it must be planted in all parts of the land. No sacrifice was too great for the accomplishment of this object. He has lived to see those sacrifices rewarded, to see his church one of the most numerous and powerful religious bodies in the country.

Being so zealous in behalf of his own church, it is not strange that he should have clashed frequently with other denominations. He got along very well with the majority, but with the Baptists and Universalists he was always on the war path. The latter especially excited his uncompromising hostility, and he never failed to attack their doctrines with all his forces wherever he encountered them. "I have thought," says he, "and do still think, if I were to set out to form a plan to contravene the laws of God, to encourage wickedness of all kinds, to corrupt the morals and encourage vice, and crowd hell with the lost and the wailings of the damned, the Universalist plan should be the plan, the very plan that I would adopt. . . . . . .

"A few years ago," he continues, "I had a neighbor who professed to be a confirmed Universalist. He contended with me that there was no devil but the evil disposition in man, and that there was no hell but the bad feelings that men had when they did wrong: that this was all the punishment any body would suffer. When this neighbor's father lay on his dying bed (a confirmed Universalist, professedly) there was a faithful minister of Christ who believed it his duty to visit this old Universalist, warn him of his danger, and try to awaken his conscience, if not seared, to a just view of his real situation. The minister, however, failed in his faithful attempt and well-meant endeavors, for the old man, then on his dying pillow, was greatly offended at the preacher, and told him that he did not thank him for trying to shake his faith in his dying moments. This neighbor of mine, and son of this old, hardened sinner, was greatly enraged at the preacher, and cursed and abused him in a violent manner. A few days after the demise of the old man, he, in a furious rage, began to abuse and curse the preacher in my presence, and said:

"'D—— him; I wish he was in hell and the devil had him.'

"I stopped him short by saying, 'Pooh, pooh, man, what are you talking about? There is no hell but the bad feelings that a man has when he does wrong, and no devil but the evil disposition that is in man.' Thus answering a fool according to his folly.

"'Well,' said he, 'if there is no hell there ought to be, to put such preachers in.'

"'Now, sir,' said I, 'you see the utter untenableness of your creed, for a man even in trying to do good honestly draws down your wrath, and, in a moment, you want a hell to put him into and a devil to torment him for giving you an offense, and for doing what no good man ought to be offended about. But God must be insulted, his name blasphemed, his laws trampled under foot, yet he must have no hell to put such a wretch in, no devil to torment him. Now I would be ashamed of myself if I were in your place, and let the seal of truth close my lips forever hereafter.'

"Although he was confounded, he still clave to his God-dishonoring doctrine, waxing worse and worse, till it was generally believed he was guilty of a most heinous crime."

Argumentative battles were not the only troubles Cartwright had to encounter from Universalists. They came to his revivals, he says, to hoot and create disturbance. At one of these meetings two sisters, Universalists in belief, were present. They came to "make fun," but one of them was overcome by Cartwright's preaching, and went up to the mourner's bench to be prayed for. When her sister heard of it, she commenced to make her way to the altar, with the angry determination to force the penitent from it. "I rose and met her in the crowded aisle," says Mr. Cartwright, "and told her to be calm and desist. She made neither better nor worse of it than to draw back her arm and give me a severe slap in the face with her open hand. I confess this rather took me by surprise, and, as the common saying is, made the fire fly out of my eyes in tremendous sparkling brilliancy, but, collecting my best judgment; I caught her by the arms near her shoulders and wheeled her to the right about, moved her forward to the door, and said,

'Gentlemen, please open the door; the devil in this Universalist lady has got fighting hot, and I want to set her outside to cool.' The door was opened, and I landed her out."

Concerning his tilts with the Baptists, he has given a mass of curious reminiscences, from which we take the following:

"We preached in new settlements, and the Lord poured out his Spirit, and we had many convictions and many conversions. It was the order of the day, (though I am sorry to say it,) that we were constantly followed by a certain set of proselyting Baptist preachers. These new and wicked settlements were seldom visited by these Baptist preachers until the Methodist preachers entered them; then, when a revival was gotten up, or the work of the Lord revived, these Baptist preachers came rushing in, and they generally sung their sermons; and when they struck the *long roll*, or their sing-song mode of preaching, in substance it was: 'Water! water! You must follow your blessed Lord down into the water!' I had preached several times in a large, populous, and wicked settlement, and there was serious attention, deep convictions, and a good many conversions; but, between my occasional appointments these preachers would rush in and try to take off our converts into the water; and indeed they made so much ado about baptism by immersion that the uninformed would suppose that heaven was an island, and there was no way to get there *but by diving or swimming.*"

He once preached a sermon on the true nature of baptism, at which were present the daughters of a Baptist minister, one of whom was converted. That night it rained violently, and all the neighboring streams overflowed their banks. Riding along the next day, he met the Baptist minister on the road.

"We've had a tremendous rain," said Cartwright.

"Yes, sir," said the Baptist brother, "the Lord sent this rain to convince you of your error."

"Ah! what error?"

"Why, about baptism. The Lord sent this flood to convince you that much water was necessary."

"Very good, sir," said Cartwright, "and in like manner he sent this flood to convince you of your error."

"What error?" asked the Baptist brother.

"Why," replied Cartwright, triumphantly, "to show you that water comes by pouring, and not by immersion."

Free and easy as he was in his manner, our preacher had a deep sense of the dignity of his mission, and he was resolved that others should share the feeling, and accord him, in his ministerial capacity, the respect and deference that were his due. His manner of accomplishing this was characteristic, as the following incident will show: Traveling on his circuit in 1805, he put up on one occasion at the house of an old man known as Father Teel, a whimsical old fellow, and supposed to be Cartwright's match in oddity. He had been warned that the old man, though a good Methodist, showed little deference to preachers. It was his custom to rise early, and, as soon as dressed, to give out his hymn, sing it himself, and then go to prayers, without waiting for his family to get up. He served preachers in the same way. Cartwright resolved to beat him at his own game, but the old man was too wary for him.

"Just as day broke," says Cartwright, "I awoke, rose up, and began to dress, but had not nigh accomplished it when I heard Teel give out his hymn and commence singing, and about the time I had got dressed, I heard him commence praying. He gave thanks to God that they had been spared during the night, and were all permitted to see the light of a new day, while at the same time I suppose every one of his family was fast asleep. I deliberately opened the door and walked out to the well, washed myself, and then walked back to my cabin. Just as I got to the door, the old brother opened his door, and, seeing me, said, 'Good morning, sir. Why, I did n't know you were up.'

"'Yes, said I, 'I have been up some time.'

"'Well, brother,' said he, 'why did you not come in to prayers?'

"'Because,' said I, 'it is wrong to pray of a morning in the family before we wash.'

"The old brother passed on, and no more was said at that time. That evening, just before we were about to retire to rest, the old brother set out the book and said to me: 'Brother, hold prayers with us.'

"'No, sir,' said I.

"Said he, 'Come, brother, take the book and pray with us.'

"'No, sir,' said I; 'you love to pray so well, you may do it yourself.'

"He insisted, but I persistently refused, saying: 'You are so fond of praying yourself, that you even thanked God this morning that he had spared you all to see the light of a new day, when your family had not yet opened their eyes, but were all fast asleep. And you have such an absurd way of holding prayers in your family, that I do not wish to have any thing to do with it.'

"He then took the book, read, and said prayers, but you may rely on it, the next morning things were much changed. He waited for me, and had all his family up in order. He acknowledged his error, and told me it was one of the best reproofs he ever got. I then prayed with the family, and after that all went well."

Among his clerical brethren was a poor hen-pecked husband, whose wife was possessed of a temper that made her the terror of the neighborhood. Cartwright had often been invited by the poor man to go home with him; "but," he says, "I frankly confess I was afraid to trust myself," but at length, yielding to his importunities, he went home with his oppressed brother, intending to spend the night with him. His visit roused the fury of the wife, and "I saw in a minute," says our preacher, "that the devil was in her as big as an alligator, and I determined on my course." The woman held her tongue until after supper, when her husband asked her kindly to join them in prayers. She flew into a rage, and swore there should be no praying in her house that night. Cartwright tried to reason with her, but she cursed him roundly. Then, facing her sternly, he said, "Madam, if you were my wife, I would break you of your bad ways, or I would break your neck."

"The devil you would," said she. "Yes, you are a pretty Christian, aint you?"

She continued cursing him, but Cartwright sternly bade her hold her peace, and let them pray. She declared she would not.

"Now," said he to her, "if you do not be still, and behave yourself, I'll put you out of doors."

"At this," says he, "she clenched her fist and swore she was one-half alligator and the other half snapping-turtle, and that it would take a better man than I was to put her out. It was a small cabin we were in, and we were not far from the door, which was then standing open. I caught her by the arm, and swinging her round in a circle, brought her right up to the door, and shoved her out. She jumped up, tore her hair, foamed, and such swearing as she uttered was seldom equaled, and never surpassed. The door, or shutter of the door, was very strongly made, to keep out hostile Indians; I shut it tight, barred it, and went to prayer, and I prayed as best I could; but I have no language at my command to describe my feelings. At the same time, I was determined to conquer, or die in the attempt. While she was raging and foaming in the yard and around the cabin, I started a spiritual song, and sung loud, to drown her voice as much as possible. The five or six little children ran and squatted about and crawled under the beds. Poor things, they were scared almost to death.

"I sang on, and she roared and thundered on outside, till she became perfectly exhausted, and panted for breath. At length, when she had spent her force, she became perfectly calm and still, and then knocked at the door, saying, 'Mr. Cartwright, please let me in.'

"'Will you behave yourself if I let you in?' said I.

"'O yes,' said she, 'I will;' and throwing myself on my guard, and perfectly self-possessed, I opened the door, took her by the hand, led her in, and seated her near the fire-place. She had roared and foamed until she was in a high perspiration, and looked pale as death. After she took her seat, 'O,' said she, 'what a fool I am.'

"'Yes,' said I, 'about one of the biggest fools I ever saw in all my life.' . . . . Brother C. and I kneeled down, and both prayed. She was as quiet as a lamb."

Six months later, our preacher tells us, this woman was converted, and became "as bold in the cause of God as she had been in the cause of the wicked one."

In 1823, Mr. Cartwright resolved to move across the Ohio, and selected Illinois as his new home. The reasons which influenced his actions are thus stated by him:

"I had seen with painful emotions the increase of a disposition to justify slavery . . . . and the legislatures in the slave States made the laws more and more stringent, with a design to prevent emancipation. Moreover, rabid abolitionism spread and dreadfully excited the South. I had a young and growing family of children, two sons and four daughters; was poor, owned a little farm of about one hundred and fifty acres; lands around me were high and rising in value. My daughters would soon be grown up. I did not see any probable means by which I could settle them around or near us. Moreover, I had no right to expect our children to marry into wealthy families, and I did not desire it, if it could be so; and by chance they might marry into slave families. This I did not desire. Besides, I saw there was a marked distinction made among the people generally between young people raised without work and those that had to work for their living. . . . . I thought I saw clear indications of Providence that I should leave my comfortable little home, and move into a free State or territory, for the following reasons: First, I would get entirely clear of the evil of slavery. Second, I could raise my children to work where work was not considered a degradation. Third, I believed I could better my temporal circumstances, and procure lands for my children as they grew up. And fourth, I could carry the Gospel to destitute souls that had, by removal into some new country, been deprived of the means of grace."

It was the last reason, no doubt, that decided our preacher. Men of his stamp were needed west of the Ohio. Kentucky was becoming too old a State for him, and he felt that his true field of labor was still on the frontier, and thither he turned his steps. Setting out first on horseback to seek an eligible location, he reached Sangamon County, Illinois, where he bought a claim on Richland Creek. He then returned to Kentucky and wound up his affairs there, obtained a regular transfer from the Kentucky Conference to the Indiana Conference, which then controlled Illinois, and in October, 1824, set out for his new home in Sangamon County. A great affliction overtook him on the way, in the death of his third daughter, who was killed by the falling of a tree upon their camp. The affliction was made more grievous by the heartless refusal of the people in the vicinity to render them any aid. "We were in great distress," he says, "and no one even to pity our condition. . . . . I discovered that the tree had sprung up, and did not press the child; and we drew her out from under it, and carefully laid her in our feed trough, and moved on about twenty miles to an acquaintance's in Hamilton County, Illinois, where we buried her."

Leaving that lonely little grave behind them, they hurried on to their new home. Springfield, the capital of the State, was but a small collection of shanties and log huts, and Sangamon County was the extreme frontier. It was the most northern county of Illinois, and just beyond it lay the unbroken Indian country. Numbers of Indians roamed through the Sangamon River bottom, and spent their winters there. It was as wild and unsettled a region as our preacher could have desired, and one which gave him a fine field for the exercise of his peculiar abilities. Mr. Cartwright was promptly received into the Indiana Conference, and he lost no time in looking about him. He at once established his family in their new home, and then set about his work. The work was hard, and money was scarce. The first year he traveled the Sangamon Circuit he received forty dollars, and the next year sixty dollars, which he says was a great improvement in his financial affairs. He was successful from the first, and in the two years referred to added one hundred and sixty persons to the Methodist Church in this thinly-settled district. For forty-six years he has labored in this region, adding many souls to the kingdom of God.

Arduous as his labors had been in the Kentucky Conference, they now increased very greatly. He had a larger amount of territory to travel over, people were more scattered, and the dangers to be encountered were greater. In 1827, he was made presiding elder, and given the Illinois District, then a very extensive region, and in 1828 Galena charge was added to this district. The district thus enlarged extended from the mouth of the Ohio River to Galena, the entire length of the present State of Illinois, and over this immense distance our preacher was obliged to travel four times in the year. The journeys were made either on horseback or in an old-fashioned sulky or one-seat gig. There were miles of lonely prairie and many rapid streams to cross, and roads, bridges, or ferry-boats were almost unknown. Yet Peter Cartwright was not the man to be deterred by obstacles. When he set out on his official journeys, he allowed nothing that it was possible to overcome to prevent him from keeping his appointments. In crossing the prairies, he would guide himself by the points of timber, for there were no roads over these vast plains. Oftentimes the streams to be crossed were swollen, and then he would swim his horse across them, or ride along the shore until he found a tree fallen over the current. Stripping himself, he would carry his clothes and riding equipments to the opposite bank, and then, returning, mount his horse and swim him across the river. Dressing again, he would continue his journey, and perhaps repeat the proceeding several times during the day. When overtaken by night, he would seek a place in some grove, and, lighting a fire with his tinder-box and steel, tie up his horse, and, throwing himself on the ground, sleep as peacefully as on a bed of down. Sometimes night would come on before he had crossed the prairie or made his way to the timber point he was aiming for, and then he would sit down on the ground, in the darkness and alone, and, holding his horse by the bridle, await the return of light to enable him to see his landmark. Sometimes he would find a little log-hut with a settler's family in it, and he says it was "a great treat" to come upon one of these lonely cabins and enjoy the privilege of a night's lodging. If the family were Methodists, there was sure to be preaching that night; and if they were strangers to that church, our preacher set to work at once to convert them. He labored faithfully, faring hard, and braving dangers from which his city brethren would have shrunk appalled. He carried the Gospel and the Methodist Episcopal Church into all parts of the great State of Illinois, and even into Iowa and the Indian country.

In 1832, the first Illinois Conference met in the town of Jacksonville, and Mr. Cartwright attended it. He had now been a traveling preacher for twenty-eight years, and, as he felt himself sorely in need of rest, he asked and obtained a superannuated relation for one year. On the same day, Bishop Soule, who presided at the Conference, came to him to ask his advice with reference to the Quincy District. It was very important, but the bishop could not find a presiding elder willing to take charge of it, as it was an almost unbroken wilderness. The bishop was in sore distress, as he feared that he would be obliged to merge it into another district. The spirit of the backwoods preacher at once took fire, and, declaring that so important a field ought not to be neglected, he expressed his willingness to relinquish his superannuated relation and accept the charge. The bishop took him at his word and appointed him to the district, which he served faithfully. His adventures in traveling from place to place to fill his appointments are intensely interesting, and I would gladly reproduce them here did the limits of this chapter permit.

It required no small amount of courage to perform the various duties of a backwoods preacher, and in this quality our preacher was not deficient. He was frequently called upon to exercise it in his camp meetings. These assemblies never failed to gather large crowds from all parts of the surrounding country, and among others came numerous rowdies, whose delight it was to annoy the preachers and worshipers in every conceivable way. Cartwright put up with the annoyance as long as he could, and then determined to put a stop to it. He believed in fighting the devil with fire, and put down many a disturbance. The following is the way he went about it:

"Our last quarterly meeting was a camp meeting. We had a great many tents and a large turnout for a new country, and, perhaps, there never was a greater collection of rabble and rowdies. They came drunk and armed with dirks, clubs, knives, and horsewhips, and swore they would break up the meeting. After interrupting us very much on Saturday night, they collected on Sunday morning, determined on a general riot. At eight o'clock I was appointed to preach. About the time I was half through my discourse, two very fine-dressed young men marched into the congregation with loaded horsewhips, and hats on, and rose up and stood in the midst of the ladies, and began to laugh and talk. They were near the stand, and I requested them to desist and get off the seats; but they cursed me and told me to mind my own business, and said they would not get down. I stopped trying to preach, and called for a magistrate. There were two at hand, but I saw they were both afraid. I ordered them to take these two men into custody, but they said they could not do it. I told them as I left the stand to command me to take them, and I would do it at the risk of my life. I advanced toward them. They ordered me to stand off, but I advanced. One of them made a pass at my head, but I closed in with him and jerked him off the seat. A regular scuffle ensued. The congregation by this time were all in commotion. I heard the magistrates giving general orders, commanding all friends of order to aid in suppressing the riot. In the scuffle I threw my prisoner down, and held him fast;

he tried his best to get loose. I told him to be quiet, or I would pound his chest well. The mob rose and rushed to the rescue of the two prisoners, for they had taken the other young man also. An old, drunken magistrate came up to me, and ordered me to let my prisoner go. I told him I should not. He swore if I did not he would knock me down. I told him to crack away. Then one of my friends, at my request, took hold of my prisoner, and the drunken justice made a pass at me; but I parried the stroke, and, seizing him by the collar and the hair of the head, and fetching him a sudden jerk forward, brought him to the ground and jumped on him. I told him to be quiet, or I would pound him well. The mob then rushed to the scene; they knocked down seven magistrates, several preachers, and others. I gave up my drunken prisoner to another, and threw myself in front of the friends of order. Just at this moment, the ringleader of the mob and I met; he made three passes at me, intending to knock me down. The last time he struck at me, by the force of his own effort he threw the side of his face toward me. It seemed at that moment I had not power to resist temptation, and I struck a sudden blow in the burr of the ear and dropped him to the earth. Just at this moment, the friends of order rushed by hundreds on the mob, knocking them down in every direction."

Once, while crossing a river on a ferry-boat, he overheard a man cursing Peter Cartwright and threatening dire vengeance against him, and boasting that he could "whip any preacher the Lord ever made." This roused our preacher's ire, and accosting the man, he told him he was Peter Cartwright, and that if he wanted to whip him he must do so then. The fellow became confused, and said he did not believe him.

"I tell you," said Cartwright, sternly, "I am the man. Now, sir, you have to whip me, as you threatened, or quit cursing me, or I will put you in the river and baptize you in the name of the devil, for you surely belong to him." "This," says Cartwright, "settled him."

Once, having gone into the woods with a young man who had sworn he would whip him, he sprained his foot slightly in getting over a fence, and involuntarily placed his hand to his side. "My redoubtable antagonist," says he, "had got on the fence, and, looking down at me, said, 'D—— you, you are feeling for a dirk, are you?'

"As quick as thought it occurred to me how to get clear of a whipping.

"'Yes,' said I, 'and I will give you the benefit of all the dirks I have,' and advanced rapidly toward him.

"He sprang back on the other side of the fence from me; I jumped over after him, and a regular foot race followed."

"It may be asked," says the old man, naïvely, "what I would have done if this fellow had gone with me to the woods. This is hard to answer, for it was a part of my creed to love every body, but to fear no one, and I did not permit myself to believe that any man could whip me until it was tried, and I did not permit myself to premeditate expedients in such cases. I should no doubt have proposed to him to have prayer first, and then followed the openings of Providence."

Mr. Cartwright was from the beginning of his ministry an ardent advocate of temperance, and, long before the first temperance society was organized in the country, he waged a fierce war against dram-drinking. This fearless advocate of temperance came very near getting drunk once. He had stopped with a fellow preacher at a tavern kept by an Otterbein Methodist, who, thinking to play them a trick, put whisky into the new cider which he offered them. Cartwright drank sparingly of the beverage, though he considered it harmless, but, "with all my forbearance," he says, "presently I began to feel light-headed. I instantly ordered our horses, fearing we were snapped for once. . . When we had rode about a mile, being in the rear, I saw Brother Walker was nodding at a mighty rate. I suddenly rode up to Brother Walker and cried out, 'Wake up! wake up!' He roused up, his eyes watering freely. 'I believe,' said I, 'we are both drunk. Let us turn out of the road and lie down and take a nap till we get sober.' But we rode on without stopping. We were not drunk, but we both evidently felt it flying to our heads."

In 1826 Mr. Cartwright was elected to the Legislature of the State, and at the expiration of his first term was reëlected from Sangamon County. He was induced to accept this position because of his desire to aid in preventing the introduction of slavery into the State. He had no liking for political strife, however, and was disgusted with the dishonesty which he saw around him. "I say," he declares, "without any desire to speak evil of the rulers of the people, I found a great deal of corruption in our Legislature, and I found that almost every measure had to be carried by a corrupt bargain and sale which should cause every honest man to blush for his country."

He was full of a quaint humor, which seemed to burst out from every line of his features, and twinkle merrily in his bright eyes. Often in the midst of his most exciting revivals he could not resist the desire to fasten his dry jokes upon one of his converts. No man loved a joke better, or was quicker to make a good use of it. He was traveling one day on his circuit, and stopped for the night at a cabin in which he found a man and woman. Suspecting that all was not right, he questioned the woman, and drew from her the confession that the man was her lover. Her husband, she said, was away, and would not return for two days, and she had received this man in his absence.

CARTWRIGHT CALLING UP THE DEVIL

Cartwright then began to remonstrate with the guilty pair upon their conduct, and while he was speaking to them the husband's voice was heard in the yard. In an agony of terror the woman implored Cartwright to assist her in getting her lover out of the way, and our preacher, upon receiving from each a solemn promise of reformation, agreed to do so. There was standing by the chimney a large barrel of raw cotton, and as there was no time to get the man out of the house, Cartwright put him into the barrel and piled the cotton over him.

The husband entered, and Cartwright soon engaged him in conversation. The man said he had often heard of Peter Cartwright, and that it was the common opinion in that part of the country that among his other wonderful gifts our preacher had the power to call up the devil.

"That 's the easiest thing in the world to do," said Cartwright. "Would you like to see it?"

The man hesitated for awhile, and then expressed his readiness to witness the performance.

"Very well," said Cartwright; "take your stand by your wife, and do n't move or speak. I 'll let the door open to give him a chance to get out, or he may carry the roof away."

So saying, he opened the door, and, taking a handful of cotton, held it in the fire and lighted it. Then plunging it into the barrel of raw cotton, he shouted lustily, "Devil, rise!" In an instant the barrel was wrapped in flames, and the lover, in utter dismay, leaped out and rushed from the house. The husband was greatly terrified, and ever afterward avowed himself a believer in Cartwright's intimacy with "Old Scratch," for had he not had ocular proof of it?

Riding out of Springfield one day, he saw a wagon some distance ahead of him containing a young lady and two young men. As he came near them they recognized him, though he was totally unacquainted with them, and began to sing camp-meeting hymns with great animation. In a little while the young lady began to shout, and said, "Glory to God! Glory to God!" and the driver cried out, "Amen! Glory to God!"

"My first impressions," says Mr. Cartwright, "were, that they had been across the Sangamon River to a camp meeting that I knew was in progress there, and had obtained religion, and were happy. As I drew a little nearer, the young lady began to sing and shout again. The young man who was not driving fell down, and cried aloud for mercy; the other two, shouting at the top of their voices, cried out, 'Glory to God! another sinner down.' Then they fell to exhorting the young man that was down, saying, 'Pray on, brother; pray on, brother; you'll soon get religion.' Presently up jumped the young man that was down, and shouted aloud, saying, 'God has blessed my soul. Halleluiah! halleluiah! Glory to God!'"

Thinking that these were genuine penitents, Cartwright rode rapidly toward them, intending to join in their rejoicings; but as he drew near them, he detected certain unmistakable evidences that they were shamming religious fervor merely for the purpose of annoying him. He then endeavored to get rid of them, but as they were all going the same direction, the party in the wagon managed to remain near him by driving fast when he tried to pass them, and falling back when he drew up to let them go ahead. "I thought," says our preacher, "I would ride up and horsewhip both of these young men; and if the woman had not been in company, I think I should have done so; but I forebore."

In a little while the road plunged into a troublesome morass. Around the worst part of this swamp wound a bridle path, by which Mr. Cartwright determined to escape his tormentors, who would be compelled to take the road straight through the swamp. The party in the wagon saw his object, and forgetting prudence in their eagerness to keep up with him, whipped their horses violently. The horses bounded off at full speed, and the wagon was whirled through the swamp at a furious rate. When nearly across, one of the wheels struck a large stump, and over went the wagon. "Fearing it would turn entirely over and catch them under," says Mr. Cartwright, "the two young men took a leap into the mud, and when they lighted they sunk up to the middle. The young lady was dressed in white, and as the wagon went over, she sprang as far as she could, and lighted on all fours; her hands sunk into the mud up to her arm-pits, her mouth and the whole of her face immersed in the muddy water, and she certainly would have strangled if the young men had not relieved her. As they helped her up and out, I had wheeled my horse to see the fun. I rode up to the edge of the mud, stopped my horse, reared in my stirrups, and shouted, at the top of my voice, 'Glory to God! Glory to God! Halleluiah! another sinner down! Glory to God! Halleluiah! Glory! Halleluiah!'

"If ever mortals felt mean, these youngsters did; and well they might, for they had carried on all this sport to make light of religion, and to insult a minister, a total stranger to them. When I became tired of shouting over them, I said to them:

"'Now, you poor, dirty, mean sinners, take this as a just judgment of God upon you for your meanness, and repent of your dreadful wickedness; and let this be the last time that you attempt to insult a preacher; for if you repeat your abominable sport and persecutions, the next time God will serve you worse, and the devil will get you.'

"They felt so badly that they never uttered one word of reply."

Our preacher was determined that his work should be recognized, and as he and his fellow traveling ministers had done a good work on the frontier, he was in no humor to relish the accounts of the religious condition of the West, which the missionaries from the East spread through the older States in their letters home. "They would come," says he, "with a tolerable education, and a smattering knowledge of the old Calvinistic system of theology. They were generally tolerably well furnished with old manuscript sermons, that had been preached, or written, perhaps a hundred years before. Some of these sermons they had memorized, but in general they read them to the people. This way of reading sermons was out of fashion altogether in this Western world, and of course they produced no effect among the people. The great mass of our Western people wanted a preacher that could mount a stump or a block, or stand in the bed of a wagon, and, without note or manuscript, quote, expound, and apply the word of God to the hearts and consciences of the people. The result of the efforts of these Eastern missionaries was not very flattering; and although the Methodist preachers were in reality the pioneer heralds of the cross through the entire West, and although they had raised up numerous societies every five miles, and notwithstanding we had hundreds of traveling and local preachers, accredited and useful ministers of the Lord Jesus Christ, yet these newly-fledged missionaries would write back to the old States hardly any thing else but wailings and lamentations over the moral wastes and destitute condition of the West."

The indignation of our preacher was fully shared by the people of the West, who considered themselves as good Christians as their New England brethren, and the people of Quincy called a meeting, irrespective of denomination, and pledged themselves to give Peter Cartwright one thousand dollars per annum, and pay his traveling expenses, if he would "go as a missionary to the New England States, and enlighten them on this and other subjects, of which they were profoundly ignorant." Circumstances beyond his control prevented his acceptance of this offer. "How gladly and willingly would I have undertaken this labor of love," says he, "and gloried in enlightening them down East, that they might keep their home-manufactured clergy at home, or give them some honorable employ, better suited to their genius than that of reading old musty and worm-eaten sermons."

Our preacher did visit New England in 1852, not as a missionary, however, but as a delegate to the General Conference which met that year in Boston. His fame had preceded him, and he was one of the marked men of that body. Every one had heard some quaint story of his devotion to his cause, his fearlessness, or his eccentricities, and crowds came out to hear him preach. But our backwoods preacher was ill at ease. The magnificence of the city, and the prim decorum of the Boston churches, subdued him, and he could not preach with the fire and freedom of the frontier log chapel. The crowds that came to hear him were disappointed, and more than once they told him so.

"Is this Peter Cartwright, from Illinois, the old Western pioneer?" they asked him once.

He answered them, "I am the very man."

"Well," said several of them, "brother, we are much disappointed; you have fallen very much under our expectations, we expected to hear a much greater sermon than that you preached to-day."

It was a regular Bostonian greeting, and it not only mortified and disheartened the old pioneer, but it irritated him. "I tell you," says he, "they roused me, and provoked what little religious patience I had. . . . I left them abruptly, and in very gloomy mood retreated to my lodgings, but took very little rest in sleep that night. I constantly asked myself this question: Is it so, that I can not preach? or what is the matter? I underwent a tremendous crucifixion in feeling."

The result was that he came to the conclusion that he *could* preach, and that the people of Boston had not "sense enough to know a good sermon when they heard it." A little later old Father Taylor, that good genius of the Boston Bethel, a man after Cartwright's own heart, came to him and asked him to preach for him, and this, after hesitating, our preacher agreed to do, upon the condition that he should be allowed to conduct the services in regular Western style.

"In the meantime," says he, "I had learned from different sources that the grand reason of my falling under the expectations of the congregations I had addressed was substantially this: almost all those curious incidents that had gained currency throughout the country concerning Methodist preachers had been located on me, and that when the congregations came to hear me, they expected little else but a bundle of eccentricities and singularities, and when they did not realize according to their anticipations, they were disappointed, and that this was the reason they were disappointed. So on the Sabbath, when I came to the Bethel, we had a good congregation, and after telling them that Brother Taylor had given me the liberty to preach to them after the Western fashion, I took my text, and after a few common-place remarks, I commenced giving them some Western anecdotes, which had a thrilling effect on the congregation, and excited them immoderately—I can not say religiously; but I thought if ever I saw animal excitement, it was then and there. This broke the charm. During my stay, after this, I could pass anywhere for Peter Cartwright, the old pioneer of the West. I am not sure that after this I fell under the expectations of my congregations among them."

Sixty-seven years have passed away since the old pioneer began his preaching, and still he labors in the cause of his Master. Age has not subdued his zeal or dimmed his eye. His labors make up the history of the West. Where he first reared his humble log-hut, smiling farms and tasteful mansions cover the fertile prairies of the West; cities and towns mark the spot where his backwoods camp-meetings drew thousands into the kingdom of God; the iron horse dashes with the speed of the wind over the boundless prairies which he first crossed with only the points of timber for his guides; the floating palaces of the West plow the streams over which he swam his horse or was ferried in a bark canoe; and stately churches stand where the little log chapels of the infant West were built by him. It is a long and a noble life upon which he looks back, the only survivor of the heroic band who started with him to carry Christ into the Western wilds. He has outlived all his father's family, every member of the class he joined in 1800, every member of the Western Conference of 1804, save perhaps one or two, every member of the General Conference of 1816, the first to which he was elected, all his early bishops, every presiding elder under whom he ever ministered, and thousands of those whom he brought into the Church. "I have lived too long," he said, in a recent lecture; but we take issue with him. He has not lived too long whose declining age is cheered by the glorious fruition of the seed sown in his youth and prime. Few, indeed, are given so great a privilege; and few, having lived so long and worked so hard, can say with him, that during such a long and exposed career, "I have never been overtaken in any scandalous sin, though my shortcomings and imperfections have been without number." A man who can boast such a record, though he be as poor in purse as this simple-hearted backwoods preacher, has earned a Great Fortune indeed, for his treasure is one that can not be taken from him, since it is laid up in Heaven, "where neither moth nor rust doth corrupt, and where thieves do not break through nor steal."

IX.

AUTHORS.

CHAPTER XXXIII.

HENRY W. LONGFELLOW.

WHEREVER the English language is spoken, the name of HENRY WADSWORTH LONGFELLOW has become a household word, and there is scarcely a library, however humble, but can boast a well-worn volume of his tender songs,—songs that

> "Have power to quiet
> The restless pulse of care,
> And come like the benediction
> That follows after prayer."

He was born in the city of Portland, Maine, on the 27th of February, 1807, and was the son of the Hon. Stephen Longfellow, a distinguished lawyer of that city. The house in which he was born was a square wooden structure, built many years before, and large and roomy. It stood upon the outskirts of the town, on the edge of the sea, and was separated from the water only by a wide street. From its windows the dreamy boy, who grew up within its walls, could look out upon the dark, mysterious ocean, and, lying awake in his little bed in the long winter nights, he could listen to its sorrowful roar as it broke heavily upon the shore. That he was keenly alive to the fascination of such close intimacy with the ocean, we have abundant proof in his writings.

He was carefully educated in the best schools of the city, and at the age of fourteen entered Bowdoin College, at Brunswick, where he graduated in his nineteenth year. He was an industrious student, and stood high in his classes. He gave brilliant promise of his future eminence as a poet in several productions written during his college days, which were published in a Boston journal called the "United States Literary Gazette." Among these were the "Hymn of the Moravian Nuns," "The Spirit of Poetry," "Woods in Winter," and "Sunrise on the Hills."

Upon leaving college he entered his father's office, in Portland, with the half-formed design of studying law, which he never carried into execution, as more congenial employment soon presented itself to him. In 1826 he was appointed Professor of Modern Languages and Literature at Bowdoin College, with the privilege of passing several years abroad for observation and study. He accepted the appointment with unaffected delight, and promptly went abroad. He passed his first year in France, studying the language and literature of that country, and the next in Spain, engaged in similar pursuits. Italy claimed his third year, and Germany his fourth. He traveled extensively, and made many pleasant acquaintances among the most gifted men and women of the Old World. Returning home toward the close of 1829, he entered upon the active duties of his professorship, and for five years held this position, winning considerable distinction by his academic labors.

During his professorship our poet married, and the years

that followed were very happy and very quiet. The life he led at Bowdoin was peaceful, and in a measure retired, giving him ample opportunity for study and for laying the sure foundation of his future fame. During this period of his life he contributed articles to the "North American Review," and extended his acquaintance gradually among the literary men of New England. He was fond of recalling the experiences of his life abroad, and being unwilling that they should be lost from his memory, determined to transmit them to paper before they faded quite away. These sketches he finally concluded to give to the public, under the title of "Outre Mer; or, Sketches from Beyond Sea." They appeared originally in numbers, and were published by Samuel Colman, of Portland. They were well received, and brought Professor Longfellow into notice in New England. Soon afterward he published a translation of the ode upon "Coplas de Manrique," by his son, Don Jose Manrique, which won him additional credit. His fugitive poems had become very popular, and had made his name familiar to his countrymen, but as yet he had not collected them in book form.

In 1835, on the resignation of Mr. George Ticknor, he was appointed Professor of Modern Languages and Belles Lettres in Harvard College, and accepted the position. Before entering upon his duties, however, he resolved to devote two years more to foreign travel and improvement, and accordingly sailed for Europe the second time. Before leaving America, however, he committed the publication of "Outre Mer" to the Harpers, of New York, who issued it complete in two volumes in 1835. Its popularity was very decided. Soon after reaching Europe, Mr. Longfellow was visited with a sad bereavement in the loss of his wife, who died at Rotterdam. He devoted this European visit to the northern part of the continent, Denmark, Sweden, Germany, and Holland, and to England, and spent some time in Paris. Returning in the autumn of 1836, he entered upon his duties at Harvard, and made his home in Cambridge. He continued his contributions to the "North American Review," and a number of fugitive pieces flowed from his pen into print.

In the summer of 1837 he went to live in the house which has ever since been his home. This is the old Craigie House, in Cambridge, famous in our history as having been the head-quarters of Washington during the siege of Boston. It had been built by Colonel John Vassal about the middle of the last century, and had finally passed into the hands of Andrew Craigie, "Apothecary General to the Northern Provincial Army" of the infant Republic. Craigie had ruined himself by his lavish hospitality, and his widow, a stately old lady, and worthy in every respect of a better fate, had been reduced to the necessity of letting rooms and parting with the greater portion of the lands which had belonged to the mansion. Mr. Longfellow had been attracted to the house not only by its winning and home-like appearance, but by its historical associations. Mrs. Craigie had decided at the time to let no more rooms, but the young professor's gentle, winning manner conquered her determination, and she not only received him into the old mansion, but installed him in the south-east corner room in the second story, which had been used by Washington as his bed-chamber.

It was just the home for our poet. Its windows looked out upon one of the loveliest landscapes in New England, with the bright river winding through the broad meadow beyond the house, and the blue Milton Hills dotting the distant background. The bright verdure of New England sparkled on every side, and the stately old elms that stood guard by the house screened it from the prying eyes of the passers on the public road. The whole place was hallowed to its new inmate by the memories of the brave soldiers, wise statesmen, and brilliant ladies who had graced its heroic age, and of which the stately hostess was the last and worthy representative. The old house was as serene and still as the dearest lover of quiet could wish. The mistress lived quite apart from her lodger, and left him to follow the bent of his own fancies; and rare fancies they were, for it was of them that some of his best works were born in this upper chamber. Here he wrote "Hyperion," in 1838 and 1839. Its publication, which was undertaken by John Owen, the University publisher in Cambridge, marked an era in American literature. Every body read the book, and every body talked of it. It was a poem in prose, and none the less the work of a poet because professedly "a romance of travel." The young read it with enthusiasm, and it sent hundreds to follow Paul Flemming's footsteps in the distant Fatherland, where the "romance of travel" became their guide-book. The merchant and the lawyer, the journalist and the mechanic, reading its pages, found that the stern realities of life had not withered up all the romance of their natures, and under its fascinations they became boys again. Even Horace Greeley, that most practical and unimaginative of men, became rapturous over it. It was a great success, and established the poet's fame beyond all question, and since then its popularity has never waned.

In 1840, he published the "Voices of the Night," which he had heard sounding to him in his haunted chamber. This was his first volume, and its popularity was even greater than that of "Hyperion," although some of the poems had appeared before, in the "Knickerbocker Magazine." In 1841, he published his volume of "Ballads, and Other Poems," which but added to his fame, and the next year bade the old house under the elms a temporary adieu, and sailed for Europe, where he passed the summer on the Rhine. On the voyage home, he composed his "Poems on Slavery," and soon after his return wrote "The Spanish Student," a drama, "which smells of the utmost South, and was a strange blossoming for the garden of Thomas Tracy."

In 1843 the stately mistress of the old house died, and Professor Longfellow bought the homestead of Andrew Craigie, with eight acres of land, including the meadow, which sloped down to the pretty river. There have been very few prouder or happier moments in his life than that in which he first felt that the old house under the elms was his. Yet he must have missed the stately old lady who first had admitted him to a place in it, and whom he had grown to love as a dear friend. She seemed so thoroughly a part and parcel of the place, that he must have missed the rustle of her heavy silks along the wide and echoing halls, and have listened some time for the sound of her old-fashioned spinet in the huge drawing-room below, and, entering the room where she was wont to receive her guests, he must have missed her from the old window where she was accustomed to sit, with the open book in her lap, and her eyes fixed on the far-off sky, thinking, no doubt, of the days when in her royal beauty she moved a queen through the brilliant home of Andrew Craigie. A part of the veneration which he felt for the old house had settled upon its ancient mistress, and the poet doubtless felt that the completeness of the quaint old establishment was broken up when she passed away.

In 1846, Mr. Longfellow published "The Belfry of Bruges, and Other Poems;" in 1847, "Evangeline" (by many considered his greatest work); in 1850, "Seaside and Fireside;" in 1851, "The Golden Legend;" in 1855, "The Song of Hiawatha;" in 1858, "The Courtship of Miles Standish;" in 1863, "The Wayside Inn;" in 1866, "The Flower de Luce;" in 1867, his translation of the "Divina Commedia," in three volumes; and in 1868, "The New England Tragedies." Besides these, he published, in 1845, a work on the "Poets and Poetry of Europe," and in 1849, "Kavanagh," a novel.

Mr. Longfellow continued to discharge his duties in the University for seventeen years, winning fresh laurels every year, and in 1854 resigned his position, and was succeeded in it by Mr. James Russell Lowell. He now devoted himself exclusively to his profession, the income from his writings affording him a handsome maintenance. In 1855, "The Song of Hiawatha" was given to the public, and its appearance may be styled an event in the literary history of the world. It was not only original in the story it told, and in the method of treatment, but the rhythm was new. It was emphatically an American poem, and was received by the people with delight. It met with an immense sale, and greatly increased its author's popularity with his countrymen.

In 1861 a terrible affliction befell the poet in his family. He had married, some years after the death of his first wife, a lady whose many virtues had endeared her to all who knew her. She was standing by the open fire in the sitting-room, one day in the winter of 1861, when her clothing took fire, and before her husband, summoned by her cries, could extinguish the flames, she was terribly burned. Her injuries were internal, and she soon afterwards died.

In 1868, Mr. Longfellow again visited Europe, and remained abroad more than a year. His reception by all classes of the people of the Old World was eminently gratifying to his countrymen. This welcome, so genuine and heartfelt, was due, however, to the genius of the man, and not to his nationality.

He had overstepped the bounds of country, and had made himself the poet of the English-speaking race. A man of vast learning and varied acquirements, thoroughly versed in the ways of the world, he is still as simple and unaffected in thought and ways as when he listened to and wondered at the dashing of the wild waves on the shore in his boyhood's home. A most gifted and accomplished artist, he has been faithful to nature in all things. Earnest and aspiring himself, he has given to his poems the ring of a true manhood. There is nothing bitter, nothing sarcastic in his writings. He views all things with a loving eye, and it is the exquisite tenderness of his sympathy with his fellow-men that has enabled him to find his way so readily to their hearts. Without seeking to represent the intensity of passion, he deals with the fresh, simple emotions of the human soul, and in his simplicity lies his power. He touches a chord that finds an echo in every heart, and his poems have a humanity in them that is irresistible. We admire the "grand old masters," but shrink abashed from their sublime measures. Longfellow is so human, he understands us so well, that we turn instinctively to his simple, tender songs for comfort in sorrow, or for the greater perfection of our happiness.

Perhaps I can not better illustrate the power of his simplicity than by the following quotations:

There is no flock, however watched and tended,
But one dead lamb is there!
There is no fireside, howsoe'er defended,
But has one vacant chair!

The air is full of farewell to the dying,
And mournings for the dead;
The heart of Rachel, for her children crying,
Will not be comforted.

Let us be patient! These severe afflictions
Not from the ground arise,
But oftentimes celestial benedictions
Assume this dark disguise.

We see but dimly through the mists and vapors,
Amid these earthly damps;
What seem to us but sad funereal tapers,
May be heaven's distant lamps.

There is no death! What seems so is transition;
This life of mortal breath
Is but a suburb of the life elysian,
Whose portal we call Death.

She is not dead—the child of our affection—
But gone unto that school
Where she no longer needs our poor protection,
And Christ himself doth rule.

In that great cloister's stillness and seclusion,
By guardian angels led,
Safe from temptation, safe from sin's pollution,
She lives, whom we call dead.

Day after day we think what she is doing
In those bright realms of air;
Year after year, her tender steps pursuing,
Behold her grow more fair.

Thus do we walk with her, and keep unbroken
The bond which nature gives,
Thinking that our remembrance, though unspoken,
May reach her where she lives.

Not as a child shall we again behold her;
For when with raptures wild

In our embraces we again enfold her,
  She will not be a child—

But a fair maiden, in her Father's mansion,
  Clothed with celestial grace,
And beautiful with all the soul's expansion
  Shall we behold her face.

And though at times impetuous with emotion,
  And anguish long suppressed,
The swelling heart heaves, moaning like the ocean,
  That can not be at rest—

We will be patient, and assuage the feeling
  We can not wholly stay;
By silence sanctifying, not concealing,
  The grief that must have way.

FROM THE GOLDEN LEGEND.

SCENE.—*The Chamber of* GOTTLIEB *and* URSULA.—*Midnight.*—ELSIE *standing by their bedside weeping.*

GOTTLIEB. The wind is roaring; the rushing rain
Is loud upon the roof and window-pane,
As if the wild Huntsman of Rodenstein,
Boding evil to me and mine,
Were abroad to-night with his ghostly train!
In the brief lulls of the tempest wild,
The dogs howl in the yard; and hark!
Some one is sobbing in the dark,
Here in the chamber.

ELSIE. It is I.

URSULA. Elsie! What ails thee, my poor child?

ELSIE. I am disturbed and much distressed,
In thinking our dear Prince must die;
I can not close my eyes, nor rest.

GOTTLIEB. What wouldst thou? In the Power Divine
His healing lies, not in our own;
It is in the hand of God alone.

ELSIE. Nay, He has put it into mine,
And into my heart.

GOTTLIEB. Thy words are wild.

URSULA. What dost thou mean? my child! my child!

ELSIE. That for our dear Prince Henry's sake
I will myself the offering make,
And give my life to purchase his.

URSULA. Am I still dreaming, or awake?
Thou speakest carelessly of death,
And yet thou knowest not what it is.

ELSIE. 'T is the cessation of our breath.
Silent and motionless we lie;
And no one knoweth more than this.
I saw our little Gertrude die;
She left off breathing, and no more
I smoothed the pillow beneath her head.
She was more beautiful than before.
Like violets faded were her eyes;
By this we knew that she was dead.
Through the open window looked the skies
Into the chamber where she lay,
And the wind was like the sound of wings,
As if angels came to bear her away.
Ah! when I saw and felt these things,
I found it difficult to stay;
I longed to die, as she had died,
And go forth with her, side by side.
The saints are dead, the martyrs dead,
And Mary, and our Lord; and I
Would follow in humility
The way by them illumined.

URSULA. My child! my child! thou must not die.
ELSIE. Why should I live? Do I not know
The life of woman is full of woe?
Toiling on, and on, and on,
With breaking heart, and tearful eyes,
And silent lips, and in the soul
The secret longings that arise,
Which this world never satisfies!
Some more, some less, but of the whole
Not one quite happy; no, not one!
URSULA. It is the malediction of Eve!
ELSIE. In place of it, let me receive
The benediction of Mary, then.
GOTTLIEB. Ah, woe is me! Ah, woe is me!
Most wretched am I among men.
URSULA. Alas! that I should live to see
Thy death, beloved, and to stand
Above thy grave! Ah, woe the day!
ELSIE. Thou wilt not see it. I shall lie
Beneath the flowers of another land;
For at Salerno, far away
Over the mountains, over the sea,
It is appointed me to die!
And it will seem no more to thee
Than if at the village on market day
I should a little longer stay
Than I am used.
URSULA. Even as thou sayest!
And how my heart beats when thou stayest!
I can not rest until my sight
Is satisfied with seeing thee.
What, then, if thou wert dead?
GOTTLIEB. Ah me,
Of our old eyes thou art the light!
The joy of our old hearts art thou!
And wilt thou die?
URSULA. Not now! not now!

ELSIE. Christ died for me, and shall not I
Be willing for my Prince to die?
You both are silent; you can not speak.
This said I, at our Saviour's feast,
After confession, to the priest,
And even he made no reply.
Does he not warn us all to seek
The happier, better land on high,
Where flowers immortal never wither;
And could he forbid me to go thither?

GOTTLIEB. In God's own time, my heart's delight!
When He shall call thee, not before!

ELSIE. I heard Him call. When Christ ascended
Triumphantly, from star to star,
He left the gates of heaven ajar.
I had a vision in the night,
And saw Him standing at the door
Of His Father's mansion, vast and splendid,
And beckoning to me from afar.
I can not stay!

GOTTLIEB. She speaks almost
As if it were the Holy Ghost
Spake through her lips and in her stead!
What if this were of God?

URSULA. Ah, then
Gainsay it dare we not.

GOTTLIEB. Amen!

The old house under the elms is still the poet's home, and dear, as such, to every lover of poetry. It is a stately building, of the style of more than one hundred years ago, and is a very home-like place in its general appearance. Entering by the main door-way, which is in the center of the house, the visitor finds himself in a wide, old-fashioned hall, with doors opening upon it on either hand.

"The library of the poet is the long north-eastern room

upon the lower floor," said a writer seventeen years ago. "It opens upon the garden, which retains still the quaint devices of an antique design, harmonious with the house. The room is surrounded with handsome book-cases, and one stands also between two Corinthian columns at one end, which imparts dignity and richness to the apartment. A little table by the northern window, looking upon the garden, is the usual seat of the poet. A bust or two, the rich carvings of the cases, the spaciousness of the room, a leopard-skin lying upon the floor, and a few shelves of strictly literary curiosities, reveal not only the haunt of the elegant scholar and poet, but the favorite resort of the family circle. But the northern gloom of a New England winter is intolerant of this serene delight, this beautiful domesticity, and urges the inmates to the smaller room in front of the house, communicating with the library, and the study of General Washington. This is still distinctively 'the study,' as the rear room is 'the library.' Books are here, and all the graceful detail of an elegant household, and upon the walls hang crayon portraits of Emerson, Sumner, and Hawthorne.

"Emerging into the hall, the eyes of the enamored visitor fall upon the massive old staircase, with the clock upon the landing. Directly he hears a singing in his mind:

"'Somewhat back from the village street,
Stands the old-fashioned country-seat;
Across its antique portico
Tall poplar trees their shadows throw,
And from its station in the hall
An ancient time-piece says to all,
"Forever—never!
Never—forever!"'

But he does not see the particular clock of the poem, which stood upon another staircase, in another quaint old mansion,—

although the verse belongs truly to all old clocks in all old country-seats, just as the 'Village Blacksmith' and his smithy are not alone the stalwart man and dingy shop under the 'spreading chestnut-tree' which the Professor daily passes on his way to his college duties, but belong wherever a smithy stands. Through the meadows in front flows the placid Charles."

So calmly flows the poet's life. The old house has other charms for him now besides those with which his fancy invested it when he first set foot within its walls, for here have come to him the joys and sorrows of his maturer life, and here, "when the evening lamps are lighted," come to him the memories of the loved and lost, who but wait for him in the better land. Here, too, cluster the memories of those noble achievements in his glorious career which have made him now and for all times the people's poet. Others, as the years go by, will woo us with their lays, but none so winningly and tenderly as this our greatest master. There was but one David in Israel, and when he passed away no other filled his place.

CHAPTER XXXIV.

NATHANIEL HAWTHORNE.

THERE came to the old town of Salem, in the Province of Massachusetts, in the early part of the seventeenth century, an English family named Hawthorne—Puritans, like all the other inhabitants of that growing town. They proved their fidelity to Puritan principles by entering readily into all the superstitions of the day, and became noted for the zeal with which they persecuted the Quakers and hung the witches. The head of the family was a sea captain, and for many generations the men of the family followed the same avocation, "a gray-haired shipmaster, in each generation, retiring from the quarter-deck to the homestead, while a boy of fourteen took the hereditary place before the mast, confronting the salt spray and the gale, which had blustered against his sire and grandsire."

Of such a race came NATHANIEL HAWTHORNE, who was born at Salem, on the 4th, of July, 1804. His father was a sea captain, and died of the yellow fever at Havana, in 1810. His mother was a woman of great beauty and extreme sensibility, and it was from her that Nathaniel derived the peculiarities of character which distinguished him through life. The death of her husband filled her with the profoundest grief, and though the violence of her sorrow subsided with time, she

NATHANIEL HAWTHORNE.

passed the remainder of her life in strict seclusion, constantly grieving in her quiet way for her departed lord. Her son grew up to the age of ten in this sad and lonely house, passing four of the most susceptible years of his life in the society of his sorrowful mother. He became a shy boy, and avoided the company of other children. His health began to suffer from the effects of such an unnatural state of affairs, and at the age of ten he was sent to live on a farm belonging to the family, on the shore of Sebago Lake, in Maine. The active out-door life which he led here entirely restored his health, which was naturally strong and vigorous; here, also, he acquired that fondness for boating which was his chief amusement in after years. Returning to Salem, he completed his studies in the preparatory schools, after which he entered Bowdoin College, where he graduated in 1825, at the age of twenty-one. He was a classmate of Longfellow and George B. Cheever, with whom he was only slightly acquainted; and he formed a warm and lasting friendship with Franklin Pierce, who was in the class next before him. Longfellow has preserved a recollection of him in his student days as "a shy youth in a bright-buttoned coat, flitting across the college grounds."

After graduating, he went back to his home in Salem, where he resided for many years, leading a life of seclusion, which he passed in meditation and study. His strong literary inclination now vented itself in efforts which were in every way characteristic of the man. He wrote numerous wild tales, the most of which he burned, but a few of which found their way into the newspapers and magazines of the country. They were full of a wild gloominess, and were told with a power which proved that their author was no ordinary man. Few, however, dreamed that they were the work of the pale recluse of Salem, for he led a life of such strict seclusion that not even the members of his own family could tell with certainty what he did. His days were passed in his chamber, and at night he took long walks alone on the sea-shore or into the woods. He shunned all society, and seemed to find companionship only in nature, and in the creations of his fancy. Yet he was not a morose or unhappy man. On the contrary, he seems to have been a very happy one, full of generous and kindly feelings, and finding only a strange pleasure where others would have found bitterness and cynicism. Like the melancholy Jacques, he might have said of his pensive shyness, "It is a melancholy of mine own, compounded of many simples, extracted from many objects; . . . which, by often rumination, wraps me in a most humorous sadness."

In 1837 he collected his published tales, which, while they had charmed a few cultivated readers, had scarcely been noticed by the masses, and published them in a volume to which he gave the name of "Twice-Told Tales." The book was well received by the public, but its circulation was limited, although Mr. Longfellow warmly welcomed it in the "North American Review," and pronounced it the "work of a man of genius and a true poet." Still it was neglected by the masses, and Hawthorne says himself that he was at that time "the most unknown author in America." There was more truth in this assertion than lies on its face, for the people who read the book supposed that the name of Nathaniel Hawthorne was merely a pseudonyme, and declared that as Nathaniel was evidently selected by the author because of the fondness of the old-time Puritans for Scripture names, so Hawthorne was chosen by him as expressive of one of the most beautiful features of the New England landscape. The merits of the book were too genuine, however, for it to lack admirers, and the small class which greeted its first appearance with delight gradually increased, and finally the demand for the book became so great that in 1842 Hawthorne ventured to issue a second series of "Twice-Told Tales," the most of which had appeared in the "Democratic Review," then edited by his friend O'Sullivan. Of these volumes, Mr. George William Curtis says: "They are full of glancing wit, of tender satire, of exquisite natural description, of subtle and strange analysis of human life, darkly passionate and weird."

In 1838 George Bancroft was Collector of the Port of Boston, and, having been deeply impressed with the genius displayed in the first volume of "Twice-Told Tales," sought out Hawthorne and offered him a place in the Boston Custom-House as weigher and gauger. Hawthorne accepted the position, and at once entered upon his duties. Leaving his solitude and the weird phantoms that had been his companions for so long, he passed immediately into the busy bustle of the great New England port. It was a new world to him, and one which interested him keenly. His duties kept him constantly on the wharf, and threw him daily into contact with captains and sailors from all parts of the world. He became a great favorite with these, and they told him many a strange story of their adventures and of the sights they had seen in distant lands, and these, as they were listened to by him, took each a distinctive form in his imagination. Not less interesting to him were the men among whom his duties threw him. They were more to him than the ordinary beings that thronged the streets of the great city, for they had been victorious in many a battle with the mighty deep, and they had looked on the wondrous sights of the far-off lands of the Old World. Queer people they were, too, each a Captain Cuttle or a Dirk Hatteraick in himself, and many an hour did the dreamy writer spend with them, apparently listening to their rude stories, but really making keen studies of the men themselves.

He discharged his duties faithfully in the Boston Custom-House, performing each with an exactness thoroughly characteristic of him, until 1841, when the accession of President Harrison to power obliged him to withdraw to make way for a Whig.

From the Custom-house he went to live at Brook Farm as one of that singular community of dreamers and enthusiasts which was to inaugurate a new era of men and things in the world, but which came at last to a most inglorious termination. He was thrown into intimate association here with many who have since become prominent in our literary history, and for some of them conceived a warm attachment. He took his share of the farm labors, to which he was very partial, but remained at the community less than a year, and then returned to Boston. In his "Blithedale Romance" he has given us a picture of the life at Brook Farm, though he denies having sketched his characters from his old associates at that place.

In 1843 he married Miss Peabody, a member of a family distinguished for their various achievements in the world of letters. Besides being an artist of no mean pretensions, she was herself a writer of considerable promise, though her writings had no other critics than her family and most intimate friends. "Her husband shrank from seeing her name in the reviews, and in this, as in all other things, his feelings were sacredly respected by her." She was a lady of rare strength of character and great beauty, and was in every respect a fitting wife for such a man. The twenty-one years of their wedded life make up a period of unbroken happiness to both. Hawthorne was very proud of his wife, and in his quiet way never failed to show it. Their friends often remarked that the wedded life of this happy pair seemed like one long courtship.

Hawthorne took his bride on his wedding-day to a new home. He had rented the old parsonage adjoining the battle-field of Concord, from whose windows the pastor of those heroic days had watched his congregation fight the British in his yard. It was a gloomy and partially dilapidated "Old Manse," and doubtless Hawthorne had chosen it because of its quaint aspect. He has himself drawn the picture of it, and given us an exquisite collection of "Mosses" from it. It lay back from the main road, and was approached by an avenue of ancient black-ash trees, whose deep shade added much to the quiet appearance of "the gray front of the old parsonage." It was just the home for him, and here passed three of the happiest years of his life. Here he wrote his "Mosses from an Old Manse," and here his first child was born.

The life he led at Concord was very secluded. He avoided the society of the village people, who sought in vain to penetrate his retirement and satisfy their curiosity concerning him. But they were disappointed. He lived on in his deep seclusion, happy in having his wife and child with him, but caring for no other society. During the day he remained in his study, which overlooked the old battle-field, or, passing down the lawn at the back of the house to the river, spent the afternoon in rowing on the pretty stream. At night he would take long walks, or row up the river to the bridge by which the British crossed the stream, and enjoy his favorite luxury—a bath. The village people were full of curiosity to know something about him, for he was absolutely unknown to them; and any one who understands what the curiosity of a New England villager is can readily imagine the feelings with which the people of Concord regarded their mysterious neighbor. They were never satisfied, however, for Hawthorne shrank from prying eyes with indescribable horror. He kept his ways, and compelled them to let him alone. He could easily avoid the town in his walks or his rides upon the river, and he was rarely seen passing through the streets unless compelled to do so by matters which needed his attention in Concord.

Yet the "Old Manse" was not without its guests. Hawthorne was a man of many friends, and these came often to see him. They were men after his own heart, and among them were Emerson, Ellery, Channing, Thoreau, Whittier, Longfellow, and George William Curtis. The last-named has left us this pleasant picture of our author in the midst of his friends:

"During Hawthorne's first year's residence in Concord, I had driven up with some friends to an esthetic tea at Mr. Emerson's. It was in the winter, and a great wood-fire blazed upon the hospitable hearth. There were various men and women of note assembled, and I, who listened attentively to all the fine things that were said, was for some time scarcely aware of a man who sat upon the edge of the circle, a little withdrawn, his head slightly thrown forward upon his breast, and his bright eyes clearly burning under his black brow. As I drifted down the stream of talk, this person who sat silent as a shadow looked to me as Webster might have looked had he been a poet—a kind of poetic Webster. He rose and walked to the window, and stood quietly there for a long time, watching the dead white landscape. No appeal was made to him, nobody looked after him, the conversation flowed as steadily on as it every one understood that his silence was to be respected. It was the same thing at table. In vain the silent man imbibed esthetic tea. Whatever fancies it inspired did not flower at his lips. But there was a light in his eye which assured me that nothing was lost. So supreme was his silence, that it presently engrossed me to the exclusion of every thing else. There was brilliant discourse, but this silence was much more poetic and fascinating. Fine things were said by the philosophers, but much finer things were implied by the dumbness of this gentleman with heavy brows and black hair. When presently he rose and went, Emerson, with the 'slow, wise smile' that breaks over his face, like day over the sky, said: 'Hawthorne rides well his horse of the night.'" Later on, after he knew him better, Curtis added to this picture, "His own sympathy was so broad and sure, that, although nothing had been said for hours, his companion knew that not a thing had escaped his eye, nor had a single pulse of beauty in the day, or scene, or society failed to thrill his heart. In this way his silence was most social. Every thing seemed to have been said."

At the close of the third year of his residence at Concord, Hawthorne was obliged to give up the "Old Manse," as the owner was coming back to occupy it. The Democrats had now come into power again under Mr. Polk, and Mr. Bancroft was in the Cabinet. The Secretary, mindful of his friend, procured him the post of Surveyor of the Port of Salem, and Hawthorne went with his little family to live in his native town. The Salem Custom-house was a sleepy sort of a place, and his duties were merely nominal. He had an abundance of leisure time, and from that leisure was born his masterpiece, "The Scarlet Letter"—the most powerful romance which ever flowed from an American author's pen. It was published in 1850, and in the preface to it the reader will find an excellent description of the author's life in Salem. He held his position in that place for three years, and then the election of General Taylor obliged him to retire.

He withdrew to the Berkshire Hills, and took a house in

the town of Lenox. It was a little red cottage, and was situated on the shore of a diminutive lake called the Stockbridge Bowl. He was now the most famous novelist in America, and had thousands of admirers in the Old World. His "Scarlet Letter" had won him fame, and had brought his earlier works more prominently before the public than ever.

During his residence at Lenox, he wrote "The House of the Seven Gables," which was published in Boston in 1851. It was not less successful than the "Scarlet Letter," though it was not so finished a piece of workmanship.

Yet, though so famous, he was not freed from the trials incident to the first years of an author's life. Mr. Tuckerman says of him at this time: "He had the fortitude and pride, as well as the sensitiveness and delicacy, of true and high genius. Not even his nearest country neighbors knew aught of his meager larder or brave economies. He never complained, even when editors were dilatory in their remuneration and friends forgetful of their promises. When the poor author had the money, he would buy a beefsteak for dinner; when he had not, he would make a meal of chestnuts and potatoes. He had the self-control and the probity to fulfill that essential condition of self-respect, alike for those who subsist by brain work and those who inherit fortunes—he always lived within his income; and it was only by a kind of pious fraud that a trio of his oldest friends occasionally managed to pay his rent." His friend and publisher, Mr. Ticknor, "received and invested the surplus earnings of the absentee author when American Consul at Liverpool, and had obtained from Hawthorne a promise on the eve of his departure for his post, that he would send him all he could spare from his official income, to be carefully nursed into a competence for his family. Never was better advice given or wiser service performed by publisher to author. The investments thus made became the means of comfort to the returned writer in the maturity of his years and his fame."

In 1852 he returned to Concord and purchased a small house which had once been the residence of the philosopher Alcott. Here he made his permanent home and gathered about him his household treasures. In the Presidential campaign of 1852, his friend Franklin Pierce was the candidate of the Democracy, and Hawthorne wrote a short biography of him which was used by the Democrats as a campaign document. It was a labor of love, for the friendship that had been begun between these two men in their college days had never been broken, and though naturally averse to every thing that savored of politics, our author made this contribution to the cause of his friend with all the heartiness of his nature. Pierce was profoundly touched by this unexpected aid, for he knew how utterly Hawthorne detested political strife, and when seated in the Presidential chair he showed his appreciation of it by offering his friend the consulship to Liverpool—one of the most lucrative offices within the gift of the executive. Hawthorne broke up his home in Concord and sailed for Liverpool in 1853, and remained there until 1857, when he resigned his consulship and traveled on the continent with his family, residing for some time in Italy for the benefit of his health. His European residence had the effect of drawing him out of his shyness and reserve to a certain extent, and during the closing years of his life he was more social with the persons about him than he had ever been. After his return he went back to Concord, where he enlarged and beautified his old home, intending to remain there for the balance of his life. He wrote the "Marble Faun" and "Our Old Home" just after his return from Europe. The former was suggested by his residence in Italy, and the latter was a collection of English sketches and reminiscences.

The war between the two sections of the country affected him very deeply. It seemed to him a terrible tragedy, to which there could be no end but utter ruin for the country. He sympathized strongly with the cause of the Union, but at the same time his heart bled at the sufferings of the people of the south. It was one long agony to him, and only those who knew him intimately can understand how much he suffered during this unhappy period.

Mr. Moncure D. Conway gives the following reminiscence of him about this time: "I passed a night under the same roof with him at the house of Mr. Fields, his publisher. He seemed much dejected. Mr. Fields had invited a little company, but, after the first arrivals, Hawthorne made his escape to his room, from which he did not emerge until the next morning at breakfast time. He then came in with the amusing look of a naughty child, and pleaded that he had become lost the night before in Defoe's ghost stories until it was too late to make his appearance in the company. He must, I should think, have been contemplating some phantasmal production at that time, for I remember his asking me many questions about the ghost-beliefs of the negroes, among whom I had passed my early life."

Besides the works already mentioned, Hawthorne was the author of "True Stories from History and Biography" and "The Wonder Book for Boys and Girls," both published in 1851; "The Snow Image and Other Twice-Told Tales," published in 1852; and "Tanglewood Tales," published in 1853, all juveniles. At the time of his death he was engaged upon a novel which was to have been published in the "Atlantic Monthly," but it was left incomplete.

In the spring of 1864 his friend and publisher, Mr. W. D. Ticknor, of Boston, seeing how feeble Hawthorne had become, asked him to accompany him on an excursion, hoping that a rapid change of scene and cheerful company would benefit him. They set out in April, and went direct to Philadelphia. Upon arriving at the hotel, Mr. Ticknor was suddenly taken very ill, and died on the 10th of April in his friend's arms. Hawthorne was profoundly shocked by this melancholy occurrence, and it is said that he never fully recovered from its effects upon him. His melancholy seemed to deepen, and though his friends exerted themselves to cheer him, he seemed to feel that his end was near. Ex-President Pierce, hoping to rouse him from his sad thoughts, induced him to accompany him on an excursion to the White Mountains. Upon reaching Plymouth, which they took on their route, they stopped at the Pemigewasset House for the night. Mr. Pierce was so full of anxiety concerning his friend, who had been quieter and sadder than usual that day, that he went softly into his room in the middle of the night to look after him. Hawthorne was lying very still, and seemed to be sleeping sweetly. Mr. Pierce stole softly away, fearing to disturb him. In the morning he went back to rouse his friend, and found him lying lifeless in the position he had noticed in the night. He had been dead some hours.

The announcement of Hawthorne's death caused a feeling of deep sadness in all parts of the Union. His body was taken to Concord for burial, and was accompanied to the grave by the best and most gifted of the land, to each of whom he had endeared himself in life.

X.

ACTORS.

CHAPTER XXXV.

EDWIN BOOTH.

THERE are many persons who remember the elder Booth, the "Great Booth," as he was called, in his palmy days, when the bare announcement of his name was sufficient to cram our old-fashioned theaters from pit to dome. He was sublime in the stormy passions which he delineated, and never failed to draw down from the gods of the gallery the uproarious yells with which they testify their approval; even the more dignified occupants of the boxes found themselves breaking into outbursts of applause which they were powerless to restrain. He was a favorite with all classes, and a deserved one, and the lovers of the drama looked forward with genuine regret to the period when he should be no longer with them. They felt that the glories of the stage would pass away with him. It was in vain that they were told that he had sons destined to the same profession. They shook their heads, and said it was impossible that the mantle of the great tragedian should rest upon any of his sons, for it was then, as now, a popular belief that great men never have great children. How very much these good people were mistaken we will see in the progress of this chapter.

One of these sons was destined in the course of time to eclipse the fame won by his father, and to endear himself to the American people as a more finished, if less stormy, actor. This was EDWIN BOOTH. He was born on his father's farm near Baltimore, Maryland, in 1833, and after receiving a good common-school education, began his training for the stage. The elder Booth was quick to see that his boy had inherited his genius, and he took great pains to develop the growing powers of the lad, and to incline them toward those paths which his experience had taught him were the surest roads to success. He took him with him on his starring engagements, and kept him about him so constantly that the boy may be said to have grown up on the stage from his infancy. He was enthusiastically devoted to his father, and it was his delight to stand at the wings and watch the great tragedian in his personations, and the thunders of applause which proclaimed some fresh triumph were sweeter to the boy, perhaps, than to the man.

In 1849, at the age of sixteen, he made his first appearance on the stage as Tyrrell, in "Richard III.," and gave great satisfaction by his rendition of the character. From this time he continued to appear at various places with his father, and in 1851 won his first great success in the city of New York. His father was playing an engagement at the Chatham Theater at the time, and was announced for Richard III., which was his masterpiece. When the hour for performance came, he was too ill to appear. The manager was in despair, for the house was filled with a large audience, who were impatient for the appearance of the humpbacked king. In this emergency Edwin Booth offered to take his father's place, and the manager, pleased with the novelty of the proposal, accepted it. Young Booth was but eighteen years old, and had not even studied the part, and it was a perilous thing to venture before an audience in a role in which one of his name had won such great fame. But he was confident of his own powers, and he had so often hung with delight upon his father's rendition of the part, that he needed but a hasty reference to the book to perfect him in the text. He won a decided triumph, and the public promptly acknowledged that he gave promise of being an unusually fine actor.

In 1852 Mr. Booth went to California, and engaged for the "utility business." He spent two years in careful and patient study in the humbler walks of his profession, learning its details, and doing much of the drudgery essential to a thorough knowledge of his art. In 1854, he went to Australia, and played a successful engagement there, stopping on his way at several of the Pacific islands. On his return, he played an engagement, with marked success, at the Sandwich Islands, and then went back to California.

In 1857 he returned to New York, and, on the 4th of May, appeared at Burton's Theater, in the character of Richard III. A writer who witnessed his performance on that occasion thus speaks of him: "The company was not strong in tragedy; the young actor came without reputation; the season was late. But he conquered his place. His Richard was intellectual, brilliant, rapid, handsome, picturesque, villainous. But the villainy was servant to the ambition—not master of it, as a coarse player makes it. The action was original; the dress was perfect—the smirched gauntlets and flung-on mantle of the scheming, busy duke, the splendid vestments of the anointed king, the glittering armor of the monarch in the field. His clear beauty, his wonderful voice—which he had not learned to use—his grace, his fine artistic sense, made all triumphs seem possible to this young man. Evidently there was great power in the new actor—power untrained, vigor ill directed. But what was plainest to be seen, was the nervous, impulsive temperament, which would leave him no rest save in achievement. He might come back to us a robustious, periwig-pated fellow, the delight and wonder of the galleries. He might come back the thorough artist, great in repose as in action. But it was clear enough that what he was then in Richard, in Richelieu, in Sir Edward Mortimer, he would never be again."

He followed this appearance by a general tour through the country, and returned to New York in 1858, where he won fresh laurels. In 1860 he reappeared at Burton's Theater, then called the Winter Garden, and added Hamlet to his role. He had improved greatly during the time that had elapsed since his last appearance at this theater, and had gained very much in power and artistic finish. The most critical audiences in the country received him with delight, crowded his houses, and hailed his efforts with thunders of applause. This season silenced all the critics, and placed him among the great actors of the American stage. He bore his honors modestly, and though he was proud of the triumphs he had won, they did not satisfy him. There were still greater successes to be achieved before the highest honors of his profession could be his, and it was upon these that his eye was fixed from the first. The applause which greeted him in every city in which he appeared only served to stimulate him to fresh exertions.

In the summer of 1861, he visited England, and played an engagement at the Haymarket Theater in London, where he was favorably received by the British playgoers. At the close of this engagement, he spent a year on the continent, in travel and in the study of his profession. He also made careful studies of the scenes of the great historic dramas of the English stage, both in England and on the continent, and of the dresses and other appointments needed for them. By thoroughly familiarizing himself with these details, he has been able to produce his plays with entire fidelity to history.

Returning once more to New York, he appeared at the Winter Garden, in the winter of 1863–64, in a series of Shakespearean revivals. He played Hamlet for over one hundred nights, and followed it during that season and the next with "Merchant of Venice" and "Othello" (in the latter playing the parts of Othello and Iago on alternate nights). During the same seasons he appeared also in "Richelieu," "Ruy Blas," "The Fool's Revenge," and "Don Cæsar de Bazan." These performances were extended into the season of 1866–67, when they were suddenly cut short by the total destruction of the Winter Garden Theater by fire on the night of the 23d of March, 1867. In this fire Mr. Booth lost his entire wardrobe, including many relics of his father, Kemble, and Mrs. Siddons.

The destruction of a theater has seldom drawn forth a more universal expression of regret than that which poured in upon Mr. Booth from all parts of the country. It was feared that the loss of his valuable wardrobe would be irremediable, as indeed it was in a certain sense. All over the Union a general wish was expressed that the great actor should have a new theater in some of our large cities, and one which should be worthy of his genius. Mr. Booth had chosen the city of New York for his permanent home, and after the destruction of the Winter Garden Theater began to arrange his plans for the erection of a new building of his own, which he was resolved should be the most magnificent and the best appointed theater in the world. The site chosen was the south-eastern corner of the Sixth Avenue and Twenty-third Street in New York, and in the summer of 1867 the work of clearing away the old buildings and digging the foundations of the new theater was begun. It was carried forward steadily, and the building was completed and opened to the public in January, 1869.

It is in the Rennaissance style of architecture, and stands seventy feet high from the sidewalk to the main cornice, crowning which is a Mansard roof of twenty-four feet. "The theater proper fronts one hundred and forty-nine feet on Twenty-third Street, and is divided into three parts, so combined as to form an almost perfect whole, with arched entrances at either extremity on the side, for the admission of the public, and on the other for another entrance, and the use of the actors and those employed in the house. On either side of these main entrances are broad and lofty windows; and above them, forming a part of the second story, are niches for statues, surrounded by coupled columns resting on finely sculptured pedestals. The central or main niche is flanked on either side by quaintly contrived blank windows; and between the columns, at the depth of the recesses, are simple pilasters sustaining the elliptic arches, which serve to top and span the niches, the latter to be occupied by statues of the great creators and interpreters of the drama in every age and country. The finest Concord granite, from the best quarries in New Hampshire, is the material used in the entire façade, as well as in the Sixth Avenue side. . . The glittering granite mass, exquisitely poised, adorned with rich and appropriate carving, statuary, columns, pilasters, and arches, and capped by the springing French roof, fringed with its shapely balustrades, offers an imposing and majestic aspect, and forms one of the architectural jewels of the city."

In its internal arrangements the theater is in keeping with its external magnificence. Entering through a sumptuous vestibule, the visitor passes into the magnificent auditorium, which is in itself a rare piece of decorative art. The seats are admirably arranged, each one commanding a view of the stage. The floor is richly carpeted, and the seats are luxuriously upholstered. Three elegant light galleries rise above the parquet. The walls and ceiling are exquisitely frescoed, and ornamented with bas reliefs in plaster. The proscenium is beautifully frescoed and carved, and is adorned with busts of the elder Booth and the proprietor of the theater; and in the sides before the curtain are arranged six sumptuous private boxes. The curtain is a beautiful landscape. The decoration of the house is not done in the rough scenic style so common in the most of the theaters of the country, but is the perfection of frescoe painting, and is capable of bearing the closest examination. The stage is very large, and slopes gradually from the rear to the footlights. The orchestra pen is sunk below the level of the stage, so that the heads of the musicians do not cut off the view of the audience. The dressing of the stage is novel. The side scenes or wings, instead of being placed at right angles to the spectator as in most theaters, are so arranged that the scene appears to extend to the right and left as well as to the rear. In this way the spectator is saved the annoyance of often looking through the wings, a defect which in most theaters completely dispels the illusion of the play. The scenery here is not set by hand, but is moved by machinery, and with such regularity and precision that these changes have very much the effect of "dissolving views." The scenes themselves are the works of highly educated artists, and never degenerate into the rough daubs with which most playgoers are familiar. The building is fire-proof, and is warmed and ventilated in a peculiar manner. The great central chandelier and the lights around the cornice of the auditorium are lighted by electricity.

The plays presented here are superbly put on the stage. The scenery is strictly accurate when meant to represent some historic locality, and is the finest to be found in America. Perhaps the grandest stage picture ever given to an audience was the grave-yard scene in "Hamlet," which "held the boards" for over one hundred nights last winter. The dresses, equipments, and general "make up" of the actors are in keeping with the scenery. Even the minutest detail is carefully attended to. Nothing is so unimportant as to be overlooked in this establishment.

It is Mr. Booth's custom to open the season with engagements of other distinguished actors, and to follow them himself about the beginning of the winter, and to continue his performances until the approach of spring, when he again gives way to others. When he is performing, it is impossible to procure a seat after the rising of the curtain. Every available place is filled, and thousands come from all parts of the country to see him. Sometimes it is necessary to secure seats a week in advance.

Mr. Booth is still a young man, being now thirty-seven years old. In person he is over the medium height, and is well built. His hair is black and is worn long, and his dark eyes are large and dreamy. His face is that of a poet, strikingly handsome, with an expression of mingled sweetness and sadness playing over it. He wears neither beard nor moustache. He dresses simply and without ornament, and is grave and retiring in his demeanor. He is exceedingly amiable in disposition, and is the center of a large circle of devoted friends. He has been married twice, and has one child, a daughter, by his first wife. He is a man of irreproachable life, and in every thing a high-toned gentleman, and it is the high character he bears not less than his genius that has enabled him to do such honor to his profession. He is very wealthy, and is in a fair way to become a millionaire.

As an actor Mr. Booth is without an equal. His impersonations are marked by rare genius and by the most careful study. His Hamlet is perhaps his most finished part, as his Richelieu is the most popular with the masses. It has been said that his Hamlet is not Shakespeare's Hamlet, and this may be true; but it is so exquisite, so perfect, that whether it be the conception of Shakespeare or Edwin Booth, it is the most powerful, the most life-like counterfeit of "the melancholy Dane" ever seen on any stage, and leaves nothing to be desired. His personation of the grim old cardinal, whose decrepit body is alone sustained by his indomitable will, is masterly, and we see before us, not Edwin Booth, the actor of to-day, but the crafty, unscrupulous, witty, determined prime minister of France, who bends kings and princes to his will. It is absolutely life-like, and to those who have seen the portraits of the old cardinal in the museums of France, the accuracy with which Booth has counterfeited the personal appearance of Richelieu is positively startling. The plays are so superbly set upon the stage that we lose sight of the little space they occupy, and seem to be gazing upon a real world. His Richard has such a strong humanity in it, that it more than half vindicates the humpbacked tyrant's memory, and the death scene of this play, as given by Booth, is simply appalling.

It is in vain, however, that we select special characters or attempt descriptions of them. No one can truly understand Edwin Booth's acting without seeing it. He has studied his heroes so profoundly, analyzed their characters so subtly, and entered so heartily into sympathy with them, that he has become able, by the aid of his wonderful genius, to entirely discard his own personality, and assume theirs at will.

Mr. Booth has steadily risen in power and finish as an actor, for his labors have been unceasing. Great as his triumphs have been, he does not regard himself as freed from the necessity of study. His studies have become more intelligent than in former years, but not the less faithful. He has the true artist's aspiration after the rarest perfection in his art, though to those of us without the charmed circle it is difficult to see how he can excel his present excellence. Yet that he does so we have undoubted proof, for we see him rising higher in the admiration and esteem of the world every year, and each year we gather fresh laurels to twine around his brows.

He has steadily educated his audiences, and has elevated the standard of his art among his countrymen. He has shown them what fine acting really is, and has taught them to enjoy it. He has kept them true to the legitimate drama, and has done more than any other man to rescue the American stage from the insignificance with which it was threatened. It speaks volumes for him as an actor and a manager, that when New York seemed wholly given up to ballet, burlesque, and opera bouffe, he was able to make the almost forgotten masterpieces of Shakespeare the most popular and most profitable dramatic ventures of the year.

JEFFERSON, AS RIP VAN WINKLE.

CHAPTER XXXVI.

JOSEPH JEFFERSON.

THE subject of this sketch is one of a race of actors. His great-grandfather was a contemporary of some of the brightest ornaments of the English stage, and was himself a famous actor and the intimate friend of Garrick, Sam Foote, and Barr. He was a man of amiable and winning disposition, and was strikingly handsome in person. He occupies a prominent place in the history of the English stage, and is said to have been, socially, one of the most brilliant men of his day. He died in 1807. In 1795 his son came to America. Of him, Dunlap, in his "History of the American Stage," says, referring to him, in February, 1797: "He was then a youth, but even then an artist. Of a small and light figure, well formed, with a singular physiognomy, a nose perfectly Grecian, and blue eyes full of laughter, he had the faculty of exciting mirth to as great a degree by power of feature, although handsome, as any ugly-featured low comedian ever seen." F. C. Wemyss has said of him at a later day: "Mr. Joseph Jefferson was an actor formed in Nature's merriest mood—a genuine son of Momus. There was a vein of rich humor running through all he did, which forced you to laugh despite of yourself. He discarded grimace as unworthy of him, although no actor ever possessed a greater command over the muscles of his own face, or the faces of his audience, compelling you to laugh or cry at his pleasure. His excellent personation of old men acquired for him, before he had reached the meridian of life, the title of 'Old Jefferson.' The astonishment of strangers at seeing a good-looking young man pointed out on the street as Old Jefferson, whom they had seen the night previous at the theater tottering apparently on the verge of existence, was the greatest compliment that could be paid to the talent of the actor. His versatility was astonishing--light comedy, old men, pantomime, low comedy, and occasionally juvenile tragedy. Educated in the very best school for acquiring knowledge in his profession, . . Jefferson was an adept in all the trickery of the stage, which, when it suited his purpose, he could turn to excellent account. . . In his social relations, he was what a gentleman should be—a kind husband, an affectionate father, a warm friend, and a truly honest man." The second Jefferson enjoyed a brilliant career of thirty-six years in this country, and died in 1832, during an engagement at the theater at Harrisburg, which was then managed by his son. This son, named Joseph, after his father, was born in Philadelphia in 1804, and died at the age of thirty-eight. He was not so famous as an actor as his father or grandfather, but like them passed his life on the stage. He had a decided talent for painting, and was partially educated as an artist, but he never accomplished any thing with his pencil. He was a man of most amiable disposition, and was possessed of scores of warm and devoted friends; but he was a poor business manager, and was always more or less involved in pecuniary troubles. He married Mrs. Burke, the famous vocalist, and mother of Burke, the comedian.

To this couple, in the city of Philadelphia, was born the Joseph Jefferson of to-day, on the 20th of February, 1829.

This boy was literally brought up on the stage, as he made his first appearance upon the boards in a combat scene at the Park Theater in New York, when he was but three years old. He soon after went with his parents to the West. Olive Logan says of him, at this period of his life, "While they were both still children, he and my sister Eliza used to sing little comic duets together on the stage of various western towns."

He received as good a common-school education as the rapid manner in which he was moved about from place to place would permit, and was carefully trained in the profession of an actor, to which he was destined by his parents, and to which he was drawn by the bent of his genius. He appeared in public frequently during his boyhood, but his first appearance as a man was at Chanfrau's National Theater, in 1849. He met with fair success, and from that time devoted himself entirely and carefully to his profession. He began at the bottom of the ladder of fame, and gradually worked his way up to his present high position. Playing engagements in various minor theaters of the United States, he at length secured a position as low comedian at Niblo's Garden in New York, where he won golden opinions from the critical audiences of the metropolis. In 1857, he closed a most successful engagement as low comedian at the theater in Richmond, Virginia, and with that engagement ended his career as a stock actor. He had by careful and patient study rendered himself capable of assuming the highest place in his profession, and these studies, joined to his native genius, had made him famous throughout the country as the best low comedian of the day.

Feeling that he had now a right to the honors of a "star" in his profession, and urged by the public to assume the position to which his genius entitled him, he began a series of engagements thoughout the Union, in which he more than fulfilled the expectations of his friends. He was received with delight wherever he went, and at once became the most popular of American comedians.

About a year or two later, he left the United States and made a voyage to Australia, through which country he traveled, playing at the principal towns. He was extremely successful. His genial, sunny character won him hosts of friends among the people of that far-off land, and his great genius as an actor made him as famous there as he had been in his own country. Australia was then a sort of theatrical El Dorado. The prices paid for admission to the theaters were very high, and the sums offered to distinguished stars in order to attract them thither were immense. Mr. Jefferson reaped a fair share of this golden harvest, and at the close of his Australian engagements found himself the possessor of a handsome sum. It was this which formed the basis of his large fortune; for, unlike his father, he is a man of excellent business capacity, and understands how to care for the rewards of his labors, so that they shall be a certain protection to him in his old age, and an assistance to those whom he shall leave behind him.

Returning to the United States, Mr. Jefferson appeared with increased success in the leading cities of the Northern and Western States. His principal success at this time was won in the character of Asa Trenchard, in the play of "Our American Cousin." His personation of the rough, eccentric, but true-hearted Yankee was regarded as one of the finest pieces of acting ever witnessed on the American stage, and drew crowded houses wherever he went. His range of characters included the most refined comedy and the broadest farce, but each delineation bore evidence of close and careful study, and was marked by great originality and delicacy. There was in his performances a freshness, a distinctiveness, and, above all, an entire freedom from any thing coarse or offensive, which charmed his audiences from the first. One of his critics has well said of him: "As Caleb Plummer he unites in another way the full appreciation of mingled humor and pathos—the greatest delicacy and affection with rags and homely speech. As Old Phil Stapleton he is the patriarch of the village and the incarnation of content. As Asa Trenchard he is the diamond in the rough, combining shrewdness with simplicity, and elevating instead of degrading the Yankee character. As Dr. Ollapod, and Dr. Pangloss, and Tobias Shortcut, he has won laurels that would make him a comedian of the first rank. His Bob Acres is a picture. There is almost as much to look at as in his Rip Van Winkle. There is nearly the same amount of genius, art, experience, and intelligence in its personation. Hazlitt says that the author has overdone the part, and adds that 'it calls for a great effort of animal spirits and a peculiar aptitude of genius to go through with it;' Mr. Jefferson has so much of the latter that he can—and to a great extent does—dispense with the former requisite. His quiet undercurrent of humor subserves the same purpose in the *role* of Bob Acres that it does in other characters. It is full of points, so judiciously chosen, so thoroughly apt, so naturally made and so characteristically preserved, that the part with Jefferson is a great one. The man of the 'oath referential, or sentimental swearing,' makes the entire scope of the part an 'echo to the sense.' Even in so poor a farce as that of 'A Regular Fix,' Mr. Jefferson makes the eccentricities of Hugh de Brass immensely funny. The same style is preserved in every character, but with an application that gives to each a separate being."

After a season of great success in this country Mr. Jefferson decided to visit England. He appeared at the Adelphi Theater, in London, and at once became as popular as he had been at home. His Asa Trenchard, in "Our American Cousin," was received by the English with delight; but his greatest triumphs were won in Boucicault's version of "Rip Van Winkle," which he has since immortalized. This play was first produced at the Adelphi, where it enjoyed an uninterrupted run of nearly two hundred nights.

Returning to the United States in the autumn of 1867, Mr. Jefferson appeared at the Olympic Theater, in New York, in the play of "Rip Van Winkle." Since then he has traveled extensively throughout the United States, and has devoted himself exclusively to the character of Rip Van Winkle; so exclusively, indeed, that many persons are ignorant of his great merits in other roles. By adopting this as his specialty, he has rendered himself so perfect in it that he has almost made the improvident, light-hearted Rip a living creature. A writer in a popular periodical draws the following graphic sketch of his performance of this character:

If there is something especially charming in the ideal of Rip Van Winkle that Irving has drawn, there is something even more human, sympathetic and attractive in the character reproduced by Jefferson. A smile that reflects the generous impulses of the man; a face that is the mirror of character; great, luminous eyes that are rich wells of expression; a grace that is statuesque without being studied; an inherent laziness which commands the respect of no one, but a gentle nature that wins the affections of all; poor as he is honest, jolly as he is poor, unfortunate as he is jolly, yet possessed of a spontaneity of nature that springs up and flows along like a rivulet after a rain; the man who can not forget the faults of the character which Jefferson pictures, nor feel like taking good-natured young Rip Van Winkle by the hand and offering a support to tottering old Rip Van Winkle, must have become hardened to all natural as well as artistic influences. It is scarcely necessary to enter into the details of Mr. Jefferson's acting of the Dutch Tam

O'Shanter. Notwithstanding the fact that the performance is made up of admirable points that might be enumerated and described, the picture is complete as a whole and in its connections. Always before the public; preserving the interest during two acts of the play after a telling climax; sustaining the realities of his character in a scene of old superstition, and in which no one speaks but himself,—the impersonation requires a greater evenness of merit and dramatic effect than any other that could have been chosen. Rip Van Winkle is imbued with the most marked individuality, and the identity is so conscientiously preserved that nothing is overlooked or neglected. Mr. Jefferson's analysis penetrates even into the minutiæ of the part, but there is a perfect unity in the conception and its embodiment. Strong and irresistible in its emotion, and sly and insinuating in its humor, Mr. Jefferson's Rip Van Winkle is marked by great vigor, as well as by an almost pre-Raphaelite finish.

The bibulous Rip is always present by the ever-recurring and favorite toast of "Here's your goot healt' and your family's, and may dey live long and prosper." The meditative and philosophic Rip is signaled by the abstract "Ja," which sometimes means *yes*, and sometimes means *no*. The shrewd and clear-sighted Rip is marked by the interview with Derrick Van Beekman. The thoughtful and kind-hearted Rip makes his appearance in that sad consciousness of his uselessness and the little influence he exerts when he says to the children, talking of their future marriage: "I thought maybe you might want to ask me about it," which had never occurred to the children. The improvident Rip is discovered when Dame Van Winkle throws open the inn window-shutter, which contains the enormous score against her husband, and when Rip drinks from the bottle over the dame's shoulder as he promises to reform. The most popular and the most thriftless man in the village; the most intelligent and the least ambitious; the best-hearted and the most careless;—the numerous contrasts which the *role* presents demand versatility in design and delicacy in execution. They are worked out with a moderation and a suggestiveness that are much more natural than if they were presented more decidedly. The sympathy of Mr. Jefferson's creation is the greatest secret of its popularity. In spite of glaring faults, and almost a cruel disregard of the family's welfare, Rip Van Winkle has the audience with him from the very beginning. His ineffably sad but quiet realization of his desolate condition when his wife turns him out into the storm, leaves scarcely a dry eye in the theatre. His living in others and not in himself makes him feel the changes of his absence all the more keenly. His return after his twenty years' sleep is painful to witness; and when he asks, with such heart-rending yet subdued despair, "Are we so soon forgot when we are gone?" it is no wonder that sobs are heard throughout the house. His pleading with his child Meenie is not less affecting, and nothing could be more genuine in feeling. Yet all this emotion is attained in the most quiet and unobtrusive manner. Jefferson's sly humor crops out at all times, and sparkles through the veil of sadness that overhangs the later life of Rip Van Winkle. His wonder that his wife's "clapper" could ever be stopped is expressed in the same breath with his real sorrow at hearing of her death. "Then who the devil am I?" he asks with infinite wit just before he pulls away at the heartstrings of the audience in refusing the proffered assistance to his tottering steps. He has the rare faculty of bringing a smile to the lips and a tear to the eye at the same time. From the first picture, which presents young Rip Van Winkle leaning carelessly and easily upon the table as he drinks his schnapps, to the last picture of the decrepit but happy old man, surrounded by his family and dismissing the audience with his favorite toast, the character, in Mr. Jefferson's hands, endears itself to all, and adds another to the few real friendships which one may enjoy in this life.

Mr. Jefferson is a thoroughly American actor. Abandoning all sensational shams, he devotes himself to pure art. His highest triumphs have been won in the legitimate branches of his profession, and won by the force of his genius, aided only by the most careful study and an intelligent analysis of the parts assumed by him. He has the happy faculty of entering into perfect sympathy with his characters, and for the time being he is less the actor than the individual he personates. It is this that gives the sparkle to his eye, the ring to his laughter, and the exquisite feeling to his pathos; and feeling thus, he is quick to establish a sympathy between himself and his audience, so that he moves them at will, convulsing them with laughter at the sallies of the light-hearted Rip, or dissolving them in tears at the desolations of the lonely old man, so soon forgot after he has gone.

Mr. Jefferson has inherited from his father the genial, sunny disposition for which the latter was famous. He is an essentially cheerful man, and trouble glances lightly off from him. He is generous to a fault, and carries his purse in his hand. Misfortune never appeals to him in vain, and many are the good works he has done in the humbler walks of his own calling. He is enthusiastically devoted to his profession, and enjoys his acting quite as much as his auditors. In putting his pieces on the stage, he is lavish of expense, and whenever he can control this part of the performance, it leaves nothing to be desired. Some years ago he brought out "A Midsummer Night's Dream" at a Philadelphia theater, in a style of magnificence rarely witnessed on any stage. The scenery was exquisite, and was a collection of artistic gems. The success of the piece was very decided in Philadelphia, but when it was reproduced, with the same scenery and appointments, in a Western city, the public would scarcely go to see it, and the theater incurred a heavy loss in consequence. Jefferson's remark to the manager, when the failure became apparent, was characteristic: "It is all right," said he. "We have done our duty, and have made an artistic success of the piece. If the people will not come to see it, it is more their misfortune than ours."

He has inherited also from his father considerable talent as an artist, and sketches with decided merit, though he makes no pretensions to artistic skill. In his vacations, which he passes in the country, his sketch-book is his constant companion. He is a famous sportsman and fisherman, and in the summer is rarely to be found without his gun and rod. It is his delight to tramp over miles of country in search of game, or to sit quietly in some cozy nook, and, dropping his line into the water, pass the hours in reveries broken only by the exertion necessary to secure a finny prize.

Not long since his love of art led him to buy a panorama merely because he admired it. He put it in charge of an agent in whom he knew he could confide, and started it on a tour throughout the country. In a month or two he received a gloomy letter from the agent, telling him that the exhibition had failed to draw spectators, and that he despaired of its ever paying expenses. "Never mind," wrote Jefferson in reply, "it will be a gratification for those who do go to see it, and you may draw on me for what money you need." The losses on the panorama, however, were so great that Jefferson was compelled to abandon it.

Several years before the death of John Sefton, Jefferson paid him a visit at his home in Paradise Valley, during one of his summer rambles. Upon reaching Sefton's farm, he found the owner "with his breeches and coat sleeves both rolled up, and standing in the middle of a clear and shallow stream, where one could scarcely step without spoiling the sports of the brook trout, which sparkled through the crystal waters. Sefton stood in a crouching attitude, watching, with mingled disappointment and good humor, a little pig which the stream was carrying down its current, and which, pig-like, had slipped from the hands of its owner in its natural aversion to being washed. Jefferson, with the true instinct of an artist, dropped his fishing tackle and took his sketch-book to transfer the ludicrous scene to paper. Sefton appreciated the humor of the situation, and only objected when Jefferson began to fill in the background with a dilapidated old barn, at which the old gentleman demurred on account of its wretched appearance. The artist insisted that it was picturesque, however, and proceeded to put it down. Sefton had to submit; but he had his revenge, by writing back to New York that 'Jefferson is here, drawing the worst "houses" I ever saw.'"

In private life, Mr. Jefferson is a cultivated gentleman, and is possessed of numbers of warm and devoted friends. He has been married twice. The first Mrs. Jefferson was a Miss Lockyer, of New York, and by her he had two children, a son and a daughter. The former is about eighteen years of age, and is destined to his father's profession, in which he has already shown unusual promise. The present Mrs. Jefferson was a Miss Warren, and is a niece of the veteran actor, William Warren, of Boston. She was married to her husband early in 1868, and has never been an actress.

Mr. Jefferson is the possessor of a large fortune, acquired in the exercise of his profession, and being thus comfortably situated, is enabled to enjoy more rest from his labors than falls to the lot of most American actors. He resides in Orange County, New Jersey, about an hour's ride from New York, where he has a handsome country seat, which he has adorned with all the attractions that wealth and taste can command.

XI.

PHYSICIANS.

CHAPTER XXXVII.

BENJAMIN RUSH.

IT is not often that a man, however gifted, is capable of rising to eminence in two distinct branches of public life, especially in two so widely separated from each other as medicine and politics. The subject of this sketch was one of the few who have achieved such distinction.

BENJAMIN RUSH was born on Poquestion Creek, néar Philadelphia, on the 24th of December, 1745. He was carefully educated at the best common schools of his native county, and then entered Princeton College, where he graduated in 1760, at the age of fifteen. He decided, upon leaving Princeton, to adopt medicine as his vocation, and began his studies in Philadelphia. He gave nine years to preparing himself for his profession, and after completing his course in Philadelphia, sailed for Europe, where he continued his studies in Edinburgh, London, and Paris. He returned home in 1769, and began the practice of medicine in Philadelphia, and was at once elected Professor of Chemistry in the medical college of that city. He was successful in rapidly acquiring a large and lucrative practice, and experienced very few of the difficulties and trials which lie in the way of a young physician.

In 1770 he began his career as an author, and for many years his writings were numerous. He devoted himself chiefly to medical subjects, but history, philosophy, and politics, and even romance, frequently claimed his attention. He adopted the patriot cause at the outset of his career, and with his pen and voice constantly advocated resistance to the injustice of Great Britain. This drew upon him the attention of his fellow-citizens, and he was chosen to a seat in the Provincial Conference of Pennsylvania. In that body he introduced a resolution setting forth the necessity of a declaration of independence of the mother country. His resolution was referred to a committee, of which he was made the chairman, and this committee having reported affirmatively, the resolution was unanimously adopted by the Conference, and was communicated to the Continental Congress, then in session in Philadelphia, about the last of June, 1776. When it became evident that the Congress would declare the independence of the colonies, five members of the Pennsylvania delegation withdrew from that body. Their places were at once supplied by Rush and four others, and when the Declaration was finally adopted Benjamin Rush affixed his signature to it as a delegate from Pennsylvania.

In 1776 Dr. Rush was married to Miss Julia Stockton, daughter of Richard Stockton, of New Jersey, also a signer of the Declaration. In April, 1777, he was made Surgeon-General of the Continental army for the Middle Department, and in July, 1777, was made Physician-General. He devoted himself to his duties with energy and intelligence, and succeeded in placing the affairs of his department in as satisfactory a condition as the means at the command of the Congress would permit. He was not able, however, to arrange every thing as his judgment assured him was best, and was subjected to many annoyances and great inconvenience by the incompetence and mismanagement of other officials, whom he could not control. The management of the hospital supplies of the army was especially defective, and was the cause of much suffering to the troops. He made repeated efforts to effect a reform in this particular, but failing to accomplish any thing, and indignant at the wrongs inflicted upon the soldiers, he resigned his commission and retired to private life.

During his connection with the army, he had watched the course of affairs in his native State with the keenest interest, and in a series of four letters to the people of Pennsylvania, called their attention to the serious defects of their Constitution of 1776, the chief of which he declared to be the giving of the legislative power to one house only. His appeals had the effect of bringing about an entire change in the form of State government, which was subsequently accomplished by a general convention of the people. After the close of the war Dr. Rush was elected a member of the State Convention which ratified the Constitution of the United States, and distinguished himself in that body by his earnest and brilliant advocacy of that instrument. He was also a member of the convention which adopted a new State Constitution, embodying the reforms he had advised in the letters referred to, and labored hard to have incorporated in it his views respecting a penal code and a public school system, both of which features he ably advocated through the public press.

With this closed his public career, which, though brief, was brilliant, and raised him to a proud place among the fathers of the Republic.

Returning to Philadelphia after resigning his position in the army, he resumed the practice of medicine, and with increased success. His personal popularity and his great skill as a physician brought him all the employment he could desire, and he soon took his place at the head of the medical faculty of the country.

In 1785 he planned the Philadelphia Dispensary, the first institution of the kind in the United States, and to the close of his life remained its warm and energetic supporter. In 1789 he was made Professor of the Theory and Practice of Medicine in the Philadelphia Medical College, and when that institution was merged in the University, in 1791, he was elected to the chair of the Institute and Clinical Medicine. In 1797 he took the professorship of Clinical Practice also, as it was vacant, and was formally elected to it in 1805. These three professorships he held until the day of his death, discharging the duties of each with characteristic brilliancy and fidelity.

The great professional triumph of his life occurred in the year 1793. In that year the yellow fever broke out with great malignancy in Philadelphia, and raged violently for about one hundred days, from about the last of July until the first of November. Nothing seemed capable of checking it. The people fled in dismay from their homes, and the city seemed given over to desolation. In the terrible "hundred days," during which the fever prevailed, four thousand persons died, and the deaths occurred so rapidly that it was frequently impossible to bury the bodies for several days. The physicians of the city, though they remained heroically at their posts, and labored indefatigably in their exertions to stay the plague, were powerless against it, and several of them were taken sick and died. Few had any hope of checking the fever, and every one looked forward with eagerness to the approach of the season of frosts, as the only means of saving those that remained in the stricken city.

At the outset of the disease, Dr. Rush had treated it in the same manner as that adopted by the medical faculty of the city; but the ill success which attended this course soon satisfied him that the treatment was wrong. He therefore undertook to subdue it by purging and bleeding the patient, and succeeded. The new practice met with the fiercest opposition from the other physicians, but Rush could triumphantly point to the fact that while their patients were dying his were getting well; and he continued to carry out his treatment with firmness and success. Dr. Ramsey, of South Carolina, estimates that Rush, by this treatment, saved not less than six thousand of his patients from death in the "hundred days." Nevertheless, the medical war went on with great bitterness, and the opposition to Rush became furious when he boldly declared that the fever was not an importation from abroad, as was popularly believed, but had been generated by the filthy condition of the city during the early part of the summer. Some time after the fever had subsided, a paper called "Peter Porcupine's Gazette," edited by William Cobbett, made a series of outrageous attacks upon Dr. Rush and his treatment of the fever. This exhausted the forbearance of the doctor, and he instituted a suit against Cobbett, in which he was successful, and secured a verdict of $5,000 damages against his defamer.

During the prevalence of the fever, Dr. Rush's labors were unceasing. He was constantly going his rounds, visiting the sick, attending sometimes over one hundred patients in a single day. He was called on at all hours of the day and night, and it may be said that he scarcely slept or enjoyed two hours, uninterrupted rest during the "hundred days."

For weeks he never sat down to his meals without being surrounded by dozens of patients, whose complaints he listened to and prescribed for as he ate. These were chiefly the poor, and at such times his house was literally thronged with them. He was a kind friend to them; rendering his services promptly and heartily, without the slightest wish to receive

PRESCRIBING AT THE BREAKFAST-TABLE.

pay in return for them; and during all this terrible summer he was to be seen ministering to these poor creatures in the foulest, most plague-stricken quarters of the city, shrinking from no danger, and deterred from his work of mercy by no thought of his own safety. He has left us the following picture of the city during this terrible summer:

The disease appeared in many parts of the town remote from the spot where it originated; although in every instance it was easily traced to it. This set the city in motion. The streets and roads leading from the city were crowded with families flying in every direction for safety, to the country. Business began to languish. Water Street, between Market and

Race Streets, became a desert. The poor were the first victims of the fever. From the sudden interruption of business, they suffered for a while from poverty as well as disease. A large and airy house at Bush-hill, about a mile from the city, was opened for their reception. This house, after it became the charge of a committee appointed by the citizens on the 14th of September, was regulated and governed with the order and cleanliness of an old and established hospital. An American and French physician had the exclusive medical care of it after the 22d of September.

The contagion, after the second week in September, spared no rank of citizens. Whole families were confined by it. There was a deficiency of nurses for the sick, and many of those who were employed were unqualified for their business. There was likewise a great deficiency of physicians, from the desertion of some and the sickness and death of others. At one time there were only three physicians able to do business out of their houses, and at this time there were probably not less than six thousand persons ill with the fever.

During the first three or four weeks of the prevalence of the disorder, I seldom went into a house the first time without meeting the parents or children of the sick in tears. Many wept aloud in my entry or parlor, who came to ask advice for their relations. Grief after a while descended below weeping, and I was much struck in observing that many persons submitted to the loss of relations and friends without shedding a tear, or manifesting any other of the common signs of grief.

A cheerful countenance was scarcely to be seen in the city for six weeks. I recollect once, on entering the house of a poor man, to have met a child of two years old that smiled in my face. I was strangely affected with this sight (so discordant to my feelings and the state of the city), before I recollected the age and ignorance of the child. I was confined the next day by an attack of the fever, and was sorry to hear, upon my recovery, that the father and mother of this little creature died a few days after my last visit to them.

The streets every-where discovered marks of the distress that pervaded the city. More than one-half the houses were shut up, although not more than one-third of the inhabitants had fled into the country. In walking, for many hundred yards, few persons were met, except such as were in quest of a physician, a nurse, a bleeder, or the men who buried the dead. The hearse alone kept up the remembrance of the noise of carriages or carts in the streets. Funeral processions were laid aside. A black man leading or driving a horse, with a corpse on a pair of chair-wheels, with now and then half a dozen relations or friends following at a distance from it, met the eye in most of the streets of the city, at every hour of the day, while the noise of the same wheels passing slowly over the pavements, kept alive anguish and fear in the sick and well, every hour of the night.

The population of Philadelphia at this time was but sixty thousand, and the reader will see that a loss of four thousand was a heavy percentage for so short a period.

Dr. Rush's skill and heroic conduct in his efforts to stay the ravages of the plague made him famous, not only in his own country, but throughout Europe, and during the latter part of his life he received most gratifying evidences of this fact. In 1805 the King of Prussia sent him a coronation medal, and the King of Spain tendered him his thanks for his replies to certain questions addressed to him concerning the causes and proper treatment of yellow fever. In 1807 the Queen of Etruria presented him with a gold medal as a mark of respect; and in 1811 the Emperor of Russia sent him a testimonial of his admiration of his medical character.

In 1799 he was made treasurer of the United States Mint, which position he held until his death.

Dr. Rush's writings were voluminous, and embraced a variety of subjects. His medical productions occupy a high place in the literature of the profession, and his political essays were one of the features of his day. He was a man of profound learning, and it is astonishing that one so constantly occupied with the duties of an engrossing profession should have found the time for such close and thorough general reading.

He was a sincere and earnest Christian, and held the Bible

in the highest veneration. He wrote an able defense of the use of it as a school-book, and for many years was vice-president of the Philadelphia Bible Society, which he helped to establish, and the constitution of which he drafted. He held skepticism and atheism in the deepest abhorrence, and in his own life affords a powerful refutation of the assertion one hears so often, that profound medical knowledge is apt to make men infidels.

He died in Philadelphia on the 19th of April, 1813, at the good old age of sixty-eight, leaving a son who was destined to render additional luster to his name by achieving the highest distinction as a statesman.

CHAPTER XXXVIII.

VALENTINE MOTT.

VALENTINE MOTT was born at Glen Cove, on Long Island, on the 20th of August, 1785. His father, Dr. Henry Mott, was an eminent practitioner in the city of New York, where he died in 1840, at the age of eighty-three. Valentine Mott was carefully educated by private tutors until he reached the age of nineteen, when he entered Columbia College, New York, as a medical student, and at the same time became a private medical pupil of his kinsman, Dr. Valentine Seaman. At the age of twenty-one he graduated with the degree of M. D.; but feeling that he had not acquired as good a medical education as the schools of the Old World could afford, he sailed for Europe in 1806, within a few weeks after his graduation at Columbia College. Proceeding to London, he was for more than a year a regular attendant upon St. Thomas', Bartholomew's, and Guy's hospitals, where he conducted his clinical studies under the direction of Abernethy, Sir Charles Bell, and Sir Astley Cooper. He chose Sir Astley Cooper as his private instructor, and became one of his favorite pupils; and also attended the lectures of Currie and Haighton. From London he went to Edinburgh, where he attended the lectures of Hope, Playfair, and Gregory, as well as the prelections of Dugald

Stewart. From Edinburgh he went to Paris, and completed his studies in the great hospitals of that city.

He gave evidence at an early day of his great surgical abilities. He was indeed a born surgeon, possessing in a remarkable degree that peculiar adaptation to this branch of his profession, without which no amount of study can make a great operator. While a student in the Old World, he performed leading operations with a skill and natural readiness which astonished his instructors as much as they delighted them. He was possessed of a firmness and dexterity of hand, a calm, cool brain, a quick, unfailing eye, a calmness of nerve, a strength of will, and a physical endurance which were Nature's gifts to him, and which rendered him a great surgeon even before he had received his diploma. He did not trust to these natural gifts alone, however, but applied himself to the theory of his profession with a determination and eagerness which nothing could daunt. He was an enthusiast in his studies, and soon became known as the most profoundly-learned *young* physician of his day. As he advanced in life, he maintained his reputation, keeping up his studies to the last. The great men under whom he studied abroad were delighted with him, and Sir Astley Cooper was loud in his praise. He exhibited so much skill as an operator that he was often called upon to perform operations which the professors would never have dreamed of intrusting to any one else, and he went through each trial of this kind with a readiness and precision which few even of his instructors excelled.

His reputation was unusually flattering to one who had not yet entered upon the practice of his profession, and upon his return to the United States, in 1809, he was met with an offer of the chair of surgery in Columbia College, his *alma mater*. He promptly accepted the position, and held it until 1813, when the medical department of Columbia College was merged in the College of Physicians and Surgeons. He was at once called to the same chair in the new college, and occupied it until 1826. In that year he resigned his place in the faculty, in consequence of a misunderstanding between the professors and the trustees of the college on the principles of college government. Withdrawing entirely from the school, he united with Drs. Hosack, Mitchell, Francis, and several others, in founding the Rutgers Medical College. This college, after a short career of four years, was compelled by the Legislature to discontinue its operations, in consequence of an alleged invalidity in its charter.

In 1830, Dr. Mott returned to the College of Physicians and Surgeons as Professor of Surgery, and in 1840 he became President of the Faculty and Professor of Surgery and Relative Anatomy in the new University Medical School. The science of Relative Anatomy is of the highest importance to the surgeon, and of this science Dr. Mott is generally regarded as the author. He held his position in the University for twenty years, and in 1860, after a period of fifty years spent in the active duties of his professorship, retired from the immediate discharge of them, and was made Professor Emeritus, in which capacity he occasionally lectured to the classes during each of the remaining years of his life.

As a professor and teacher of surgical science Dr. Mott won a brilliant reputation, and was considered one of the most thoroughly successful instructors in the Union. He had the power of winning the attention of his pupils at the opening of his lectures and of retaining it until the close. He made even the most difficult operations so clear and simple in his lectures that the dullest intellects could comprehend them; and his system of practical demonstration of his subjects was vastly superior to any thing that had ever been seen in America. He was the first to introduce into this country the system of delivering clinical lectures, or lectures at the bedside of the patient, whose ailments were operated upon during the course of his remarks. This system is naturally the most repugnant to the patient, but its advantages to the student are so great that they outweigh all other considerations. Other professors had shrunk from subjecting their patients to such an ordeal, but Dr. Mott had seen enough, during his attendance upon such lectures abroad, to satisfy him that it was the only method by which a thorough knowledge of the profession of surgery could be imparted, and immediately upon establishing himself in this country he introduced it. He met with opposition at first, but he gradually overcame it, and made the advantages of his system so apparent to all that at length the opposition entirely ceased.

The greatest difficulty to which American medical schools have always been subject has been the almost utter impossibility of procuring dead bodies for dissection. It was this want that compelled Dr. Mott, as it has compelled so many others, to seek a practical education in Europe; and when he came back to the college as professor, he was met by the same drawback to thorough instruction. The law forbade the taking of dead bodies for dissection, under severe penalties. If a student was ever found in possession of a limb, he was liable to fine and imprisonment; and popular sentiment was so strong against the practice of dissection that those who engaged in it ran serious risk of incurring violence at the hands of the mob. Dr. Mott was often driven to desperate expedients in the procuring of subjects. He was fond of relating one of his adventures of this kind, which will show the reader how he was enabled to carry on his lectures.

It was in the winter of 1815, and it had been found impossible to procure a supply of subjects for the season. They could not be obtained at any price, and it was evident that if any were to be had, the doctor and his pupils would have to take the matter in their own hands. There was a grave-yard just outside the city, in which a number of interments had recently been made, and the doctor resolved upon securing these bodies for his dissecting-room. It was a dangerous undertaking, as discovery would subject all engaged in it to the direst penalties of the law, if, indeed, they should be lucky enough to escape being lynched by the people. In spite of the dangers, however, the students volunteered to assist the doctor in the attempt, and at an appointed time proceeded to the cemetery, properly disguised, and began the removal of the bodies from the graves. The night was intensely dark, and the wind was high, both of which circumstances favored their undertaking, but every sound, every snapping of a twig or rustling of a leaf caused them to start with alarm and gaze anxiously into the darkness. It was near midnight when they had finished their task, and, this done, they waited in anxious silence for the arrival of the means of removing their prey. Their movements had been accurately timed, and they had scarcely completed their labors when a cart, driven by a man dressed in the rough clothing of a laborer, approached the cemetery at a rapid pace. Signals were exchanged between the driver and the students, and the latter fell to work to place the bodies, eleven in number, in the cart. Having accomplished this, they covered them over in such a manner as to make it appear that the cart was loaded with country produce, bound for the city markets. When every thing was properly arranged, the students disappeared in the darkness, each seeking the means by which he had come out from the city, and the driver, turning his cart about, drove off rapidly in the direction of New York. It was a long ride, and to an imaginative man, carrying eleven dead bodies that had been torn from their quiet graves through the darkness of that winter night would have been a terrible undertaking. But this man was not imaginative, and, besides this, he was keenly alive to the tremendous consequences of discovery. He knew that he was carrying his life in his hand, and that he needed all the coolness and decision of which he was master. Reaching the city long after midnight, he drove rapidly down Broadway and turned into Barclay Street. The lights of the college shone out brightly, and they had never seemed so welcome as then. The cart was driven rapidly to the college entrance, where the students were in readiness to receive it. In a few moments the bodies were removed from the cart and conveyed to the dissecting-room, and the cart turned over to its owner. The driver accompanied the students to the dissecting-room, and, throwing off his disguise, revealed the handsome but excited and eager countenance of Dr. Mott. He had shared the dangers to which his pupils had subjected themselves, and had even borne the part in the enterprise attended with the greatest risk. The affair had succeeded admirably, a winter's supply of "subjects" had been obtained, and after this the lectures went on without interruption.

"A story is told of his readiness in the lecture-room. A mother brought into the amphitheater, one morning, an extremely dirty, sickly, miserable-looking child, for the purpose of having a tumor removed. He exhibited the tumor to the class, but informed the mother that he could not operate upon the child without the consent of her husband. One of the students, in his eagerness to examine the tumor, jumped over into the little inclosure designed for the operator and his patients. Dr. Mott, observing this intrusion, turned to the student and asked him, with the most innocent expression of countenance: 'Are you the father of this child?' Thunders of applause and laughter greeted this ingenious rebuke, during which the intruder returned to his place crestfallen."

He was equally as successful in his private practice as in his labors in the medical school. His brilliant reputation preceded him in his return to his native country, and immediately upon opening his office in New York he entered upon a large and lucrative practice. His skill as a surgeon was in constant demand, and it is said that during his long career he tied the common carotid artery forty-six times, cut for stone one hundred and sixty-five times, and amputated nearly one thousand limbs. His old preceptor, Sir Astley Cooper, proud of the distinction won by his favorite pupil, said of him exultingly: "He has performed more of the great operations than any man living, or that ever did live."

When he was but thirty-three years old (in 1818) he placed a ligature around the bracheo-cephalic trunk or arteria innominata, within two inches of the heart, for aneurism of the right subclavian artery. This was the first time this wonderful operation had ever been performed, and the skill and success with which he accomplished it stamped him as one of the brightest lights of his profession. "The patient survived the operation twenty-eight days, and thus demonstrated the feasibility of this hazardous and thus far unparalleled undertaking. He discovered in this case that, though all supply of blood to the blood-vessels of the right arm was apparently cut off, the circulation was kept up by the interosculating blood-vessels, the pulsation at the wrist maintained, and no evidence of loss of vitality or warmth manifested in the limb. The patient finally died from secondary hemorrhage."

In 1828 he performed successfully the most difficult and dangerous operation known to surgery. A clergyman called upon him to remove an enormous tumor in the neck, in which were imbedded and twisted many of the great arteries. In this operation it became necessary to take out entire the right clavicle or collar bone, to lay bare the membrane which surrounds the lungs, to search for and dissect around the arteries which ran through the tumor, to make forty ligatures, and to remove an immense mass of diseased matter. This terrible operation had never been attempted before, and was performed by Dr. Mott without the aid of chloroform; yet it was done so skillfully that the patient survived it, and in 1865 was still living and discharging his ministerial duties. It was thirty years before it was attempted again in any part of the world. It was a great triumph of the genius of the operator, and won him praises from men of science in all countries.

In 1821 "he performed the first operation for osteo-sarcoma of the lower jaw. In 1822 he introduced his original operation for immobility of the lower jaw. He was the first surgeon who removed the lower jaw for necrosis, and the first to tie successfully the primitive iliac artery for aneurism. Other of his original operations were cutting out two inches of the deep jugular vein, inseparably imbedded in a tumor, and tying both ends of the vein, and closing, with a fine ligature, wounds of large veins of a longitudinal or transverse kind, even where an olive-sliced piece had been cut out."

It was invariably his practice before attempting an operation on a living subject to perform it on a dead body, and by the most minute and patient examination to render himself absolute master of the anatomy of the parts to be operated upon. He was a thoroughly conscientious man in the exercise of his profession, and was always on his guard to resist that greatest danger of the skillful surgeon—the temptation to use the knife needlessly. It was his practice to investigate his cases thoroughly, and never to use the knife unless his judgment was satisfied that an operation was necessary. "That he decided in favor of operating when some of his associates hesitated, was due rather to his large experience than to an overweening fondness for the use of the knife." In his operations he was firm and decided. Gifted with an unusual steadiness of nerve and strength of muscle, he never allowed his sympathy for the patient to cause him to hesitate or inflict one pang less than the case required. He was prompt and ready in the event of unforeseen complications, and never permitted any thing to take him by surprise. His manner toward his patients was tender and sympathizing to a remarkable degree, and his brother surgeons used to say of him, that he seemed to have the power of cutting with less pain to the patient than was possessed by most operators. During forty years of his practice anæsthetics were unknown, and he had to operate with the full consciousness that his patient was suffering the keenest agony. Besides attaining such an exalted position as a surgeon, Dr. Mott won an enviable reputation as a physician. His practice was confined almost entirely to the best class of the people of New York, and he was for many years the favorite accoucheur in a large circle of families in that city.

He was an eminently progressive man. He fully recognized the advance of science with the growth of the world, and was always prompt to welcome any valuable discovery in medicine or surgery. He was among the first to adopt and advocate the use of anæsthetics, for no man had had more cause to understand the necessity of such assistants. He was himself the inventor of many valuable surgical instruments, but he gladly welcomed the introduction of others, even though they superseded his own in use. To the close of his life he was a diligent student, and watched the progress of his science with a keen and intelligent eye. He was the author of several works of merit, including a volume of travels, and the translator of "Velpau's Operative Surgery," to which he made extensive and valuable additions and annotations. He received numerous literary and scientific honors from colleges, universities, and learned bodies in the United States and Europe.

In 1835 he visited Europe for the purpose of resting from his arduous labors, and spent several years in traveling extensively in England, on the continent, and in the East. His great achievements had made him as famous in the Old World as at home, and he was received wherever he went with great distinction. He was cordially welcomed by the most eminent surgeons of Paris, and Louis Philippe conceived a warm friendship for him. During his visit to Constantinople, he was called upon to attend professionally the reigning Sultan Abdul Medjid, who was suffering from a tumor in the head. Dr. Mott successfully removed this tumor, and was afterwards invested by the Sultan with the order of Knight of Medjidechi, of Constantinople.

During his visit to Paris, a circumstance occurred which he related upon his return home, and which will serve to show the extremes to which professional skill and vanity will sometimes carry men. One of the most eminent surgeons in Paris asked him if he would like to see him perform his original operation. Dr. Mott replied that nothing would give him more pleasure. "Then you shall see it to-morrow," said the Frenchman. "But stay," he added, "now I think of it, there is no patient in the hospital who has that malady. No matter, my dear friend, there is a poor devil in ward No. —— who is of no use to himself or any body else, and if you 'll come to-morrow, I 'll operate beautifully on him." Dr. Mott at once declined to attend the operation or to countenance in any way so horrible an outrage.

In person Dr. Mott was a thorough gentleman of the old school. He was an exceedingly handsome man, and was possessed of an erect and well-developed figure. His hair was as white as snow, and his dress, which consisted of a simple suit of spotless black, with linen of matchless purity, was in the most perfect taste. He was grave and dignified in his deportment, and polished and courteous in every action. Even in his most difficult and trying operations the services of the assistants were always promptly acknowledged with scrupulous politeness. He was possessed of many friends, and was regarded with pride and veneration by his profession throughout the world.

During the last winter of his life he had lectured once or twice at the Medical School, and had performed several operations of importance in his private practice. Although nearly eighty, he was still erect and vigorous, and was far from considering himself too old for his work.

On the morning of the 15th of April, 1865, he sent for his barber, as was his custom, and submitted himself to the hands of the man who had been his attendant in this capacity for years. He was sitting in his dressing-room, and, being in fine spirits, began conversing with the barber, who, during the conversation, asked him if he had heard the terrible news of the day.

"What is the news?" asked the doctor.

"President Lincoln was killed last night at the theater in Washington," was the reply.

The doctor turned as pale as death, and, trembling violently, motioned the barber aside, and tottered into the chamber adjoining, in which his wife was dressing.

"My dear," he gasped, scarcely able to speak, "I have received such a shock. President Lincoln has been murdered."

His agitation had now become so great that he could say no more. He sank down into a chair, pale and trembling, and so feeble that he could scarcely sit up. He was seized in a short

"PRESIDENT LINCOLN HAS BEEN MURDERED!"

time with acute pains in the back, and at the same time his vigor seemed to desert him entirely, and he became a weak and broken old man. He was obliged to seek his bed, from which he never rose. He grew feebler every day, and died on the 26th of April, 1865.